JOSEPH SMITH AND THE BEGINNINGS
OF MORMONISM

Portrait of Joseph Smith by William Whitaker.

JOSEPH SMITH
AND THE BEGINNINGS
OF MORMONISM

RICHARD L. BUSHMAN

UNIVERSITY OF ILLINOIS PRESS
Urbana and Chicago

For
Leonard Arrington

© 1984 by the Board of Trustees of the University of Illinois
Manufactured in the United States of America
5 6 C P 9 8 7

This book is printed on acid-free paper.

Library of Congress Cataloging in Publication Data

Bushman, Richard L.
  Joseph Smith and the beginnings of Mormonism.

  Bibliography: p.
  Includes index.
  1. Smith, Joseph, 1805–1844. 2. Mormon Church — History
— 19th century.   I. Title.
BX8695.S6B87   1984   289.3'09'034   84-2451
ISBN 0-252-01143-0 (cloth : alk. paper)
ISBN 0-252-06012-1 (pbk. : alk. paper)

UNIVERSITY OF ILLINOIS PRESS
1325 SOUTH OAK STREET
CHAMPAIGN, ILLINOIS 61820-6903
WWW.PRESS.UILLINOIS.EDU

CONTENTS

Acknowledgments

I have received a great deal of assistance from other scholars working in early Mormon history. Two of those who know the early years best, Larry C. Porter and Marvin Hill, read the entire manuscript. I also received expert help and insight on particular problems from Dean Jessee, Richard L. Anderson, and Jan Shipps. Nathan O. Hatch and Timothy L. Smith, though not entirely sympathetic to my perspective, offered useful critiques. The staff at the Church Archives was always cooperative.

On the editorial side, Richard L. Wentworth of the University of Illinois Press made special efforts to remove obstacles in the way of publication. Claudia Bushman advised on the subtleties of tone and style. Bonnie Depp, the copyeditor, had a sharp eye for small errors. David Ferguson checked the footnotes. Marsha Nielsen typed the manuscript. Lowell Durham, Jr., offered encouragement at an early stage.

Work was begun under a fellowship from the John Simon Guggenheim Memorial Foundation, that enduring supporter of scholarship in America.

Leonard Arrington, the patron of virtually all contemporary scholarship in the field of Mormon history, sustained and inspired this work from beginning to end.

JOSEPH SMITH
AND THE BEGINNINGS
OF MORMONISM

INTRODUCTION

In the first stages of composition this book was titled "The Origins of Mormonism." The word "Origins" was dropped when the actual complexities of identifying the sources of Mormon belief and experience bared themselves. An attempt to trace all the images, ideas, language, and emotional structure of a movement as elaborate as Mormonism became more evidently elusive and futile as the work went on. The word "Beginnings" in the title signifies a more modest purpose: to narrate what happened as Mormonism came into being in the early nineteenth century.

The problem of Joseph Smith's visions complicates even this simplified undertaking. Believing Mormons like myself understand the origins of the Book of Mormon quite differently from others. How can a description of Joseph Smith's revelations accommodate a Mormon's perception of events and still make sense to a general audience? My method has been to relate events as the participants themselves experienced them, using their own words where possible. Insofar as the revelations were a reality to them, I have treated them as real in this narrative. General readers will surely be left with questions about the meaning of these experiences, but at least they will have an understanding of how early Mormons perceived the world.

I have not attempted an all-encompassing social or cultural analysis. Explication of the cultural influences on Joseph Smith has been limited to demonstrable connections between his writings and beliefs and the culture of his immediate society. Abstract relationships with Puritanism and Romanticism, for example, though significant from some perspectives, have been subordinated to the influences that are known to have played upon him through actual persons in the villages where he lived.

Mormonism, it must be remembered, began with one family, the family of Joseph Smith, Sr., and Lucy Mack Smith of Vermont and New York. Joseph Smith, Jr., the fourth child among nine, became the Prophet and First Elder of the Church of Christ when it was organized on April

6, 1830, but three of the six original organizers were Smiths, just as previously three of the eight witnesses to the golden plates were family members.

Young Joseph Smith's culture was predominantly family culture. So far as the record shows, he had little schooling until he was past twenty. The necessity of work on the family farm kept him at home where someone, probably his father, at one time a school teacher, taught the children. Nor is there a record of church attendance until religious ex-citement stirred the neighborhood in his early teen years. As a boy and youth, Joseph was almost entirely under the influence of his family and a small circle of acquaintances in the villages of Palmyra and Manchester, New York.

On both the mother's and father's sides, family culture had borne the strains of migration for two generations. Joseph Smith's grandparents were among the large number of migrant pioneers who left the fringe of settlements along the New England coast after the middle of the eighteenth century to clear farms in the heavily forested interior. After a century of relative stability in New England's population a combination of crowding and better opportunities propelled many young men west and north in search of new land. In the 1760s Solomon Mack, Lucy Smith's father, left Lyme, at the mouth of the Connecticut River, for New Hampshire and northern Massachusetts. In the 1770s Asael Smith, Joseph Smith Jr.'s pa-ternal grandfather, moved from Topsfield, Massachusetts, just north of Salem, to New Hampshire, and later to Vermont. Joseph Smith's parents, Joseph Smith, Sr., and Lucy Mack, met and married in Tunbridge, Vermont.

When the Smiths moved to Palmyra, New York, in 1816, they chose an area settled for twenty-five years but still heavily forested. Young Joseph spent his teen-age years cutting trees, burning brush, and plowing virgin soil. In a newspaper interview in 1843, Joseph said that when he became confused about the churches as a boy, he chose a place in the woods where his father had a clearing and "went to the stump where I had stuck my axe when I had quit work, and I kneeled down, and prayed. . . ."[1]

The removal from old settlements to new ones separated the Smiths and the Macks from the religion of their fathers. Most eighteenth-century New England towns had one dominant church, the Congregational, still deeply inbued with Calvinist theology and committed to strict church discipline. As new parishes grew on the town periphery, they modeled themselves after the parent church. Only a sprinkling of Baptists, Quakers, and Anglicans here and there interrupted the basic uniformity of belief and practice.

Migration, war, and economic adversity detached Joseph Smith's ances-tors from Congregationalism. Solomon Mack, an indentured servant from age four to twenty-one, learned no religion from his master, and lived without religion until age seventy-five, when he was at last converted. His wife, the daughter of a deacon in the Congregational church, taught her children to worship but apparently without formal church connections. Her daughter Lucy was not baptized as a child and joined no church until she finally became a Presbyterian in Palmyra around 1820. On Joseph Smith Sr.'s side, Asael Smith became a Universalist, a believer in salvation for all, and, though associated with the Congregational church from time to time, always dissented from its theology. His son, Joseph Smith, Sr., though privately religious, attended church only sporadically.

The Smiths were religious without being church people. Lucy Smith solemnly promised to serve God with all her heart when an illness brought her close to death in 1803, and then was unable to find a pastor to suit her. She at last persuaded a minister to baptize her without requiring church membership. For seventeen years she read the Bible and prayed with her family before becoming a Presbyterian. Although averse to ministers and churches, Joseph Smith, Sr., had seven inspirational dreams over a span of years, all exhibiting a desire for belief, healing, and direction, all showing dissatisfaction with religion as it existed.

The multiplication of denominations complicated the problem. There were five churches vying for members in Palmyra in 1820 in contrast to the traditional uniformity in New England towns. To Smith eyes, the religious world was in turmoil, marred by hypocrisy and corruption, far removed from the purity and simplicity of the Bible.[2]

In its precarious descent to Joseph Smith, Jr., the Calvinism of his forefathers lost its strength. Asael Smith's Universalism was explicitly heterodox, and all along the line Calvinist belief was diluted. By Joseph Smith's generation, the family could scarcely connect with mainstream Protestantism, which in the nineteenth century was absorbed with evangelical revivalism. Revivalism depended on a Calvinist sense of alienation from God and the belief that grace alone could redeem people. Without the theological foundation the Smiths could not respond, and were destined to live along the margins of evangelical religion.

On the strength of revival conversions, the Baptists and the Methodists grew from tiny minorities in 1780 to the most populous Protestant churches in 1850. Congregationalists and Presbyterians were not far behind. Every major city and almost every rural town saw not just one revival but a succession of them in the decades after 1800. No Smiths of Joseph Sr.'s family were converted. Solomon Mack underwent a classic spiritual rebirth in Vermont in 1811, and for a time Lucy and Joseph attended meetings, but Joseph, Sr., soon withdrew and Lucy did not persist. Lucy and three of the children were sufficiently caught up in the revival in 1820 to join the Presbyterians, but none mentioned conversion in the usual sense. Joseph Smith, Jr., complained that "he wanted to get Religion too, wanted to feel and shout like the rest but could feel nothing."[3]

Aspects of the first vision resembled a conversion experience — the forgiveness of sins and the joy and elation afterward — and Joseph may have first interpreted the experience as conversion. But in later accounts the conversionist elements faded in the telling, and the opening of a new dispensation overshadowed all else. After the church was organized in 1830, evangelical revivalism had no place in Mormon worship. Mormon theology, as it developed in the revelations and in discourses, showed few signs of having wrestled free of Calvinism. A common biblicism united Mormonism and Calvinism, but Calvinism did not establish the framework for Joseph Smith's thought.

The Smiths were more directly affected by Enlightenment skepticism than by Calvinist evangelism. Skepticism had influence within the family itself and figured still more largely in the village through newspaper editors and other local intellectuals. As a percentage of the population, free-thinkers and deists were rare in America, but skeptical attitudes cast a long shadow. In 1828 Robert Owen, the atheistic founder of the unsuccessful utopian community at New Harmony, Indiana, offered to debate anyone on the proposition that religion was founded on ignorance and was the chief source of human misery. Alexander Campbell, the leading spirit in the incipient Disciples of Christ movement, agreed to meet Owen in a Methodist meetinghouse in Cincinnati. For eight days in April they debated. Campbell's concluding speech took twelve hours. Through all fifteen sessions the meetinghouse, with seating for a thousand, was filled to capacity. On the last day Campbell called for a standing vote of those favorable and those opposed to Christianity. Only three listeners stood against Christianity.[4]

The vote probably represented the distribution of sentiment in the country. Few Americans were infidels, but the full house day after day spoke for their fascination with skepticism. Moreover, both contenders made their arguments on the basis of reason. Campbell attempted to prove that hard evidence — well-attested miracles — supported Christian belief. His mode of defense illustrated how faith as well as doubt had embraced the Enlightenment by the beginning of the nineteenth century. Christianity claimed to be as reasonable by Enlightenment standards as science or philosophy.

All of this affected Joseph Smith when he told his family and friends about Moroni and the gold plates. The reaction was quite confused. The price Christianity had paid for assimilating the Enlightenment was to forgo belief in all supernatural happenings except the well-attested events of the

Bible. Witchcraft, dreams, revelations, even healings were thrown indiscriminately on the scrapheap of superstition. While in 1692 Cotton Mather, the leading intellectual of his day, could discourse learnedly on the manifestation of witchcraft, no leading divine fifty years later would countenance such talk. The Enlightenment drained Christianity of its belief in the miraculous, except for Bible miracles. Everything else was attributed to ignorant credulity. Joseph Smith's story when it became known was immediately identified as one more example.

A movement among the intellectual elite, of course, could not entirely suppress popular belief in divine and satanic forces affecting everyday life. Common people, surreptitiously to some extent, still entertained traditional beliefs in water-witching and in spells to locate hidden treasure. Many more yearned for a return of the miraculous powers of the original Christian church. A group of practitioners of traditional magic in Palmyra thus reacted quite differently from the newspaper editors to Joseph's story of the golden plates and a protecting angel. They saw Joseph Smith as one of them, tried to absorb him into their company, and grew angry when he drew back.

Joseph was assaulted from two sides in this struggle between modern rationalism and traditional supernaturalism. He had to answer to demands for proof from the newspaper editors and ministers, on the one hand, and extricate himself from the schemes of the Palmyra magicians and money diggers, on the other. At times his closest followers and his own family were confused. One of Joseph Smith's tasks in the years before 1830 was to define his calling and mission so as not to be misunderstood, and to set his own course, apart from rationalism or superstition.

The perspective of this work is that Joseph Smith is best understood as a person who outgrew his culture. The usual purpose of historical analysis is to depict persons and ideas as the sum total of the historical forces acting on them. Mormonism has customarily been seen as the product of the culture emanating from upstate New York and Puritan-Yankee New England. The shortcoming of this form of analysis is that it exaggerates similarities and suppresses differences. Everything in Mormonism that resembles the local culture assumes importance, and everything unusual fades into insignificance. The original and innovative, a great deal of what is most interesting, are obscured.

The viewpoint of this book is that parts of early Mormonism did resemble aspects of the environment; other parts were alien and peculiar. In some passages the Book of Mormon and the Book of Moses appear to come from another world entirely. Single-minded attribution of these works to upstate New York culture blinds us to many of their most interesting qualities. We can understand Mormonism better if it is seen as an independent creation, drawing from its environment but also struggling against American culture in an effort to realize itself.

Joseph Smith astounded and offended the people of Palmyra. His achievements, even before he left New York, were hardly what they expected from the son of Lucy and Joseph Smith, Sr. When he was just twenty-four, he organized a church, published a large and complex book of sacred writings, and began to teach a Christian gospel familiar yet strange. All this is more than could be attributed to their own small-town rural culture. Mormonism appeared to be, as the scripture said, a stone cut out of the mountains without hands.

The aim of this volume is to recognize the unusual as well as the common in Joseph Smith's early work, to tell how Mormonism unloosed itself from its immediate locale in those critical first years, and to portray as accurately as possible what it had become by the time the Prophet, his family, and his followers left New York for Ohio early in 1831.

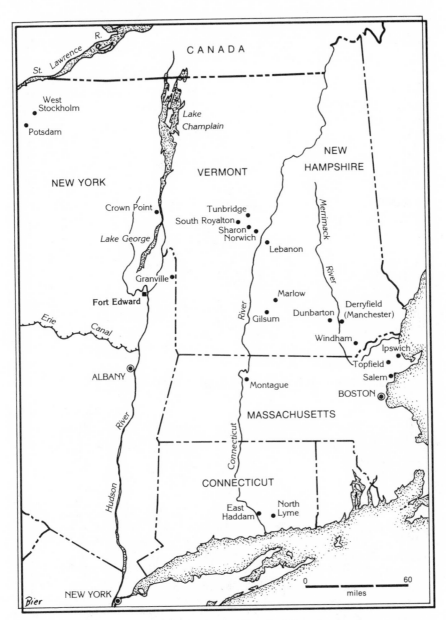

The Mack and Smith Families in New England

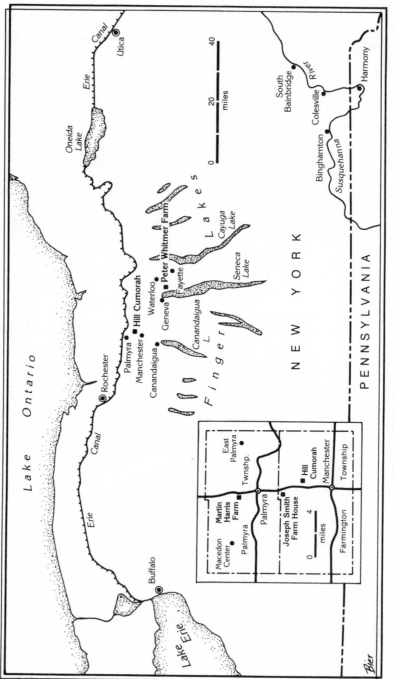

The Joseph Smith, Sr., Family in New York

CHAPTER I

THE JOSEPH SMITH FAMILY

Lucy Mack Smith bade farewell to her sons Hyrum and Joseph a few days after their deaths in Carthage in June, 1844. Willard Richards had brought the bodies back to Nauvoo, and after the corpses were washed and dressed in burial clothes, the Smith family was admitted to the room. "I had for a long time braced every nerve," Lucy wrote, "roused every energy of my soul, and called upon God to strengthen me; but when I entered the room, and saw my murdered sons extended both at once before my eyes, and heard the sobs and groans of my family, and the cries of 'Father! Husband! Brothers!' from the lips of their wives, children, brother, and sisters, it was too much, I sank back, crying to the Lord, in the agony of my soul, 'My God, my God, why hast thou forsaken this family!'"[1]

At that moment the scenes of sorrow and distress through which they had passed together flashed through her mind, and she recalled "the innocence and sympathy which filled their guileless hearts." The two young men seemed to say, "Mother, weep not for us, we have overcome the world by love." Lucy thought back on a promise she had received in Missouri that in five years Joseph should have power over all his enemies. "The time had elapsed," she wrote, "and the promise was fulfilled."[2]

Six months later Lucy began the narrative that contains most of what is known of the early life of Joseph Smith. She was sixty-eight, afflicted with disease and infirmities, and burdened with sorrow brought on "by the cruelty of an ungodly and hard hearted world."[3] Within a month she had lost three sons: Joseph and Hyrum by vigilante bullets at Carthage and Samuel from fever contracted while trying to escape the mob. Of her seven sons, only the unpredictable William survived. Joseph, her husband, had died in Nauvoo four years earlier. She lived with a daughter or with Emma, the Prophet's wife, who carried Joseph Jr.'s unborn son.

It was a troubled and uncertain moment for the church. The question

9

of the Prophet's successor remained unsettled. Lucy's own son William was soon to be among the contenders. The gentile countryside expected the kingdom to crumble and the Saints to disperse. When they proved inconveniently adamant, the mob rose again and forced the Mormons to flee. Lucy could not ease her own pain with the thought of the church's favorable prospects. The vicissitudes of the moment, however, did not color her dictation to Martha Coray through the winter of 1844-45.[4] Infirmities and sorrows had not dampened her spirits. The words flowed easily. One crisply told story after another covered the pages. Her narrative remains the central source for the early life of Joseph Smith.

Lucy Smith's reaction to the sorrows and distresses of her life was indignation, not regret. When she recollected the murder of her sons, she wrote, "my blood curdles in my veins." In the closing lines of the book she consigned the malicious and indifferent government officials who had darkened her family's lives to the judgment of God: Lilburn W. Boggs, Thomas Carlin, Martin Van Buren, and Thomas Ford. She was a proud, high-strung woman, belligerent when she had to be, capable of anger, grief, and sublime confidence in the final triumph of the innocent. She concluded the sketches like a Book of Mormon prophet: "And I shall leave the world to judge, as seemeth them good, concerning what I have written. But this much I will say, that the testimony which I have given is true, and will stand for ever. . . ."[5]

Lucy's pride did not arise solely from the overawing achievements of her most famous son. The name of Joseph Smith, Jr., is not mentioned in the narrative until page fifty-six. On the first page of the original draft she cast a momentary glance in his direction with the observation that one reason for undertaking her sketch was her familiarity with "some" whose lives and death excited curiosity in the minds of those who knew them. Even that slight acknowledgment was omitted from the final draft. Nor was Joseph's birth accompanied by signs or portents as Lucy told the story. She announced simply in the course of narrating other matters that "in the meantime we had a son, whom we called Joseph, after the name of his father; he was born December 23, 1805. I shall speak of him more particularly by and by."[6] Joseph's revelations and writings, his part in constructing the city of Nauvoo, the tens of thousands of followers, the high honor and respect paid him by men of the strongest character did not overwhelm Lucy Smith's narrative.

The Smith family as a whole more than any single individual stood at the center of the story — its hardships, triumphs, sorrows, and happiness. Lucy's pride was the pride of family. Her spontaneous reaction when she saw the bodies of Hyrum and Joseph was "My God, my God, why hast thou forsaken this family?" Her narrative began with her father Solomon and devoted five chapters to her brothers and sisters before telling about herself. Lucy calculated that six Smith martyrs had fallen because of persecution, not just one: Joseph, Sr., Don Carlos, Hyrum, Samuel, and William's wife Caroline, as well as Joseph the Prophet.[7]

Hers was not a wordly pride, although she sensed acutely the "attention and respect which are ever shown to those who live in fine circumstances." She never forgot that her family for three generations commanded little of this kind of attention. Her narrative opens with a recollection that Ebenezer Mack "was a man of considerable property, and lived in good style," but a "series of misfortunes" visited the grandparents, and they were reduced to poverty.[8] Lucy's father, Solomon, struggled manfully through a lifetime and seemed to verge perpetually on prosperity without securing it. Only Stephen of Lucy's brothers accumulated substantial property. The others lived modestly. Lucy and her husband, Joseph, Sr., lost their farm in 1803, and after a succession of odd jobs, rentals, mortgage payments, and unremitting toil, twenty-five years later still lacked a house and land of their own.

Her pride arose not from the family's success but from the way in which they met adversity. Joseph and Hyrum lay in triumph in their coffins because justice and charity gave them power over all their enemies. Of her sister Lydia, who "sought riches and obtained them," Lucy wrote but two paragraphs: not that Lydia was less loved, "but she seemed to float more with the stream of common events."[9] Lucy Smith honored those who overcame. She made her narrative the story of many troubles, turning the misfortunes of Smith family history into exemplifications of their character.

SOLOMON AND LUCY MACK

Lucy Mack Smith was the last of eight children born to Solomon Mack. She opened her biographical sketches with an excerpt from Solomon's brief autobiography in which he related various adventures in the two wars in which he fought, the French and Indian War and the Revolution. Beyond that, little mention is made of him, perhaps because he was absent for years at a time while Lucy was growing up. Until late in his life when he experienced a drastic change of heart, Solomon was preoccupied solely with the pursuit of wealth.

Solomon Mack was born September 15, 1732, in Lyme, Connecticut, the grandson of John Mack (1682-1734), one of Lyme's prospering traders. When Solomon was four, during a steep decline in the economy, his father, Ebenezer Mack, lost the land he had inherited in Lyme. Solomon and his two brothers and a sister were indentured to various households in the village.[10] This was the beginning of Solomon's sorrows. "I was treated by my master as his property and not as his fellow mortal. He taught me to work and was very careful that I should have little or no rest. . . . His whole attention was taken up on the pursuits of the good things of this world; wealth was his supreme object. I am afraid gold was his God." Solomon said that the man never spoke of anything else, and never of religion. Solomon was not even given the simple learning that the law required masters to provide. When the eventual falling out came, the mistress of the house feared Solomon might sue them. "She took me aside and told me I was such a fool we could not learn you." The man called the doctor when Solomon was scalded and fell ill afterward, but only to enable him to keep on working. Solomon felt that he grew up "like the wild ass's colt," feeling "no obligation with regard to society." Two months before he was twenty-one and his indentures expired, he ran away, but he returned at the master's request to finish out the term.[11]

Having earned his freedom, Solomon Mack knew no better, as he later reflected, than to try "to make myself great and happy in the way I was educated," that is, by making money. He later regretted his single-minded devotion to economic enterprises, but the simple narrative that he wrote when he was seventy-nine is an unconscious tribute to his irrepressible courage and optimism. Defeated in one venture after another, wounded by falling trees and spills from horses, afflicted with fits and permanently lame after the most severe accident, shipwrecked, betrayed by business associates, he always recovered his health and courage and set forth on new undertakings. After his conversion in 1811 he turned his energies to telling the folly of worldly pursuits, and traveled the countryside describing the peace that faith had at last brought to his life: "My friends, when you read this journal, remember your unfortunate friend Solomon Mack, who worried and toiled until an old age to try to lay up treasures in this world, but the Lord would not suffer me to have it. But now I trust I have treasures laid up that no man can take away. . . ."[12]

Solomon Mack got his start in life in the war with the French and Indians. The war opened with young George Washington's skirmishes in the Ohio Valley in 1754 and quickly spread along the line from Maine to Kentucky that separated the swelling English population from the fur regions claimed by the French. On September 10, 1755, Solomon Mack, not yet twenty-three, enlisted for two and half months' service at Fort Edward on the upper Hudson just south of Lake George. At Fort Edward he re-enlisted for another six months under Israel Putnam, a fellow Connecticut man later to gain fame in the Revolution. A tragedy for many, war was an opportunity for Solomon. After discharge, his military pay enabled him to purchase a farm in Lyme and two teams of oxen that he drove back to the combat zone to help transport the army's baggage and supplies. In 1758 he enlisted again, saw action, and then set up a small shop at Crown Point on Lake Ticonderoga. For two years he sold supplies to the army. Despite losses when a team of oxen was stolen and a dishonest clerk took advantage of his illiteracy, Solomon accumulated enough to add two more plots to his acreage in Lyme. When he closed out his holdings after 1762, they amounted to 127 acres with houses and outbuildings. The war enabled an enterprising young man still not thirty who began life with nothing to acquire a larger than average farm. In 1759 at age twenty-seven he married Lydia Gates, the daughter of Deacon Daniel Gates in nearby East Haddam.[13]

War also loosened Solomon Mack's ties to the village of his father, his grandfather, and his own unhappy childhood. After service on the upper Hudson, his imagination ranged freely across the whole of New England in search of opportunities. Whether from necessity or ambition, Solomon could not content himself with the cultivation of his Lyme holdings and the round of modest town offices that property and prudence would have inevitably brought. In the fifteen years between his last service in the French and Indian wars and the outbreak of the Revolution, he made all of the country between the Hudson and the Connecticut his field of activity. Immediately after he closed his shop at Crown Point, he purchased rights to 1,600 acres in Granville, New York, and began building the log houses required before issuance of a clear title.[14] Shortly after that he freighted a vessel and sailed for New York City. Beginning in 1762 he divested himself of his Lyme property and bought a proprietary right in Marlow, a southern New Hampshire town just west of the Connecticut River. This was pioneering: four families in forty miles and trees to be cleared from every acre. By 1767 he owned 100 acres and in 1770 acquired another seventy-six. But still dissatisfied, in 1773 the Macks moved from Marlow to nearby Gilsum, where Solomon's brother Elisha owned saw- and gristmills and many of his Mack cousins from Lyme had settled. Joseph and Abner Mack of Lyme were among the original proprietors who laid out Gilsum (then called Boyle). In 1772 three other Macks, Obijah, Josiah, and John, were also grantees.[15]

What had Solomon Mack to show for his enterprise in 1775 at age forty-three? Eight children were born between 1759 and 1775. He had cleared scores of acres and owned hundreds more. He had risked his capital and labor in a variety of ventures, and yet his terse comment that, despite all his efforts to make himself "great and happy," "the Lord would not suffer me to prosper," tells the sad tale. Although Solomon owned land in Gilsum and was not penniless, industry and ingenuity had not brought its accustomed rewards. Why? Solomon's own analysis probably comes close to the truth. Life in eighteenth-century America was mined with hazards beyond the capacity of calculation or hard work to avoid. At Granville he gashed his leg while felling trees, and the man hired to raise the required houses while Solomon recovered left with his wages before finishing the job. The 1,600 acres were forfeited, and doctor bills ate further into Solomon's resources. Although the New York cargo fetched a good price, a gale damaged the vessel on the return trip. Solomon limped into a Long Island port and returned home without the boat or the profits. Subsequently a broken wrist halted his labors and brought more doctor bills. Time after time the vicissitudes of nature and the vices of human nature defeated his efforts.[16]

Lucy Mack was born in Gilsum, New Hampshire, July 8, 1775, when the town was still a primitive frontier area.[17] The threat of Indians had prevented settlement until the French wars ended. The first settlers were on the land in 1763 but still had not met the rudimentary requirements to make their titles good. The legislature confirmed the charter anyway, and the proprietors commissioned one of Solomon's Lyme kinsmen, Joseph Mack, along with two others, to lay out roads and lots. When Lucy was born, Gilsum claimed 178 inhabitants, most of them accounted for by twenty to thirty young to middle-aged families. About half of the population was under seventeen. Only ten of eighty-seven males were over fifty. Solomon, with eight children under seventeen, had more than most, but there were plenty of boys and girls for the Mack children to swim and ride with.[18]

Lucy called Gilsum a "rocky region." Land was plentiful but not fertile enough to make anyone rich or to draw many settlers. By 1793, when Lucy was eighteen, the population had risen to over 300 and presumably the number of families had about doubled to forty or fifty. In the agricultural census of that year Gilsum listed sixty-eight acres of arable or tillage land. If that figure can be believed, the average family plowed and planted only one or two acres. No orchards were listed. All the rest of the improved land, 619 acres in total, was given to pasture and mowing. There were 269 animals: horses, oxen, cows, cattle. Probably each family owned a cow, some an ox or two for plowing and meat, and all a couple of beef cattle that would provide the main surplus for the market.[19]

Small wonder that Solomon Mack chose not to remain in the village for long, especially when events afforded better prospects elsewhere. The Battle of Bunker Hill took place in Boston a little over three weeks before Lucy's birth, and Washington took command of the army a few weeks later. The general's greatest need was for supplies. Sensing a renewal of the opportunities of the French and Indian War, Solomon learned from his brother-in-law in Connecticut how to make saltpeter for gunpowder and earned a dollar a day teaching the art from town to town.[20]

For the next fourteen years Solomon lived at home less than half of the time. His insatiable yearning to accumulate an estate and the pressure of sheer necessity carried him from one venture to another, leaving Lydia at home to tend the farm with the eight children. Solomon was one of the seven men in Gilsum who had enlisted in the army in 1775. Following his pattern in the French and Indian War, he signed up for a short term and then mustered two teams to carry the army's baggage to the Lake Champlain area, a part of the country he had learned well in the previous war. Then he enlisted again, this time in the artillery, and served until taken sick.[21]

When he was home, Solomon was an invalid much of the time. In 1777 a tree his son was cutting fell on Solomon, stripped the skin off his back, and broke his bones. For four months he lay in bed or was carried in a sheet by six men. When he was well enough to get about, he hobbled around on crutches. While still lame and directing repairs of the family sawmill, he fell on the waterwheel. More months of painful recuperation failed to heal him. Solomon never fully recovered the use of his limbs. He had to ride side-saddle and was subject to occasional "fits," as he called them. Looking back as he wrote his life story in 1811, Solomon saw little to rejoice in. These painful, crushing accidents, which brought him to the edge of death on two or three occasions without killing him, led him to conclude grimly that he was not meant to die young: "There was yet more trouble for me to pass through."[22]

Four years into the Revolutionary War, Solomon was "destitute of property, and without my natural strength to get my bread, with a young and dependent family whose daily wants were increasing and none to administer relief." What choice had he but to seek the most profitable occupation he could find? In 1779, with sons Jason and Stephen, ages thirteen and nineteen, he joined the crew of the privateer *Beaver* under Captain William Havens. In an exceptional run of luck the *Beaver* captured eight British vessels in Long Island Sound between April and June, 1779. Solomon and his sons probably received three shares of the prizes divided among the crew of eighty. With that money in his pocket, Solomon returned to Gilsum and moved his family forty miles south to Montague on the Connecticut River. The next four or five years at home were the longest period Lucy ever had with him.[23]

After the war Solomon freighted a vessel bound for Liverpool, Nova Scotia. He had received word that a large debt due him had been collected there. Taking Jason with him, he was gone for four years, most of it spent at sea. He and Jason signed on as crew of a fishing schooner, and ended up purchasing the vessel after it was damaged in a hurricane and abandoned. They carried passengers to New London and back, conducted a coasting trade between Halifax, Nova Scotia, and St. John, New Brunswick. They lost the ship when it ran aground on a reef, purchased it again, and then he and Jason both fell sick. For four years Solomon heard nothing from his family. Finally around 1788, after recovering from his illness, he returned home with little to show for his exertions. He was fifty-six, and after all his "hard labor and perplexity of mind, I had won nothing." "The best of my days were past and gone and had to begin entirely anew." More dispiriting than anything, he discovered on his return that Lydia and the children had been turned out of their house in Montague. Solomon thought he had taken care of an old debt from Lyme with a debt owed to him for the same amount. A misunderstanding and the underhanded dealings of one Samuel McCurdy, who fell heir to Solomon's promissory note, led to the ejection. This news took the heart out of him. "I now thought all was gone, and I did not care whether I lived or died."[24]

Solomon's doleful account of his life should not be read as a narrative of unmitigated failure. His reason for writing was to show that God had repeatedly humbled him and showed him the vanity of the world, and yet he had remained blind and deaf to the Lord's call. Solomon's purpose required that he emphasize his defeats and despair. Although they suffered reverses, the Mack family did not dwell in mean poverty. At various times they owned farms and houses. Solomon had the capital to purchase land, freight vessels, buy a schooner, and to owe and be owed hundreds of dollars. In 1786 his daughter Lydia married Samuel Bill from one of Gilsum's prominent families. Moreover, Solomon's disappointments never broke his spirit. After lamenting that he cared not whether he lived or died, he reported that nevertheless "I went to work and shifted from plan to plan till at length I moved to Tunbridge." Neither failure, old age, nor broken bones defeated him. By 1792 at age sixty he was ready to move again, this time back to Gilsum where Stephen had opened a store. A few years later Solomon admitted that he had "gained some property."[25]

The significance of Solomon's account lies less in his actual success or failure in acquiring wealth than in his sense of life as made up of toil, hurt, defeat, and death. Outside of the war episodes there is no happiness or triumph until the end, when "God did appear for me and took me out of the horrible pit and mirey clay, and set my feet on the rock of Christ Jesus." Lucy's emotional range was broader and deeper than Solomon's—pride, triumph, and tenderness radiate from her sketches—but much of Solomon's grim endurance passed to his daughter. While her life was not a "horrible pit and mirey clay," Lucy measured the early years not by happy friendships or childish adventures but by deaths and illnesses.

Her memories, she said, were "engraved upon my heart with a pen of Iron." When a chance meeting reminded her of her youth, the thought would come to her, " 'The friends of my youth! Where are they?' The tomb replies, 'here are they!' "[26]

The bare facts of Lucy's life justify her somber outlook. She was in her third year when Solomon was carried home half-dead from the falling tree, and she watched while he suffered from the waterwheel fall and the blow on the head from the tree limb that started his fits. Solomon left for Nova Scotia when Lucy was about eight. Soon after, her mother suffered a "severe fit of sickness" and came so near death that, in the absence of Solomon, she assigned eight-year-old Lucy to her brother Stephen for safekeeping.[27] When Lucy was fourteen, her married sister Lovisa fell ill with consumption, and the family underwent a five-year period when either Lovisa or Lovina, a year younger, hovered on the edge of death.

Lucy nursed Lovina, and at age sixteen or seventeen was able to carry her twenty-nine-year-old sister from chair to bed. The circumstances of Lovina's death after two years burned into Lucy's memory. She reported with awed fascination Lovina's telling of the cold creeping into her fingers and face. A few months later in 1794 Lovisa's consumption flared up again after a three-year remission. Solomon went at once to South Hadley, where she lived with her husband, and, finding her improved, tried to bring her back to Gilsum. She died in an inn four miles along the road. Lucy remarked at the end of her "mournful recital" that the feelings evoked by these events "must last while life endures." In summing up her life, near the end, Lucy told almost nothing of her childhood other than her part in these illnesses and deaths.[28]

Lovina and Lovisa probably died in 1794 when Lucy was nineteen. The succession of deaths bore her to the ground. The grief began to prey upon her health. "I was pensive and melancholy, and often in my reflections I thought that life was not worth possessing." Depressed and restless, Lucy sought comfort in religion. "I determined to obtain that which I had heard spoken of so much from the pulpit—a change of heart." She gave herself to Bible reading and prayer but kept stumbling over one obstacle. "If I remain a member of no church, all religious people will say I am of the world; and if I join some one of the different denominations, all the rest will say I am in error. No church will admit that I am right, except the one with which I am associated."[29]

It was a logical dilemma, but only for one whom life had carried to a certain religious position. For others the question of which church could never be a question. They knew only one church in town and, when needed, religion was found there. Parents were members and the family attended weekly. When a change of heart was sought, the pastor ministered to the soul's hungers. Life had dealt differently with Lucy. A church had been organized in Gilsum in 1772, but for twenty-two years the town could not afford a pastor. The church invited ministers from neighboring towns, particularly Keene, to preach. Not until the year of Lovina's and Lovisa's death did Elisha Fish accept an invitation to settle. Whatever associations Lucy had in Montague, her other home, they were not accessible when she needed help in 1794.[30]

Solomon had little to offer. At sixty-two he was still seeking happiness in an elusive prosperity, the false hope of his faithless upbringing. Not until 1811 at age seventy-five was he converted. Lucy's mother Lydia was the only source of religious instruction in the Mack household. Lydia was reared in the home of Deacon Daniel Gates of East Haddam, and joined the Congregational church there at age thirty after she was married to Solomon. He gave her full credit for instructing the children in habits of "piety, gentleness, and reflection," and for calling them together morning and evening to pray. Lucy said that all of her religious instruction came from her "pious and affectionate" mother.[31]

The Mack children bore their mother's imprint. The oldest son, Jason, became a lay preacher at age twenty, and at the end of his life was practicing faith-healings and "holding meetings, day and night, from place to place." As they approached death, Lovina and Lovisa each warned their hearers to prepare for eternity. Lydia imparted faith to her children, but she did not give them a church. Jason became a seeker before he was sixteen and pursued the spiritual gifts of early Christianity outside of established churches. The only mention of a church in Lucy's childhood reminiscences occurs in the reference to Lovisa after her marriage to Joseph Tuttle.[32]

Yet religious currents ran deep in Lucy. She believed that the power of God healed her sister and her mother, and she recorded in awe the account of Lovisa's vision of "the Saviour, as through a veil."[33] The deaths of her sisters drove her thoughts to eternity, judgment, and the worthlessness of life. She groped through her depression looking for a church and a change of heart and found nothing. Mack religion was family religion, and when Lucy desired an association beyond that circle, she was at a loss.

The only social organization to register on Lucy's memory before her twentieth year, besides perhaps the army, was the family. Looking back from 1844, she organized her thoughts around the experiences of brothers, sisters, father, and mother. The memorable events were the deaths of Lovina and Lovisa, the heartbreak of Jason, the heroism of Daniel. When Solomon went off to war, his only noteworthy companions were his sons. Almost no one outside the family was mentioned in the published version of the *Biographical Sketches.*

Lucy's impressions seem to have followed the actual contours of her life. The migrations from Lyme to Marlow followed a family track cut by other Macks, then to Gilsum settled by still more Macks from Lyme, and to Montague where brother Elisha lived. Later Solomon moved to Tunbridge, where son Stephen was set up in business. He died at Gilsum with Solomon, Jr. When Lovisa fell ill in her husband's house in South Hadley, Solomon was off at once to bring her back to Gilsum at her own request, to die and be buried with her family. Lydia sickened while Solomon was at sea, and Stephen received the assignment to care for Lucy the youngest.[34] For these mobile, insecure New Englanders, pursuing one hopeful, desperate plan after another, always in danger of debilitating accident or sickness, disappointed by creditors, business partners, and employees, family was the network through which information passed, the safety net when risks were taken, the retreat when fate turned against them. Whatever the level of sentiment or affection, trust and need bound member to member in a resilient chain.

Stephen Mack took to heart his mother's charge to look after Lucy. When she succumbed to depression after the sisters' deaths, he insisted that she visit him in Tunbridge, eighty miles north and across the Connecticut River in Vermont. Stephen had gone into business for himself in Gilsum in 1787 when he was twenty-one. In 1793 he had transferred his operations to Tunbridge, where he was on his way to a successful career. After the turn of the century he moved to Detroit and then Pontiac, where he opened a number of stores, farmed, was a builder, and ran saw and flour mills. Near the end of his life he moved to Rochester, Michigan, and again operated mills before he died. In 1794, at twenty-eight, he was a partner with John Mudget in a mercantile and tinning business.[35]

Tunbridge was a new town, like Gilsum or Marlow thirty years earlier when Solomon had moved there from Lyme. Among the new settlers was Asael Smith, who first acquired land in 1791 and was clearing and settling his sons on it when Lucy visited Stephen. Asael became Stephen's "intimate acquaintance," though twenty-two years separated the two men. Stephen spoke of the Smiths as "a worthy, respectable, amiable, and intelligent family." Asael was a selectman of Tunbridge, one of the three active men chosen to look after the town's affairs. During her visit Lucy met Joseph Smith, Asael's second son, a strong, tall young man of twenty-three. After a year she returned to Gilsum by way of Marlow where Mack relatives still lived, but was hardly home when Stephen came again and "insisted so hard upon my returning with him" that she agreed. In the dead of the Vermont winter, January 24, 1796, justice of the peace Seth Austin married Lucy Mack and Joseph Smith.[36]

ASAEL SMITH

Until Asael's generation scattered to the north and west, the Smith ancestors of the Prophet Joseph were rooted in Topsfield, Massachusetts. Fifteen-year-old Robert Smith had sailed from England in 1638 at the height of the Puritan migration and ended up in Topsfield, a farm village eight miles north of Salem. Asael was the fourth generation of Smiths in the town. His father, Samuel, had received all the honors the town could bestow. He was repeatedly chosen assessor, selectman, town clerk, representative to the General Court (the Massachusetts name for the legislature), and delegate to the Provincial Congress. Most important, he was chosen twenty times as moderator of the town meeting, a position reserved for one who commanded universal respect. During the Revolution he served on the Committee of Safety. When he died on November 14, 1785, his obituary in the *Salem Gazette* noted that he "was esteemed a man of integrity and uprightness. . . . a sincere friend to the liberties of his country, and a strenuous advocate for the doctrines of Christianity."[37]

Samuel's distinction in Topsfield gave Asael no particular economic advantage in getting started in life. Selectmen, though respected, were not necessarily the richest men in town. Asael was the youngest of five children, each of whom had to be provided for: land for the two boys and marriage portions for the three daughters. After helping the older children and holding back enough to carry him through old age, Samuel lacked the resources to set Asael up in Topsfield. He cast loose from the old village moorings and thereafter scrambled to gain a toehold in the spare New England economy, much like Solomon Mack, who began with nothing.

In 1767, at age twenty-three, Asael married Mary Duty. For five years they lived with Samuel and his second wife Priscilla. The first three children were born in Samuel's house, including Joseph on July 12, 1771. In May, 1772, Asael moved with wife and children to Windham, New Hampshire, where Mary's family had migrated. Two years later Asael and Mary were a few miles north in Dunbarton on the Merrimack River. In the summer of 1776 Asael enlisted for a few months' service along the northern New York frontier. During the early years of the Revolution the family was probably in Salem, New Hampshire. In 1777, when the sixth child was born, Asael was thirty-three and still in search of a place to sink his roots.[38]

Not until their move to Derryfield, New Hampshire (later Manchester), did Asael and Mary Smith find a modicum of security. In 1778 they purchased 100 acres on the Merrimack River and opened a coopering business. A year after acquiring property in Derryfield, Asael was elected town clerk. Four more children were born in Derryfield, bringing the total

to ten (one more was yet to come). For three years ill health prevented
Asael from doing any work beyond his clerk duties but, despite sickness
and a large family, from 1778 to 1786 Asael and Mary kept body and soul
together and saw no reason to move.[39]

In 1785 Asael visited his father, Samuel, in Topsfield in his last
sickness, and saw the old man at seventy-two jump out of bed in a delirium
and head for the door, saying he must go to the mill or his family would
suffer. Asael assured Samuel the family would be watched after. After
Samuel's death on November 14, 1785, care of his widow first fell to
Samuel, Jr. He was executor of the estate and initially took over the family
farm. His listing as gentleman in the land records as compared to Asael's
cooper may reflect an aspiration to follow Samuel, Sr., into the town
aristocracy. Within a few months of Samuel Sr.'s death, however, Samuel,
Jr., was ready to rid himself of the farm and settle for less. With the farm,
he had inherited the responsibility for seeing that Priscilla Smith received
one-third of its income, her widow's portion. In addition, he soon discovered
that the estate was actually insolvent. The two burdens were greater than
he chose to carry.[40]

The insolvency of Samuel's estate is not surprising. In the absence
of currency, New Englanders conducted their exchanges through debts and
credits with neighbors, storekeepers, tradesmen, and city merchants. An
active man could easily owe money to fifty or a hundred individuals and
be owed by as many in turn. Debts were paid with services, commodities,
and occasionally with small sums of money if any happened to come
along. At a given moment it was difficult to know where one stood,
because it was never certain which debtors would make good or when
creditors would demand payment. Creditors were lenient while a man
had earning power and closed in when he was in trouble. A person could
be prospering while alive and working, and suddenly be insolvent at death.[41]

Sometime in the winter of 1786 Samuel came to Asael with the bad
news that their father's debts came to more than the total worth of all
the real estate, receivables, and personal property combined. Samuel was
convinced that, with his own large family, he could not succeed in Topsfield. The low state of the economy and the shortage of money, which
in the west was driving farmers to close the courts to prevent debt collection,
made the prospect still more gloomy. Asael was more optimistic and,
perhaps more important, did not want his father's name tarnished. Asael's
son John remembered him saying, "I am not willing that my father, who
has done so much business, should have it said of him that he died
insolvent." The two of them arranged a trade. Samuel purchased Asael's
Derryfield farm for £120, and Asael, who had inherited half of his father's
Topsfield land, paid Samuel £250 for the other half. In the spring of 1786

Asael, Mary, and their ten children moved into Samuel and Priscilla's house in Topsfield.[42]

For five years Asael and his boys raised cattle and sheep for the market and grain, potatoes, vegetables, and fruit for the family. Priscilla received her one-third, the creditors an occasional payment, and the children were fed. Only gradually did Asael accept the inevitable: he could not pay the debts and keep the farm too. In 1791 the farm was sold. With considerable effort the debts were paid, Priscilla received her share, and Mary and Asael were once more looking for a new home.[43]

Asael's son said the family was destitute when they left Topsfield, but they were not without recourse. The Topsfield property was sold in March, 1791; in June Asael purchased eighty-three acres of uncleared land in Tunbridge, Vermont, for £26. His plan was to send the two oldest sons, Jesse and Joseph, ages twenty-three and twenty, to clear the Tunbridge land in preparation for the family's arrival the next spring, while he and Mary and the others leased land with a dairy herd in Ipswich, a few miles from Topsfield. They followed their plan through the summer but then amended it in the fall. "My father changed his mind," John wrote later, "as he could not bear to have his boys so far from him, as he always loved to have his children close by." In October Asael sold his Ipswich crops on the ground, hired three yoke of oxen and a wagon, and set out with the family on the 140-mile journey to Tunbridge. En route they met Joseph on his way back to Ipswich with a "partly fractured" leg bone. By November the Smiths were crowded into the fourteen-by-ten-foot hut built by Jesse and Joseph, and ready to face the Vermont winter on their new property.[44]

Because of boundary disputes Vermont had not attracted many settlers until a few years before. Solomon Mack might have settled in Vermont in 1763 rather than in Marlow on the New Hampshire side of the Connecticut River were it not for the uncertainty of land titles in Vermont. Both New York and New Hampshire laid claim to the territory between the Connecticut and the New York line. Farmers who purchased land under a grant from New Hampshire risked court battles with settlers with titles derived from New York. In an attempt to end the disruptive suits, Vermont broke free of the United States immediately after independence. In 1777 the settlers set up an independent republic under the name "New Connecticut." In 1790 a payment of $30,000 to quiet the New York claims removed that obstacle, and in March, 1791, Vermont was admitted to the Union as an independent state. Asael was one of thousands of prospective migrants who felt they could now purchase land without fear of loss.

People had trickled into Vermont soon after English victory in the French and Indian wars reduced the hazard of Indian attack. Most of them settled along the southern border above Massachusetts, and just west of the Connecticut River. In 1791 the state contained 85,425 inhabitants. The most thickly settled counties were Windham and Windsor, along the river in the southeast corner. Tunbridge lay just north of Windsor in Orange County. When the Smiths arrived, 487 inhabitants, perhaps eighty to a hundred families, had scattered themselves over the town's thirty-six square miles of hilly, broken land. Over the next decade Vermont's somewhat exaggerated reputation for fertility more than doubled the state's population and nearly tripled the size of Tunbridge to 1,324 people.[45]

They came primarily to raise cattle, augmenting their economy with other enterprises. A new family first cut the virgin white pines covering virtually every acre and made what profit they could from the harvest. They were not likely to haul out the trees as lumber. The trouble and expense of getting planks to the Connecticut and past the falls to markets on the lower river were more than the price warranted. After constructing their own house and sheds, and piling up the winter's fuel supply, a new settler burned the trees and converted them to pot and pearl ash for soap making. In that compact form Vermont exported its trees to markets in Springfield and Hartford. A family also commonly tapped the maples each spring, and in a few weeks in February and March made as much as 200 or 300 pounds of sugar.[46]

With the trees down, a kitchen garden went in and cows, beef cattle, sheep, and hogs were put out to graze. When the stumps were out, the farmers plowed the land and sowed hay and wheat. Vermont's major exports were pot and pearl ash, pork, beef, wheat flour, grain, butter, cheese, lumber, and horses. After the turn of the century it was reported that Vermonters drove from 12,000 to 15,000 head of beef cattle to Boston each year.[47]

Asael had seven sons when he arrived in Tunbridge. Their strength was his greatest resource, their need for farms as they came of age his greatest responsibility. Jesse married a year after their arrival at age twenty-four, and set up on fifty acres received from his father. The rest of the boys labored alongside Asael until they married. By 1796 he could report to an old friend in Topsfield that one farm was ready and a new house built on a second. Joseph, the second son, received the first farm when he married Lucy Mack in 1796 and worked it on halves. Asael used his half to support his family while he brought in new farms for the others. In 1794 and 1795 he purchased two additional 100-acre lots close to the first farm and a third soon followed. By the time the third son, Asael, Jr., married in 1802, the Smiths had a 300-400-acre compound of adjoining farms.[48]

By the end of the century Asael could look back with satisfaction on his accomplishments. Two sons and two daughters had married since his arrival and were raising children of their own. He had hewn four farms out of the forest and won the respect of the village. Beginning in 1793 he was frequently elected one of three selectmen to manage town affairs, and occasionally served as moderator and highway surveyor. Jesse was trustee of the school district opened in the southern portion of the town near the Smith farms, and in his time was to be selectman and town clerk. Asael had come close to replicating in Tunbridge the life his father had led in Topsfield.[49]

Each of Asael's four married children bore him a grandchild in 1799. Perhaps moved by the fact that he was soon to have eight grandchildren in all, Asael composed at age fifty-five "A few words of advice" to his family, "whom I expect ere long to leave." Addressed to "My Dear Selfs," it was intended to be a testament, but it was also a revelation of his character, beginning with the melancholy tone of the opening sentence: "I know not what leisure I shall have at the hour of my death to speak unto you, and as you all know that I am not free in speech especially when sick or sad; and therefore now speak my heart to you, and would wish you to hear me speaking to you as long as you live (when my tongue shall be mouldered to dust in the silent tomb) in this my writing. . . ." Though he desired to speak his heart, Asael was a quiet man and one known to feel sadness. "I never found anything too hard for me in my calling," he said, "but discouragement and unbelief." "Above everything," he advised his children, "avoid a melancholy disposition. That is a humor that admits of any temptation and is capable of any impression and distemper. Shun as death this humor, which will work you to all un-thankfulness against God, unlovingness to men, and unnaturalness to yourselves and one another." He spoke as one who knew firsthand how depression alternated with surges of anger.[50]

One cannot help wondering where the melancholy came from. One thing we know is that he felt abused by the woman who raised him. Asael's mother died when he was six months old. His mother's cousin, who married his father a year later, "did not treat him so kindly as some mothers treat their children." Perhaps the fact that his neck was somewhat awry did not endear him to her. In "A few words of advice," he asked his wife, if she should remarry following his death, to "remember what I have undergone by a stepmother, and do not estrange your husband from his own children or kindred, lest you draw on him and on yourself a great sin." He also advised his children to show no partiality for their offspring. "If nature hath made no difference, do you make none in your affections, countenances nor portions; partiality this way begets envy, hatred, strife and contention." Asael remembered a hard childhood and was conscious of personal deficiencies. He urged his children to remember that their father "had never your parts nor helps."[51]

Though touched with bitterness and memories of strife, the current of sadness in Asael's life did not harden him. It did make him cautious and circumspect. "Do not talk and make a noise to get the name of forward men, but do the thing and do it in a way that is fair and honest, which you can live and die by and rise and reign by." There may be some hurt in his counsel to "abandon all infectious, flattering, self-serving companions. When once you have found them false, trust them no more."[52]

On the other hand, there is still more evidence of an open and generous heart, particularly with regard to his family. To the family as a group he gave the fullest and most forceful instructions:

My last request and charge is that you will live together in an undivided bond of love. You are many of you, and if you join together as one man, you need not want anything. What counsel, what comfort, what money, what friends may you not help yourselves unto, if you will all as one contribute your aids.

Wherefore my dear children, I pray, beseech, and adjure you by all the relations and dearness that hath ever been betwixt us and by the heart-rending pangs of a dying father, whose soul hath been ever bound in the bundle of life with yours, that you know one another. Visit as you may each other. Comfort, counsel, relieve, succor, help and admonish one another. And while your mother lives, meet her if possible once every year. When she is dead, pitch on some other place, if it may be, your elder brother's house; or if you cannot meet, send to and hear from each other yearly and oftener if you can. And when you have neither father nor mother left, be so many fathers and mothers to each other, so you shall understand the blessing mentioned in the 133 Psalm.[53]

Those sentiments were distilled from his own life. Asael was the one to look after a stepmother whose love he had never trusted. When the family moved to Vermont, Asael left a daughter behind to take care of his ailing older sister. The love for his children that made it impossible for Asael to leave Jesse and Joseph alone in Vermont for the winter welded his own offspring to him and to each other. He told them "to join together as one man" as they had done in clearing their Vermont farms. A few years later the family showed that their capacity for a grand venture had not dissipated with time. Between 1811 and 1820 Asael and Mary and at least seven of the eleven children moved from Tunbridge. Six of the seven settled around their parents once again, this time in Stockholm and Potsdam in St. Lawrence County, New York, where presumably with the aid of grandchildren they opened new farms.[54]

They were living close together in 1828 when Joseph Smith, Sr., wrote the news of the visions of his son. In 1830 he came personally with copies of the Book of Mormon. Faith and belief seemed to flow along family lines. Asael and Mary and eventually three of the four surviving sons and all but two daughters believed the teachings of their nephew and grandson. Only Jesse the eldest held back. In 1836 the clan moved again, this time without Asael, who died in 1830. Asael, Jr., Silas, John, and Mary Duty Smith gathered in Kirtland. At the end of the 500-mile journey Joseph, Jr., and Hyrum met their ninety-two-year-old grandmother in her Fairport hotel room. "Joseph blessed her and said she was the most honored woman on earth." Mary told Lucy, "I am going to have your Joseph [Jr.] baptize me, and my Joseph [the patriarch] bless me." Life did not last long enough for that family event, but there was time for a reunion with four sons, grandsons, and a score of great-grandchildren which fulfilled Asael's admonition that the children meet yearly and "live together in an undivided bond of love."[55]

Asael gave more religious direction to his children than did Solomon Mack, whose conversion did not occur until his offspring were long dispersed. Unlike Solomon's irreligious master, Asael's father saw to the baptism of all his four children in the Topsfield Congregational church. At eighteen Asael was assigned a seat in the meetinghouse, and in 1772 husband and wife owned the convenant.[56] Owning the convenant did not make them full members of the church. One had to show evidence of supernatural grace and have an assurance of salvation before becoming a voting member. Owning the church covenant meant that they believed the doctrines outlined in the covenant and promised to live an upright and moral life. That degree of commitment allowed them to present Jesse, Joseph, and Priscilla for baptism.

The absence of assurance of divine grace did not mean that Asael and Mary lacked religious convictions. In the third paragraph of "A few words of advice," Asael said, "And now my dear children, let me pour out my heart to you and speak first to you of immortality in your souls. Trifle not in this point: the soul is immortal. You have to deal with an infinite majesty; you go upon life and death. Therefore, in this point be serious. Do all to God in a serious manner. When you think of him speak of him, pray to him, or in any way make your addresses to his great majesty, be in good earnest." Asael's piety and faith, however, did not flow entirely in the well-worn channels of New England Congregationalism. Asael went on to admonish his children to "search the scriptures and consult sound [reas] on" in the formation of their beliefs. By joining the two, reason and faith, he signaled his independence of conventional orthodoxy.[57]

While New England Puritans had always employed right reason to open the true meaning of the scriptures, in the eighteenth century dissenters from strict Calvinist orthodoxy justified their departures on the basis of reason. They did not turn reason against the scripture or ground their beliefs on reason alone, but they insisted that the scriptures be interpreted reasonably. A group of Harvard-educated ministers, mostly settled in churches near Boston, argued that Calvinism read ideas into the scripture which were not there. It seemed unscriptural and dangerous to believe that God saved men arbitrarily. What good were human strivings? The scriptures, they said, taught that grace came in response to an effort to obey. Their reasoning brought these men around to the position of the Dutchman Jacobus Arminius, who raised similar objections to Calvinism in the early seventeenth century, and thus they were labeled Arminians.[58]

This reasonable spirit was in the air when Asael Smith began forming his beliefs. Reason freed him from an unthinking acceptance of traditional Puritan beliefs, but he did not follow the path of the Arminians. His teachings to his children show more of the influence of the Universalist John Murray. Murray arrived in America from England in 1770 and settled in Gloucester, Massachusetts, in 1774, about fifteen miles from Topsfield. Not Boston-born and not Harvard-bred, his teachings were more widely accepted by the common people of New England than the Arminians.' He taught that Christ assumed the sins of all men and redeemed them all by his atonement. They did not merit grace by their good works; Christ's grace alone redeemed them, but it was powerful enough to redeem everyone without exception. Murray carried the Calvinist idea of irresistible grace to its logical conclusion and included every soul within the circle of divine love.[59]

Asael, like Murray, put his trust in salvation by grace alone. In "A few words of advice" he tried to bring his children step by step to the same conclusion. Consider, he said, "whether you can by outward forms, rites and ordinances save yourselves, or whether there is a necessity of your having help from any other hand than your own." The question was whether Christ came "to save mankind because they were sinners and could not save themselves or whether he [came] to save mankind because they had repented of their sins, so as to be forgiven on the score of their repentance." In Asael's opinion, and here he was on safe ground because it was the common Congregational belief, "he came to save sinners merely because they were such," not because of repentance. Having gone that far, Asael saw no reason why God should favor Vermont Christians over "the worst heathen in the darkest corner of the deserts of Arabia." "And if you can believe that Christ [came] to save sinners and not the righteous Pharisees or self-righteous; that sinners must be saved by the righteousness of Christ alone, without mixing any of their own righteousness with his, then you will see that he can as well save all as any."[60]

The Universalist followers of Murray organized an association in Massachusetts in 1785 for the purpose of gaining exemption from the state's ecclesiastical taxes. In 1793 a New England convention of Universalists met. From all reports Vermont was one of their strongholds. The Green Mountains were reputed to be the lair of all manner of heresies. Ethan Allen in 1784 published an attack on the Bible and Christian doctrines in *The Only Oracle of Man.* Tom Paine's *Age of Reason* was "greedily received in Vermont." Orthodox critics lumped Universalism and Paine's deism together among the state's great errors, even though the two were miles apart. Timothy Dwight, the Calvinist president of Yale, said Vermont's settlers were "men of loose principle and loose morals. They were either professed infidels, Universalists, or people who exhibited the morals of these two classes of mankind." Actually deists denied revelation, the inspiration of the Bible, the divinity of Christ, and the efficacy of the atonement, while Universalists were believing Christians. They appeared as one to the conservative clergy because together they signified that the grip of the old Puritan faith had been broken in Vermont.[61]

In 1790 five Congregational clergymen on the upper Connecticut converted to Universalism not many miles from Tunbridge. Asael had no trouble in finding kindred spirits in his own village. In 1797 the town clerk recorded a request from seventeen members of the Tunbridge Universalist Society to be exempted from ecclesiastical taxes. Asael was moderator of the group, and Joseph and Jesse were among the seventeen. The society came to nothing. Two years later one of the number denied that he had ever signed the document; in 1798 Asael occupied a pew in the newly built Congregational meetinghouse.[62]

In 1774 Connecticut's General Association of Ministers resolved to send representatives to Vermont. Following the Revolution Connecticut clergymen toured the state to test the religious atmosphere and returned with horrifying reports. Vermont needed a major missionary effort. The Congregational and Presbyterian ministers in the state organized in 1796 to combat "infidelity and other hurtful errors," and in 1798 Connecticut organized a missionary society with an eye on Vermont. Revivals began in the western counties in 1801 and increased in frequency through the next ten years. "The gospel chariot rolls" in Vermont, the *Connecticut Evangelical Magazine* told its readers in 1802. "Universalism, Deism and atheism are less threatening than in past years."[63]

Asael's family felt the effects of the revivals. His children apparently gravitated toward orthodoxy. Asael's Universalism was an overlay on family religion, not the heart and soul of it. In "A few words of advice" Asael dropped the confident exhortatory tone when he came to Universalism, and reasoned with his children as if he knew some had yet to be persuaded.

Jesse, a member of the Universalist Society in 1797, was stiffly orthodox when Joseph, Sr., brought the Book of Mormon to the family in 1830. Asael's own convictions did not waver; his grandson George A. Smith remembers him writing "quires of paper on the doctrine of universal restoration" before his death. But of all the children, apparently only Joseph remained aloof from conventional religion. He stubbornly refused to embrace any church until his own son showed the way.[64]

JOSEPH AND LUCY SMITH

Thanks to help from both sides of the family, Joseph and Lucy Mack began married life under favorable circumstances. Asael provided his son with part ownership of a "handsome" four-year-old farm, and her brother Stephen Mack and his partner John Mudget presented Lucy with $1,000 for a wedding present. Lucy bought her household furnishings with other means at her disposal and laid away the money as a cash reserve. After visiting Solomon and Lydia Mack in Gilsum, she and Joseph set to work on their farm in a most promising year. Wheat prices in Tunbridge in 1796 were up by a third. The New England farm economy had left the doldrums of the 1780s far behind. A first son died in childbirth, and then two years after their marriage Lucy bore a second son, Alvin, and two years later almost to the day a third boy, Hyrum.[65]

They remained in Tunbridge for six years. Perhaps in hopes of advancing their fortunes still further, perhaps prodded by the ambitious Stephen Mack, Joseph and Lucy in 1802 left the farm and turned to storekeeping. Early in the year they rented their Tunbridge house and land and moved to Randolph, a neighboring village seven miles to the west. It was a favorable moment to move and a good location for a store. Randolph was larger than Tunbridge; in 1800 it had 1,841 inhabitants to Tunbridge's 1,324. The numbers seem small now, but in 1800 Randolph was the largest town in Orange County and the fourteenth largest in the state. Nor was its growth cycle exhausted. By 1810 Randolph held 2,255 inhabitants and was the eighth largest town in Vermont. Topography favored the village. Instead of the usual hills that rumple most of Vermont's landscape and make large portions useless, a broad plateau stretched between the two rivers running through the town. Nearly 20,000 acres of arable land attracted settlers. Randolph's growth after 1800 was further stimulated by the opening of a canal at Bellows Falls in 1802, which gave Vermont water access to the lower Connecticut, and by the institution in 1801 of a weekly Vermont-Boston stage line.[66]

Joseph Smith opened his Randolph store with a line of goods purchased on credit from Boston. His inventory sold quickly, not for cash but for promise of payment in commodities at harvest. Joseph meanwhile turned his thoughts to ginseng, the root that grew wild in Vermont and was prized in China for its supposed capacity to prolong life and restore virility. The *Empress of China*, the first American ship to reach Canton after the Revolution, carried forty tons of ginseng. The next year the Americans shipped twice as much without satisfying the demand or lowering the price. Joseph collected the root, probably from local farmers, and crystalized it. He did well enough that a merchant named Stevens from Royalton, a few miles south of Randolph, offered $3,000 for the ginseng, but Joseph preferred to handle it himself and obtain the full price.[67]

It was a fateful turning point in the Smith family fortunes. Joseph took the ginseng to New York and contracted for shipment on consignment. He stood to make as much as $4,500 by circumventing the middlemen, but he also assumed the whole burden of risk. As it turned out, he lost. The son of the Royalton merchant who made the original offer for the root sailed for China on the same ship with a cargo of his father's. On his return he reported the sad news that the venture had failed. He presented Joseph with a chest of tea as his only compensation. The venture, in fact, was a failure, but not because of a poor market. Stephen Mack smelled foul play when the young Stevens shortly after his return opened works for crystalizing ginseng and hired seven or eight men. Catching Stevens in his cups, Stephen deftly extracted the information that the ginseng had brought a chestful of money. Joseph had been cheated of his just returns. Coming to his senses, Stevens fled for Canada, and though Joseph set out after him, the pursuit was in vain. Joseph returned from the chase disheartened, perhaps wiser, and financially ruined.[68]

Meanwhile the debt for the original inventory of store goods was due. With his shelves empty, Joseph found he had $2,000 in bad debts from his customers and nothing to pay the $1,800 owed in Boston. Forced to the wall, he took the step that blighted the Smith family fortunes for thirty years. He sold the farm. Lucy contributed her $1,000 wedding gift, and the farm went for $800. Lucy said they made the sacrifice to avoid the "embarrassment of debt," but they soon knew the "embarrassment of poverty." They crossed the boundary dividing independent ownership from tenancy and day labor. It was a line that for all their industry and ingenuity the Smiths were not to recross until after the organization of the church in 1830.[69]

One of the misfortunes of the propertyless was the necessity for frequent moves. Tenants ofttimes rented farms that were in process of being sold and available only for a few years. When the farm was not sold out from under them, a better opportunity elsewhere impelled a move. Over the next fourteen years the Smiths moved seven times. Between 1803 and 1811 all the moves were in a tiny circle around Tunbridge, Royalton, and Sharon, immediately adjoining towns, and probably never involved a distance of more than five or six miles. Then the circle widened. In 1811 they moved twenty miles across the Connecticut River to Lebanon, New Hampshire, and finally, after a few years back in Vermont in Norwich, the Smiths broke entirely free of the network of family and friends and in 1816 migrated to New York.[70]

Until that final break, family members smoothed the way for Joseph and Lucy. In the spring of 1803 the Smiths were back on their Tunbridge farm, amidst Asael's children, for the birth of Sophronia in May. After the sale of the farm they spent a few months in Royalton and then rented a farm from Solomon Mack, who on August 27, 1804, purchased 100 acres bridging the Sharon-Royalton line. They were still in familiar territory. The Smith clan lived but a few miles north of the new farm; Stephen Mack remained in Tunbridge for a few years yet; Daniel Mack, Lucy's brother, married in Tunbridge in 1799; and Solomon and Lydia Mack were close at hand. However poor Joseph and Lucy were, they would never starve or be short-handed when they needed help.[71]

Joseph taught school in Sharon in the winter and farmed in the summer. There is no record of his own education, but whether or not Joseph, Jr., ever attended school, his father certainly could have taught him at home. Joseph's brother Jesse was judged a fit man to appoint as trustee of schools in the southern part of Tunbridge, and presumably Joseph benefited from the family reputation. With Joseph working both jobs, the Smith family circumstances, as Lucy reported, "gradually improved." She was feeling optimistic when another son arrived on December 23, 1805, whom they named Joseph Smith, Jr.[72]

Young Joseph probably had no memories of the sloping hill farm which now bears his name. His family moved when he was barely two. They were in Tunbridge on March 13, 1808, for the birth of Samuel Harrison. Two years later to the day Ephraim was born and exactly one year later William, both in Royalton. Little Ephraim died eleven days after birth, the second of Lucy's children lost in childhood.[73]

Despite the frequent moves and occasional sorrows, there is no evidence of stress in the Smith family during Joseph's early years. Lucy remembered them as happy, progressive times. Joseph probably had enough schooling from Deacon Jonathan Finney in Royalton to learn his letters. When they crossed the Connecticut to Lebanon, New Hampshire, in 1811, the Smiths congratulated themselves upon their prosperity. "We looked around us and said what do we now lack. There is nothing which we have not a sufficiency of to make us and our children perfectly comfortable both for food and raiment as well as that which is necessary to a respectable appearance in society both at home and abroad." Not content with what they had, they renewed their exertions "to obtain a greater abundance of this worlds goods." They purchased 100 pounds of candles, to permit them to work into the winter nights, and 200 yards of cloth for a stock of family clothing. None of the children had yet attended school. Hyrum, age eleven, was sent a few miles north to Moor's Charity School, associated with Dartmouth. Alvin, age thirteen, and Sophronia, age eight, went to public school. Joseph, five, and his two younger brothers, Samuel and William, three and six months, remained at home. In the summer of 1812 a baby girl, Catherine, joined the family.[74]

For all of its modest comfort, the life of the Smith family, as Lucy well knew, was far from secure. She and Joseph were driven by the knowledge that they were still unprepared for the two great economic challenges of every nineteenth-century farm family: provision for children as they came of age, and provision for their own old age. Adult life was a race to accumulate sufficient goods to give the children a start, and still have enough to be independent and comfortable in old age. "We doubled our diligence, in order to obtain more of this world's goods, with the view of assisting our children, when they should need it; and, as is quite natural, we looked forward to the decline of life, and were providing for its wants. . . ." Ultimately they had to own property to make it over both hurdles. Without land, the margin between comfort and mean poverty was all too thin. A single calamity could consume their resources and leave them penniless.[75]

In 1812 calamity struck. Typhoid fever swept through the upper Connecticut Valley and left 6,000 dead. One after another the Smith family fell ill, until all but the parents were prostrate. Sophronia, who was hit hardest, went through a ninety-day siege that left her at last limp, wide-eyed, and motionless. Joseph and Lucy clasped hands, knelt, and uttered a grief-stricken prayer. Then Lucy caught the apparently dead girl up in a blanket, pressed her close, and paced the floor until the child sobbed and began to breathe. Mother and daughter sank to the bed. Lucy was exhausted but the fever had broken. None of the children died.[76]

The fever left seven-year-old Joseph after two weeks, but a sore formed in his armpit and was wrongly diagnosed as a sprain. After two weeks of intense pain Dr. Parker identified the true cause of the suffering and lanced the sore, which discharged a quart of purulent matter. Though that infection healed, Joseph complained immediately of a pain in his left shin and ankle. After three weeks Dr. Stone, a surgeon, was called in and this time an eight-inch incision was made between ankle and knee. Opening the infection helped temporarily, but infection had now entered the bone. As the wound healed over, the infection flamed up again. The doctor made another, larger incision, going down to the bone.

When the healing wound began to swell once more, Dr. Stone consulted a "council of surgeons," headed by Nathan Smith and Cyrus Perkins from the Dartmouth Medical College. They proposed amputation, the sensible treatment of osteomyelitis in the age before antibiotics. Lucy remembered seven physicians riding up to the house in Lebanon; Joseph remembered eleven. To a seven-year-old they must have seemed like a small army, all there to deal with his leg. Probably some were medical students who came to witness the surgery. Lucy refused to accept the idea of amputation, and young Joseph protested too. As she remembered the event, Lucy appealed to the doctors to cut out the diseased portion of bone and, by refusing to let them into Joseph's room, won their consent. Lucy also remembered young Joseph refusing wine or brandy and assuring the doctors that cords were unnecessary. Fortunately for him, Joseph had come under the the care of one of the most renowned surgeons in New England. Nathan Smith, in his extensive practice with typhoid patients suffering from bone infection, had developed a surgical procedure far in advance of his time. He may have suggested amputation to prepare the family for accepting an alternative that, though unconventional, he knew to be sound.[77]

As the operation began, Lucy went out into the fields and left Joseph, Jr., in his father's arms, the infected leg resting on folded sheets. The surgeons bored holes on each side of the leg bone and chipped off three large pieces. Joseph screamed when they broke off the first piece, and Lucy rushed back into the room. Sent away, she came back again as the third piece came off. Blood gushed from the open wound, and Joseph lay on the bed drenched in blood. He was "pale as a corpse, and large drops of sweat were rolling down his face, whilst upon every feature was depicted the utmost agony."[78]

After three months of constant pain Joseph had passed the crisis and the leg began to mend. The ordeal, however, was not over. While the wound healed cleanly this time, fourteen additional pieces of bone worked their way to the surface. The disease and pain so wasted his body that his mother easily carried him about in her arms. Convalescence dragged on for three years. To speed his recovery, the family sent him to Salem, on the Massachusetts coast, with his uncle Jesse to enjoy the sea breezes. In due time Joseph was able to get about, but until the family moved to New York he hobbled around on crutches. During those three active years from seven to ten, he was either in bed or on crutches. To the end of his life he limped slightly, possibly because the trauma stunted the growth of the invaded leg.[79]

The typhoid fever episode laid bare relationships in the Smith household that were less visible in placid times. Mostly we know about Lucy because she was the only one to leave an account, save for a paragraph in Joseph Jr.'s manuscript history. The predominant impression is of her boldness and determination. When the seven medical men walked into her house in Lebanon with the intention of cutting off Joseph's leg, Lucy blocked the way. As she told the story, after they were seated she posed the crucial question: "Gentlemen, what can you do to save my boy's leg?" When they answered, "We can do nothing," she took them on and proposed another procedure.[80]

Lucy obviously enjoyed the part and took pleasure in the memory of what she had done. On the long journeys from Norwich to Palmyra, and again from New York to Kirtland, she took the same role. She was the one to know the right thing to do, to set matters in order, to stand up to error when it presented itself, and eventually to save the day. Beyond any question she was a woman of great spirit, outspoken and candid, forceful under pressure. Her concluding words to the doctors were, "You will not, you must not, take off his leg until you try once more. I will not consent to let you enter his room until you make me this promise."[81]

When the doctors entered young Joseph's room, his father was with him. Lucy said her husband "was constantly with the child." Lucy reported that after learning of the decision to operate again, Joseph, Sr., "seemed for a moment to contemplate my countenance; then turning his eyes upon his boy, at once all his sufferings together with my intense anxiety rushed upon his mind; and he burst into a flood of tears, and sobbed like a child." The scene suggests the tenderness of the elder Joseph in contrast to the resoluteness of Lucy Smith. She contended with the doctors while he sat by the boy.[82]

Lucy was a comforter too. She was the one to pace the floor with Sophronia clasped to her bosom until the child began breathing again. When Joseph's leg began to swell, Lucy carried him much of the time. She had convenanted with God during an earlier religious crisis to comfort her family to the best of her ability, but her comfort was more intense and high-strung. After Sophronia caught her breath, Lucy sank to the bed, "completely overpowered by the intensity of my feelings." She carried Joseph so much that she was taken ill herself. "The anxiety of mind that I experienced, together with physical overexertion, was too much for my constitution, and my nature sunk under it."[83]

Her husband's strength was of another kind. He cried at the thought of an operation on his son, but he also held the child while the doctors cut into his leg. When the pain first struck, Joseph, Jr., cried out to his father, not to Lucy, and in refusing to be tied with cords, said, "I will have my father sit on the bed and hold me in his arms." He sent his mother from the room, telling her, "I know you cannot bear to see me suffer so;

father can stand it, but you have carried me so much, and watched over me so long, you are almost worn out." The steadier father stood by when Lucy's nerves could not bear the strain.[84]

Even though she saw herself as the fighter in the family, Lucy recognized and needed her husband's kind of strength. In retelling the story, she gave him full credit for his part in the operation. In the flinty fashion of nineteenth-century Yankees, she was circumspect about her feelings for him, but her affection and admiration were all the more evident because she revealed them unconsciously. A few years earlier, when she was trying to interest her husband in religion, she dreamed of Joseph, Sr., and his brother Jesse. She saw herself standing in a beautiful meadow which "wore an aspect of peculiar pleasantness." In the "magnificent meadow" stood two large trees which she later understood represented Joseph and his brother. "These trees were very beautiful, they were well proportioned, and towered with majestic beauty to a great height. Their branches which added to their symmetry and glory, commenced near the top, and spread themselves in luxurious grandeur around. I gazed upon them with wonder and admiration." One of the trees was fixed and rigid in the wind, the other flexible and joyous. The dream comforted Lucy, because her Joseph was the flexible tree, which she took to mean he would embrace the gospel, while the unbending Jesse stubbornly refused. The unconscious point of the dream was the beauty of her husband in Lucy's eyes and the admiration with which she beheld him.

I saw one of them was surrounded with a bright belt, that shone like burnished gold, but far more brilliantly. Presently, a gentle breeze passed by, and the tree encircled with this golden zone bent gracefully before the wind, and waved its beautiful branches in the light air. As the wind increased, this tree assumed the most lively and animated appearance, and seemed to express in its motions the utmost joy and happiness. . . . Even the stream that rolled beneath it, shared, apparently, every sensation felt by the tree, for, as the branches danced over the stream, it would swell gently, then recede again with a motion as soft as the breathing of an infant, but as lively as the dancing of a sunbeam. The belt also partook of the same influence, and as it moved in unison with the motion of the stream and of the tree, it increased continually in refulgence and magnitude, until it became exceedingly glorious.[85]

This happy tribute to the radiance of Joseph must have magnified Lucy's pleasure after each separation "in once more having the society of my husband, and in throwing myself and children upon the care and affection of a tender companion and father."[86]

That deep affection and regard for her husband seem to have opened the channels of emotion in the Smith household. Lucy instinctively pulled her children to her when they were suffering. After carrying the ailing

Joseph exhausted her, thirteen-year-old Hyrum, "who was rather remark-able for his tenderness and sympathy," sat beside Joseph for long stretches, night and day, "holding the affected part of his leg in his hands, and pressing it between them, so that his afflicted brother might be enabled to endure the pain. . . ." Joseph, Jr., himself later loved children and enjoyed holding them as he had been held as a child. Lucy's high-strung temper-ament did not inhibit the spontaneous flow of emotion in her or her children.[87]

Lucy's only explicit reservation about her husband was his diffidence about religion. After his brief flirtation with Universalism in 1797, Joseph, Sr., hovered on the margins of the churches. Her own quest for peace of mind and a church had not slackened since girlhood, and her husband's refusal to become involved troubled her. Her concern culminated during the stay in Randolph in 1803 while they were operating the store. She came down with a cold and then a hectic fever that the doctor diagnosed as consumption. The sickness so wore on her that she could not bear the sound of a footfall or voices above a whisper. The knock of a well-meaning Methodist exhorter come to visit agitated her nerves unbearably.[88]

As the man sat there, Lucy dreaded to hear him speak, for she feared he would ask if she was prepared to die. "I did not consider myself ready for such an awful event, inasmuch as I knew not the ways of Christ; besides, there appeared to be a dark and lonesome chasm, between myself and the Savior, which I dared not attempt to pass."[89] In that frame of mind she was a ready mark for the Methodist exhorter or for any evangelical preacher, although Lucy's mother forbade that unfortunate man to speak for fear of jangling Lucy's nerves again.

The main purpose of evangelical preaching was to set people on a quest for salvation exactly like Lucy's. The conventional method was to convict people of their sins, to persuade them that they were utterly unable to please God through sheer obedience. Lucy's sense of "a dark and lone-some chasm, between myself and the Savior," was a classic expression of the feeling the preachers wished to engender. Having been brought so low, she should have been prepared to throw herself entirely on the mercy of God and plead for grace. In the ideal case, as the scriptural message of divine mercy began to dawn, a new hope arose in the heart, and the person began to rejoice in the glory and goodness of God in accepting even unworthy souls through His grace. That realization often opened a flood of happiness and love and an overwhelming sense of the beauty of the world. The scriptural phrase "born again" described exactly the renewal that had occurred.

In the evangelical churches this process was called conversion or new birth. It did not entail a change in one's ideas. A person might believe in

Christ and in every principle of the Gospel before conversion. This was known as historical faith, and meant that the facts of Christ's life and resurrection were acknowledged and the principles of the Gospel intellectually accepted. In conversion the person applied the principles to his own life where they transformed his being. Mere belief became personal and immediate faith.

The Congregational churches of New England, the descendants of Puritan churches, and the Presbyterian churches of the middle colonies had always made conversion one of the aims of preaching. Calvinist doctrine identified the reception of divine grace as the crucial moment in the religious life of an individual, and the emotional crisis of conversion came to be seen as the moment when grace triumphed over pride and indifference. During the Great Awakening of the 1740s entire churches had passed through seasons of grace. Thousands of persons had felt first the anxiety and then the peace of conversion. Leaders of the revival such as Jonathan Edwards had taken these mass conversions as a hopeful sign that God was leading the world into the millennium. Although in the eighteenth century no revival season after 1740 matched the Great Awakening, evangelical preachers had not lost hope. They still sought to shatter false confidence in their congregations, to bring them low before Christ, and in that mood to teach the promises of the Gospel.

In 1803 another season of revivals was beginning that would soon surpass the Great Awakening. Congregations in Connecticut and Vermont had already experienced a flurry of conversions, and in the west and south vast camp meetings were just then being organized at which hundreds and thousands of persons came under evangelical preaching. Lucy's very personal concern in 1803 connected her with a vast movement that was spreading across the nation, that would course in great waves through the entire nineteenth century, and not spend itself completely to this day.[90]

Lucy did not have the benefit of evangelical preaching during her illness, but doubtless she had heard the doctrines of new birth many times. Without any direction, she reached her own peace with God. At the height of her illness, when her husband despaired of her life, she pleaded with the Lord to spare her that she might bring up her children and comfort her husband.

My mind was much agitated during the whole night. Sometimes I contemplated heaven and heavenly things; then my thoughts would turn upon those of earth — my babes and my companion. During this night I made a solemn covenant with God, that, if he would let me live, I would endeavor to serve him according to the best of my abilities. Shortly after this, I heard a voice say to me, "Seek, and ye shall find; knock, and it shall be opened unto you. Let your heart be comforted, ye believe in God, believe also in me."

In a few moments her mother entered the room and said, "Lucy you are better."[91]

That experience brought surcease but not perfect equanimity. She recovered her health, but her mind still was "considerably disquieted" and "wholly occupied upon the subject of religion." When she was able, she looked for someone to give her direction "in the way of life and salvation." Her attempts to connect with a church, however, were scarcely more successful this time than during the crisis which followed the deaths of her sisters. She visited Deacon Davies, a local man noted for piety, but he was wholly concerned for her physical warmth and comfort and said nothing "in relation to Christ or godliness." Lucy returned to her house disgusted and sorrowful. Out of anxiety to abide the covenant which she had made, she looked on every side for a congenial spirit. A notable itinerant Presbyterian preacher whom she heard only convinced her that he "neither understood nor appreciated the subject upon which he spoke." His discourse was all "emptiness vanity vexation of spirit," and palled her heart "like the chill night air." The cold words could "not fill the aching void." She concluded "that there was not upon the earth the religion" she sought. She resigned herself to Bible reading and self-instruction. Eventually she found a minister to baptize her without requiring that she join a church. Like her brother Jason in his early life, Lucy was a seeker.[92]

While she was still searching for direction, Lucy attended Methodist meetings in Tunbridge, and Joseph obligingly accompanied her. The news of this activity angered Joseph's father and brother Jesse, who pressed Joseph to stop. Lucy reported that one day Asael came to the door "and threw Tom Paine's *Age of Reason* into the house and angrily bade him read it until he believed it."[93] While the details are somewhat out of character for Asael (Lucy told the story only in her draft manuscript), it is not surprising that Asael should oppose Joseph's association with an evangelical church. Universalists thought the evangelical belief that grace visited only part of God's children slandered a loving heavenly father. Grace was sufficiently powerful to save all sinners if it was adequate for even one. That conviction put the Universalists in opposition to the entire revival tradition. There simply was no need for the anxiety, humiliation, and depression of rebirth. Conversion was necessary only if God granted grace sparingly and withheld it from many. Asael was understandably disgusted with Joseph for listening to Methodists, who preached little else than conversion. Asael may have thrown Paine at his son to startle him into reconsideration.

Joseph Smith, Sr., was not totally lacking in religion. He spontaneously knelt with his wife to pray for Sophronia in her illness and insisted on morning and evening prayers in his house. He was himself stimulated to religious concern during revival seasons. Solomon Mack was converted during the revival of 1810 and 1811, turning away at last from his fruitless pursuit of wealth, and Joseph, Sr., "became much excited upon the subject of religion" about the same time. In the midst of this excitement he dreamed two prophetic dreams, and four other such visions came to him later in New York. Nothing in his temperament or principles cut him off from faith in divine power or a concern for salvation.[94]

What he could not embrace was the institutional religion of his time. The reason became clear in one of the prophetic dreams, which Lucy took seriously enough to record verbatim. In the first dream in Royalton around 1811, Joseph, Sr., found himself traveling in a barren field covered with dead fallen timber. "Not a vestige of life, either animal or vegetable, could be seen; besides, to render the scene still more dreary, the most death-like silence prevailed, no sound of anything animate could be heard in all the field." What did this silent, lifeless desert represent? The attendant spirit told him that "this field is the world which now lieth inanimate and dumb, in regard to the true religion or plan of salvation. . . ." Joseph, following instructions, ate the contents of a box to gain "wisdom and understanding," when immediately "all manner of beasts, horned cattle, and roaring animals" sprang up, "tearing the earth, tossing their horns, and bellowing most terrifically." They pressed so close he was forced to drop the box and fly. That was the religious world as Joseph, Sr., saw it: either empty and silent or fiercely hostile to true wisdom and understanding. Lucy said he concluded from his dream that the "class of religionists" knew no more of the Kingdom of God than "such as made no profession of religion whatever." Even after Lucy and most of the children joined the Presbyterians in New York, Joseph, Sr., held aloof.[95]

Partly because of Joseph's attitude, Lucy was caught in a dilemma. Besides feeling a deep personal need for religion, she yearned for a church association. Yet her husband's ingrained aversion to evangelical religion and the churches confirmed her own skepticism and alienation. She hovered on the edge of respectable religion, attracted and repelled at the same time. There was no satisfactory resolution for either Joseph or Lucy until their own son brought life and sound to the desolate world. In the meantime the family had prayers together, and as William Smith remembered later, his mother "made use of every means which her parental love could suggest, to get us engaged in seeking for our souls' salvation. . . ."[96]

Typhoid fever and Joseph's leg infection lasted through a full year of the Smiths' stay in Lebanon. At the end, medical bills had broken them financially. Pressing immediate needs for provisions forced them to give up work on future prospects. Time closed in around them as they struggled to stay alive. Around 1814 they moved back across the Connecticut River to Norwich, Vermont, where they rented a farm from "Squire Moredock" and went into "business." Their low condition and residence in a new village may have left them without credit to tide them over until their first crop, and compelled them, like other poor people, to truck for a living. Sometime before the move to New York Lucy learned to paint oil cloths, which were popular for table coverings. Joseph could have peddled small items and hired out as a farm hand. When their crops failed the first year, they lived on the sale of fruit from their orchard and took work in the town.[97]

The Smiths came closer to destitution from 1814 to 1816 than at any point in their lives. Unfortunately, the Mack and Smith back-up was ebbing away. Solomon Mack was nearing eighty and unable to help. The Smith clan in Tunbridge were uprooting themselves and moving west. By 1815 all of Joseph's brothers had migrated to St. Lawrence County in northern New York, except Jesse, and he and Asael followed before 1820. Joseph and Lucy walked a thin line, more and more on their own.[98]

In the next two years nature conspired to drive them from Vermont. Crops failed again the second year on the Norwich farm. Joseph planted the third spring with a resolve to try just once more. The outcome was conclusive. 1816 was ever after known as the year without a summer. Lucy spoke modestly of an "untimely frost." Actually on June 8 several inches of snow fell all across the highlands of northern New York and New England, and ice formed on the ponds. The entire summer was cold and dry. Famine compelled farmers to pay $3 a bushel for imported corn. As Lucy remembered it, "This was enough: my husband was now altogether decided upon going to New York." Thousands of other Vermonters made the same decision. Migration in 1816 and 1817 drained the state, a blow to its prospects from which it did not recover for a century. The population in Orange County, which contained Tunbridge, had more than doubled between 1790 and 1800 and grown by another 50 percent in 1810. After the cold summer the 1820 census showed 600 fewer people than in 1810, and thereafter growth was spasmodic at best. In 1880 Orange County had shrunk by more than 3,000 people from its size in 1810.[99]

The many reasons for leaving Norwich did not make the decision easy for Joseph. Lucy had borne a son, Don Carlos, in March, 1816, and would be traveling with a babe at her breast. While Joseph was locating a new place, she would have to handle the family's business affairs and prepare for the trip. There was also the question of where to resettle. Joseph's brothers and father had all made St. Lawrence County on the northern rim of New York their new home. If he were to follow, Joseph and Lucy could turn to their kinsmen in emergencies, but was it the best place? It might also be difficult to extricate themselves from Norwich. By

1816 the Smiths had woven themselves into the web of debts and credits that substituted for money at that period. All of the debts would have to be paid; it was a point of honor with the Smiths not to run out on their creditors as others did.[100]

Lucy assured Joseph of her ability to make the preparations and suggested that "he might get both his creditors and debtors together, and arrange matters between them in such a way as to give satisfaction to all parties concerned. . . ." That satisfactorily accomplished, Joseph felt free to go. A local man, a Mr. Howard, was going to Palmyra, and the offer of a traveling companion seems to have made Joseph's mind up concerning where to look. The Vermont papers advertised new land in the Genesee country for $2 to $3 an acre. Palmyra looked promising. In the summer of 1816 he set out. Alvin and Hyrum walked out along the road with their father to say goodbye.[101]

Lucy had the help of her mother and the older boys to collect provisions and clothing and pack the wagon. She had sewn woolen clothing for the children and "had on hand a great deal of diaper and pulled cloth in the web." When the word came, they were ready to go. Joseph arranged for Caleb Howard, the cousin of his traveling companion, to come with a team. There was just one more hurdle. The family was about to depart when the old debts rose to plague them. Some of the creditors had not brought their books to the first settlement and waited until the last to make their claim. A departing family was particularly vulnerable at the moment of leave-taking. Under ordinary circumstances creditors knew that the scarcity of money made collection impractical and waited patiently for credits to balance the account. Departure was, of course, the last opportunity to collect, and furthermore it was a time when the family, having sold all of its possessions to obtain cash for the trip, was most liquid. Apparently some of Joseph's creditors unscrupulously held back their accounts until this moment when they could hope for a better settlement than earlier. Two well-wishers offered to take Lucy's case to court, but to avoid delay she chose to settle. The creditors took $150 of the funds Lucy had painstakingly assembled to pay expenses, leaving her only $60 or $80. By the end of the trip she was paying innkeepers with clothing and bits of cloth.[102]

Snow covered the ground when Lucy and the eight children left Norwich. They went by sleigh to Royalton where they left Lucy's mother with Daniel Mack. Lydia Mack wept over her daughter and admonished her to "continue faithful in the service of God to the end of your days, that I may have the pleasure of embracing you in another and fairer world above." Transferring their goods to a wagon, the little party turned their backs on family and familiar places and headed for Palmyra, 300 miles distant.[103]

The driver, Caleb Howard, proved troublesome from the start. The Smiths fell in with a Gates family traveling west in sleighs, and Howard wanted the Gates daughters to ride beside him. To make room, he drove Joseph from his place. For days at a time Joseph, who had just discarded his crutches and was still lame, limped along in the snow. When Alvin and Hyrum protested, Howard knocked them down with the butt of the whip. A few miles west of Utica, still nearly 100 miles from Palmyra, the Smiths ran out of money. Seeing no hope for more from Lucy, Howard threw their goods into the street and was about to set off with the Smiths' wagon and team. Lucy confronted him in the bar room before a company of travelers and demanded the reason for his outrageous action. When he attempted to drive off, Lucy grabbed the reins and shouted to the bystanders that she was being robbed and left destitute with eight children. "As for you sir," she announced to Howard, "I have no use for you and you can ride or walk the rest of the way as you please but I shall take charge of my own affairs."[104]

Howard left them, but Joseph's hardships were not at an end. He was assigned to the Gates sleigh, and one of the sons in the Gates family knocked him down as he attempted to find a place. Joseph was "left to wallow in my blood until a stranger came along, picked me up, and carried me to the Town of Palmyra."[105]

Lucy arrived at Palmyra, after a journey of three to four weeks, with a few possessions and 9¢ in money. Her last payment to the innkeepers was made with Sophronia's eardrops. At last the strain of caring for the family passed partly back to Joseph. "The joy I felt in throwing myself and My children upon the care and affection of a tender Husband and Father doubly paid me for all I had suffered. The children surrounded their Father clinging to his neck, covering his face with tears and kisses that were heartily reciprocated by him." Refreshed by that reunion, energy returned and all eyes looked forward. "We all now sat down, and counselled together relative to the course which was best for us to adopt in our destitute circumstances...."[106]

CHAPTER II

THE FIRST VISIONS

NEW YORK

The area in western New York south of Lake Ontario where the Smith family arrived late in 1816 had opened for settlement just twenty-five years earlier. During the Revolution Massachusetts and New York contested control of western New York (because of a sea-to-sea clause in Massachusetts's original charter), just as New York and New Hampshire fought over Vermont. A 1786 agreement awarded the right of government to New York and ownership of the land to Massachusetts. Eager to liquidate the property to avoid further trouble and expense, the Massachusetts government in 1788 sold 6 million acres in a huge square west of Seneca Lake and south of Lake Ontario to two Massachusetts speculators, Oliver Phelps and Nathaniel Gorham, who headed a syndicate of speculators. In the same year Phelps paid the Indians $5,000 and a $500 annuity for their title to 2,500,000 acres between Seneca Lake and the Genesee River, and the land was ready for sale. The first permanent settlers moved on the land north of Lake Canandaigua in the area of Palmyra in the early 1790s at the same time that Asael Smith moved his family to Tunbridge, Vermont.[1]

After the Revolution the growing American population pressed against the wilderness frontier from Vermont to Kentucky. People poured into fertile regions like western New York as soon as the states, the speculators, and the Indians settled title and boundary disputes. Because of superior soils and climate, New York grew more rapidly than Vermont. Palmyra quickly increased from a mere handful of inhabitants to 2,614 residents in 1810. Tunbridge by comparison held just 1,640 inhabitants in 1810, and Randolph, the largest town in Orange County, had 2,255. Although the move from Vermont to New York carried the Smiths west, it did not carry them to the frontier. In 1812 Palmyra offered its residents the services of two tailors, a blacksmith, several saddlers, a cooper, two lawyers, and a physician. Along the main street there were a harness shop, a tannery, a distillery, a clothiery, two drugstores, a bookstore, eight other stores of unspecified contents, and four taverns. Located in a region notable for its weaving, Palmyra farm families produced 33,719 yards of cloth annually on home looms.[2]

The major settlements in western New York formed at the tips of the Finger Lakes, where goods carted from the east could be boated southward to the villages along the lakes. Geneva, in Seneca township at the head of Seneca Lake, and Canandaigua, fifteen miles directly south of Palmyra on Canandaigua Lake, took shape at about the same time. Before selling out to another speculator, Robert Morris, in 1790, Phelps and Gorham established their land offices at Canandaigua on the eastern boundary of their holdings. Canandaigua was the natural county seat when New York State organized Ontario County in 1789, encompassing the entire western territory from Canandaigua to Lake Erie. Canandaigua also became the major entry point for migrants into the new country. The central artery west from Albany, the Great Genesee Road, which reached Buffalo in 1803, skirted the tops of the Finger Lakes, passing through Geneva and Canandaigua. In the early days some traffic also went south down the lakes from these two centers toward the tributaries of the Susquehannah and thence by raft or barge to Harrisburg and Baltimore.[3]

By 1824 Canandaigua was characterized as a "populous and opulent" town, and the author of the gazetteer for that year already feared that "extravagance and fashion" would corrupt its farmers. In 1812, 137 houses and stores lined a two-mile main street. An academy, housed in a three-story building, educated Canandaigua's young people, and two newspapers circulated to surrounding towns. As county seat, Canandaigua was the focus of legal as well as commercial business. Merchants and farmers in surrounding towns directed their trade toward this bustling little center, which promised to become "the Metropolis of the Western Counties." The main street south from Palmyra was called Canandaigua Street. By 1824 a stage ran daily between the two towns.[4]

Between Palmyra and Canandaigua lay Farmington, a large rectangular township with various village centers. One of the most prosperous, Manchester Village, was to become the nucleus of a new township in 1822. The chief natural advantage of Manchester Village was its location near the falls on the Canandaigua outlet. Since boats could navigate the outlet from the lake to Manchester Village, the founders dreamed of a manufacturing center, using power from the river and distributing products up the outlet to Canandaigua Lake and thence south. They named the village after England's great industrial center. In 1811 the Ontario Manufacturing

Company constructed a woolen factory with a spinning jenny and a spinning jack, six looms, and a coloring and dye shop. About a mile away at another fall, a flour mill, a sawmill, a paper mill, and another woolen factory went up. Although western New York's rich soils were the main attraction for migrants, and grains were its major product, the picture of a complete village in this generation included a host of small manufacturing enterprises. In a day when high transportation costs made decentralized manufacturing practical, the ambitions of Manchester's manufacturers were not unfounded. The spectacular growth of population in the counties west of Canandaigua from a total of 16,973 in 1800 to 108,981 in 1820 added substance to the dreams.[5]

These speculative prospects collapsed after 1820. The Erie Canal dashed the hopes of Manchester's entrepreneurs. Farmington, the township containing Manchester, tripled in size between 1800 and 1810 (rising to 2,215 inhabitants) and doubled again by 1820. From 1820 to 1830 population only grew from 4,214 to 4,584, an increase of a mere 370 people. While the canal was a boon to farmers who shipped their harvests to New York City, it was death to many small manufacturers. They were thrown into competition with more efficient producers in major centers. The marketing range of the small factories was limited to the immediate area, where they enjoyed the greatest advantage in transportation costs.[6]

The canal had a different impact on Palmyra. The canal route paralleled Mud Creek, on which Palmyra had been settled, and passed just a few hundred feet north of the village center at the corner of Main and Canandaigua. Construction began in 1817, and the Palmyra section was completed in 1822. In October, 1825, cannons placed at intervals along the canal signaled the news from Albany to Rochester that the channel was completed, and water flowed the entire 363 miles from Albany to Buffalo on Lake Erie. Well before that time local traffic along the canal foreshadowed the benefits Palmyra would enjoy.[7]

Palmyra entertained its own industrial pretensions. In 1820 the census listed 748 persons in agriculture, eighteen in commerce, and 190 in manufacturing. An 1824 gazetteer credited the town with three gristmills, eight sawmills, one fulling mill, an iron works, five distilleries, two asheries, and two tanneries. But Palmyra's hopes for the future rested more on commerce. The village's fortuitous location close to the canal put Palmyra in a position to become a trading center for the entire region southward. The townspeople aspired to replace Canandaigua as the major entrepôt for the area. Instead of commerce flowing westward along the Seneca Pike and north from Canandaigua, the main current would flow along the Erie. Canal boats would unload at Palmyra, and the goods move southward. Forward-looking residents built docks and warehouses. Thirteen dry goods stores appeared by 1824, and the proprietors of the Phelps tavern enlarged it to three stories and renamed it the Eagle Hotel. Population growth, instead of slowing as in Manchester, continued upward. The old town of Palmyra divided in 1823 into Palmyra and Macedon, but the total population within the old town boundaries increased from 3,724 in 1820 to 5,416 in 1830. In that year 2,000 people, 60 percent of the whole town of Palmyra, lived in the center on the canal.[8]

And yet Palmyra's prosperity fell short of its residents' expectations. The town suffered a major setback in the failure to be designated a county seat. In 1820 Horace Spafford, compiler of a state gazetteer, predicted that when a new county was formed, the "steeples of its capital" would rise at Palmyra. A courthouse meant added business for everyone—taverners, hotel keepers, storekeepers, lawyers, stable owners—as well as symbolic leadership. To the dismay of Palmyra's townspeople, when Wayne County was organized in 1823, the legislature selected Lyons, fifteen miles to the east, to be the county seat. Lyons enjoyed the same proximity to the canal as Palmyra, plus the added advantage of a water connection to Canandaigua. The Canandaigua outlet joined Mud Creek at Lyons. By 1820 Lyons's population had reached 3,972 compared to Palmyra's 3,427. The business of a county seat propelled Lyons still further ahead, while Palmyra lagged behind.[9]

The canal not only stimulated internal growth but reoriented the western villages geographically. Before 1820 Palmyra and Lyons looked southward to Canandaigua and Geneva. Besides giving the canal towns a direct eastward orientation, the Erie turned them westward toward Rochester. No place benefited more from the canal than this straggling little village near the mouth of the Genesee River. In 1815 Rochester contained just 331 inhabitants, a fraction of Palmyra's population. By 1830 it had 9,207, two and a half times as large and still growing at a phenomenal rate. Hindsight clearly reveals why. It stood at the juncture of the canal, the Genesee River valley, one of the richest farm areas in the country, and Lake Ontario. Rochester's destiny was to become a flour export center. Wheat shipped into Rochester in canal boats and carted up the Genesee Valley was ground into flour and sent northward via Lake Ontario and the St. Lawrence River for European markets, or east to Albany and New York City. Less than twenty-five miles away along the canal, Palmyra fell within Rochester's commercial and cultural sphere of influence. Before 1820, to the north and west of Palmyra, settlements thinned and forest clearings grew less frequent. After the canal the west pulsed with commerical and cultural activity.[10]

Canandaigua and Geneva merchants quickly recognized Rochester as a rival for control of western commerce and resisted its growth. Citizens of the older communities fought the organization of an independent county and the formation of rival banks. Canandaigua and Geneva were destined to drop far behind, but this fate did not befall them all at once. Traffic on older routes continued for many years. Indeed, activity along the canal sent energy into all the tributary trade paths. The Chemung Canal, completed in 1833, connected Seneca Lake with the Susquehannah, thus offering continuous water transport north to Geneva. Daily stages from Palmyra to Canandaigua and twice weekly to Geneva indicated the continued importance of the southerly route. Palmyra operated on two axes, east-west to Rochester and Albany along the canal, and north-south toward Canandaigua and Geneva.[11]

As it turned out, Smith family affairs moved mainly along the southerly route. Joseph went southward along the area's earliest roads to the Susquehannah for work, for a wife, and eventually for converts to the church. Martin Harris applied for a loan in Geneva to finance the Book of Mormon. The Rochester route figured much less prominently in the lives of the Smiths until events compelled them to pack all of their belongings on a canal boat and move west via Lake Erie to Kirtland, Ohio.[12]

For a year and a half after their arrival the Smiths lived in Palmyra without a farm. Since the loss of their own property in 1803, they had rented acreage as a base for their personal economy, supplementing farming with labor for others and small business enterprises. In Palmyra they lived by their labor alone. Lucy painted oil table cloths and paid for the food from the proceeds. The family sold refreshments from a small shop and peddled them from a cart on public occasions. Joseph, Sr., and the older sons hired out for haying, harvested in the peak seasons when every farmer needed extra hands, and took on odd jobs gardening and digging wells. The contributions of Alvin, aged nineteen, and Hyrum, aged fourteen, made a big addition to the family income. Canal contractors paid workers 50¢ a day, or $8 to $12 a month, and the opportunity of alternative employment probably drove up farm wages. With wheat prices high from 1812 to 1819, farmers willingly paid well in the expectation of a generous return on their harvest.[13]

The combination of Palmyra's flourishing economy, the added contribution of Alvin and Hyrum, and their own industry put the Smiths in a better position by 1818 than they had occupied for fifteen years. For the first time they were able to contract for a farm and begin payments on land they hoped to make their own. They did not have to look far. The growing population had not yet occupied all of Palmyra's and Farmington's virgin land. The Smiths located a wooded tract less than two miles south of Palmyra village on Stafford Street. The property was part of the Phelps and Gorham purchase and had passed through the hands of various speculators until purchased by Nicholas Evertson of New York City in 1798. Evertson, who bought 3,000 acres in all, sold it off in farm-sized plots. Joseph Smith, Sr., contracted with the Evertson land agent to pay $100 annually for 100 acres, the last payment to be made in December, 1825. The total cost was between $700 and $900.[14]

Before moving out of the village, the Smiths raised a log house near their farm. By mistake it was constructed on a site fifty feet inside the Palmyra town line, even though the farm itself lay just over the line in Farmington (later, in 1822, to be Manchester). An early visitor described the house as having two rooms on the ground floor, one doubtless a kitchen–dining room, and a low garret divided in two. When they first moved in 1818, the Smiths had to find sleeping spaces for ten people in four rooms: six boys from nineteen to two, two girls fifteen and six, and the partents. They soon added a bedroom wing of sawed slabs. Crowded though it was, the "snug log house, neatly furnished," with "the means of living comfortably," satisfied Lucy.[15]

The acquisition of property changed the tempo of family life. Instead of odd jobs and shopkeeping, interspersed with stretches of arduous work in harvest and hay seasons, father and sons now faced daily the unrelenting necessity to clear the land and cultivate a crop. To prepare the land for planting, new settlers cut the underbrush, grubbed up small trees, and piled the cuttings into huge piles. When the ground was cleared, they felled the large trees and dragged them away or girdled them and let them die. When the piles of brush dried out, the farmers burned them in roaring conflagrations that left only blackened stumps, charred logs, and seared ground. Rather than work out the stubborn stumps, most farmers let them rot and plowed or dug around them. A skilled woodsman took seven to ten days to clear a single acre. A pioneer working alone could probably clear ten acres the first year, though at the risk of neglecting fences, garden, and the construction of barn and outbuildings. Lucy remembered that "something like thirty acres of land were got ready for cultivation the first year," a herculean achievement even with the aid of Alvin, Hyrum, and Joseph, Jr.[16]

The farm began to produce a little income at once. The asheries in Palmyra purchased the remains of brush and log fires for working into potash. As late as 1822 Governor DeWitt Clinton listed ashes along with wheat as the two leading exports of the state. The Smiths probably derived some profit from ashes loaded into a cart and hauled into the village. They also sold cord wood in the village and made maple sugar. Other than that, they may not have had a money crop for two years. Most farmers planted corn for family and animals on the first cleared land. Wheat followed in the second year with the possibility of a small surplus beyond the family needs.[17]

The Smiths had to think about a cash crop because of the one dark cloud in the sky: the annual $100 payment on the farm. Failure to meet the payment gave the land agent the legal right to reclaim the farm, improvements and all, with no compensation for the family's labor. In a trade deficit area like western New York where cash was scarce, the agents rarely held to the exact letter of the contract as long as the occupant showed signs of industry. Lucy reported that after the first year the Smiths made "nearly all" of the first payment without being ejected. But repeated shortfalls stretched an agent's patience and endangered all the family had worked for. The Smiths manufactured small items for sale—black ash baskets and birch brooms—and kept up their refreshment business with cakes, sugar, and molasses. The boys and their father may have fished, hunted, and trapped. Joseph said that all of the children who "were able to render any assistance . . . were obliged to labor hard" to support the family. He took an occasional odd job at a village store when he was there on an errand, and probably worked for nearby established farmers. Lucy credited Alvin, the eldest, with making the second payment. "Alvin went from home to get work, in order to raise the money, and after much hardship and fatigue, returned with the required amount." Alvin set the pattern for the other boys, who in subsequent years regularly dispersed across the countryside in search of employment.[18]

Lucy took pride in the Smiths' accomplishments since they entered Palmyra "destitute of friends home or employment." She spoke happily of their "snug comfortable though humble habitation built and neatly furnished by our own industry." Neighbors, accustomed to the regular appearance of new faces and perhaps newcomers themselves, readily accepted the family. "If we might judge by external manifestations," Lucy said later, "we had every reason to believe that we had many good and affectionate friends for never have I seen more kindness or attention shown to any person or family than we received from those around us." At social gatherings with the wives of merchants or the minister, she took pride in her family and forgot their primitive cabin. "Again we began to rejoice in our prosperity," she wrote, "and our hearts glowed with gratitude to God for the manifestations of his favor that surrounded us."[19]

REVELATIONS

Material improvements could not satisfy the family's spiritual longings. Lucy interrupted her narrative of the Palmyra beginning with three more of Joseph Sr.'s visions. There were seven in all. Two she could not remember "distinctly enough to rehearse them in full." The other five she narrated in first person as if she were transcribing Joseph Sr.'s words. In introducing the first of the visions, Lucy reported that her husband fell asleep one night "and before waking had the following vision, which I shall relate in his own words, just as he told it to me the next morning." Since no other member of the family gave an account of the visions or even referred to them, there is no way to test the accuracy of Lucy's memory. One of the recitals shows strong evidence of Book of Mormon influence. Lucy elsewhere exhibited an ability to absorb Book of Mormon language into her own style of speaking and thinking. Questions must be raised about the details of wording and imagery, but in all likelihood the visions do indicate the religious mood of the Smith household. In that respect their testimony is unanimous.[20]

One that Lucy remembered to have occurred about the time they built the log cabin typified the dreams' characteristic message. Joseph, Sr., found himself traveling on foot. "I was very sick, and so lame I could hardly walk." As always, a guide attended him. The lameness increased until Joseph, Sr., believed he could go no farther. The guide encouraged him to press on until he came to a large gate. "Open this," the guide said, "and you will see a garden, blooming with the most beautiful flowers that your eyes ever beheld, and there you shall be healed." Joseph, Sr., limped along until he came to the garden and entered the gate. Inside, besides "the most delicate flowers of every kind and color," he found walks lined with marble stones and on each side of the central walkway a "richly-carved seat" with six wooden images the size of a man on each seat. The twelve images arose and bowed to him in turn as he passed, "after which I was entirely healed." "I then asked my guide the meaning of all this, but I awoke before I received an answer."[21]

Though emphasis varied from dream to dream, the same themes recurred. Joseph, Sr., found himself alone, decrepit, desolate, or ill, on a vaguely defined quest. In the sixth vision he traveled alone and fatigued, toward judgment. "Presently I found that my flesh was perishing. I continued to pray, still my flesh withered upon my bones." In earlier visions he traveled alone "in the desolate world," on a road "so broad and barren that I wondered why I should travel in it," or in a "gloomy desert" amidst "the most death-like silence." The desolation defined the quest and prepared him for the redemption ahead: the flower-filled garden where the regard of the images healed his lameness, or the fruit of an "exceedingly handsome" tree representing the love of God which rose at the end of a path leading away from the desolate field. In one vision he came to the door of a great building. "On arriving at the door, I found it shut; I knocked for admission and was informed by the porter that I had come too late. I felt exceedingly troubled, and prayed earnestly for admittance." "I was almost in a state of total despair, when the porter asked me if I had done all that was necessary in order to receive admission. I replied, that I had done all that was in my power to do. 'Then,' observed the porter, 'justice must be satisfied; after this, mercy hath her claims.' " Joseph, Sr., cried out "in the agony of my soul, 'Oh, Lord God, I beseech thee, in the name of Jesus Christ, to forgive my sins.' " "I was now made quite whole, and the door was opened, but, on entering, I awoke."[22]

In every dream a yearning for relief or redemption or beauty moved the dreamer. Each vision held the promise that beyond a gate, through a door, under a tree, could be found healing and salvation. Two dreams permitted Joseph, Sr., the satisfaction of enjoying his redemption. In others it hovered just beyond reach, promised but not embraced. In the last vision a messenger in the guise of a peddler commended Joseph, Sr., for his honesty and generosity and then told him "there is but one thing which you lack, in order to secure your salvation." In his eagerness for the answer Joseph, Sr., asked the peddler to write the words on a paper. "He said he would do so. I then sprang to get some paper, but, in my excitement, I awoke," and never heard the answer. Although pleased with farm, cabin, and friends, the Smiths traveled a barren land, believing that through a gate somewhere lay a blooming garden which they earnestly desired to enter and where they would be healed.[23]

In Palmyra as in Vermont, the churches offered the hope of salvation and religious peace. Four groups met within a few miles of the Smiths' house. Presbyterians had the largest congregation in Palmyra village and in 1820 the only meetinghouse. The Methodists, the next largest group, constructed a building of their own in 1822, and the Society of Friends one in 1823. Two miles west of the village a large congregation of Baptists had met in a meetinghouse of their own since 1808, and in the eastern part of Palmyra stood a second Presbyterian church.[24]

The churches kept the questions of salvation before the settlers as they cleared the trees and brought in their crops. Most of the residents came from New England, where they had been taught Calvinist Christianity as children in their homes or had heard it in the churches. Although migration and arduous toil may have forced concerns of the soul into the background, periodic religious revivals stirred the memories of the hardened or indifferent. Once aroused, religious feeling could engulf a congregation or an entire village. James Hotchkin, who wrote the history of Presbyterianism in western New York largely as an account of these revivals, described the effect on the congregations in West Bloomfield, where he was ministering in 1802:

The congregation was small, and met for worship in a moderate sized school-house. The first symptoms of a revival were manifested in a more than usual attendance on public worship, and earnest attention to the word preached. In a short time it was known that a number of individuals were deeply convicted of their guilty, wretched condition. With some their convictions came on gradually; others, from a state of entire stupidity, were suddenly brought into a state of deep conviction; but all were brought to consider themselves as heinous sinners against God. In this state of feeling, and with an increasing conviction of the desperate depravity of their own hearts, and their utter helplessness in themselves, they generally continued for some days, perhaps weeks, and finally with penitent hearts were led to cast themselves on the mercy of God through a Mediator, and thus found rest to their souls.[25]

One of the ministers' purposes was to halt what was then called "infidelity," a general term for various kinds of unbelief. Hotchkin believed that the great revival of 1799, which began among the Palmyra Presbyterians and spread through western New York, rolled back "the tide of infidelity which was setting in with so strong a current." "Western New York was delivered from the moral desolation which threatened it."[26]

The effect of a revival on a community can be imagined from Hotchkin's description of its greatest achievement. "The reality of religion, and its holy nature, had been exhibited, and the glory of the gospel had been set before the eyes of mankind, in the exhibitions of its transforming power on the hearts of lives of those who embraced it." Indifferent or calloused souls who ventured within the sound of the minister's voice found themselves the object of the preaching. The recurrence of revivals meant that the urgent question, "What must I do to be saved?" was on everyone's mind.[27]

Revivals occurred periodically from 1799 on, touching first one town and then another. Ministers had every incentive to preach for revivals, since membership grew more in the few months of a revival season than in many years of normal times. One hundred people joined the Baptist church in Palmyra during a revival in 1808, making it necessary and possible to construct a meetinghouse. Six years earlier just seventy people formed the congregation. The great revival of 1816 and 1817 in Palmyra doubled the number of Presbyterians and led to the formation of a new congregation. Beyond the material benefits, a pastor's greatest triumph was to see people yield to grace under his preaching. The clergy understandably pressed for conversions and noted happily each sign of an awakening.[28]

The great revival of 1816 and 1817 was in progress when the Smiths arrived in Palmyra, renewing the pressures Joseph, Sr., and Lucy felt during the 1810-11 revival in Vermont. Joseph Sr.'s dreams reveal how powerfully the revival appealed to him despite his refusal to join a church. He dreamed of judgment day, and he and others were going to meeting, as if a church meeting was the place where his life was judged. "When I came in sight of the meeting-house, I saw multitudes of people coming from every direction, and pressing with great anxiety towards the door of this great building; but I thought I should get there in time, hence there was no need of being in a hurry." But as in real life, others entered into the church, and the door was shut to him. He knocked and the porter told him he had come too late. Only after calling on the Lord in the name of Christ did he feel comforted. The porter gave Joseph, Sr., precisely the instructions he would have heard at a revival meeting: "it was necessary to plead the merits of Jesus, for he was the advocate with the Father, and a mediator between God and man." With that, the door opened and Joseph, Sr., entered, just as he would have entered a church had he made the same confession in a waking moment at a meetinghouse. Was peace to be found in a church? Joseph, Sr., dreamed it must be so.[29]

Joseph Smith, Jr., began to be concerned about religion "at about the age of twelve years." That would have been in late 1817 and early 1818, when the after-effects of the revival of 1816 and 1817 were still felt in Palmyra. "My mind became seriously imprest with regard to the all important concerns for the wellfare of my immortal Soul," he reported later, "which led me to searching the scriptures."[30] A few years later, in July, 1819, the Methodists of the Genesee Conference met for a week in Vienna (later Phelps), a village thirteen miles southeast of the Smith farm on the road to Geneva. About 110 ministers from a region stretching 500 miles from Detroit to the Catskills and from Canada to Pennsylvania met under the direction of Bishop R. R. Robert to receive instruction and set policy. If we are to judge from the experience at other conferences, the ministers preached between sessions to people who gathered from many miles around. It was a significant year for religion in the entire district. Joseph later spoke of "an unusual excitement on the subject of religion." In 1819 the Manchester Baptists increased their numbers 25 percent. The Geneva Presbytery, which included the churches in Joseph's immediate area, reported in February, 1820, that "during the past year more have been received into the communion of the Churches than perhaps in any former year." Methodists kept no records for individual congregations, but in 1821 they built a new meetinghouse in town.[31]

In their sensitive and unsettled frames of mind, the Smiths responded to the stimulus of the revival preaching much as they had before. At some unspecified date Lucy finally overcame her reservations and joined the Western Presbyterian Church in Palmyra, probably the best established church in the village and before 1823 the only one with a building of its own. Hyrum, Sophronia, and Samuel joined with her.[32] Joseph, Sr., and the other sons held back. Joseph, Jr., "became somewhat partial to the Methodist sect," and came close to joining, but could not overcome his reservations. Two printer's apprentices at the *Palmyra Register* who knew Joseph remembered his Methodist leanings. One said he caught "a spark of Methodism in the camp meeting, away down in the woods, on the Vienna road." The other remembered that Joseph joined the probationary class of the Palmyra Methodist Church. Joseph himself confessed "some desire to be united with them." He later said "he wanted to get religion too, wanted to feel and shout like the rest but could feel nothing."[33]

From his observation point outside the churches, Joseph, like his mother in earlier years, was more aware of hypocrisy and contradiction than harmony or Christian devotion. He saw the revivals create a "stir and division amongst the people" where there was supposed to be love.

For, notwithstanding the great love which the converts to these different faiths expressed at the time of their conversion, and the great zeal manifested by the respective clergy, who were active in getting up and promoting this extraordinary scene of religious feeling, in order to have everybody converted, as they were pleased to call it, let them join what sect they pleased; yet when the converts began to file off, some to one party and some to another, it was seen that the seemingly good feelings of both the priests and the converts were more pretended than real; for a scene of great confusion and bad feelings ensued; priest contending against priest, and convert against convert; so that all their good feelings one for another, if they ever had any, were entirely lost in a strife of words and a contest about opinions.[34]

His mother remembered Joseph as a "remarkably quiet, well-disposed child," "much less inclined to the perusal of books than any of the rest of our children, but far more given to meditation and deep study." To others who knew him less well, Joseph seemed slow, "destitute of genius," but between twelve and fifteen he seriously searched the scriptures, "believeing as I was taught, that they contained the word of God." He was confused by the failings of the Christians in the town. "My intimate acquaintance with those of differant denominations led me to marvel excedingly for I discovered that they did not . . . adorn their profession by a holy walk and Godly conversation agreeable to what I found contained in that Sacred depository. This was a grief to my Soul. . . ." The failings of the church people made him wonder where salvation was to be found and forced him to search.[35]

Joseph had two questions in his mind: which church was right, and how to be saved. The two questions were actually one. His anguish for himself mingled with his anguish for the world, for the corruption in the churches seemed to stand in the way of his own salvation.

From the age of twelve years to fifteen I pondered many things in my heart concerning the sittuation of the world of mankind the contentions and divions [*sic*] the wickeness and abominations and the darkness which pervaded the minds of mankind my mind become excedingly distressed for I became convicted of my Sins and by Searching the Scriptures I found that mankind did not come unto the Lord but that they had apostatised from the true and liveing faith and there was no society or denomination that built upon the Gospel of Jesus Christ as recorded in the new testament and I felt to mourn for my own Sins and for the Sins of the world.[36]

How could a young person in that frame of mind find salvation? Quite obviously an answer for himself must be an answer for the entire world.

Joseph's acquaintances in the newspaper office seem to have complicated the situation. Orasmus Turner, one of the apprentices, said Joseph came to the meetings of a "juvenile debating club," which met in the red school house on Durfee Street, to "solve some portenous questions of moral or political ethics." Very likely the young debaters raised the question of how to know of God's existence, an issue the deists had given currency. Deists did not seriously doubt the reality of God but wished to base their belief on reason. Young debaters would have rehearsed the classic arguments about the existence of an ordered world, proving the existence of a divine creator. Oliver Cowdery later said that Joseph wondered for a time whether "a Supreme Being did exist." In any event, in recounting his thoughts in the time of confusion, Joseph partly rested his faith on the beauty of the created universe: "the sun the glorious luminary of the earth and also the moon rolling in their magesty through the heavens and also the Stars shining in their courses and the earth also upon which I stood and the beast of the field and the fowls of heaven and the fish of the waters. . . ." "All these," he said, using rationalist language, bespoke "an omnipotent and omniprasant power a being who makith Laws and decreeeth and bindeth all things in their bounds. . . ."[37]

Although Joseph came out of the debating club discussions believing in God, the discussions began with questions that, however lightly entertained, added to the confusion, and made it all the more important to find the right way. Recounting the experience eighteen years later, Joseph vividly recalled how his "mind at times was greatly excited, the cry and tumult were so great and incessant." Young as he was, he saw no way of resolving his questions, and yet he could not lay them aside: "In the midst of this war of words and tumult of opinions, I often said to myself: What is to be done? Who of all these parties are right; or, are they all wrong together? If any one of them shall be right, which is it, and how shall I know it?"[38]

In this state of mind he came across the Bible verses that promise that "if any of you lack wisdom, let him ask of God that giveth to all men liberally... and it shall be given him." The words seemed made for him. "Never did any passage of scripture," he recalled later, "come with more power to the heart of man than this did at this time to mine. It seemed to enter with great force into every feeling of my heart. I reflected on it again and again, knowing that if any person needed wisdom from God, I did. . . ." In his desperation he saw no other way. The contradictory views of the clergy had destroyed his confidence "in settling the question by an appeal to the Bible." "At length I came to the conclusion that I must either remain in darkness and confusion, or else I must do as James directs, that is, ask of God."[39]

Joseph came to a determination to pray for help in the early spring of 1820. With no hope of privacy in the little cabin filled with children and household activity, he went to a place in the woods where his father had a clearing and where Joseph had left his axe in a stump.[40] In the minds of Latter-day Saints today, the events of that morning marked the beginning of the restoration of the Gospel and the commencement of a new dispensation. The vision is called the First Vision because of its place at the beginning of a series of revelations. But to understand how Joseph Smith's life unfolded, it must be kept in mind that in 1820 he did not know this was the First Vision, nor could he be expected to grasp fully everything that was said to him. Like anyone else, he first understood a new experience in terms of his own needs and his own background.[41]

By 1832, when he first wrote it down, Joseph knew that his vision in 1820 was one of the steps in "the rise of the church of Christ in the eve of time," along with Moroni's visit, the restoration of the Aaronic Priesthood, and the reception of the "high Priesthood." But even twelve years after the event the First Vision's personal significance for him still overshadowed its place in the divine plan for restoring the church. In 1832 he explained the vision as he must have first understood it in 1820 — as a personal conversion. What he felt important to say in 1832 was that a "pillar of light" came down and rested on him, and he "was filld with the spirit of God." "The Lord opened the heavens upon me and I Saw the Lord and he Spake unto me Saying Joseph my Son thy Sins are forgiven thee, go thy way walk in my statutes and keep my commandments." It was the message of forgiveness and redemption he had longed to hear. "Behold I am the Lord of glory I was crucifyed for the world that all those who believe on my name may have Eternal life. . . ."[42]

That was half of it. He had also mourned the sins of the world and pondered "the contentions and divions [sic] the wickeness and abominations and the darkness which pervaded the minds of mankind." The Lord gave Joseph less to hope for with regard to mankind. "Behold the world lieth in sin at this time and none doeth good no not one they have turned asside from the Gospel and keep not my commandments they draw near to me with their lips while their hearts are far from me and mine anger is kindling against the inhabitants of the earth. . . ." The Lord promised "to visit them acording to this ungodliness and to bring to pass that which hath been spoken by the mouth of the prophets and Apostles behold and lo I come quickly as it is written of me in the cloud clothed in the glory of my Father. . . ."[43]

Like countless other revival subjects who had come under conviction, Joseph received assurance of forgiveness from the Lord, and, in the usual sequence, following the vision his "soul was filled with love and for many days I could rejoice with great joy and the Lord was with me. . . ." In actuality there was more in the vision than he first understood. Three years later in 1835, and again in another account recorded in 1838, experience had enlarged his perspective. The event's vast historical importance came to overshadow its strictly personal significance. He still remembered the anguish of the preceding years when the confusion of the churches puzzled and thwarted him, but in 1838 he saw the vision was more significant as the opening event in a new dispensation of the Gospel. In that light certain aspects took on an importance they did not possess at first.[44]

Joseph recognized, for one thing, that he had confronted satanic power. Difficulties in praying were the result of demonic opposition. As he tried to speak, he recalled in 1835, "my tongue seemed to be swoolen in my mouth, so that I could not utter. . . ." Just then he heard a noise behind him like someone walking toward him. "I strove again to pray, but could not; the noise of walking seemed to draw nearer, I sprang upon my feet and looked round, but saw no person. . . ."[45] It seemed then "as if I were doomed to sudden destruction . . . not to an imaginary ruin, but to the power of some actual being from the unseen world."[46]

Deliverance came when the pillar of light or pillar of fire descended from heaven and fell on him. In his first narrative Joseph said only that he saw the Lord in the light and heard His words of forgiveness. In 1835 he said that first one personage appeared and then another, and in 1838 he reported that the first pointed to the other and said, "This is my beloved Son, Hear him." By 1838 Joseph understood how significant it was that God the Father had appeared to introduce the Son. A new era in history began at that moment. Joseph's personal salvation paled in comparison to the fact that the God of Heaven had set His hand again to open a new dispensation. The promise of forgiveness through faith in Christ was dropped from the narrative, and the apostasy of Christian churches stood alone as the message of the vision. When Joseph asked "which of all the

sects was right," he was told, "I must join none of them, for they were
all wrong, and the personage who addressed me said that all their creeds
were an abomination in His sight: that those professors were all corrupt;
that they draw near to me with their lips but their hearts are far from
me; they teach for doctrines the commandments of men: having a form
of godliness but they deny the power thereof."[47]

When Joseph came to, he found himself lying on his back. Returning
to the house, he spoke to his mother but apparently did not tell her about
the vision. When she asked about his evident weakness, Joseph said, "Never
mind all is well — I am well enough off." All he reported of the content
was that he had learned for himself that Presbyterianism was not true.
Like other boys, Joseph held back intimate experiences from his family.[48]
Three years later when the angel appeared to him, he said nothing until
explicitly commanded to speak to his father. The failure to tell his mother
about the First Vision gave Lucy a misunderstanding of the sequence of
Joseph's vision that she had trouble correcting. In the draft of the *Biographical Sketches* she connected Joseph's confusion about the churches
with the visit of Moroni. In her account Moroni was the one to tell Joseph
that "the churches that are now upon the earth are all man made churches."
William, who probably got the story from his mother, made the same
mistake. Neither intended to contradict Joseph, but the confusion in their
accounts indicates that Joseph's silence about the First Vision at the time
prevented them from getting the story straight. To be on the safe side in
the published version of her *Sketches,* Lucy simply quoted at length from
Joseph's own narrative.[49]

Joseph did tell a Methodist preacher about the vision. Newly reborn
people customarily talked over their experiences with a clergyman to test
the validity of the conversion. The preacher's contempt shocked Joseph.
Standing on the margins of the evangelical churches, Joseph may not have
recognized the ill repute of visionaries. The preacher reacted quickly, not
because of the strangeness of Joseph's story but because of its familiarity.
Subjects of revivals all too often claimed to have seen visions. In 1825 a
teacher in the Palmyra Academy said he saw Christ descend "in a glare
of brightness exceeding tenfold the brilliancy of the meridian Sun." The
Wayne Sentinel in 1823 reported Asa Wild's vision of Christ in Amsterdam,
New York, and the message that all denominations were corrupt. At various
other times and places, beginning early in the Protestant era, religious
eccentrics claimed visits from divinity. Nathan Cole, a Wethersfield, Connecticut, farmer and carpenter, recorded in his "Spiritual Travels" that in
1741 "God appeared unto me and made me Skringe: before whose face
the heavens and the earth fled away; and I was shrinked into nothing. . . ."[50]

The visions themselves did not disturb the established clergy so much as the messages that the visionaries claimed to receive. Too often the visions justified a breach of the moral code or a sharp departure in doctrine. By Joseph's day, any vision was automatically suspect, whatever its content. "No person is warranted from the word of God," a writer in the *Connecticut Evangelical Magazine* said in 1805, "to publish to the world the discoveries of heaven or hell which he supposes he has had in a dream, or trance, or vision. Were any thing of this kind to be made known to men, we may be assured it would have been done by the apostles, when they were penning the gospel history." The only acceptable message was assurance of forgiveness and a promise of grace. Joseph's report on the divine rejection of all creeds and churches would have sounded all too familiar to the Methodist evangelical, who repeated the conventional point that "all such things had ceased with the Apostles and that there never would be any more of them."[51]

The peremptory dismissal widened the gulf between Joseph and the evangelical ministry, which had been narrowing in the months prior to the vision. For a time they may have concentrated on him in an effort to rid him of his visionary notions. In any event, it seemed to Joseph that the clergy picked him out for persecution. The reviling angered him all the more because he spoke from direct experience. "I had actualy seen a light and in the midst of that light I saw two personages, and they did in reality speak unto me, or one of them did. And though I was hated and persecuted for saying that I had seen a vision, yet it was true. . . ." Like his mother and father before him, Joseph learned early to trust his own experiences above the influence of established authorities and institutions. His vision, instead of bringing him into the evangelical mainstream like most conversions, set him on a course of his own.[52]

The 1820 vision did not interrupt the Smith family round of work. "I continued to pursue my common vocation in life," Joseph later wrote. William Smith remembered sixty acres being cleared and fenced, and an orchard planted. By the middle 1820s the Smiths were contracting with grain dealers for the sale of their wheat crops. Joseph rose each morning to chores in the barnyard, followed by a day of work in the fields. In 1820 he was entering the years of greatest usefulness to the family when he brought in income and was not yet laying aside money to start his own farm. When the census taker came to the Smith farm in 1820, Joseph, Sr., and Lucy did not list Joseph, Jr., as a resident, probably because he lived elsewhere during the growing season while earning money for the annual payment on the contract. Regular schooling was out of the question so long as the danger of losing the farm hung over their heads. "As it required the exertions of all that were able to render any assistance for the support of the Family," Joseph recalled in 1832, "we were deprived of the bennifit of an education. Suffice it to say I was mearly instructed in reading writing and the ground rules of Arithmatic which constuted my whole literary acquirements." John Stafford remembered the Smiths hold-ing school in their house and studying the Bible.[53]

At age twenty-two Alvin, the eldest, was probably laying plans for a house and farm of his own. After he left, Hyrum and Joseph, Jr., would have to bring in outside income while Joseph, Sr., ran the farm. Alvin's departure would be a great loss to the family. In the meantime he showed all the serious attention to duty characteristic of a model oldest son. Joseph, Jr., said of him that "from the time of his birth he never knew mirth. He was candid and sober and never would play; and minded his father and mother in toiling all day. He was one of the soberest of men. . . ."[54]

In 1822 Alvin began to build a frame house for the Smith family. The birth of a new baby, named Lucy, on July 18, 1821, added to the complexity of life for the other ten people living in the small cabin. Alvin took responsibility for the "management and control" of construction, which began in November after the fall harvest. With the three older boys bringing in income, the Smiths were able to purchase the materials and hire a carpenter. In his usual serious way Alvin looked ahead to the declining years of his parents and wished to provide for them before he left. "I am going to have a nice pleasant room for father and mother to sit in," Lucy remembered him saying, "and everything arranged for their comfort, and they shall not work any more as they have done." Had Alvin lived, the Smiths might have enjoyed the comfort he envisioned. Lucy said they planted a large orchard and "made every possible preparation for . . . [the time] when advanced age should deprive us of the ability to make those physical exertions which we were then capable of." In a couple's old age a farm provided income whether worked by a son or a tenant, and a house offered both shelter and dignity.[55]

Joseph, Jr., said little about his spiritual thoughts and feelings in the years immediately after the vision. He left the clearest record of the treatment he received from the clergy "and all classes of men, both religious and irreligious, because I continued to affirm that I had seen a vision." Eighteen years later when he wrote the account, the memories of the injustices still rankled.[56] The abuse, however, did not depress him for long or turn him within himself entirely. He remembered himself as enjoying a "cheery temperament" in adolescence. His very congeniality caused some twinges of conscience. Evangelical morality placed severe restraints on reborn individuals. Besides forbidding drunkenness and sexual immorality as might be expected, evangelical ministers condemned fiddling, dancing, and night walks. Converts were expected to deny themselves the usual forms of good times and keep their thoughts fixed on eternity. Brigham Young later said he found his cheerless upbringing in a Methodist household nearly unbearable. If not in the Smith home, in the community at large, similar values worked on Joseph's conscience. To the end of his life he had compunctions about loud laughter. At age fifteen and sixteen he worried about small indulgences in light-minded pleasure with his friends. "I was left to all kinds of temptations, and mingling with all kinds of society I frequently fell into many foolish errors and displayed the weakness of youth and the foibles of human nature which I am sorry to say led me into divers temptations offensive in the sight of God." "I was guilty of levity and sometimes associated with jovial company, etc., not consistent with that character which ought to be maintained by one who was called of God as I had been." The Methodists called converts who returned to their sins backsliders. Joseph felt the guilt of one forgiven by God who then made himself unworthy again. "In consequence of these things, I often felt condemned for my weakness and imperfections."[57]

His remorse came to a head in the fall of 1823. On September 21, after the others in the crowded little cabin had gone to sleep, Joseph, Jr., remained awake to pray "to Almighty God for forgiveness of all my sins and follies."[58] He wanted another manifestation to assure himself of his "state and standing" before God. While praying he noticed the room growing lighter until it was brighter than broad daylight. Suddenly, as Joseph later reported the event, a person appeared in the light standing above the floor.

He had on a loose robe of most exquisite whiteness. It was a whiteness beyond anything earthly I had ever seen; nor do I believe that any earthly thing could be made to appear so exceedingly white and brilliant. His hands were naked, and his arms also, a little above the wrist; so, also, were his feet naked, as were his legs, a little above the ankles. His head and neck were also bare. I could discover that he had no other clothing on but this robe, as it was open, so that I could see into his bosom. Not only was his robe exceedingly white, but his whole person was glorious beyond description, and his countenance truly like lightning.

The being, who identified himself as Moroni, assured Joseph that his sins were forgiven and that he still enjoyed acceptance with God. The rest of Moroni's words completely overshadowed Joseph's personal concern for salvation. If Joseph initially understood the First Vision as his personal conversion, similar to thousands of other evangelical conversions, the vision of Moroni wrenched Joseph out of that track. The first thing said was that God had a work for Joseph that would result in his name being "had for good and evil among all nations, kindreds and tongues." He was to expect opposition, including rejection by the ministry. Furthermore, he was to carry out a mission quite unlike any evangelical had ever envisioned.[59]

The startling part of the vision was Moroni's report of a book "written upon gold plates, giving an account of the former inhabitants of this continent, and the sources from whence they sprang. He also said that the fulness of the everlasting Gospel was contained in it, as delivered by the Savior to the ancient inhabitants." Besides that "there were two stones in silver bows — and these stones, fastened to a breastplate, constituted what is called the Urim and Thummim — deposited with the plates, and the possession and use of these stones were what constituted 'seers' in ancient or former times; and that God had prepared them for the purpose of translating the book."[60]

The rest of the vision was more familiar and comprehensible. Moroni quoted Old and New Testament prophecies related to the final days of the earth and the coming of Christ: the third and fourth chapters of Malachi, Acts 3:22 and 23, Joel 2:28-32, Isaiah 11. These were the texts the clergy used to teach of the millennium. Joseph knew them well enough to notice small departures from the words in the Bible. Hearing the familiar texts from Moroni confirmed what was commonly preached — that the last days were near. More important, Joseph learned that he was to prepare for the return of Christ.[61]

Moroni concluded with a warning about showing the plates or the Urim and Thummim, and then the light began to gather around him until the room was dark except near his person. "Instantly, I saw, as it were, a conduit open right up into heaven, and he ascended till he entirely disappeared." Joseph lay back in astonishment, trying to understand what had happened, when the room began to brighten again, and the angel reappeared. Moroni repeated every word he had said before and then added comments about "great judgments which were coming upon the earth with great desolations by famine, sword and pestilence." Moroni again ascended but soon after appeared a third time to repeat again all he had said. This time he added the warning that "Satan would try to tempt me, (in consequence of the indigent circumstances of my father's family,) to get the plates for the purpose of getting rich." Joseph was to have no other object "but to glorify God."[62]

Not long after the third appearance day broke and the family began to stir. As after the First Vision, Joseph said nothing to his parents but went to the fields as usual. Reaping wheat alongside Alvin and William, Joseph stopped and seemed to be in a deep study. As Lucy Smith later told the story, Alvin chided him, saying, "We must not slacken our hands or we will not be able to complete our task." Joseph went back to work but stopped again. Noticing his son's drained face, Joseph, Sr., sent the boy back to the house. In attempting to climb over a fence, Joseph, Jr., fainted and for a time lay unconscious. The first thing he recognized was a voice calling his name. Looking up, he saw Moroni standing above him in a bright light. The angel repeated the entire message of the previous night and commanded Joseph to tell his father. Joseph returned to his father in the field and, overcoming fears of not being believed, told him all. Joseph, Sr., expressed no skepticism. Having learned himself to trust in visions, he accepted his son's story and counseled him to do exactly as the angel said.[63]

The hill where the plates lay buried stood in Manchester about three miles south and east of the Smith farm and just a few hundred feet to the east of the main road between Palmyra and Canandaigua. Joseph had seen the hill in vision the night before in enough detail to know exactly where the plates were. The steep northern side was an open pasture while to the south trees grew. The stone covering the plates lay in scattered trees on the western slope near the top. Joseph dug away the earth and pried up the stone with a lever. Under the top stone was a box made of five stones set in cement with their flat sides turned in. Inside lay the plates, the Urim and Thummim, and the breastplate. Oliver Cowdery and Joseph gave similar descriptions of the box, but Joseph said the plates and the other things sat on two stones laid cross ways in the bottom and Oliver said the plates were on three pillars of cement.[64]

Thoughts of the money value of the plates troubled Joseph when he saw the heavy pile. The angel had cautioned him the previous night about the temptation "to get the plates for the purpose of getting rich" because of "the indigent circumstances of my father's family." He was told he must have "no other object in view in getting the plates but to glorify God, and must not be influenced by any other motive than that of building his kingdom. . . ." Despite the warning, the sight of the gold was too much, and Joseph gave way to the very temptation he had been cautioned about. Oliver Cowdery and Lucy Smith said that Joseph felt a severe physical shock when he touched the plates, and that the angel appeared and severely rebuked him. Joseph merely reported that he was "forbidden by the messenger" and informed that "the time for bringing them forth had not yet arrived." He was to come to the hill the next year for further instructions. Lucy Smith said Joseph's disobedience was the reason for the delay. He had to wait "until he had learned to keep the commandments of God— not only till he was willing, but able, to do it."[65]

Joseph Sr.'s acceptance of his son's story of Moroni overcame Joseph

Jr.'s reserve about his religious experiences. The evening after the visit to the hill he told all of the family about the angel and the plates. The interest in Joseph's story went beyond mere curiosity: "The whole family were melted to tears, and believed all he said." In subsequent evenings the family continued to gather. Lucy Smith remembered with great happiness the family "all seated in a circle, father, mother, sons and daughters." It struck her that her "family presented an aspect as singular as any that ever lived upon the face of the earth," all "giving the most profound attention to a boy, eighteen years of age; who had never read the Bible through in his life. . . ." "The sweetest union and happiness pervaded our house, and tranquility reigned in our midst." Joseph warned of troubles ahead for the Smiths. "The world was so wicked that when they came to a knowledge of these things they would try to take our lives." For that reason all he told them had to be kept to themselves. And yet they rejoiced to know that God was about to give them "a more perfect knowledge of the plan of salvation and the redemption of the human family." At last, as Lucy said, the Smiths had "something upon which we could stay our minds."[66]

MONEY

The tranquility of those first evenings after Moroni's visit soon ended. The misfortunes and sorrows that followed the Smiths in Vermont and that had receded after the move to New York descended upon them again. Less than two months after Joseph went to the hill, Alvin fell sick. About ten o'clock in the morning of November 1, he came into the house in great pain. Joseph, Sr., went at once for a doctor and came back with a Dr. Greenwood, the Smiths' usual physician, Alexander McIntyre, not being available. The diagnosis was bilious colic, and the doctor prescribed a large dose of calomel, a compound of mercury and chlorine thought to promote the discharge of bile. Alvin objected strenuously but finally gave way. Lucy said that the calomel lodged in Alvin's stomach, and the combined exertions of four physicians who came with Dr. McIntyre three days later could not remove it.[67]

Alvin felt at once that he would die and called the family to the bedside to say farewell. He charged Hyrum to finish the house and care for the parents, and Sophronia to "be kind to them and remember what they have done for us." Little Lucy, just over two, clung to her brother and cried out, "Amby, Amby," her pet name for him. Alvin urged Joseph, Jr., "to be a good boy, and do everything that lies in your power to obtain the Record."[68] On November 19, 1823, Alvin died, a terrible loss to his family. He had been a model for them all. Lucy said, "Alvin was a youth of singular goodness of disposition—kind and amiable. . . ." Joseph, Jr., remembered him as a man in whom "there was no guile. He lived without spot from the time he was a child." Later in life Joseph, Jr., saw Alvin in vision in the company of Adam and Abraham in the celestial kingdom.[69]

His death brought an end to the family gatherings to discuss the record. Alvin had taken a greater interest than any of the other family members, Lucy said, and consequently they could not bear to hear anything said upon the subject. When Joseph, Jr., spoke of the record, they thought of Alvin, "with all his zeal, and with all his kindness; and, when we looked to his place, and realized that he was gone from it, to return no more in this life, we all with one accord wept over our irretrievable loss, and we could 'not be comforted, because he was not.' "[70]

A large number of neighbors came to the funeral and joined in the family mourning, and yet someone was not above playing on the family grief. On September 30, 1824, Joseph, Sr., published a statement in the *Wayne Sentinel* to discredit reports that Alvin had been exhumed and dissected. To quiet the rumors, Joseph, Sr., and a few neighbors dug into the grave and found the body to be undisturbed.[71]

In 1824, the year following Alvin's death, another revival struck Palmyra and nearby towns, this one even closer to the Smiths' home than the one in 1819. All of the churches in Palmyra showed growth in membership. Once again Lucy was drawn toward the churches as she had been in previous revivals. She and most of the family took particular interest in a minister who attempted to "effect a union of the different churches in order that all might be agreed, and thus worship God with one heart and with one mind." Even Joseph, Sr., attended two or three meetings before refusing to go again. Joseph, Jr., however, quietly held his own course. He told his mother he could learn more in the woods from the Bible than from any number of meetings. He saw too much greed among purported Christians to be comfortable in church. You are "mistaken in them," he told his mother, "and do not know the wickedness of their hearts." By 1824 Joseph, Jr., had sloughed off the family's traditional ambivalence about the churches and come down firmly on the side of his father.[72]

Work on the new frame house slowed down after Alvin's death. It was not completed until late in 1825 or early 1826, three years after construction began. Alvin's loss also added to the difficulty of meeting the burdensome annual contract payment. The responsibility fell on Joseph, Jr., and Hyrum to scout the countryside for work. That is probably the reason why Joseph took a position digging for Josiah Stowell in Pennsylvania in October, 1825. Hyrum's value to the family was lessening as he began saving for his own marriage. On top of the land contract, the carpenter had to be paid. Tradesmen were accustomed to working on credit, but sooner or later the Smiths had to meet their demands or face a court suit.[73]

In the fall of 1825 the family determined to borrow on next year's wheat crop. Sometime after November 17, when Joseph came back from the digging expedition in Pennsylvania, Josiah Stowell of South Bainbridge, with whom Joseph had been working, and Joseph Knight of Colesville visited Palmyra looking for wheat or flour, as they may have been doing for a number of years. Stowell and Knight agreed to lend the Smiths money for the contract payment with next year's wheat crop as collateral. With the load off their backs, Hyrum was able to go to Canandaigua to tell the land agent that the final payment would be made on December 25.[74]

Probably Hyrum made the special trip because the 25th fell beyond the due date. The owners of the land, the Evertsons of New York City, had also appointed a new agent, and possibly the Smiths were not entirely sure of him. Agents had a legal right to reclaim property and evict the occupants if they missed a payment, without compensation for their improvements. Few agents acted so harshly as a general rule. Most of the migrants to western New York lacked capital, and cash was hard to raise. After 1819 falling prices for grain, cows, and butter put hundreds of farmers in jeopardy. The president of the Genesee County Agricultural Society estimated in 1819 that the interest alone on the farm debt amounted to $350,000, and only $150,000 was paid that year. "The inhabitants of this village," a resident of Rochester said in 1818, "are half of them no better than bankrupts, and the rest can hardly pay." By 1828 over 700 debtors were in the Rochester prison. Rarely were contract payments made on time. Agents did foreclose, as the advertisements for public sale attest, but they gained little so long as there was no one else to buy the land. Instead, they usually added additional interest to the total cost and exercised patience with farmers who showed good faith. Ejectments were reserved, as one owner said, for "men of bad character and bad habits." So long as the land was being improved, the owners' investment appreciated. Without occupants to keep it up, the land quickly lost value. Although they understood this, the Smiths wished to make sure the new agent trusted them and would not act rashly.[75]

Unfortunately, as Lucy tells the story, Stoddard, the carpenter on the house, had designs on the property. Lucy Smith said he offered them $1,500 for it at one point. Perhaps also he doubted the Smiths' capacity to pay for the house with Alvin dead and Joseph, Sr., growing old. The right purchase arrangement would give Stoddard the farm and payment for his labor as well. Most original contractors for land in western New York ended up unable to finish the payments and had to reassign the contract to a second party. Stoddard probably thought the Smiths would follow the well-worn path.[76]

Having been rebuffed, Stoddard raised money for the purchase from his neighbors and tried another angle. He persuaded the agent that Joseph, Sr., and Joseph, Jr., were running away (they had gone to southern New York to get the money from Stowell and Knight), and Hyrum was cutting the sugar orchards and tearing down the fences. Lucy says the agent panicked. He may also have seen an unusual opportunity. Stoddard offered full payment for the farm instead of the $100 the Smiths owed, and he offered cash. In a difficult time, when other farmers were slow in their payments, here was good news to report to the Evertsons.[77]

Stoddard and two friends arrived at the farm while Joseph, Sr., was still away. They asked again if the Smiths wished to sell out and then informed Lucy and Hyrum of the agreement with the agent. Stoddard told the Smiths to get off the property so that the lawful owners could take occupancy. Lucy nearly fainted. She pled with the threesome to relent, but they were adamant. Hyrum hurried off to Dr. Gain Robinson, a friend of the family and one of the physicians who attended Alvin during his sickness. Since one important factor was the Smiths' character, Dr. Robinson wrote out a testimonial to their industry and circulated it himself until he had sixty signatures. If the agent could be persuaded of the Smiths' trustworthiness, he might reverse himself.[78]

The land agent at least appeared chagrined when Hyrum presented the testimonial. It is not recorded if he offered to buy back the land from Stoddard and his associates, but he did try to reason with them. They refused to see the agent until he threatened to bring them in with a warrant, and then they saw no reason to give up the deed. Lucy Smith remembered them taunting Hyrum with sneering remarks. "Oh, no matter about Smith, he has gold plates, gold bibles, he is rich—he don't want anything." Under prodding they ultimately agreed to return the farm if Hyrum could raise $1,000 by Saturday at 10 P.M. Since it was then Thursday noon, Stoddard yielded very little.[79]

Hyrum rode home at full speed and found Joseph, Sr., back from seeing Knight and Stowell. Hyrum had left notes at various inns en route informing his father of the crisis, and one of these reached him. The Smiths had no expectation of being able to raise the money that had been demanded. At best they hoped to persuade a friendly party to buy the farm and permit the family to harvest the crop and perhaps allow them to stay on as tenants. By Friday morning they had a plan. Joseph, Sr., sent Lucy to an old Quaker gentleman, a friend of the family who had admired the farm. Unfortunately, he had just that day laid out all of his cash to redeem the land of another friend. Lucy returned home ten miles through the forest in the mid-December night with the bad news. The Quaker did agree to look for another possible purchaser. Hearing that Lemuel Durfee, Sr., might be able to help, the Quaker took the trouble to ride to the Smiths that very night, arriving less than twenty-four hours before the Saturday deadline. Joseph, Sr., took the advice and set off immediately. Before daybreak, he was talking to Durfee, who asked Joseph to fetch one of Durfee's sons who was a sheriff. The three hurried back to the Smiths' farm and were there to inspect it by 10 A.M. Saturday. Liking the appearance of the place, the Durfees and Joseph, Sr., went on to Canandaigua. A few minutes before the 10 P.M. deadline, Stoddard was asked to appear. After feebly protesting that the deadline was actually past, he yielded up the deed. Lemuel Durfee, Sr., purchased the Smith farm for $1,135 on December 20, 1825. The Smiths lost the property but may eventually have received $700 for their improvements.[80]

The loss of the farm in 1825 hurt Lucy much more than the sale of their Tunbridge property in 1803. Then "we were young," she said, "and by making some exertions we might improve our circumstances." In 1825 Lucy was fifty and Joseph, Sr., fifty-four, both weary from lives of endless toil. They no longer had the help of Alvin, and Hyrum and Joseph were nearing the age of marriage. The moment had passed when the unified effort of father and sons could raise the money to buy a farm. They were doomed to revert to tenancy, and when old age overtook them, instead of the dignity of a house and land of their own, they would live as guests in the home of one of the children. Durfee permitted Joseph, Sr., and Lucy to work the farm until 1829, when with five of the younger children they moved in with Hyrum and his wife,[81] who had married in 1826.

The loss of the farm did not end Joseph's work excursions. The family had to pay rent in place of the contract payment and Joseph at age twenty was looking ahead to marriage and a house and farm of his own. He had to make provisions for himself as well as for his parents. Samuel and William, ages eighteen and fifteen, could handle the work on the Smith farm while Joseph took employment elsewhere.[82] Joseph was drawn back to the properties where he had been working before the loss of the farm. Josiah Stowell paid him $14 a month plus room and board to do farm chores and perhaps work in his mills. Stowell, who was fifty-six in 1826, owned hundreds of acres of woodlots and ran a number of sawmills in the southern part of the state. Joseph's experience in clearing the Smith farm would have made him a useful hand in the Stowell enterprises. When he was not employed by Stowell in 1826, Joseph worked for Joseph Knight, who ran carding machinery and a gristmill in addition to his farms. Stowell's property lay on the Susquehannah River in South Bain-

bridge (now Afton), Chenango County, and Joseph Knight lived in Colesville, Broome County, on the south (or east) side of the river, three and a
half miles downstream and just a few miles north of the Pennsylvania
line.[83]

Joseph Knight, Jr., said his father thought Joseph Smith, Jr., was "the
best hand he ever hired." But that was not the reason why Stowell and
Knight initially brought young Joseph all the way from Palmyra to South
Bainbridge to work in 1825. Stowell believed that he had located the site
of an ancient Spanish mine where coins had been minted and buried.
Through the summer of 1825 he put his hired hands to work on the site,
which lay some twenty-six miles southwest from his farm near Harmony,
Pennsylvania. When his men failed to locate the cache, Stowell enlisted
the Smiths' help, and Joseph Smith, Sr., and Joseph, Jr., agreed to join the
diggers in Harmony. A set of "Articles of Agreement," dated November
1, 1825 (though published only much later), indicated that Joseph and his
father were to receive two-elevenths of the ore in the mine or "the coined
money and bars or ingots of Gold or Silver" reputed to lie hidden under-
ground. The articles created a company to share the profits and bear the
labor and expenses of mining. Lucy recalled that after less than a month
Joseph prevailed upon Stowell to stop digging. In mid-November the group
dispersed, and Joseph and his father returned to Manchester during the
crisis over the farm. After he returned later in the winter, Joseph seems
to have been engaged in more conventional labor.[84]

Stowell and Knight went to the trouble of bringing Joseph Smith, Jr.,
150 miles from Palmyra, Lucy Smith explained, "on account of having
heard that he possessed certain keys by which he could discern things
invisible to the natural eye." Around 1822 Joseph had discovered a stone
while digging a well with Willard Chase a half-mile from the Smith farm.
The stone enabled Joseph to see things, as Lucy said, "invisible to the
natural eye."[85] Emma Smith said it was "a small stone, not exactly black,
but was rather a dark color." In 1841 Joseph showed the stone to the
Council of the Twelve in Nauvoo and told them, Brigham Young reported,
"that every man who lived on the earth was entitled to a seerstone and
should have one, but they are kept from them in consequence of their
wickedness. . . ." After Brigham Young showed the stone to Hosea Stout
in 1856, he described it as "dark color almost black with light colored
stripes. . . . It was about the size but not the shape of a hen's egg." In 1888,
when Wilford Woodruff consecrated the seerstone upon the altar in the
Manti Temple, he wrote in his journal that it was the stone "that the
Prophet Joseph Smith found by revelation some thirty feet under the earth
(ground) and carried by him through life."[86] For a time Joseph probably
used the stone to help people find lost property and other hidden things,

and his reputation reached Stowell. Having failed on his own to find the Spanish bullion, he thought Joseph could help.[87]

All of this was later turned against Joseph Smith. In 1833 an excommunicated Mormon apostate named Philastus Hurlbut collected affidavits in Palmyra and Manchester from people who claimed to remember the Smith family. One of the repeated charges in the affidavits was that Joseph, Sr., and his sons hunted for treasure and looked in the seerstone. From that day to this the neighbors' accusations of money digging and glass looking have cast a shadow over Joseph Smith.[88]

Although the conscious intent was to expose Joseph, the neighbors revealed even more about themselves and the folk culture of western New York in the early nineteenth century. All of the firsthand observations of the treasure seeking of necessity came from people who had gone on the expeditions. Thus the affidavits that are most explicit about the Smiths are reports from individuals who were themselves participants. They provide a glimpse into a netherworld of magical belief and practice that polite members of society had long ago repudiated but that many people still believed in. The stories told in the affidavits so rarely corroborate one another that it would be presumptuous to reconstruct a narrative of events, but taken as a whole they certainly attest to fascination with spirits, treasure, and magic.

Willard Chase's affidavit did not mention firsthand observation of treasure hunting, but it disclosed an intense interest in the seerstone. Most of his anger against Joseph, Jr., arose from Chase's claim that he found the stone, not Joseph, and that the Smiths refused to return it. Chase said he let Joseph take it home, but as soon as it was known "what wonders he could discover by looking in it," Chase wanted it back. As late as 1830 Chase was still trying to get his hands on the stone. Willard Chase's younger brother Abel later told an interviewer that their sister Sally had a stone. A nearby physician, John Stafford, reported that "the neighbors used to claim Sally Chase could look at a stone she had, and see money. Willard used to dig when she found where the money was." After Joseph obtained the plates, Willard Chase led the group that attempted to find them in the Smiths' house, guided by Sally Chase and a "green glass, through which she could see many very wonderful things."[89]

A clan of Staffords who lived about a mile and a half from the Smiths had their own money-digging operations that peripherally involved the Smiths. William Stafford told Hurlbut about twice hunting for treasure with Joseph, Sr., but after a time the "people of this vicinity" lost faith in the Smiths, and presumably the Staffords fell back on their own resources. Joshua Stafford, Dr. John Stafford's father, reportedly had a stone "which looked like a white marble and had a hole through the center."

Cornelius Stafford said "there was much digging for money on our farm and about the neighborhood. I saw Uncle John and Cousin Joshua Stafford dig a hole twenty feet long, eight broad and seven deep." Although apparently unconnected with the Staffords, Peter Ingersoll, according to his own testimony, was another to take part. W. D. Purple knew a Chauncy Hart, who had a "small peculiar stone like Smiths" that he used to find lost objects.[90]

Circling outward from Palmyra and Manchester, traces of similar belief are found throughout the region. The appearance of the Book of Mormon reminded a correspondent to the *Rochester Gem* of an eighteen-year-old boy who in 1815 used a seerstone to hunt for treasure. The historian of Susquehannah County knew of a Jack Belcher, who found lost objects with a stone. Folklorists find tales of spirits guarding buried treasure deeply enmeshed in rural culture throughout New York State. Vermont in the same era had its buried treasures and lost mines detected through dreams, divining rods, or stones. The Nathaniel Woods family in the Wells-Putney area of Vermont set out with one Winchell, who used St. John's rod to find treasure guarded by a hostile spirit. Supposedly Oliver Cowdery's father was a follower of the Woods.[91]

The lore of buried treasure was tied into a great stock of magical practices that went back many centuries. A play published in Philadelphia in 1767, called the *Disappointment; or, the Force of Credulity,* turned on the attempt of a fraudulent magician to find a treasure, and depicted the rite of drawing a magic circle on the ground to ward off the evil spirit. The playwright ridiculed the credulity of those who fell prey to Rattletrap the bogus magician, but the comedy of the play derived from the fact that people believed. The author said "people to this day," "like so many mischievous muskrat's spoilt the pastures and bank along shore" in search of buried money. Not a hundred years earlier Goodwin Wharton, a Whig member of Parliament, spent twenty-five years searching for treasure with the aid of spirits and angels, while pursuing a career in the House of Commons that culminated in appointment as a Lord of Admiralty. Before 1650 the search for treasure with stones and rods was still more common and, like most magic, blended imperceptibly with orthodox Christian faith in the minds of common people.[92]

The forces of eighteenth-century rationalism were never quite powerful enough to suppress the belief in supernatural powers aiding and opposing human enterprise. The educated representatives of enlightened thought, newspaper editors and ministers particularly, scoffed at the superstitions of common people without completely purging them. The scorn of the polite world put the Palmyra and Manchester money diggers in a dilemma. They dared not openly describe their resort to magic for fear of ridicule from the fashionably educated, and yet they could not overcome their fascination with the lore that seeped through to them from the past. Their embarrassment shows in the affidavits Hurlbut collected. William Stafford, who admitted participation in two "nocturnal excursions," claimed he thought the idea visionary all along, but "being prompted by curiosity, I at length accepted of their invitations." Peter Ingersoll made much more elaborate excuses. One time he went along because it was lunchtime, his oxen were eating, and he was at leisure. Secretly, though, he claimed to be laughing up his sleeve: "This was rare sport for me." Another time he said he "thought it best to conceal my feelings, preferring to appear the dupe of my credulity, than to expose myself to his resentment. . . ." Willard Chase and the Staffords said nothing about their personal quests for treasure and reliance on stones other than Joseph's.[93]

Despite the disdain of the educated, ordinary people apparently had no difficulty reconciling Christianity with magic. Willard Chase, perhaps the most vigorous of the Palmyra money diggers, was a Methodist class leader at the time he knew the Smiths, and in his obituary was described as a minister. When Josiah Stowell employed Joseph to use his seerstone to find Spanish bullion, Stowell was an upright Presbyterian and an honored man in his community. The so-called credulity of the money diggers can be read as a sign of their faith in the reality of the invisible powers described in scripture. Christian belief in angels and devils made it easy to believe in guardian spirits and magical powers.[94]

The Smith family at first was no more able to distinguish true religion from superstition than their neighbors. Standing on the margins of instituted churches, they were as susceptible to the neighbors' belief in magic as they were to the teachings of orthodox ministers. Joseph's discovery of the seerstone and the revelation of Moroni and the gold plates confused them even further. The visit of the angel seemed to confirm the beliefs of their superstitious neighbors. When she drafted the *Biographical Sketches,* Lucy seemed to understand how the story of Moroni might be mistakenly understood as a tale of money digging. She prefaced her narrative of the discovery of the plates with the declaration that

I shall change my theme for the present, but let not my reader suppose that because I shall pursue another topic for a season that we stopt our labor and went at trying to win the faculty of Abrae drawing Magic circles or sooth saying to the neglect of all kinds of buisness we never during our lives suffered one important interest to swallow up every other obligation but whilst we worked with our hands we endeavored to remember the service of and the welfare of our souls.[95]

Lucy Smith's main point was that the Smiths were not lazy as the affidavits claimed — they had not stopped their labor to practice magic — but she also revealed a knowledge of magic formulas and rituals. It seems likely that Joseph, Sr., stimulated by his son's supernatural experiences, searched for treasure with the help of his family. Understandably, Moroni's visit and the discovery of the seerstone appeared to confirm the entire culture of magic.[96]

On his first appearance, Moroni warned Joseph, Jr., against the spirit of treasure hunting. "Satan would try to tempt me," Joseph was told, "(in consequence of the indigent circumstances of my father's family,) to get the plates for the purpose of getting rich. This he forbade me, saying that I must have no other object in view in getting the plates but to glorify God. . . ." If heeded, the admonition would have separated Joseph from the money diggers, but, according to Oliver Cowdery's 1835 report, Joseph was not entirely able to suppress his baser motives on the first walk to Cumorah. When he saw the "sacred treasure," he began to calculate how to "add to his store of wealth . . . without once thinking of the solemn instruction of the heavenly messenger, and that all must be done with an express view of glorifying God." When stopped from lifting out the plates, Oliver said, Joseph's mind flashed back to the tales of the treasure hunters: "He had heard of the powers of enchantment, and a thousand like stories, which held the hidden treasures of the earth, and supposed that physical exertion and personal strength was only necessary to enable him to yet obtain the object of his wish." Despite the warnings, Joseph spontaneously connected the plates with money-digging lore.

When he failed after three attempts, Joseph spontaneously cried out, "Why can I not obtain this book." Moroni then appeared to say, "Because you have not kept the commandments of the Lord." In an instant the earlier warning came back to mind, and Joseph was filled with contrition. Moroni opened to Joseph a vision of the prince of darkness and told him, "All this is shown, the good and the evil, the holy and the impure, the glory of God and the power of darkness, that ye may know hereafter the two powers and never be influenced or overcome by that wicked one." Lucy's sketches also told of Moroni describing "the operation of a good Spirit and an evil one" and urging Joseph to "keep your mind always staid upon God that no evil may come into your heart." The angel's instructions connected the greed of the money digger with the powers of Satan. Joseph was to walk a different course. "You now see why you could not obtain this record." Oliver reported Moroni as saying, "The Commandment was strict, and . . . if ever these sacred things are obtained they must be by prayer and faithfulness in obeying the Lord."[97]

Moroni's warning may have led to a rift in the Smith family over the next few years. Although he did not repudiate the stone or ever deny its power to find treasure, Joseph, Jr., began to orient himself toward a new mission — obtaining and translating the Book of Mormon. Martin Harris later remembered Joseph saying that "the angel told him he must quit the company of the money-diggers. That there were wicked men among them. He must have no more to do with them. He must not lie, nor swear, nor steal."[98] Joseph, Jr., began to pull back, while his father still hoped to find wealth through the seerstone. The affidavits describe just four incidents of money digging actually observed by the neighbors: two reported by William Stafford and one each by John Stafford and Peter Ingersoll. All four involved Joseph, Sr., and not Joseph, Jr. William Stafford depicts Joseph, Sr., hunting for gold and going back to the house to seek further instructions from Joseph, Jr., as if the son was trying his best to keep out of it. John Stafford saw Joseph, Sr., and Hyrum digging one day, "but Joseph was not there." Peter Ingersoll does not mention Joseph, Jr., in the incident he retells.[99] Two articles in the Palmyra *Reflector* in February, 1831, appearing nearly three years before the earliest affidavit, say that Joseph, Sr., "evinced a firm belief in the existence of hidden treasures," but do not accuse Joseph. In 1825, when the family needed money, Joseph agreed to use the seerstone to help Stowell find the Spanish gold, but Joseph may soon have had misgivings. Lucy said of Stowell's operation that "Joseph endeavored to divert him from his vain pursuit."[100]

Joseph Jr.'s reservations about digging may account for Isaac Hale's observation of arguing between father and son while they boarded at Hale's house during the brief mining operation. Their normally amicable relations broke down under their disagreement over treasure hunting. Alva Hale, a son in the household where the Smiths stayed, said Joseph, Jr., told him that the "gift in seeing with a stone" was "a gift from God" but that " 'peeping' was all d——d nonsense." Alva did not grasp the difference and apparently neither did Joseph, Sr.[101]

The transcript of a purported trial in March, 1826, in South Bainbridge sheds further light on the Smith family's state of mind on the eve of receiving the plates. While the evidence that such a trial actually took place is not beyond question, the circumstances and portions of the recorded trial testimony are not out of character.[102] According to the most trust-worthy of the three accounts of the trial, Peter Bridgeman, nephew of Josiah Stowell, entered a complaint against Joseph Smith, Jr., as a disorderly person in South Bainbridge, Chenango County, New York. Joseph continued working for Stowell after the abortive mining operation in November, 1825, and presumably Bridgeman believed that Joseph exercised undue influence on his uncle. Stowell did say in the court record that he "had the most implicit faith in the prisoner's skill."[103]

The very existence of a trial record, if it is indeed authentic, attests to the popular interest in stone looking and treasure hunting. Ordinarily the trial of a disorderly person before a justice of the peace left no further trace than a few lines in the court records. Albert Neely, the presiding justice, asked W. D. Purple, a local physician and a friend, to take notes, which as published came to over a thousand words. The townspeople shared Neely's fascination with the subject. Purple said "there was a large collection of persons in attendance, and the proceedings attracted much attention." Two of the witnesses in the record believed in Joseph's gifts; the other two were intrigued enough to test Joseph before rejecting him.[104]

What the trial record reveals is that Joseph Smith, as he had always admitted, did help Josiah Stowell search for treasure. Stowell said Joseph used the stone to locate "hidden treasures" in various locations. Three other witnesses associated with Stowell testified to the same thing. The record has Joseph saying that "he had a certain stone, which he had occasionally looked at to determine where hidden treasures in the bowels of the earth were . . . and while at Palmyra he had frequently ascertained in that way where lost property was. . . ."[105]

The record is equally explicit that Joseph did not like treasure hunting. Purple has Joseph conclude his testimony by saying that "he did not solicit business of this kind, and had always rather declined having anything to do with this business." Why then did he get involved? It seems clear that Joseph was under pressure—from neighbors, from the enthusiastic and well-off Josiah Stowell, from his own father, and from cruel, unrelenting poverty. Joseph appears to have extricated himself from the local money-digging operations before his family did, perhaps as early as 1825. His interests were changing, but as a twenty-year-old he was not impervious to pressures from his circumstances and friends. The trial may have been a turning point. W. D. Purple published a fuller account in 1877 after he had been telling the tale for years. There are so many contradictions with the earlier trial record that the 1877 account is not to be trusted entirely. But Purple said the solemn sincerity of one statement made a strong impression. Joseph, Sr., testified that "both he and his son were mortified that this wonderful power which God had so miraculously given him should be used only in search of filthy lucre, or its equivalent in earthly treasures. . . ." "His constant prayer to his Heavenly Father was to manifest His will concerning this marvelous power. He trusted that the Son of Righteousness would some day illumine the heart of the boy, and enable him to see His will concerning Him." Those words, remembered by a hostile and skeptical observer, suggest a change of perspective. By 1826 Father Smith was beginning to discern the deeper purpose of Joseph's gifts. A neighbor who knew Joseph, Sr., around 1827 reported that the old man "stated their digging was not for money but it was for the obtaining of a Gold Bible. Thus contradicting what he had told me before. . . ." Despite the ongoing fascination of treasure hunting, the Smiths by 1826 were ready to take a greater interest in the translation of the plates.[106]

MARRIAGE

Joseph spent most of 1826 in southern New York. He went to school, and worked for Stowell in South Bainbridge, and possibly labored in Joseph Knight's carding mills, three and a half miles down the Susquehannah River in Colesville.[107] He made a good impression while there. John Reid, a noted lawyer who later defended Joseph in the local courts, said Joseph was truthful and intelligent. Josiah Stowell, Jr., said Joseph was "a fine likely young man and at that time did not profess religion. He was not a Profane man although I did once in a while hear him swair. He never gambled to my knowledge. I do not believe he ever did . . . I never new him to get drunk." The Knight boys, Joseph, Jr., and Newel, had the same impression. Joseph Smith, Jr., formed lifelong friendships with both families. Stowell, Sr., believed in Joseph to the last. In 1843, through his son, Stowell wrote of Joseph that "he never knew anything of him but that was right; and also know him to be a seer and a Prophet and believe the Book of Mormon to be true." In November, 1826, Joseph, Jr., told the Knights about Moroni and a "gold book of ancient date." At first the two older boys had no faith in the story, but Joseph Knight, Jr., and his father believed at once. The Knights later became the nucleus of a small branch in Colesville and migrated to Ohio with the church.[108]

Joseph had to return to Manchester in the fall to comply with Moroni's instructions to report at Cumorah every year on September 22. He did not stay at home for long, possibly not even for Hyrum's marriage to Jerusha Barden on November 2, since Joseph Knight, Jr., remembered Joseph being at their house in Colesville in November.[109]

Work on the Stowell and Knight farms was not the only magnet drawing Joseph Smith back. While at home, Joseph told his mother of Miss Emma Hale, who "would be my choice in preference to any other woman I have ever seen." Joseph had kept company with two of Stowell's daughters, but he had been most attracted to the tall, dark-haired Emma while he and his father boarded at the Hale home in Harmony during the treasure-hunting expedition, and could not forget her. Isaac Hale, a Connecticut-born man, sixty-two years old, had moved into the area around 1790, acquired land, and won notoriety as a hunter. Hale was close enough to the Stowell mining venture to witness the signatures on the agreement which Stowell, the Smiths, and others signed on November 1, 1825. Later, however, he turned against the treasure seekers. When Joseph came to court Emma and eventually ask for her hand, Hale objected that Joseph was "a stranger, and followed a business that I could not approve."[110]

Despite the opposition, the two young people were not to be thwarted. In January, 1827, Emma visited Josiah Stowell in Bainbridge and saw Joseph. He was a handsome young man, over six feet tall with broad chest and shoulders, light brown hair, blue eyes, and long thick lashes and bushy brows. She later told her son, "I had no intention of marrying when I left home; but during my visit at Mr. Stowell's, your father visited me there. My folks were bitterly opposed to him; and being importuned by your father, aided by Mr. Stowell, who urged me to marry him, and preferring to marry him to any other man I knew, I consented." Joseph was twenty-one and Emma twenty-two when they were married in the house of Zechariah Tarble in South Bainbridge, January 18, 1827.[111]

Apparently without returning to Harmony, the young couple moved to Manchester, where Joseph farmed with his father. The next summer Emma timidly wrote home to ask if she might obtain her clothing and some furniture and cows that belonged to her. When Isaac Hale assured her of the availability of her belongings, Joseph hired his neighbor Peter Ingersoll to accompany him and Emma and haul the goods back to Manchester. In Harmony Joseph and Emma met Isaac Hale for the first time since the marriage. The old man tearfully rebuked Joseph for stealing his daughter and said he would rather follow her to her grave than have her married to Joseph. His chagrin came from his belief that Joseph was a fraudulent money digger and glass looker. Joseph assured his father-in-law that all that was behind, and "he expected to work hard for a living, and was willing to do so." Isaac offered to let Emma and Joseph live on the Hale property in Harmony and to help Joseph get started in business.[112]

Joseph, of course, had long since been trying to free himself from the money diggers. He told Peter Ingersoll on the way back to Manchester that he intended to keep the promise he had made to his father-in-law, but "it will be hard for me, for they will all oppose, as they want me to look in the stone for them to dig money. . . ." Ingersoll observed that Joseph's predictions came true. "They urged him, day after day, to resume his old practice of looking in the stone."[113] After four years the hands of the treasure hunters still clutched at Joseph. He was yet to endure their curses, the invasion of his house, and sometimes their blows and attempts on his life. When he actually had the plates, Sally Chase would be there with her stone to try to find the hiding place, and Willard Chase not far behind. But Joseph was determined to break free.

Joseph experienced the years from 1820 to 1827 as a succession of personal struggles with the evangelical clergy, ridiculing townspeople, and superstitious neighbors. It was a troubled time. Lucy later remembered Joseph warning the family after he first saw the plates, "They will want to kill us for the sake of the gold if they know we have them and as soon as they do find that we pretend to have any such thing our names will be cast out as evil and we shall be scoffed at. . . ." That all proved true. On one occasion he was mysteriously shot at in his own dooryard. Sometimes it was a lonely ordeal. For the three years from 1823 to 1826 Joseph stood alone against aggressive and demanding neighbors, the overwhelming need to make money, and the entreaties of his father.[114]

The struggle was an education for a young man not yet twenty-two in September, 1827, and for his family. He could never escape the libels of his enemies, whose culture preconditioned them to conceive of Joseph as a glass looker and his followers as "profound believers in witchcraft, ghosts, goblins, etc." But he and his family knew by the time he received the plates that the seerstone was not merely a license for money digging. They had begun to realize the plates were to be valued more for their history than as bullion. Joseph was to use his powers in the service of God, not for the enrichment of the family.[115]

After Joseph and Emma's return to Manchester in 1827, Joseph, Sr., sent his son into the village on business. When it grew dark and Joseph was still not back, the parents started to fret. At last an exhausted Joseph came through the door and dropped into a chair. For a long time he sat silent while his father plied him with questions. Mother Smith held back. "The fact was, I had learned to be a little cautious about matters with regard to Joseph, for I was accustomed to see him look as he did on that occasion, and I could not easily mistake the cause thereof."[116]

Finally Joseph said quietly, "I have taken the severest chastisement that I have ever had in my life." The angel had met Joseph on the road near Cumorah and warned him that he "had not been engaged enough in the work of the Lord; that the time had come for the Record to be brought forth; and that I must be up and doing, and set myself about the things which God had commanded me to do." The angel had been angry and insistent, but by the time Joseph got home he was calm. "I now know the course that I am to pursue, so all will be well." The moment had come for Joseph to take the plates from their ancient hiding place.[117]

CHAPTER III

TRANSLATION

By the fall of 1827 events had carried Joseph Smith into the turbulence of a contested cultural boundary—the one dividing superstition from rational belief. Through the eighteenth century Enlightenment theologians worked to discredit the visions, dreams, seerstones, witchcraft, spells, and healings that had bounteously flourished in Christian countries until the end of the seventeenth century. Rationalists scoffed at this effusion of supernatural manifestations as the imaginings of ignorance, unrelated to either divine or demonic power. The established clergy acknowledged only the gift of grace as an acceptable form of divine intervention. All else was unholy, unscriptural, and irrational.

But though practitioners of magic among the common people became objects of ridicule, the yearning for contact with powers beyond this world could not be quenched. Many Christians hoped for a return of primitive Christianity's divine gifts, and water witching, stone gazing, treasure hunting, and spiritualism went on despite the scorn of newspaper editors, ministers, and physicians who spoke for Enlightenment values in New York villages.

Joseph Smith stood on the line that divided the yearning for the supernatural from the humanism of rational Christianity—one of the many boundaries between the traditional and modern world passing through American culture in the early nineteenth century. Culturally Joseph looked backward toward traditional society's faith in the immediate presence of divine power, communicating through stones, visions, dreams, and angels. On the other hand, Joseph repudiated the superstitions of the past, particularly the Palymyra money diggers' exploitation of supernatural power for base purposes. In the end he satisfied neither religionists nor the local magicians. Joseph Smith, Sr., said at the trial in 1826 that the family believed "that the Son of Righteousness would some day illumine the heart of the boy, and enable him to see His will concerning him." Joseph's desires were religious, but the supernatural powers that played about his life scandalized rational Christianity, while the religious impulse confused the money diggers.

Inevitably Joseph Smith was misunderstood. Editors and clergymen vilified him for reviving old superstitions that they believed should be suppressed. The Palmyra magicians harassed him for not playing their game. It was hard for either group to believe that Joseph's powers were meant solely to advance the purposes of the God of the Bible. Even the men most strongly inclined to believe—Oliver Cowdery and Martin Harris— questioned at times. They heard the story with a mixture of amazement, joy, and cautious disbelief. In their first encounters they wavered between fascination and incredulity, devising one test after another to safeguard themselves against deception. Though not sophisticated nor truly skeptical, they asked for proof of Joseph's gifts in the same spirit of doubt that moved his enemies.

As Joseph Smith became better known after 1827, both friends and enemies repeatedly measured him against standards of humanistic ratio- nality. Just as he had extricated himself from revivalist Christianity, and then distinguished his quest for the golden plates from local folk magic, he was compelled after 1827 to define his convictions over against the Enlightenment. Particularly he had to react to the demand for rational proof in the form of miracles, and to establish a basis of his own for soliciting belief. He had to provide a foundation for faith in a modern angel and in a new scripture written on plates of gold.

THE PLATES

The events preceding publication of the Book of Mormon can be pieced together from the recollections of a dozen or so contemporaries. A few non-Mormons wrote—Pomeroy Tucker, Charles Anthon, and Willard Chase—but mainly they were Mormons: Lucy Smith, Joseph Knight, Joseph Knight, Jr., David Whitmer, Oliver Cowdery, Joseph Smith, Jr., Emma Smith, William Smith, and Martin Harris. The story to emerge from these accounts may in one respect perplex readers who are not Mormons. All the extant Mormon sources accept as fact Joseph Smith's possession of the plates and his effort to translate. Interspersed with de- scriptions of journeys, illnesses, business deals, and lost horses are trips to Cumorah, efforts to conceal the plates, long translating sessions, and read- ings from the completed manuscript. Some readers may wish to separate the easily believable mundane details from the extraordinary supernatural events, and to find another explanation for the unusual experiences. The account that follows does not make that separation or attempt an explanation beyond that given in the sources. It tells the story as the Mormons remembered it, in the hope that an account reconstructed from the participants' memories will be useful in some degree to every reader.

In September, 1827, according to Joseph Knight, Joseph Smith's Colesville friend, he along with Josiah Stowell, the South Bainbridge employer, visited the Smiths in Manchester. Knight had arranged a business trip to Rochester to coincide with the date of Joseph's next visit to Cumorah. Knight remembered Joseph saying that the angel told him "if he would Do right according to the will of God, he mite obtain [the plates] the 22nt day of September Next and if not he never would have them." According to Knight, he was at the Smith house on the evening of September 21 and observed the preparations Joseph made. Joseph foresaw the possibility that Samuel Lawrence, a neighbor who had pretensions to seership and knew about the plates and the annual visits, would try to interfere. Joseph asked his father to scout the Lawrence house in the late afternoon and, if he saw signs of movement, to warn Lawrence off. Joseph, Sr., returned at nightfall with nothing to report.[1]

The angel had commanded Joseph to come to the hill on September 22. To be precise in his compliance and still to throw off meddlers who knew of the date, Joseph chose to go to Cumorah in the dead of night, almost the minute September 22 arrived. Lucy stayed up until past midnight on September 21. Around twelve o'clock Joseph came into the room to ask if his mother had a chest with lock and key. Knowing at once why he wanted it, Lucy was upset when she was unable to provide one. "Never mind," Joseph assured her, "I can do very well for the present without it—be calm—all is right." Minutes later Emma passed through the room in her bonnet and riding dress, and Lucy heard the two of them drive off in Joseph Knight's wagon.[2]

Joseph and Emma did not return until after breakfast the next morning. When the men were seated at the table, Joseph, Sr., asked after his son. Lucy tried to put him off, but her husband insisted. "I must have Joseph sit down here and eat with me." "Well, now, Mr. Smith," Lucy came back, "do let him eat with his wife this morning; he almost always takes breakfast with you." A few minutes later Joseph Knight came in with the disturbing news that his horse was missing. "Never mind the horse," Lucy parried. "Mr. Knight does not know all the nooks and corners in the pastures; I will call William, he will bring the horse immediately." Satisfied for a moment, Knight soon discovered his wagon gone and was convinced that some rogue had taken both. Lucy put him off again until finally Joseph got back.[3]

Lucy was trembling as Joseph came into the house, fearful that

through some failure of obedience all was lost. When she left the room
to conceal her feelings, Joseph stepped aside with her. "Do not be uneasy
mother, all is right—see here, I have got a key," and handed her an object
covered with a silk handkerchief. Lucy said she felt "two smooth three
cornered diamonds set in glass" and fixed in bows that were connected,
as she said, like old-fashioned spectacles. After breakfast Joseph called his
good friend Joseph Knight into another room and, with the happy en-
thusiasm of a young man, told Knight that everything was "ten times
Better then I expected." He described the plates but was more excited about
the Urim and Thummim. "I can see any thing; they are Marvelus." As
for the plates, they were "writein in caracters," Joseph said, "and I want
them translated."[4]

Probably to forestall interference, Joseph did not bring the plates home
on September 22. Lucy said he concealed them in an old birch log by
cutting out a segment of bark, carving out the interior, depositing the
plates, and replacing the bark. This interim hiding place also gave him
time to have a box made. Lucy directed him to a cabinetmaker who had
made furniture for Sophronia. Always short of cash, the Smiths worried
a little about how to make payment. Lucy told Joseph to promise half
cash, half produce, the same arrangement as for the furniture, but to their
delight Joseph learned the next day of a well-digging job in Macedon, just
east of Palmyra. The following day he left to go to work.[5]

It soon appeared that the Smiths' efforts to keep news of the plates
from getting out were in vain. The day after Joseph left for Macedon, a
neighbor questioned Joseph, Sr., about them. He soon learned that ten or
twelve men working with Willard Chase were conspiring to find the
plates, and had sent sixty miles for a conjuror whom they believed could
discover the hiding place. Brigham Young said the conjuror traveled the
sixty miles three times that season. "The man I refer to was a fortune-
teller," Brigham said, "a necromance, an astrologer, a sooth sayer, and
possessed as much talent as any man that walked on the American soil,
and was one of the wickedest men I ever saw."[6] The next morning Joseph,
Sr., walked over the hill east of the Smith farm to the Samuel Lawrence
place and found Willard Chase, Samuel Lawrence, the conjuror, and a
group of others laying plans. Joseph, Sr., heard enough to learn that the
gang aimed at getting the "gold bible," as they called it. When he got
back, Emma went off at once to fetch Joseph from Macedon. Joseph left
the well, borrowed a horse, and hastily the two of them rode through
Palmyra to the Smith farm. Joseph reassured the family that the plates
were safe but decided that now was the time to bring them home.[7]

Joseph set out to get the plates alone, still dressed in the linen smock
in which he had been digging the well. Lucy Smith said he wrapped the

plates in the smock and put them under his arm. Martin Harris later estimated that the plates weighed forty or fifty pounds, and Joseph had to carry them three miles. Wary of interference, Joseph thought it better to leave the road after a short distance and travel in the woods. His caution proved of no avail. While scrambling over a tree that had fallen across the path, he was assaulted by a large man and struck with a gun. Joseph turned and knocked the man down and ran off at full speed, still with the heavy plates under his arm. A half-mile further he was assaulted again and made his escape. Still a third time someone tried to stop him before he finally reached home, speechless with fright and fatigue and suffering from a dislocated thumb.[8]

Carlos ran off at once to get Hyrum, who came with a cherry chest. Once the plates were safely locked inside, Joseph told his father, Knight, and Stowell what had happened. A number of neighbors gathered to listen, for word of the plates had spread, and curiosity ran high. All wanted to know "something in regard to the strange circumstance which had taken place." Offers of cash and property were made to be given a glimpse of the plates.[9]

Some of the neighbors were more than curious. Willard Chase's gang had not given up their efforts to get possession. Lucy Smith said the angel warned Joseph as the record was turned over to him that "wicked men" would "lay every plan and scheme that is possible to get it away from you, and if you do not take heed continually, they will succeed." Lucy said Joseph kept the seerstones on his person to keep track of the plates. Alerted to an approaching danger, Joseph decided to counsel with his mother and Mr. Braman, a friend from Livonia, to take up some of the hearthstones in the west room and bury the box of plates there. They had scarcely replaced the stones when a company of armed men rushed up to the house. Thinking quickly, Joseph threw open the doors, yelled loudly, and all the men in the house, including fifteen-year-old Carlos, ran out in a fury. Surprised and disorganized, the mob fell back, ran for the woods, and disappeared.[10]

Besides trying to intimidate the Smiths, treasure seekers like Chase laid claim to Joseph Smith as a former partner. "The money-diggers," Martin Harris explained, "claimed they had as much right to the plates as Joseph had, as they were in company together." Over a year later David Whitmer met a group of incensed young men in Palmyra who claimed that before Joseph got the plates, "he had promised to share with them." One of them, Samuel Lawrence, and one Beeman, who worked with divining rods, came to the Smith house to try to persuade Joseph to give them a share. Joseph Knight, who was still at the Smiths', said "they Proposed to go shares with him and tried every way to Bargain with him

But Could not." Whereupon Beeman held up his rods until they pointed to the hearth where the plates were hidden.[11]

To throw off Chase and Lawrence, Joseph moved the plates from the hearth to the cooper's shop in the yard where Joseph, Sr., carried on his trade. He took the precaution to bury the box under a floor board and hid the plates themselves in a pile of flax in the shop loft. Fortunately, the device worked. Willard Chase brought his gang again that very night and his sister Sally Chase with her green glass. They rummaged around outside but did not come in. Lucy learned later that Sally Chase told the men the plates were in the coopering shop. The next morning the Smiths found the floor torn up and the box smashed. To their relief, the plates buried in the flax were safe.[12]

MARTIN HARRIS

Joseph saw by this time that changes had to be made. He asked his mother to go to the village and ask Martin Harris to come out to the Smith farm. The Harrises lived on a farm less than a half-mile north of Palmyra village. As the son of an early settler of Palmyra and a prosperous farmer, Harris was in a position to be of real help.[13] He knew of Joseph's gifts as a seer, and talk of the plates was all over the village. Martin was laying a hearth when Lucy arrived, and while she waited for him to finish up, she talked to Mrs. Harris about the plates. Lucy Harris was enthralled. She immediately tried to press money on Lucy Smith to assist in the translation. Lucy put her off and asked that Martin pay them a visit.[14]

Lucy Harris was the first to come. Her curiosity about the plates ran high. She first pled and then offered payment for a glimpse of them. Joseph had to tell her, as he had all the villagers, that he was forbidden to show them. Lucy Smith said that Mrs. Harris dreamed of an angel and the plates that night, and awoke the next morning believing. She offered to lend Joseph $28 and, to satisfy her, Joseph accepted. Martin himself arrived a few days later when Joseph was off working for Peter Ingersoll to earn some flour. Martin took the occasion of Joseph's absence to test the veracity of Emma and the Smiths. "I talked with them separately," he later reported, "that I might get the truth of the matter." When Martin first heard of the plates in the village, he had stood up for Joseph in the face of prevailing scorn. "He that answereth a matter before he heareth it," he had cautioned the detractors, "it is foolishness unto him. I do not wish to make myself a fool." Now he no more wished to be made the fool by Joseph.[15]

When Joseph came home, Martin pulled him aside and asked again to hear the story without telling Joseph of the previous conversations. To

Martin's surprise, Joseph told him the angel had revealed that Martin Harris was to assist in the translation. "If it is the devil's work," Martin answered, "I will have nothing to do with it; but if it is the Lord's, you can have all the money necessary to bring it before the world." Martin made it clear that he did not wish to be taken in. "You must not blame me for not taking your word." Martin hefted the box containing the plates and went home. He later said that he went to his bedroom, prayed, and was shown by God that "it was his work, and that it was designed to bring in the fullness of his gospel to the gentiles. . . . He showed this to me by the still small voice spoken in the soul."[16]

Meanwhile, pressure was building in the village. Martin heard of a mob with plans to tar and feather Joseph unless he showed them the plates, and advised Joseph to move. Joseph could see that he would have no peace in Palmyra and so asked Alva Hale, Emma's brother, to come up from Harmony with a wagon to transport their belongings.[17]

Joseph and Emma had trouble getting away. Joseph had to pay off the debts which every farmer accumulated in those days of barter. Fortunately, Martin was able to help out. One day when Joseph and Alva were in town on business with the Smiths' landlord, Martin presented them with $50 to do the Lord's work and publicly witnessed it as a gift, not a loan.[18]

A few townsmen were determined to see the plates before Joseph left. Lucy said a mob of fifty men asked Dr. Alexander McIntyre to lead them in an effort to get the "gold bible." He dismissed them as a "pack of devilish fools." Quarreling over a substitute leader, the group broke up. Still, precautions had to be taken. Martin advised Joseph to start two days in advance of the announced day of departure. They put the plates in a barrel one-third full of beans and topped it off. Joseph and Alva cut cudgels for themselves. Then on a Saturday night in the late fall they loaded their belongings into the wagon, helped in the two-month-pregnant Emma, and set out for Harmony.[19]

Isaac Hale was not entirely pleased with Joseph on his return. He had agreed the previous August to help Joseph get started and exacted a pledge that Joseph would settle down to serious work. The story of the "wonderful book of Plates," as Isaac Hale called them, was not what he had hoped for. "I was allowed to feel the weight of the box," he said, "and they gave me to understand, that the book of plates was then in the box — into which, however, I was not allowed to look." Hefting the box was not enough for Hale. He told Joseph "that if there was any thing in my house . . . which I could not be allowed to see, he must take it away. . . ." The neighbors also pestered Joseph, Joseph Knight said, and offered money for a glimpse of the plates. To placate his father-in-law and escape the demands of the curious, Joseph temporarily hid the plates in the woods. That winter he and Emma moved into a small two-room house owned by Emma's brother Jesse, standing on her father's land about 150 yards from the main house. There the translation could begin at last, and there the two of them lived for the next two and a half years. In August, 1830, Joseph purchased the house and thirteen acres for $200.[20]

Though finally settled, Joseph still had to learn how to translate the curious characters on the plates. He had told his friend Joseph Knight on the day the plates came out of their hiding place, "I want them translated." But now they were there before his eyes, how was he to begin? The interpreters, he had been told, were prepared "for the purpose of translating the book," but as Oliver Cowdery later learned, translating required more than possession of the plates and the translating instrument. After Oliver's attempt failed, he was told that he had wrongly "supposed that I would give it unto you, when you took no thought save it was to ask me." "You must study it out in your mind," and then ask for confirmation. Joseph had to learn how to study it out with the aid of the interpreters and work toward a translation. As his mother remarked of him at this period, "Joseph was very solicitous about the work but as yet no means had come into his hands of accomplishing it." With Emma's help, he began by copying off "a considerable number" of the intricate figures and translating "some of them."[21]

Martin Harris arrived in Harmony in February, 1828, two months after the Smiths. In his 1832 account Joseph said that because of Martin's righteousness "the Lord appeared unto him in a vision and shewed unto him his marvilous work which he was about to do and mediately came to Susquehannah and Said the Lord had shown him that he must go to New York City with some of the characters...." The vision may have confirmed a plan already agreed on, for Lucy Smith said Joseph had previously arranged with Martin to join the Smiths in Harmony and then take the characters east to a linguist.[22]

Why he went is unclear. Joseph Knight, who from his home in nearby Colesville aided Joseph while the translation went on, said that Joseph and "his wife Drew of[f] the Caricters exactley like the ancient and sent Martin Harris to see if he Could git them Translated." Lucy gave the same reason. She said Joseph was instructed "to take off a facsimile of the characters composing the alphabet which were called reformed egyptian Alphabetically and send them to all the learned men that he could find and ask them for the translation of the same." Lucy implied that once Joseph had a translation of all the basic characters, he could carry on by himself—thus the need to copy a great number of characters. Lucy Smith said, sarcastically, that Martin went to the "professed linguists" to give them "an opportunity to display their talents in giving a translation of the characters." The *Rochester Gem,* with Martin Harris for its source, reported on September 5, 1829, that he went in search of someone to interpret the hieroglyphics but found "no one was intended to perform that all-important task but Smith himself." In 1830 Fayette Lapham interviewed Joseph Smith, Sr., and later reported him as saying that his son, "not being able to read the characters, made a copy of some of them, which he showed to some of the most learned men of the vicinity." Joseph himself did not say why Martin went to the linguists, except that he was commanded to go, nor did Martin. But one of the questions Martin asked when he found an authority was, is the translation correct? The answer would interest Martin and the citizens of Palmyra. Perhaps even Joseph wanted some check on his work.[23]

Where Martin Harris went, whom he saw, and what happened are clouded in contradictory reports. He stopped at Albany, probably to see Luther Bradish, a New York State assemblyman with a reputation for knowledge of the Middle East. Someone referred Martin to the illustrious philomath Samuel Latham Mitchill, then vice-president of Rutgers Medical College in New York City and famed as a "living encyclopedia," a "chaos of knowledge." Accounts vary as to whether he saw Mitchill or Anthon first, or if he saw Mitchill before and after Anthon, but the Mitchill episode was of slight importance. According to Harris, Mitchill apparently gave him encouragement and referred him to another scholar, Charles Anthon, where a more important exchange took place.[24]

Anthon was professor of classical studies at Columbia College from 1820 until his death in 1867. In February, 1828, when Martin arrived, the scholarly work that was to establish Anthon as "the principal classical bookmaker of his time" lay ahead of him, but he was already noted for his 1825 edition of *A Classical Dictionary,* really an encyclopedia, first published by John Lempriere in 1788. Anthon added 4,000 entries to the dictionary, among the most notable many on Egypt. In the preface he professed familiarity with the most eminent authorities on Egypt and cited Jean Francois Champollion's "elaborate treatise on Hieroglyphics of Egypt." Anton was probably as well equipped as anyone in America to answer Martin's questions.[25]

Anthon and Harris differ drastically in their accounts of what happened. Anthon wrote letters in 1834 and 1841 to critics of the Mormons, denying that he had verified Joseph's translation or the authenticity of the characters. Anthon claimed he saw through the hoax at once, feared that Martin was about to be cheated of his money, and warned the "simple-hearted farmer" to beware of rogues. Unfortunately, Anthon contradicts himself on an important detail. In the first letter Anthon said he refused to give Harris a written opinion; according to the second, the opinion was written "without any hesitation," in an attempt to expose the fraud.[26]

There is confusion about what he actually saw as well. Anthon said that on the paper Martin showed him was a "singular medley" of Greek and Hebrew letters with other strange marks, with "sundry delineations of half moons, stars, and other natural objects, and the whole ended in a rude representation of the Mexican zodiac." In actuality the characters on the "Anthon Transcript" as it was published in 1844 seem to be Egyptian. They are not put together to form Egyptian sentences, but the individual characters closely resemble characters from Egyptian sources.[27]

Martin Harris said he showed Anthon both Joseph's translation and the untranslated characters and received confirmation of both. According to Harris, Anthon then said that the characters were Egyptian, Chaldaic, Assyriac, and Arabic, and gave Harris "a certificate certifying to the people of Palmyra that they were true characters, and that the translation of such of them as had been translated was also correct."[28] Satisfied with the professor's observations, Harris was leaving when Anthon inquired about the origins of the plates. When he was told that an angel had revealed their location, he asked for the certificate and tore it up. Anthon wanted to see the plates themselves, but Harris said they could not be shown because part was sealed. "I cannot read a sealed book," Harris reported Anthon to say. With that they parted.[29]

Whatever the exact truth about the encounter may be, Martin Harris came back more convinced than before. Sometime in the succeeding months it became evident to the small band around Joseph that Harris and Anthon had inadvertently fulfilled Isaiah's prophecy of the "words of a book that is sealed, which men deliver to one that is learned, saying, Read this I pray thee: and he saith, I cannot; for it is sealed: And the book is delivered to him that is not learned, saying, Read this, I pray thee: and he saith, I am not learned." The early pages of the Book of Mormon contain a long exposition of Isaiah by the prophet Nephi that made still more explicit the parallels with Martin's interview with Anthon. When Joseph began the history of the church in 1832 or 1833, he referred to Isaiah 29:11, 12, when he came to the Anthon incident. Martin Harris

took his journey to the Eastern Cittys and to the Learned Saying read this I pray thee and the learned Said I cannot but if he would bring the plates they would read it but the Lord had forbid it and he returned to me and gave them to me to translate and I said I cannot for I am not learned but the Lord had prepared Spectacles for to read the Book therefore I commenced translating the characters and thus the prophecy of Isaia was fulfilled which is written in the 29 Chapter concerning the book. . . .[30]

The scripture must have struck Joseph with all the more power if at first he did not know how to translate, as his mother said. The protest "I am not learned" would then have expressed Joseph's situation in 1827 exactly. Joseph Knight thought the circumstances fit the scripture. "He Bing an unlearned man did not know what to Do. Then the Lord gave him Power to Translate himself. Then ware the Larned men Confounded, for he, By the means he found with the plates, he Could translate those Caricters Better than the Larned."[31]

The fulfillment of the prophecy, however, meant less to Martin Harris in 1828 than the fact that Joseph could translate at all. Martin began telling his New York experience soon after he got back. References to it appeared in newspapers in Palmyra and Rochester in August, 1829. W. W. Phelps, a printer in Canandaigua, knew about Anthon by late 1830. The story circulated in Painesville, Ohio, a year before the missionaries went there in the fall of 1830 and later prompted a local editor, E. D. Howe, to make inquiries about its authenticity. In none of these accounts was Isaiah's sealed book prophecy mentioned. The first known reference to Isaiah 29 as a proselyting point is 1836. While the passage may have been used earlier, it is doubtful that E. D. Howe would have passed it by in his attempted refutation of Mormonism had it been used around Kirtland.[32]

Martin seemed more impressed with the proof that Joseph had ancient writings and that he could translate characters better than the learned doctor. What the *Rochester Gem* got out of his story was that Martin discovered from his search for an interpreter that "no one was intended to perform that all-important task but Smith himself." Pomeroy Tucker, the Palmyra printer's devil and later historian, said Martin's conclusion was that "God hath chosen the foolish things of the world to confound the wise." "The very fact that Smith was an obscure and illiterate man" and could translate, the local Episcopal priest remembered Martin saying, was proof that Joseph "must be acting under divine impulses." The type-setter for the Book of Mormon said Martin returned satisfied that Joseph "was a little smarter than Professor Anthon." Martin's conclusion was actually consonant with prophecy. The book was sealed to the learned, and translation was left to the unschooled Joseph Smith.[33]

Martin stopped to see Joseph briefly in Harmony on his way back from New York City and then hurried home to Palmyra. Lucy Harris still hovered on the edge of believing while worrying that Joseph was scheming to cheat Martin of his property. She had wanted to go to New York with her husband, but he had slipped off without her. When he returned, she made him sleep in a separate room. To undermine the effect of the Anthon visit, Lucy Harris had her daughter's suitor copy the characters for her.

When Martin pulled out his transcript, Lucy put hers on the table at the same time to diminish the effect of the strange figures.[34]

When Martin told his wife he planned to help translate the plates, Lucy insisted on going with him. The two departed for Harmony in March, 1828. This time she was more determined than ever to see the plates and settle the question of their existence for herself. She ransacked every possible hiding place in the Smith cabin in Harmony and then searched the ground outside. As a precaution, Joseph concealed the plates away from the house. Frustrated and angry, Lucy Harris took lodging nearby and told people of her fear that Joseph intended to cheat her husband of his farm. When the Harrises returned to Palmyra after two weeks, Lucy tried to persuade Martin to give up the translation and stay home, but in vain. After he left for Harmony again, Lucy hid the movable articles in the house to put them out of reach of Joseph's supposed design.[35]

Martin was back in Harmony by mid-April, 1828, and for the first time the translation began in earnest. For three months, from about April 12 to June 14, 1828, Joseph and he were hard at work. Joseph translated using the interpreters, and Martin wrote down the text as it was dictated. A curtain divided them to prevent Martin from seeing the plates. Even in the midst of the translation questions flickered across Martin's mind. During a break the two men sometimes went to the river to throw stones. Once Martin found one that resembled the seerstone and made a substitution without Joseph's noticing. When translation resumed, Joseph paused for a long time and finally exclaimed, "Martin! What is the matter? All is as dark as Egypt." Martin confessed he wished "to stop the mouths of fools, who had told him that the Prophet had learned the sentences and was merely repeating them."[36]

By the middle of June, 1828, Martin had covered 116 pages of foolscap with text from the golden plates, and yet uncertainty still beset him. The ever-lengthening manuscript and the little tests to which he put Joseph did not quiet his doubts. He could not forget his wife's skepticism or the hostile queries of Palmyra's tavern crowd. Was Joseph making a fool of him? Was he the classic dupe, to be cheated of his money and farm when the fraud was complete? Martin wanted more evidence to set his own mind at ease and to quiet the doubters at home. Lucy Smith said that Martin asked Joseph for a look at the plates, for "a further witness of their actual existence and that he might be better able to give a reason for the hope that was within him. . . ." When that desire was denied, he asked about the manuscript. Could he at least take it home to reassure his wife? Joseph asked on Martin's behalf through the interpreters and was told no. Martin pressed again and received the same answer. Still he was not satisfied. Joseph said, "After much solicitation, I again inquired of the Lord, and permission was granted him to have the writings," on the condition that Martin show the pages only to his brother Preserved, his wife, his father and mother, and his wife's sister, Abigail Cobb. Uneasy about the whole proceeding, Joseph required Martin to bind himself in a solemn covenant to comply before he set off.[37]

Joseph immediately turned his attention to other matters. The day after Martin left, Emma, after an exhausting labor, gave birth to a son. Whatever happiness the child brought was short-lived. The baby, named Alvin after Joseph's older brother, died that very day, June 15, and was buried near Emma's grandparents in sight of the cabin. For a time Emma seemed to be close to death, and Joseph had to attend her night and day. After two weeks, as she began to mend, Joseph's mind turned back to the manuscript. Sensing his anxiety, Emma suggested that he go to Manchester to check up on Martin. Emma's mother agreed to watch after her daughter, and Joseph caught the first stagecoach north.[38]

The stage stopped twenty miles from the Smith house at ten in the evening. Exhausted and depressed, Joseph stumbled along the forest road through the night. He was supported by a generous passenger who, seeing Joseph's condition, offered to accompany him. They reached the Smith farm at dawn. Lucy Smith hurriedly made a little pepper tea to warm Joseph's stomach. When it grew light, someone went to fetch Martin Harris.[39]

The family expected Harris at eight for breakfast. The morning hours dragged by, and he did not come. At half past twelve, Lucy reported, "we saw him walking with a slow and measured tread towards the house, his eyes fixed thoughtfully upon the ground. On coming to the gate, he stopped, instead of passing through, and got upon the fence, and sat there some time with his hat drawn over his eyes." When he finally came in and sat down for the long-delayed breakfast, Martin "took up his knife and fork as if he were going to use them, but he immediately dropped them." He "pressed his hands upon his temples, and cried out, in a tone of deep anguish, 'Oh, I have lost my soul! I have lost my soul!' " Joseph sprang up and demanded to know of the manuscript. "Have you broken your oath, and brought down condemnation upon my head, as well as your own?" "Yes, it is gone," replied Martin, "and I know not where."[40]

Lucy said that seeing the manuscript had placated Mrs. Harris, as Martin had hoped. She was so pleased that she let him lock the papers in her bureau, from which the manuscript was retrieved from time to time to show to the relatives named in the covenant. Martin's first mistake came when he wished to show the pages to a close friend. His wife was away and, having no key, Martin picked the lock, marring the bureau. Having broken his promise once, he showed the manuscript to any friend who came along. Lucy Harris castigated Martin when she returned and found her bureau damaged, but that was not the worst. When the Smiths sent for Martin, the manuscript had disappeared from the place where Martin had transferred it. He spent the morning frantically searching, without success. Joseph demanded that he go back and look again, but Martin said further search was useless. "I have ripped open beds and pillows; and I know it is not there." Lucy Smith surmised that Mrs. Harris stole the manuscript with the intention of altering it. The discrepancies between the second translation and the first would make the whole appear as a fraud. Whatever the reason, the manuscript was gone, never to be recovered.[41]

"O, my God!" moaned Joseph, clenching his hands, "All is lost! all is lost! What shall I do?" Joseph blamed himself as much as Martin. "It is I who tempted the wrath of God. I should have been satisfied with the first answer. . . ." What would Emma think? "Then must I return to my wife with such a tale as this? I dare not do it, lest I should kill her at once." No one could comfort Joseph, Lucy said; everyone felt his despair. "Sobs and groans, and the most bitter lamentations filled the house." "I will remember that day of darkness," Lucy recalled, "both within and without. To us, at least, the heavens seemed clothed with blackness, and the earth shrouded with gloom." Joseph paced the floor, weeping and grieving, until sunset when he finally consented to eat.[42]

In his 1838 narrative Joseph himself said nothing of his anguish and fear for the loss of his privileges, but the revelation received soon after made plain the situation in the summer of 1828: "For although a man may have many revelations, and have power to do many mighty works, yet if he boasts in his own strength, and sets at naught the counsels of God, and follows after the dictates of his own will and carnal desires, he must fall and incur the vengeance of a just God upon him." The danger was real that he would "be delivered up and become as other men, and have no more gift."[43]

Joseph went back to Harmony in July, 1828, and at once engaged in "mighty prayer before the Lord." The angel appeared and gave him the interpreters, which had been taken from him when Martin went off with the manuscript.[44] Through them Joseph received his chastisement: "The works, and the designs, and the purposes of God cannot be frustrated, neither can they come to naught. For God doth not walk in crooked paths, neither doth he turn to the right hand nor to the left, neither doth he vary from that which he hath said, therefore his paths are straight, and his course is one eternal round. Remember, remember that it is not the work of God that is frustrated, but the work of men." The burden of Joseph's fault was his weakness in yielding to Martin: "Behold, you have been entrusted with these things, but how strict were your commandments; and remember also the promises which were made to you, if you did not transgress them. And behold, how oft you have transgressed the commandments and the laws of God, and have gone on in the persuasion of men. For, behold, you should not have feared man more than God. Although men set at naught the counsels of God, and despise his words — yet you should have been faithful. . . ."[45]

The old problem had returned in a new form. Joseph had listened to his associates rather than to the Lord. He valued Martin Harris's friendship and needed his aid, and had not depended on God alone. "Behold, thou art Joseph, and thou was chosen to do the work of the Lord, but because of transgression, if thou art not aware thou wilt fall." The words were hard for a young man who had lost his first-born son and nearly lost his wife, and whose chief error was to trust a friend, but there was comfort in the revelation as well: "Remember, God is merciful; therefore, repent of that which thou hast done which is contrary to the commandment which I gave you, and thou art still chosen, and art again called to the work. . . ." Lucy said Joseph was then put on probation. If he showed proper penitence, the interpreters would be returned on September 22, the day of his annual interview with Moroni for the past four years.[46]

In the history of the church the revelation printed as section 3 of the current Doctrine and Covenants holds a significant place. So far as can be told, the words of that section are the first revelation written down by the Prophet. He and others remembered earlier revelations, but they were written later. The current section 3 appeared as section 2 in the first printed edition of revelations, immediately following the introduction, which was revealed in 1833.[47] This revelation gave the first inkling of how Joseph would speak in his prophetic voice. With a few exceptions, the revelations are not reports of experiences written in the first person by the author, as in Joseph's narrative of his life. The speaker stands above and outside Joseph, sharply separated emotionally and intellectually, talking to the Prophet or his associates. The rebuke of Joseph in the revelation of July, 1828, is as forthright as the denunciation of Martin Harris. There is no effort to conceal or rationalize, no sign of Joseph justifying himself to prospective followers. The words flow directly from the messenger to Joseph and have the single purpose of setting Joseph straight.

The force and style of the revelation are surprising when it is recalled that two and a half years earlier Joseph was entangled with the money diggers while struggling to scrape together rent money for his family. Where had he learned the confidence of attack in the opening sentence? "The works and the designs, and the purposes of God cannot be frustrated, neither can they come to naught." The words have a scriptural flavor and yet are not direct quotation. His mother said that Joseph read the Bible less than her other children, and since 1820, like his father, he stayed away from preachers, but some of the words could not have been imitated even if he had been exposed to sermons. "For although a man may have many revelations, and have power to do many mighty works, yet if he boasts in his own strength, and sets at naught the counsels of God, and follows after the dictates of his own will and carnal desires, he must fall and incur the vengeance of a just God upon him." At age twenty-two Joseph knew how to speak prophetically.[48]

What does the revelation tell us about Joseph Smith's life in 1828? Quite clearly the events of the year — the visit to Anthon, the first translation, the loss of the baby, Martin's terrible mistake — were only half the story. The revelation in a few brief allusions suggests the dimensions of Joseph's internal world as it was unfolding through revelation and vision. Perhaps most significant was the sense of mighty forces pouring out of heaven into the earth. Those forces encompassed more than the Smith family and their friends, the region where they lived, or even the United States. In fact, nothing parochial has any place in the picture. The work was for ancient peoples and tribes: "Nevertheless, my work shall go forth, for inasmuch as the knowledge of a Savior has come unto the world, through the testimony of the Jews, even so shall the knowledge of a Savior come unto my people — And to the Nephites, and the Jacobites, and the Josephites, and the Zoramites, through the testimony of their fathers. . . ." The revelation sketches a complex and densely peopled past where covenants made long ago were now to be fulfilled. Joseph was to play a part, but he was not at the heart of the movement. If he faltered, he would be cast aside, and the purpose of God would sweep on, "that the promises of the Lord might be fulfilled." The end was more important than the means. The descendants of the ancient tribes were to learn of the promises of the Lord, "that they may believe the gospel and rely upon the merits of Jesus Christ, and be glorified through faith in his name and that through their repentance they might be saved."[49]

OLIVER COWDERY

Sometime in this dark period Joseph attended Methodist meetings with Emma, probably to placate her family. One of Emma's uncles preached as a Methodist lay minister, and a brother-in-law was class leader in Harmony. Joseph was later said to have asked the circuit preacher to be enrolled in the class. Joseph Lewis, a cousin of Emma's, rose in wrath when he found Joseph's name, objecting to inclusion of a "practicing necromancer." Lewis confronted Joseph and demanded repentance or removal of his name. For some reason Joseph Smith's name remained on the roll for another six months, although there is no evidence of his attendance.[50]

Lucy said that Joseph received the interpreters again on September 22, and he and Emma did a litle translating, but the need to prepare for winter intervened.[51] Emma's family was still suspicious and gave no aid. In the fall of 1828 Joseph worked the land that Isaac Hale lent him and tried to collect supplies. In the early winter he and Emma visited their old friend Joseph Knight in Colesville and told him that they were in need. Knight could do very little between his own straitened circumstances and his wife's lack of sympathy. He gave Joseph some food, a pair of shoes out of the store, and $3.[52]

Joseph, Sr., and Lucy Smith, having heard nothing from their son since his gloomy departure in July, grew anxious for news. In October they set off to see Joseph, Jr., and were much relieved to learn that he had not lost his gift and had the plates back. Lucy said they enjoyed meeting Isaac and Elizabeth Hale and their eight children. "They were an intelligent and highly respectable family. They were pleasantly situated, and lived in good style. . . ."[53] After nearly three months in Harmony the elder Smiths got back to Manchester on January 22.

Joseph, Sr., did not stay home long. In late January he and Samuel were off again. They stopped at Joseph Knight's house on the way to Harmony and the three of them sleighed the rest of the way. On this visit Joseph, Sr., received a revelation through his son, possibly in answer to a question about the father's place in the work. Through the next few months a number of individuals came to the Prophet with the same inquiry. The answer to Joseph Sr.'s question formed the basis for many of the subsequent replies. The same words with slight variations were repeated in four revelations. The key lay in the first verse: "Now behold, a marvelous work is about to come forth among the children of men." The revelation went on to enjoin many virtues and to promise salvation to those who complied, but the essential theme was the great work that was about to begin. "Faith, hope, charity, and love, with an eye single to the glory of God" were valued as qualifications for the work. Salvation came to him who "thrusteth in his sickle with his might." To "stand blameless before God at the last day," one must serve God with "heart, might, mind, and strength." The message was the same as to Joseph himself. The inward orientation of the evangelical was reversed. The point was not to rid oneself of the burden of sin but to make oneself worthy of the great work that lay ahead.[54]

Amidst all the comings and goings, Joseph took up the translation again. Emma wrote his dictation most of the time, although she says her brother Reuben Hale helped. Emma had none of Martin's trouble in believing Joseph. When the plates were not in her red morocco trunk, they lay on the table wrapped in a linen table cloth. "I once felt of the plates, as they thus lay on the table," she later told Joseph Smith III, "tracing their outline and shape. They seemed to be pliable like thick paper, and would rustle with a metalic sound when the edges were moved by the thumb, as one does sometimes thumb the edges of a book." She occasionally moved them around on the table as her work required it. When Joseph III asked if his father might have written the manuscript beforehand or memorized what he dictated, Emma said no. Joseph at that time of his life "could neither write nor dictate a coherent and well worded letter; let alone dictating a book like the Book of Mormon." Furthermore, "he had neither manuscript nor book to read from." "If he had had anything of the kind he could not have concealed it from me." The whole thing was as marvelous to Emma as to any one.

I am satisfied that no man could have dictated the writing of the manuscripts unless he was inspired; for, when acting as his scribe, your father would dictate to me hour after hour; and when returning after meals, or after interruptions, he would at once begin where he had left off, without either seeing the man-uscript or having any portion of it read to him. This was a usual thing for him to do. It would have been improbable that a learned man could do this; and, for one so ignorant and unlearned as he was, it was simply impossible.[55]

Near sunset on the first Sunday evening in April, the 5th, Samuel Smith arrived at the Smith cabin accompanied by a stranger named Oliver Cowdery. Samuel had just recovered from a period of sickness and was coming to spend the spring with Joseph, probably to help with the planting. Cowdery came seeking information about the plates. Twenty-two years old, a year younger than Joseph, and unmarried, Oliver had learned of Joseph's work while teaching the district school in Palmyra and boarding with the Smiths. Lucy Smith said Oliver became so obsessed with the story he heard from the Smiths that he could think of nothing else. When he learned that Samuel was going to Harmony, Oliver asked to go along.[56]

Oliver was born in Wells, Rutland County, Vermont, not fifty miles from Joseph's birthplace. His brothers first moved to western New York and the rest of the family followed. The district school committee on which Hyrum Smith served first hired Lyman Cowdery but accepted Oliver in his place when Lyman was unable to honor the contract. Oliver had blacksmithed, clerked in a store, and worked in New York City, doubtless like the Smith boys, trying to help his family and to accumulate enough for a start in life himself.[57]

Cowdery met twenty-four-year-old David Whitmer in Palmyra and learned of the plates through him. Joseph, Sr., had been reluctant to say much when Oliver first inquired. Bad experiences had taught caution. Oliver finally won the family's trust and was told enough to whet his curiosity. After praying for understanding, he was persuaded there was a work for him with Joseph. In early April he and Samuel set out in the rain to walk 150 miles to Harmony on the muddy spring roads. They stopped at the Whitmer residence in Fayette on the way south, and Oliver promised to send back information about the plates to David.[58]

Joseph and Oliver talked late into the evening the Sunday of his arrival. Joseph told more of the story, and Oliver decided to stay. On Monday there were business affairs to attend to, but on Tuesday, April 7, the translation began again, to go on with only a few pauses until the book was completed in early July. "Day after day I continued, uninterrupted," Oliver reported in 1834, "to write from his mouth, as he translated with the Urim and Thummim. . . ." When Martin had taken dictation from Joseph, they hung a blanket between them to prevent Martin from inadvertently catching a glimpse of the plates contrary to the angel's instructions. By the time Oliver arrived, they did not always follow that practice. Emma said she sat at the same table with Joseph, writing as he dictated, with nothing between them.[59] When Oliver took up the job of scribe, he and Joseph translated in the same room where Emma was working. There was no problem with the plates because Joseph looked in the seerstone or the interpreters, and the plates lay covered on the table.[60]

"These days were never to be forgotten," Oliver reflected in 1834. "To sit under the sound of a voice dictated by the inspiration of heaven, awakened the utmost gratitude of this bosom." The young prophet more than fulfilled Oliver's expectations. On the other hand, the shock of the sudden immersion in a supernatural work now and then gave Oliver pause, and he needed further reassurance.[61] A revelation put Oliver's doubts to rest. The revelation told Oliver about two experiences that he had never mentioned to Joseph. The first was Oliver's practice of inquiring of the Lord for direction and the fact that he had "received instruction" of the Spirit. The second was his specific inquiry about Joseph and the plates. "Verily, verily, I say unto you, if you desire a further witness, cast your mind upon the night that you cried unto me in your heart, that you might know concerning the truth of these things. Did I not speak peace to your mind concerning the matter? What greater witness can you have than from God?" After the revelation was given, Oliver admitted having received just such a manifestation, "but he had kept the circumstance entirely secret, and had mentioned it to no one; so that after this revelation was given, he knew that the work was true, because no being living knew of the thing alluded to in the revelation, but God and himself."[62]

Oliver had come to Harmony the possessor of a supernatural gift, alluded to in another revelation as the "gift of Aaron." The first printing of the Book of Commandments said this was "the gift of working with the rod." Most likely Oliver used the rod to discover water and minerals as was common in New England and New York at that time. The Book of Commandments spoke of divine power causing "this rod of nature, to work in your hands." The revelation to Oliver recognized his special powers and encouraged him. "Behold thou has a gift, and blessed art thou because of thy gift. Remember it is sacred and cometh from above —." Rather than repudiating Oliver's claims, the revelation redirected the use of the gifts.

Oliver received the same caution the angel gave to Joseph at Cumorah: "Seek not for riches but for wisdom. . . ." The gift was to be used not for trivial purposes — "trifle not with sacred things" — but to gain knowledge of God. "Therefore thou shalt exercise thy gift, that thou mayest find out mysteries, that thou mayest bring many to the knowledge of the truth. . . ." Above all Oliver was not to become obsessed with the pleasure of exercising supernatural power. His gift was a means to an end — the ultimate acquisition of a much greater gift. "If thou will do good, yea, and hold out faithful to the end, thou shalt be saved in the kingdom of God, which is the greatest of all the gifts of God; for there is no gift greater than the gift of salvation." Oliver had to learn the purposes of supernatural power just as Joseph had done. Joseph first used his seerstone to find lost objects and treasures. Oliver worked the rod, presumably like other such practitioners. The revelation admonished him, as Joseph had learned painfully years before, to seek not for riches and to trifle not with the gifts of God. Gifts were to "find out mysteries" of godliness and to "bring many to the knowledge of the truth."[63]

Joseph's was, of course, the far greater gift. He had come to prize the power to translate. In his darkest moment, after the loss of the 116 pages, his punishment was to lose the interpreters. In the succeeding months he feared most the permanent loss of the power to translate. Except he repent, the Lord warned, "thou shalt be delivered up and become as other men, and have no more gift." Not long after Oliver began work on the Book of Mormon, he also came to yearn for the gift of translation. The first revelation directed to him promised "a gift, if you desire of me, to translate, even as my servant Joseph." The revelation spoke of records "which contain much of my gospel," held back because of wickedness. "And now I command you, that if you have good desires — a desire to lay up treasures for yourself in heaven — then shall you assist in bringing to light, with your gift, those parts of my scriptures which have been hidden because of iniquity." Joseph and Oliver were both to hold "the keys of this gift," that "in the mouth of two or three witnesses shall every word be established."[64]

Joseph said that after hearing those words, Oliver "became exceedingly anxious to have the power to translate bestowed upon him. . . ." Later in April, in a subsequent revelation, Oliver was promised that by asking in faith he would receive "a knowledge concerning the engravings of old records. . . ." He would know through the Holy Ghost, which was none other than the spirit of revelation that guided Moses and the children of Israel through the Red Sea on dry ground. "Therefore this is thy gift; apply unto it."[65]

The experiment was less than successful. Oliver was no more able to translate on his first attempt than Joseph was. Oliver began all right and then stopped. He had mistakenly believed that he needed only to ask God and look in the stones. "Behold, I say unto you," the revelation gently chided him, "that you must study it out in your mind; then you must ask me if it be right, and if it is right I will cause that your bosom shall burn within you." Oliver had underestimated the concentration of mind Joseph exercised as he dictated day by day. "You feared," the revelation said, "and the time is past, and it is not expedient now." Oliver was to go back to writing for Joseph and continue to the end. "And then, behold, other records have I, that I will give unto you power that you may assist to translate."[66]

By May Joseph and Oliver had not yet translated what are now the opening books of the Book of Mormon. In the winter of 1829 Joseph and Emma took up the translation where he and Martin had broken off the previous June, that is, around the first part of the Book of Mosiah in the reign of King Benjamin. Joseph and Oliver kept on in sequence. Sooner or later Joseph had to decide what to do about the gap left by the loss of the previous manuscript, in which was written the first 400 years of Book of Mormon history. In May he received a revelation telling him not to retranslate. The people who had stolen the manuscript intended to alter the words and trap him. Were he to bring out a new translation contradicting the first version, they would say that "he has lied in his words, and that he has no gift," and claim "that you have pretended to translate, but that you have contradicted yourself." The plates of Nephi, the revelation said, covered the same period. Joseph was to translate them instead and publish them as the record of Nephi. In June, probably after the rest of the book was done, he and Oliver began work on I Nephi.[67]

Events in Palmyra may have precipitated this revelation. Lucy Smith had always suspected Mrs. Harris of stealing the manuscript. According to Lucy Smith, sometime before Joseph moved to the Whitmers' in June, Mrs. Harris brought a suit against him for attempting to defraud her husband. Lucy Smith said that Mrs. Harris "mounted her horse, flew from house to house through the neighborhood, like a dark spirit," collecting information and stirring up feelings. Lyman Cowdery, Oliver's brother, was asked to accompany the court officers to Pennsylvania to apprehend Joseph. To Mrs. Harris's dismay, the judge dismissed the case after hearing from Martin Harris himself. Joseph probably heard of Mrs. Harris's scheme from his mother and wondered how the lost pages might be used against him. Lucy Smith said Mrs. Harris aimed to prove that "Joseph never had the record." The revelation said that unspecified conspirators wanted to show that Joseph only "pretended to translate." Joseph sought guidance on how to escape the trap. The revelation answered his question and warned him, as he had been warned so many times before concerning enemies, that "Satan stirreth them up, that he may lead their souls to destruction."[68]

Amidst all of their spiritual exertions, the Smiths had to keep food on the table. Spring was the bleakest time for farmers. Provisions from the previous season were at low ebb, and the ground had not yet produced anything edible. Oliver and Joseph had to take off a few days from translating to get help. They trudged twenty-six miles to Joseph Knight's place in Colesville but found him away. Back in Harmony, they went out in search of work, a frustrating dissipation of time when so much translation remained. One day, after looking unsuccessfully, they arrived home to find that the good-hearted Knight had brought nine or ten bushels of grain, five or six of potatoes, a pound of tea, and a barrel of mackerel. Knight also remembered lined paper.[69]

Despite the hard work and the spartan diet, the two young men enjoyed the two months they spent translating in Harmony. They watched with interest the unfolding story of the Nephites, pausing occasionally to talk over what they learned. In April they differed over the question of whether John the ancient apostle died or continued to live, a question raised perhaps by passages in the text on prophets who were never known to die. They agreed to settle the matter through the interpreters, and learned that the Lord permitted John to tarry until the Second Coming.[70]

By mid-May the translators had reached III Nephi and Christ's visit to the Nephites and were reflecting on its meaning. "After writing the account given of the Savior's ministry to the remnant of the seed of Jacob upon this continent," Oliver remembered, "it was easily to be seen, that amid the great strife and noise concerning religion, none had authority from God to administer the ordinances of the gospel." Joseph said the question disturbed them enough that they broke off the translation and went down to the river to pray about it. In the middle of the prayer, in the brightness of day, an angel descended in a cloud of light. He said he was John the Baptist and that he had been sent by Peter, James, and John. Then he laid his hands upon their heads to ordain them. "Upon you my fellow servants, in the name of Messiah I confer the Priesthood of Aaron, which holds the keys of the ministering of angels, and of the gospel of repentance, and of baptism by immersion for the remission of sins; and this shall never be taken again from the earth, until the sons of Levi do offer again an offering unto the Lord in righteousness." John told Oliver and Joseph they would later receive a higher priesthood, the Melchizedek Priesthood, and the power to lay on hands for the gift of the Holy Ghost. At this time they were to baptize one another and ordain each other again to the Priesthood of Aaron. Foreshadowing future events, Joseph was told that his title was to be First Elder of the church, and Oliver's Second Elder.[71]

Joseph took Oliver into the Susquehannah and baptized him as directed and Oliver did the same for Joseph. Then they ordained one another. It was a happy time for them.

Immediately on our coming up out of the water after we had been baptized, we experienced great and glorious blessings from our Heavenly Father. No sooner had I baptized Oliver Cowdery, than the Holy Ghost fell upon him, and he stood up and prophesied many things which should shortly come to pass. And again, so soon as I had been baptized by him, I also had the spirit of prophecy, when standing up, I prophesied concerning the rise of this church, and many other things connected with the Church, and this generation of the children of men. We were filled with the Holy Ghost, and rejoiced in the God of our Salvation.

Subsequently their study of the scriptures yielded more knowledge than ever before. "Our minds being now enlightened, we began to have the Scriptures laid open to our understandings, and the true meaning and intention of their more mysterious passages revealed unto us in a manner which we could never attain to previously, nor ever before had thought of."[72]

Joseph told twenty-one-year-old Samuel, his younger brother who was still living with them, about the experience. Samuel had reservations and pressed Joseph with doubtful inquiries, forcing him to reason out of the Bible. At length Samuel was sufficiently persuaded to go to the woods and pray for understanding, and was convinced. Oliver baptized Samuel on May 25, 1829.[73]

Hyrum came to Harmony a few days later to learn more about what was happening. Joseph received a revelation for Hyrum as he had for Joseph, Sr. Hyrum was told to put your trust in that Spirit which leadeth to do good — yea, to do justly, to walk humbly, to judge righteously; and this is my Spirit. Verily, verily, I say unto you, I will impart unto you of my Spirit, which shall enlighten your mind, which shall fill your soul with joy; And then shall you know, or by this shall you know, all things whatsoever you desire of me, which are pertaining unto things of righteousness, in faith believing in me that you shall receive.

Hyrum was more eager to become involved than Samuel. The revelation had to caution him about moving ahead too fast. "Behold, I command you that you need not suppose that you are called to preach until you are called. Wait a little longer, until you shall have my word, my rock, my church, and my gospel, that you may know of a surety my doctrine." Hyrum was baptized a month later in Seneca Lake.[74]

WITNESSES

Joseph's activities had not gone unnoticed in the neighborhood. He and Oliver said nothing publicly about the vision of John the Baptist, but people disliked the translating. "We had been threatened with being mobbed from time to time," Joseph said, "and this, too, by professors of religion." He had sufficiently won over the Hale family by this time to receive their protection, but he needed more time to complete the translation.[75]

Sometime in the latter part of May Oliver Cowdery wrote David Whitmer, asking if they could work in his father's house in Fayette. Situated between Seneca Lake and Lake Cayuga, the Whitmer farm lay about seven miles southeast of Geneva. Both Oliver and Joseph knew the Whitmers. Joseph had met David's father, Peter Whitmer, soon after the translation began, and the Smiths traveled by way of the Whitmer farm on their way to visit Joseph in February, 1829. Oliver became acquainted with David Whitmer in Palmyra in 1828 when he was there on business and both young men were just learning about the plates. Oliver stopped at the Whitmer farm on the way from Palmyra earlier in the spring and later wrote from Harmony to say he was sure Joseph had the records. The Whitmers were interested enough to welcome Joseph and Oliver into their home. Oliver asked David to come with his wagon and carry them back.[76]

The request for help came at an awkward moment. The Whitmers were in the middle of spring plowing, and the round trip to Harmony would take five or six valuable days. In later accounts David told of what seemed to him miraculous help in completing the work. Plowing that should have taken two days was accomplished in one. Lucy Smith said that three strangers sowed his plowed land without orders from him. David also remembered that on his arrival in Harmony, Oliver told him "when I started, where I put up at night and even the name on the sign board of the hotel where I stayed each night." Oliver said that he had asked Joseph to look in the seerstone and then recorded what the Prophet told him. Oliver had written down the names of owners whom David did not know, and on the way back they proved accurate.[77]

David marveled at these signs of supernatural power. He told of meeting an old man on the return trip who told them he was going to Cumorah. David said he looked inquiringly at Joseph, and when he looked back the old man had disappeared. David believed "it was the messenger who had the plates, who had taken them from Joseph just prior to our starting from Harmony." In marked contrast to David Whitmer's stories of marvels, Joseph, who was spare in his reporting, simply said David Whitmer came to Harmony "and brought with him a two-horse wagon, for the purpose of having us accompany him to his father's place. . . ."[78]

The Whitmers were Pennsylvania Germans who moved to Fayette around 1809 when other Pennsylvanians were settling there. They purchased a farm and joined the German Reformed church. The town elected Peter Whitmer, Sr., overseer of highways and a school trustee. Christian, the eldest son, received an appointment as ensign in the militia. Mary and Peter Whitmer had seven children when Oliver and Joseph arrived in early June, 1829. Three were married and living close by; three boys — Peter, Jr., age nineteen, David, twenty-four, and John, twenty-six — and fourteen-year-old Elizabeth Ann still lived at home.[79]

The whole family took an interest in the translation. The five older boys including the two married sons later became witnesses of the plates. Another witness, Hiram Page, was the Whitmers' son-in-law, the husband of their oldest daughter, Catherine. Young Elizabeth Ann was to marry Oliver Cowdery three years later in Jackson County, Missouri.[80]

Mary Whitmer, Peter Sr.'s wife, experienced her own miracle, according to David. Burdened with two extra persons in her household, plus Emma Smith, who soon joined Joseph in Fayette, Mrs. Whitmer began to feel the strain. Going to milk the cows one morning, she met an old man who said, "You have been very faithful and dilligent [sic] in your labors, but you are tired because of the increase of your toil, it is proper therefore that you should receive a witness that your faith may be strengthened." The old man then showed Mary Whitmer the plates, which had been hidden in the barn for safekeeping. David, John, and Peter Whitmer, Jr., each received a private revelation on his behalf like other friends of the Prophet earlier. In June Oliver baptized Peter Whitmer, Jr., and Joseph baptized David Whitmer and Hyrum Smith in Seneca Lake.[81]

Joseph and Oliver began to translate again the day after arriving at the Whitmer farm. David Whitmer thought they worked hard. "It was a laborious work for the weather was very warm, and the days were long and they worked from morning till night." Various persons relieved Oliver as clerk. David remembered Emma and Christian each taking a turn. One of the hands in the manuscript of I Nephi looks like John Whitmer's, and Joseph said, "John Whitmer, in particular, assisted us very much in writing during the remainder of the work." But Oliver still did most of the transcribing.[82]

Occasionally circumstances interrupted the flow of translation. David said sometimes Joseph "found he was spiritually blind and could not translate. He told us that his mind dwelt too much on earthly things, and various causes would make him incapable of proceeding with the translation."

One morning when he was getting ready to continue the translation, something went wrong about the house and he was put out about it. Something that Emma, his wife, had done. Oliver and I went upstairs and Joseph came up soon after to continue the translation but he could not do anything. He could not translate a single syllable. He went downstairs, out into the orchard, and made supplication to the Lord; was gone about an hour — came back to the house, and asked Emma's forgiveness and then came upstairs where we were and then the translation went on all right. He could do nothing save he was humble and faithful.[83]

The people living around Fayette and elsewhere in Seneca County showed more interest in Joseph's work than any of his previous neighbors. Doors opened for meetings. "We met with many from time to time," Joseph remembered, "who were willing to hear us, and who desired to find out the truth as it is in Christ Jesus, and apparently willing to obey the Gospel, when once fairly convinced and satisfied in their own minds. . . ." The number of believers grew, and some were baptized.[84]

Joseph knew that his story was difficult to accept. Outside of his immediate family and close associates, a thick wall of doubt and ridicule enclosed him. Even Martin Harris, Joseph's most willing assistant for a year and a half after reception of the plates, could not conquer his doubts. First he had grilled the Smith family about Joseph's story, then he checked on the characters with authorities in New York City, then he asked for the manuscript to show his wife. When he asked again in March for proof that Joseph had the plates, a revelation came back saying, "Behold if they will not believe my words, they would not believe you, my servant Joseph, if it were possible that you should show them all these things which I have committed unto you." There was no satisfying querulous curiosity. Oliver had troubled Joseph less after obtaining a witness at the senior Smith's house, but he too needed the benefit of a small miracle to assure him.[85]

The March revelation answering Martin's query emphasized that "I, the Lord, am God, and have given these things unto you, my servant Joseph Smith, Jun., and have commanded you that you should stand a witness of these things. . . ." The burden lay squarely, but not entirely, on Joseph. He learned that "in addition to your testimony, the testimony of three of my servants, whom I shall call and ordain, unto whom I will show these things" should "go forth with my words that are given through you." "Yea, they shall know of a surety that these things are true, for from heaven will I declare it unto them." Martin was to be patient and "if he will bow down before me, and humble himself in mighty prayer and faith, in the sincerity of his heart, then will I grant unto him a view of the things which he desires to see."[86] As the translation neared completion at the Whitmer house in June, 1829, Joseph and Oliver came to three passages that again referred to witnesses, one in the Book of Ether, 5:2-4, and the other two in II Nephi, 11:3 and 27:12, which, because the translators did the small plates of Nephi last, came near the end of the translation period.[87]

Oliver, David, and Martin (who came over to Fayette to see about the progress of the translation) began to wonder, now that the three of them were close to Joseph, if they might be the ones to see the plates. Joseph was slow to respond to their inquiries. His earlier requests for such things had brought admonitions of patience. Finally the three solicited him so ardently that he asked for a revelation, which promised them a view not only of the plates but of the breastplate, the Urim and Thummim, and the other sacred objects accompanying the plates — the sword of Laban and the miraculous directors given to Lehi by the Red Sea, presumably still in Cumorah.[88]

Joseph, Sr., and Lucy Smith came over to the Whitmers' after the translation was completed and spent their first evening reading the manuscript. The next morning after the usual daily religious services, reading, singing, and praying, Joseph stood, as Lucy remembered it, and turned to Martin Harris. "Martin Harris, you have got to humble yourself before your God this day, that you may obtain a forgiveness of your sins. If you do, it is the will of God that you should look upon the plates, in company with Oliver Cowdery and David Whitmer."[89]

David was plowing the field when Joseph and Oliver came to say they were to seek a witness that day. David tied his team to the fence and when Martin joined them, the four men entered the nearby woods. They had agreed to take turns praying, first Joseph, then the other three. The first attempt brought nothing, and they tried again. Again nothing. Before they made a third attempt, Martin Harris offered to leave, saying he was the obstacle. The remaining three knelt again and before many minutes, according to their account, saw a light in the air over their heads. An angel appeared with the plates in his hands. David Whitmer said the breastplate, Lehi's directors, and the sword of Laban lay on a table. The angel said to David Whitmer, "David, blessed is the Lord, and he that keeps his commandments." That was all David could remember him saying. Then a voice out of the light said, "These plates have been revealed by the power of God, and they have been translated by the power of God. The translation of them which you have seen is correct, and I command you to bear record of what you now see and hear."[90]

Martin had gone further into the woods when Joseph went searching for him. Martin asked Joseph to pray with him, and at length, they later reported, their desires were fulfilled. Joseph said he saw the same vision as before, and Martin cried out "in an ecstasy of joy," "'Tis enough; 'tis enough; mine eyes have beheld. . . ." At the close of the vision he jumped up, shouted "Hosanna," and blessed God.[91]

When the company reassembled in the Whitmer house, Martin overflowed with happiness. The years of uncertainty at last had ended. The surges of faith that ebbed and flowed now gave way to knowledge. "I have now seen an angel from Heaven who has of a surety testified of the truth of all that I have heard concerning the record and my eyes have beheld him." "I bless God in the sincerity of my soul that he has con-descended to make me even me a witness of the greatness of his work and designs in behalf [of] the children of men."[92]

Lucy remembered that Joseph seemed immensely relieved. He threw himself down beside her and exclaimed that "the Lord has now caused the plates to be shown to more besides myself." "They will have to bear witness to the truth of what I have said, for now they know for themselves, that I do not go about to deceive the people. . . ." The strain of the prevailing skepticism was at last distributed around a little. "I feel as if I was relieved of a burden which was almost too heavy for me to bear, and it rejoices my soul, that I am not any longer to be entirely alone in the world."[93]

The signed testimony of the three appeared in the first edition of the Book of Mormon and remained a support for Joseph from then on. Al-though personal vicissitudes drove all three out of the church, none ever went back on that statement. It was not a perfect answer for the skeptics, but it helped to protect Joseph Smith from the doubt and ridicule he constantly faced.[94]

Lucy said that a few days later Joseph, Oliver, and the Whitmers went over to Palmyra to make printing arrangements. By that time the elder Smiths had left their old house and moved in with Hyrum, whose eighty-acre farm immediately adjoined their former property.[95] The whole company of Whitmer and Smith men, including the four Whitmer sons, a son-in-law, Hiram Page, and Hyrum, Samuel, and Joseph Smith, Sr., walked out to the place where the family went to pray. There Joseph, Jr., showed them the plates. They turned over the leaves, examined the characters and the workmanship, and held the plates in their own hands. They later signed a statement saying what they had seen and testifying that they knew "of a surety that the said Smith has got the plates of which we have spoken."[96]

While he was finishing up the translation at the Whitmers', Joseph thought a lot about the promise of a higher priesthood mentioned by John the Baptist.[97] He and Oliver "had for some time made this matter a subject of humble prayer, and at length we got together in the chamber of Mr. Whitmer's house, in order more particularly to seek of the Lord what we now so earnestly desired. . . ." Here, to their "unspeakable satisfaction," their prayers were answered, "for we had not long been engaged in solemn and fervent prayer, when the word of the Lord came unto us in the chamber, commanding us that I should ordain Oliver Cowdery to be an Elder in the Church of Jesus Christ; and that he also should ordain me to the same office; and then to ordain others, as it should be made known unto us from time to time." They were not to ordain each other immediately but to await a time when all who had been baptized could be assembled to accept Joseph and Oliver as "spiritual teachers." At that time they were to bless bread and wine, call out others to be ordained, and, by laying on hands, give the gift of the Holy Ghost to those who had been baptized.[98]

PUBLICATION

On June 11 Joseph deposited the title page of the Book of Mormon in the office of R. R. Lansing, clerk of the Northern District of New York, and obtained a copyright. At the same time he was negotiating with Egbert B. Grandin, a Palmyra bookseller, printer, and publisher of the *Wayne Sentinel*, to print the book. Grandin held back out of religious compunction and from doubt about the book's commercial feasibility, since he knew that many citizens of Palmyra felt that the book should be suppressed. Joseph and Martin were forced to go to Rochester looking for a printer. They twice applied to Thurlow Weed, publisher of the *Rochester Telegraph*, without success. Finally Elihu F. Marshall, another Rochester publisher, agreed to print the book. Pomeroy Tucker said that, before signing with Marshall, Joseph and Martin made a last appeal to Grandin, pointing out that the book was to appear anyway. Some of Grandin's friends urged him to go ahead, and an agreement was reached.[99]

Martin Harris mortgaged his farm for $3,000 as security in case the books did not sell. Mrs. Harris refused to be a party to the mortgage. In a sense she was right about the consequences of Martin's involvement with Joseph. Joseph never profited personally from the Book of Mormon, but Martin did sell his farm on April 7, 1831, even though Pomeroy Tucker, the Palmyra editor, judged that Martin could have paid the bill from other resources.[100]

With financial arrangements complete, printing could begin. Oliver, Joseph, and Martin stood together in the printing office when the printer drew the first proof-sheet of the title page and celebrated the "dawning of a new gospel dispensation." Joseph foresaw trouble during the printing. Hostility was growing among the citizens of Palmyra. As a security measure, Joseph told Oliver to recopy the entire manuscript and never take both copies to the printing office at once. Someone was to accompany him while he carried the pages back and forth, and a watch was to be kept at the house. Oliver set to work, and about the middle of August delivered the first twenty-four pages to Grandin's printshop on the third floor of the Exchange Building on Palmyra's Main Street. One of Grandin's typesetters said the copy came "on foolscap paper closely written and legible, but not a punctuation mark from beginning to end." Oliver spent time in the office, and now and again he would pick up a stick and set type. In December he wrote to Joseph, "It may look rather Strange to you to find that I have so soon become a printer. . . ." Grandin's typesetter said that Oliver set ten or twelve pages in all of the first edition.[101]

Joseph arrived back in Harmony on October 4 where Emma awaited him. He wrote to Oliver that the neighbors were friendly and showed great interest in the book now that he actually had a copyright. Josiah Stowell planned to buy $500 or $600 worth of books. Joseph purchased a horse from Stowell and asked for someone to come for it, but he was soon required to return to Palmyra himself.[102]

Trouble in Palmyra brought Joseph back. On September 2, Abner Cole, a one-time justice of the peace, began publishing a Palmyra weekly entitled *The Reflector*, under the pseudonym O. Dogberry. Through the fall Cole inserted brief observations on the "Gold Bible," sarcastically exaggerating its success: "Thousands are already flocking to the standard of Joseph the Prophet. The Book of Mormon is expected to astonish the natives!" On December 22 Cole changed the paper's format and began a new series. For the December 29 issue he filled the front page with the present chapter 1 of I Nephi and the first three verses of chapter 2. Reading the manuscript moderated his criticism. He urged his readers to judge the book after they saw it, and reported that he found nothing "treasonable, or which will have a tendency to subvert our liberties."[103]

The Smiths were forewarned about Cole's pirating of the manuscript.

Acting on a hunch, Oliver and Hyrum discovered the editor hard at his labors in Grandin's shop one Sunday afternoon. Cole worked on his paper on Sundays when the press was free. There they found a prospectus promising subscribers excerpts from the Book of Mormon before its appearance. Hyrum warned Cole about the copyright but to no avail. "I don't care a d—n for you," Lucy reported him saying. "That d—d gold bible is going into my paper, in spite of all you can do." All efforts to persuade him otherwise failing, the family decided they must send for Joseph. Joseph, Sr., set off at once for Harmony and returned the next Sunday.[104]

On Sunday afternoon Joseph found Esquire Cole once more at work in Grandin's shop. Joseph apprised Cole again of the copyright and told him to stop meddling. As Lucy reported the incident, the feisty Cole rose to the occasion. He threw off his coat, rolled up his sleeves, and came at Joseph smacking his fists together. "Do you want to fight, sir? do you want to fight?" Smiling, Joseph told Cole to put his coat back on. "It is cold, and I am not going to fight you." " 'Sir,' bawled out the wrathy gentleman, 'if you think you are the best man, just pull off your coat and try it.' " "There is law," Joseph returned, "and you will find that out, if you do not understand it." At length Cole cooled off and agreed to arbitration. The next two issues of *The Reflector,* dated January 13 and 22, copied more of the Book of Mormon text, but Cole ran no more, and that ended it.[105]

The imminent publication of the Book of Mormon raised the ire of Palmyrans more than ever. Judging from newspaper comments even before it came off the press, the book was seen as a blasphemous rival to orthodox Christianity. Lucy Smith believed the ministers feared a loss of members. The officers of her own church, the Western Presbyterian congregation in Palmyra, thought the matter serious enough to send Deacon George Beckwith and two others to visit the Smiths. Finding Lucy adamant in her convictions, Beckwith tried to persuade her at least not to talk about the Book of Mormon. "Deacon Beckwith," she replied, "if you should stick my flesh full of faggots, and even burn me at the stake, I would declare, as long as God should give me breath, that Joseph has got that Record, and that I know it to be true." Beckwith had no more luck with Hyrum and Samuel. Samuel quoted Isaiah 56:9-11: "His watchmen are blind: they are all ignorant, they are all dumb dogs . . . yea they are greedy dogs, which can never have enough . . . ," and the committee left discouraged. The Presbyterians asked Lucy, Hyrum, and Samuel to appear before a church court on March 24 for eighteen months' neglect of worship. None of the three appearing, on March 29 they were all suspended from the sacrament of the Lord's Supper and censured for their contumacy.[106]

Abner Cole was surprised, as he said in his January 2 issue, that people "should give themselves *quite* so much uneasiness about matters that so little concern them." The very reasonableness of the Book of Mormon text as it appeared in Cole's paper may have worried the Christians of the neighborhood more than a transparent fraud. Cole himself moderated his scorn after he set part of the book in type, though his disdain returned after Joseph's rebuke. By early March Luther Howard, the bookbinder who worked on the floor below Grandin's printshop and who had a chance to read the Book of Mormon before it appeared, was accused of privately advocating the "gold bible." Joseph reported a favorable reception in Harmony and Fayette. Cole's pirated excerpts gave people a taste of the book's actual contents and showed them what they had to contend with.[107]

The alarmed inhabitants of "the surrounding country" called a meeting to deal with the problem. As a group they resolved never to purchase one of the books and called on Grandin to tell him of their opposition. They argued that, since the Smiths had lost their farm, they could not pay him unless the book sold. The boycott on purchases would prevent Grandin from getting his money. Having entered the contract reluctantly in the first place, Grandin was easily persuaded. In November he had told Oliver the printing would be done by February 1. Sometime in January he stopped work until he could be assured of payment.[108]

In the early part of the year Joseph again made the long trip up from Harmony to confer with his friends and the printer. Martin consented to sell part of his farm to raise some cash, although only after getting a signed agreement from Joseph, Sr., giving Martin the right to sell books on his own account. Hyrum grew impatient with Martin's reluctance and urged Joseph to leave him out entirely. Hyrum thought they could raise the money themselves. He had heard that the copyright could be sold in Canada and asked Joseph to inquire of the Lord. David Whitmer later reported that Joseph told Oliver and Hiram Page to go to Toronto and promised them success, but the two returned empty-handed. They had to depend on Martin after all. Lucy says that Joseph and Martin together allayed Grandin's fears and the work went on.[109]

In the March 26, 1830, edition of the *Wayne Sentinel,* Grandin published the title page of the Book of Mormon, and announced: "The above work, containing about 600 pages, large Deuodecimo, is now for sale, wholesale and retail, at the Palmyra Bookstore, by E. B. Grandin."[110]

Martin soon discovered, to his sorrow, that the citizens' boycott was effective. The book did not sell well. Joseph Knight brought Joseph up from Harmony in the spring. As they approached the elder Smiths' house, the two of them spotted Martin crossing the road with a pile of books in his arms. "The Books will not sell for no Body wants them," Martin reported dejectedly. "I think they will sell well," Joseph replied encouragingly. "I want a Commandment," Martin said, presumably a revelation assuring him he was doing the right thing. "Why, fullfill what you have got," Joseph said. "I must have a Commandment," Martin insisted three or four times. The next morning after a night at the Smiths', Martin repeated his demand. According to Joseph Knight, later in the day Joseph received a revelation on Martin's behalf in which he was told he must not covet his own property but to "impart it freely to the printing of the Book of Mormon, which contains the truth and the word of God." "Pay the debt thou hast contracted with the printer. Release thyself from bondage."[111]

The publication of the Book of Mormon made Joseph Smith a minor national figure. He first received newspaper attention on June 26, 1829, two weeks after he registered the title page with the clerk of the Northern District. The *Wayne Sentinel,* one of Palmyra's papers, published the title page and a brief notice. In late August and early September two Rochester papers picked up the news from another article in the *Palmyra Freeman,* and other papers, such as the *Painesville* (Ohio) *Telegraph,* took notice. In the spring of 1830, after publication of the book, the *Rochester Republican,* the *Rochester Daily Advertiser,* and the *Rochester Gem,* all published substantial comments. The appearance of the "gold bible" was noticed in Boston and Manchester, Vermont, in April and May. By the summer of 1831 James Gordon Bennett, writing for the *New York Morning Courier and Enquirer,* could say, "You have heard of MORMONISM — who has not? Paragraph has followed paragraph in the newspapers, recounting the movements, detailing their opinions and surprising distant readers with the traits of a singularly new religious sect. . . ."[112]

At best the papers gave Joseph Smith notoriety. The editors elevated him from an obscure money digger of limited neighborhood fame to the rank of full-blown religious impostor. The *Rochester Daily Advertiser* and the *Horn of the Green Mountains* headed their reports, "Blasphemy" and "Fanaticism." Six months before the book appeared, with no knowledge of its actual contents beyond what was given on the title page, a Rochester editor quoted the *Palmyra Freeman,* setting the tone for editors and publicists for the rest of the century. "The greatest piece of superstition that has come within our knowledge now occupies the attention of a few individuals of this quarter." The *Freeman* reported that the "Golden Bible" "was almost invariably treated as it should have been — with contempt."[113]

The explanation for the book was obvious to the editors and required no investigation of Joseph Smith or the book itself. The "gold bible" was an "impudent" imposition. Obviously it had been gotten up as a money-making scheme. The Palmyra *Reflector* called it priestcraft. The *Rochester*

Daily Advertiser said a "viler imposition was never practiced. It is an evidence of fraud, blasphemy, and credulity, shocking both to Christians and Moralists." And why would anyone believe it? "It is frequently remarked that any scheme, however gross, will find more or less dupes —." A "certain class" of people, "blindly enthusiastic" like Martin Harris, could be made to believe by the exercise of "hocus pocus." The editors classed Joseph Smith and his followers with other fraudulent claimants to supernatural power. "It partakes largely of Salem Witchcraft-ism and Jemima Wilkinson-ism . . . ," one said. Superstition, impudent frauds, and credulous believers had been known before. Joseph Smith may have been "the very summit" of such impositions, but he fell into a well-defined category. As the editor said, there was only one way to treat him and his book — with contempt.[114]

The Smiths seemingly paid no notice to the newspapers. Neither Lucy nor Joseph mentioned any of the articles in their histories. Abner Cole upset them all when he pirated the Book of Mormon itself, but his snide comments through the fall and winter did not register. Deacon Beckwith's visit meant much more to Lucy than the newspaper articles. She told in detail the schemes of the neighbors to lay hold of the manuscript and the plates and to malign her family. The hostility of people whom she knew personally hurt more than the jibes of remote editors.

Joseph seemed most sensitive to the possible appearance of a doctored version of the lost 116 pages. The preface to the Book of Mormon informed readers that some persons had stolen the account translated from the "Book of Lehi," and despite his "utmost exertions" the pages had not been recovered. He had been instructed not to retranslate that part, "for Satan had put it into their hearts to tempt the Lord their God, by altering the words," and "if I should translate the same over again, they would publish that which they had stolen, and Satan would stir up the hearts of this generation, that they might not receive this work. . . ."[115] A translation from the plates of Nephi he explained, replaced the missing part.

For all the effort and trouble he put into the translation, Joseph made little of the book's appearance. Neither he nor his mother named the day when bound copies were available or mentioned any celebration. (Perhaps Joseph was in Pennsylvania on March 26.) The first edition said virtually nothing about Joseph himself. The preface contained one sentence about his part in the work: "I would also inform you that the plates of which hath been spoken, were found in the township of Manchester, Ontario county, New York." His own name appeared only on the title page and in the testimony of the eight witnesses at the back. It was an unusually spare production, wholly lacking in signs of self-promotion. Joseph presented his handiwork to the public and moved on. The book thenceforth had a life of its own.[116]

CHAPTER IV

THE BOOK OF MORMON

The Book of Mormon explains itself as largely the work of Mormon, a military figure who led his people, the Nephites, from 327 to 385 A.D. in the twilight of their existence as a nation. Two others wrote long segments to begin and end the book: Moroni, Mormon's son and the last recordkeeper, and Nephi, one of the first migrants from Palestine to America around 600 B.C. But the bulk of the remainder is Mormon's narrative, drawn from the records that passed into his hands from previous chronicles.

Mormon was appointed to lead the armies at age fifteen, giving no other reason for his precocious elevation to eminence than the fact that "notwithstanding I being young was large in stature." In the same year, "being somewhat of a sober mind," he was "visited of the Lord." From then until he was cut down by the Lamanites, still fighting at age seventy-three, Mormon moved with his people across North America, swept this way and that by the tides of battle.[1]

Mormon wrote at a time when Nephite civilization had fallen into decay and was headed toward extinction. He led his people in hopeless desperation, knowing that peace and security would never come until they turned to God.[2] Writing from the perspective of a man standing at the verge of cultural desolation, Mormon's purpose was anything but academic. He used the history to teach his readers why his nation sometimes prospered and why it eventually destroyed itself. "Inasmuch as they shall keep my commandments they shall prosper in the land. But remember, inasmuch as they will not keep my commandments they shall be cut off from the presence of the Lord."[3]

Sometime during his harried life Mormon worked through the pile of records and wrote the Book of Mormon. Nephite history began with the migration of Lehi and his family from Jerusalem through the wilderness along the Red Sea around 600 B.C., on the eve of the Babylonian captivity. After eight years of wandering, Lehi, his wife, Sariah, their six boys, along with one other family, launched a vessel and voyaged to a new land. One of the sons, Nephi, followed his father as prophet and won the loyalty of three other sons, Samuel, Jacob, and Joseph. The other brothers, Laman and Lemuel, were jealous, proud, and indifferent to Lehi's prophecies. The rebellious pair contended with Nephi from the start. When Lehi died after arriving in the promised land, the remaining family ties broke. For the safety of his followers, Nephi separated from Laman and migrated to another part of the land. The great division in the nation arose from that fateful decision.

The animosity between the original brothers never died out. The Lamanite nation persisted in the tradition that Nephi usurped authority over their ancestors, perhaps because Nephi was a younger son and Laman the eldest. The Lamanites repeatedly invaded Nephite territory seeking conquest. The periodic wars that broke out right down to Mormon's time formed the skeleton of Mormon's history. Because of Lamanite wickedness, the Lord cursed them. "For behold they had hardened their hearts against him, that they had become like unto a flint," Nephi said, "and wherefore, as they were white, and exceeding fair and delightsome, that they might not be enticing unto my people the Lord God did cause a skin of blackness to come upon them." Modern readers of the Book of Mormon assumed that the American Indians were descendants of the Lamanites.[4]

From the beginning, the doom of the Nephites had been foretold. The Lord said to Nephi shortly after the departure from Jerusalem in 600 B.C. that the Lamanites would be "a scourge unto thy seed, to stir them up in remembrance of me; and inasmuch as they will not remember me, and hearken unto my words, they shall scourge them even unto destruction." A thousand years later that prophecy came to pass in Mormon's day.[5]

Over the intervening centuries, and even from year to year, the faith of the Nephites fluctuated, and their prosperity and happiness rose and fell accordingly. At one point the Lamanites were converted and exceeded the Nephites in righteousness. A Lamanite prophet Samuel came to the Nephites, called them to repentance, and prophesied of Christ's coming. In one of the most startling sections of the book, the resurrected Christ appeared among the Nephites immediately following the crucifixion, and as a result of his teachings the entire population, Nephites and Lamanites, lived together in peace for nearly 200 years. But in the century before Mormon's birth society deteriorated once more into warring tribes. The Lamanites became a scourge as prophesied, and nothing Mormon could say or do would bring his people to their senses. He mourned that "they were once a delightsome people, and they had Christ for their shepherd;

yea, they were led even by God the Father. But now behold, they are led about by Satan, even as chaff is driven before the wind, and as a vessel is tossed about upon the waves, without sail or anchor. . . ."[6]

As the Lamanite armies pressed relentlessly down upon the Nephites, Mormon appealed to the Lamanite king for time to gather his people for one conclusive battle. They pitched their tents around the hill Cumorah "in a land of many waters, rivers, and fountains; and here we had hope to gain advantage over the Lamanites." At age seventy-three Mormon felt his years and knew he must make provision for the records "handed down by the fathers." He hid the large collection of plates in the hill Cumorah, gave his own brief history of the Nephites to Moroni his son, and then prepared for battle.[7]

The Lamanites slaughtered the Nephites. Mormon himself fell wounded, and the onrushing armies passed him over. When the enemy had returned to their camps, a straggling band of twenty-four survivors, including Moroni, gathered with Mormon on the top of Cumorah and surveyed the destruction. Mormon wrote his final address to the descendants of the Lamanites admonishing them to remember that they were of the house of Israel and must return to the God of Israel and believe in Christ.[8] Then he handed over the plates to his son. Writing in 400 A.D. some fifteen years after the great battle, Moroni reported that the Lamanites hunted down and slew the Nephites who escaped southward. "And my father also was killed by them, and I even remain alone to write the sad tale of the destruction of my people." He renewed the record merely to fulfill the command of his father. "I will write and hide up the records in the earth; and whither I go it mattereth not." There was little room left on the plates, and he lacked ore to make more. With his father gone and all his kinsfolk, he had "not friends nor whither to go; and how long the Lord will suffer that I may live I know not."[9]

Moroni lived at least another twenty-one years, secreting himself away from the Lamanites, who while fighting ferociously among themselves also put to death every Nephite who refused to deny Christ. In those years Moroni acquired more plates and devoted himself, like his father, to history. Among the records in Cumorah were twenty-four gold plates discovered some 500 years previously in a land covered with the bones of men and beasts and the ruins of buildings. King Mosiah, a Nephite monarch-prophet and a seer, possessed the two interpreter stones that enabled him to read the record. He found on the plates the story of a lost people that went back to the "building of the great tower, at the time the Lord confounded the language of the people and they were scattered abroad upon the face of all the earth," and thence back to the creation of Adam.[10]

In the last years of his life Moroni translated these plates. They were called the plates of Ether, after the prophet who watched the final destruction of his people and wrote their history. Ether hid in a "cavity of a rock" by day and came out at night to observe the results of the havoc that had overtaken the society. His attempts to call the people to God only aroused anger, and he had to flee for his life back to his hiding place. Eventually, when the last man had apparently perished, Ether closed his record with resignation much like Moroni's: "Whether the Lord will that I be translated, or that I suffer the will of the Lord in the flesh, it mattereth not, if it so be that I am saved in the kingdom of God."[11] Moroni translated and summarized Ether's record.

Moroni said he wrote only a hundredth part of the story in the book called the Book of Ether in the Book of Mormon. He omitted entirely the portion of the record going from Adam to the great tower, and abbreviated even the period from the tower to the destruction of Ether's people. Moroni called the people Jaredites after their first leader. Through the faith of Jared's brother, "a large and mighty man, and a man highly favored of the Lord," the Lord did not confound the Jaredites' language at the tower but led them to the edge of the "great sea which divideth the lands," where they pitched their tents and lived for four years. By commandment they built eight barges, "tight like unto a dish," and "light upon the water, even like unto the lightness of a fowl upon the water." For illumination, the brother of Jared "did molten out of rock sixteen small stones; and they were white and clear, even as transparent glass," and asked the Lord to touch them. When the Lord did, the brother of Jared saw his finger and fell to the earth with fear. "And he saith unto the Lord: I saw the finger of the Lord, and feared lest he should smite me; for I knew not that the Lord had flesh and blood." Because of Jared's brother's faith, the Lord allowed him within the veil and revealed himself as Jesus, who would come in the flesh and in whose image man was created. The brother of Jared then saw "all the inhabitants of the earth which had been, and also that would be; and he withheld them not from his sight, even unto the ends of the earth."[12]

Moroni wrote on his plates the complete vision of the brother of Jared and sealed it. The plates that Joseph Smith received, he reported, included these pages on which was written a vision of the world down to the very end. Moroni said the translation was to be held back from the gentiles "until the day that they shall repent of their iniquity, and become clean before the Lord."[13] They would have to have the faith of the brother of Jared to see what he saw. That portion of the plates was sealed, and Joseph Smith was told not to touch them.

In Moroni's own book, the last in the Book of Mormon, written after he completed the Book of Ether, he reported that to his surprise he had not perished. The wars of the Lamanites were "exceedingly fierce among themselves; and because of their hatred they put to death every Nephite that will not deny the Christ . . . wherefore, I wander whithersoever I can for the safety of mine own life." He added a few things he thought might "be of worth unto my brethren, the Lamanites, in some future day," including practices of the church established during Christ's ministry, and two epistles from Mormon. Then Moroni wrote his farewell to the future readers, admonishing them to "come unto Christ, and be perfected in him, and deny yourselves of all ungodliness," and closed the record. In Joseph Smith's history the person who appeared on September 22, 1823, said that "he was a messenger sent from the presence of God to me, and that his name was Moroni."[14]

CRITICS

By any standard the Book of Mormon is a narrative of unusual complexity. Scores of characters like Ether and Moroni, Jared and the brother of Jared, move through the story. The pronunciation guide in the current edition lists 284 proper names: Paanchi, Pachus, Pacumeni, Pagag, Pahoran, Pathros, Pekah, Rahab, Ramath, Rameumpton. Intricate and shattering events are compressed into a few sentences. Migration, war, and intrigue alternate with prophecy, sermon, and conversion. Mormon, as warrior, historian, and prophet himself, interwove political and military events with the history of salvation.[15]

Besides the intricacy of plot, the narrative perspective is complicated. The first six books are pure source material, written by the original prophets and untouched by later editors. But then with only a slight introduction, Mormon takes up the story himself. In his narrative, derived from the available source materials, he quotes other prophets and sometimes quotes them quoting still others. Moroni injects a letter from his father, and Nephi inserts lengthy passages from previous scriptures. Mormon moves in and out of the narrative, pointing up a crucial conclusion or addressing readers with a sermon of his own. Almost always two minds are present and sometimes three, all kept account of in the flow of words.[16]

This was the book that Joseph Smith published and Martin Harris began to sell in late March, 1830. The Book of Mormon was more than the citizens of Palmyra were prepared to comprehend. The volume still receives slight attention in cultural histories of the United States. The origin of the Indians, the similarities of Masonry to Book of Mormon robber bands, and the apparent republican tone in certain spots have been noted as connecting with America in 1830, but the whole Book of Mormon, with its multiplicity of stories and characters, its sketches of an ancient civilization, its involved conception of history, and its unrelenting religious message, has eluded analysis.[17] Small wonder that the citizens of Palmyra and village newspaper editors dealt with it summarily and superficially.

How did people make sense of this creation, suspended in its web of marvelous stories and yet entirely tangible and real itself, printed on E. B. Grandin's press just like the weekly newspaper? Joseph said the book "was accounted as a strange thing" and caused "no small stir." Abner Cole, editor of the short-lived Palmyra *Reflector,* more than anyone else, tried to characterize the Book of Mormon for the public in the first few months after publication. The two satires he attempted under the heading "Book of Pukei," published in June and July, 1830, gave an idea of what Palmyra thought should result when someone of Joseph Smith's background attempted a history of America's ancients. Cole had the figure of a little old man appear to Joseph dressed "in Egyptian raiment, except his Indian blanket and moccasins," and announce he was sent by Mormon "the great apostle to the Nephites" and "chief among the last [*sic*] ten tribes of Israel." This same apostle conducted the Nephites "to these happy shores in bark canoes," where smallpox "killed two-thirds of them, and turned the rest to Indians." The reference to "Egyptian" came from the description of Nephite language as "reformed Egyptian," a fact that intrigued many readers. The other commonplace symbols of Indians—the bark canoes, the blankets and moccasins, decimation by smallpox—should have been in the story but for some reason were not. In their absence Cole fabricated them himself. He had the Nephites descend from the lost ten tribes, when the Book of Mormon perversely overlooked this common explanation for Indian origins. Cole made the book comprehensible by adding all the elements Palmyra readers expected and were disappointed to find missing.[18]

Cole handled the whole business scornfully and humorously. Without making a direct accusation, he surmised that Joseph worked under the inspiration of "Walters the Magician," apparently an actual person who had caused a stir in Palmyra somewhat earlier. As Cole told the story, the Book of Mormon was the latest production of a talented money digger working in the tradition of vernacular magic. In Cole's imaginary scenario Walters dubbed Joseph "the *ignoramus,*" and promised him the title of greatest of the money diggers. Cole ridiculed the healing of Newel Knight by saying that "no prophet, since the destruction of Jerusalem by Titus, has performed half so many wonders as have been attributed to that *spindle shanked* ignoramus JO SMITH."[19]

After the first flurry of attention, Cole said little about the "Golden Bible" until events in the fall of 1830 made the Mormons newsworthy again. Oliver Cowdery, Peter Whitmer, and two other missionaries left for the West to teach the Indians in October, 1830. On the way they stopped at Kirtland, Ohio, to tell the friends of one of the missionaries about the new church. The *Painesville Telegraph,* published just nine miles from Kirtland, noted on November 16 that twenty or thirty had been baptized. Two weeks later there was a "rising of 100 in this and an adjoining county who have embraced the ideas and assertions of Joseph Smith, Jr. many of them respectable for intelligence and piety." The *Telegraph* liberally sprinkled the word "pretended" through its reports and warned that, if a fabrication, the Book of Mormon was of "infamous and blasphemous character," but admitted it would be useless to condemn it out of hand. "Time will discover in it either something of vast importance to man, or a deep laid plan to deceive many." The *Telegraph* editor quickly decided in favor of the deception thesis, but in the meantime Mormon numbers were growing. Thomas Campbell, father of Alexander Campbell and a well-known minister through middle America, took Mormonism seriously enough to publish a lengthy letter to his former friend Sidney Rigdon, a recent Mormon convert, challenging him to a debate. No scorn or ridicule tinctured Campbell's arguments. He was intent on proving the Book of Mormon to be a fraud.[20]

News of the Ohio conversions caused Abner Cole to look at the "Gold Bible" and Joseph Smith in a new light. Besides using Mormonism to sell the *Reflector* in the vicinity of Palmyra, he saw an opportunity to become a source of information for a much wider audience. A letter from "Plain Truth" in the January 6, 1831, issue observed that "this most clumsy of all impositions, known among us as Jo Smith's 'Gold Bible,' is beginning to excite curiosity abroad. . . ." Since the other Palmyra papers refused to print anything on the subject, Plain Truth advised, "to you, and you alone, do we look for an expose of the principal facts, and characters, as connected with this singular business." In that very issue Cole began a six-part series on the Book of Mormon to satisfy the "curiosity of our friends at a distance." Although he did not change his scornful tone, and never quite brought his material under control, Cole did replace satire with argument and attempted to make a case against Joseph Smith that would appeal to his enlarged readership.[21]

In this second round of comments Cole took a position commonly assumed by Enlightenment Christians when confronted with supernatural phenomena. Like so many other subsequent writers on Mormonism, Cole began "by way of introduction, and illustration," with "brief notices and sketches of the superstitions of the ancients," the "pretended science of alchymy," "Mahomet" and "other ancient impostures" down to more recent legends, "the Morristown Ghost, Rogers, Walters, Joanna Southcote, Jemima Wilkinson, etc." To make sense of unwanted claims to divine power, Christian apologists had adopted the practice of grouping religious frauds together and dismissing them all as the products of human ignorance. Alexander Campbell, in his critique of the Book of Mormon, started off with a similar string of bogus miracle workers. The *Painesville Telegraph* elaborated on the seventeenth-century French prophets. Joseph Smith could be accounted for more readily if it was understood that people had always believed in religious imposture. "The page of history informs us, that from time immemorable, Man has more or less been the dupe of superstitious error and imposition." Mormons were one more example of human gullibility.[22]

The impostures were believed to succeed because of ignorance. "Where ignorance is found to prevail, superstition and bigotry will abound. . . ." Reason was the only antidote. In the modern era people were less susceptible because enlightenment had steadily spread its beneficent influence. It was a little surprising that Joseph Smith should win converts in the enlightened age, but then Joanna Southcote, the London prophetess, had won adherents not long before. If she could enjoy success "in the great metropolis of England, and spread over a considerable portion of that kingdom, it is not surprising that one equally absurd, should have its origin in this neighborhood. . . ."[23]

The cultural perspective affected much of what Cole wrote about Joseph Smith. He, of course, identified himself and his readers as people of reason who penetrated the absurdities of Joseph Smith's pretensions. The Smiths, on the other hand, were the epitomé of ignorance. Cole described Joseph Smith as "having but little expression of countenance, other than that of dullness; his mental powers appear to be extremely limited. . . ." The same held true for the rest of the Smiths. "We have never been able to learn that any of the family were ever noted for much else than ignorance and stupidity. . . ." Cole felt no need to provide evidence of the Smiths' limitations. They had to be dull because it was axiomatic that superstition flourished in ignorance.[24]

This disdain for superstitious belief in supernatural happenings, though convenient for disposing of Joseph Smith, presented a problem to enlightened Christians. What about Christianity itself? How was Christ to be distinguished from Muhammad and innumerable other impostors? An answer had been developed over the past century by Christian apologists who were compelled by skeptics and deists to defend the Bible against the same criticism that Cole directed against the Book of Mormon. The critics depicted biblical happenings as the superstition of ignorant and credulous primitives. What could be said in reply? Enlightened Christians chose to place their reliance on miracles, amazing events like the opening of the Red Sea that could not be explained without positing divine intervention.

The Bible was to be believed because its prophets worked genuine miracles. That basic outlook affected the reaction to the Mormons. The *Painesville Telegraph* on first discussing the Book of Mormon noted that "we have not been able to discover testimony which ought to elicit faith in any prudent or intelligent mind." By contrast, "when Jesus sent his disciples to preach, he gave them power against all unclean spirits, to cast them out, to heal all manner of diseases, and to raise the dead." Not so with the Mormons. "These newly commissioned disciples have totally failed thus far in their attempts to heal, and as far as can be ascertained, their prophesies have also failed." When Rigdon told a correspondent to the *Painesville Telegraph* that the new revelation was not to be confirmed by miracles, the man wanted to know "How then are we to obtain faith?"[25]

Both Cole and the editor of the *Telegraph* were particularly alert to miracles, because for enlightened Christians they were the evidence separating true faith from imposture. But miracles alone did not suffice. There were countless claims to miracles attested by witnesses. Healings, appearances, miraculous transformations studded Roman Catholic history. As Christian apologists honed their arguments, they worked down to a single fine point: Christianity was *founded* on miracles. The first disciples believed solely because the evidence of their senses — the miracles of Jesus — first persuaded them. The disciples were not previously committed nor did they foresee personal advantage. Prevailing belief and established religious authority opposed Jesus; the disciples were bound to suffer by following Him. As William Paley, the classic exponent of rational Christianity, put it, "Miraculous pretensions, and miraculous pretensions alone, were what they had to rely upon." The disciples had no other incentive, while fraudulent miracle workers and their witnesses already had established a religion or had something to gain from miraculous proofs. The hope for personal advantage polluted their testimonies. In no case except Christianity did "miraculous evidence lay at the bottom of the argument."[26]

False religions, even those that claimed miracles, began with a hope for gain and then later assumed a more religious demeanor. Cole's presentation of Joseph Smith was shaped to fit this pattern. The Mormon prophet developed his claims just like that other false prophet, Muhammad. In one paragraph Cole pointed out that "Mahomet had a regular plan from the beginning." Only later did he claim miracles, and even those were suspect. In the next paragraph Joseph Smith was said to have his plan also. He was a money digger and did not even pretend "to have any communion with angels." The search for treasure preceded any claim to miracles, so Cole said. Joseph Smith's whole design from the beginning was to make money, and the witnesses and other claims to miracle working were added afterward when the scheme was well underway. The witnesses were all in on the design and, if not conspirators themselves, were strongly inclined to believe already. By establishing the timing of the visions to fit the pattern, Cole discredited Mormonism and at the same time preserved Christianity's unique claim to a miraculous beginning.[27]

At first oblivious to newspaper attacks, Joseph Smith refused to rise to the challenge to produce miracles. The public questions were no different from the private requests of Martin Harris and Oliver Cowdery. Their desires for proof had been met with the vision of the three witnesses, and that was all Joseph offered in support of the Book of Mormon. In a revelation in July, 1830, giving instructions to Oliver Cowdery as he went out to preach, Joseph was told to "require not miracles, except I shall command you. . . ." A year later in Kirtland, after the newspaper attacks had stepped up, a revelation warned, "There are those among you who seek signs, and there have been such even from the beginning: But, behold, faith cometh not by signs, but signs follow those that believe." Miracles were the reward of faith, not its foundation. "I, the Lord, am not pleased with those among you who have sought after signs and wonders for faith, and not for the good of men unto my glory." The Mormon revelations had no sympathy for the perplexity of Alexander Campbell, who thought it absurd that "I must believe it first, and then ask God if it be true."[28]

While Book of Mormon critics complained about the absence of miraculous proof, they had some explaining of their own to do. How did these 584 pages of text come to issue from the mind of an untaught, indolent ignoramus, notable only for his money-digging escapades? That caricature had to be reconciled with the large, complex, intense volume that Mormons carried in their satchels. W. W. Phelps, a Canandaigua newspaper editor, said in a letter to E. D. Howe, January 19, 1831, that Joseph Smith was certainly a person of "limited abilities in common learning — but his knowledge of divine things, since the appearance of his book, has astonished many."[29]

Abner Cole attributed the idea of a book to Walters, the "vagabond fortune-teller" from the town of Sodus, who was reputed to have shown his followers a copy of Cicero's *Orations* in Latin and claimed it was a "record of the former inhabitants of America," telling where they deposited their treasures. Cole could not make an actual connection between Walters and the Smith family, but he surmised there must have been one. Under the license of satire, Cole said that "the mantle of Walters the Magician" fell on Joseph. In a more sober account for the *Painesville Telegraph*, a letter from Palmyra said that "the first idea of a 'Book' was doubtless suggested to the Smiths by one Walters."[30]

The contents were another matter. The Palmyra critics simplified the task by saying that the Book of Mormon was almost entirely borrowed from the Bible. "The book is chiefly garbled from the Old and New Testaments," the Palmyra letter to the *Telegraph* observed, "the Apocraphy having contributed its share. . . ." "A quarto Bible now in this village, was borrowed and nearly worn out and defaced by their dirty handling. Some seven or eight of them spent many months in copying, Cowdrey being principal scribe." The letter implied wholesale plagiarizing by a committee of authors to produce a cheap imitation of scripture. Nephi and his brothers did insert seventeen chapters of Isaiah and the resurrrected Christ repeated a portion of the Sermon on the Mount, but the copying theory was an inadequate explanation because it left so much of the text unaccounted for.[31]

As the months went by, others offered more likely hypotheses. Alexander Campbell read at least part of the book and suggested an explanation that became the kernel of the modern view. Campbell was founder of the Disciples of Christ and one of the country's most notable theologians and preachers. When his father, Thomas Campbell, challenged Rigdon to debate Mormonism in early February, 1831, Thomas specified that both contestants should be allowed "every assistance that can be contributed by the friends on each side."[32] His son Alexander, well known for his debating ability from a famous encounter with the atheist Robert Owen, had already begun a study of the Book of Mormon. The young Campbell published his critique in his own paper, the *Millennial Harbinger,* on February 7, 1831. The *Painesville Telegraph* reprinted the essay, and it appeared again as a pamphlet in Boston in 1832 under the title *Delusions: An Analysis of the Book of Mormon; with an Examination of Its Internal and External Evidences, and a Refutation of Its Pretences to Divine Authority.*

Alexander Campbell proved his knowledge of the Book of Mormon by summarizing about half of the plot, enough to give his readers a sense of the narrative. Campbell exhibited the customary contempt of Joseph Smith, "as ignorant and as impudent a knave as ever wrote a book," but he saw no need for a committee of authors. Joseph Smith definitely wrote it himself. "There never was a book more evidently written by one set of fingers, nor more certainly conceived in one cranium since the first book appeared in human language, than this same book." "It is as certainly Smith's fabrication as Satan is the father of lies. . . ." Campbell found signs of Joseph's culture scattered through the book, a touch of Masonry and republican government, a few characteristic Yankee phrases, and opinions on many of the theological controversies of his time: "infant baptism, ordination, the trinity, regeneration, repentance, justification, the fall of man, the atonement, transubstantiation, fasting, penance, church government, religious experience, the call to the ministry, the general resurrection, eternal punishment. . . ." Still more revealing were the grammatical errors, which Campbell noted down in great number and copied into his essay, gaffes like "Ye are like unto they" and "We did arrive to the promised land." "Smithisms," as Campbell called them, were sure evidence of human composition.[33]

In contrast to the Palmyra critics, Campbell downplayed the similarity to the Bible. What most impressed him was how unbiblical the Book of Mormon was. Partly it was style: "I would as soon compare a bat to the American eagle, a mouse to a mammoth . . . as to contrast it with a single chapter in all the writings of the Jewish or Christian prophets." More striking still was theology. He did not like the fact that Nephi and his brothers exercised the priesthood when they were not descendants of Levi or Aaron, that another land besides Palestine was a promised land, or that descendants of tribes other than Judah became kings. What most appalled him was that the Book of Mormon "represents the christian institution as practised among his Israelites before Jesus was born." The Nephites preached "baptism and other christian usages hundreds of years before Jesus Christ was born!" There was no regard for the divide between Old and New Testaments. Joseph Smith's "Jews are called christians while keeping the law of Moses, the holy sabbath, and worshipping in their temple at their altars, and by their high priests." Campbell has Joseph writing the Book of Mormon in simple-minded ignorance of the basic facts of Jewish and Christian history, and spreading across its pages "every error and almost every truth discussed in N. York for the last ten years."[34]

As for the intricate plot and the huge array of characters, Campbell dismissed all that as "romance." Subsequent critics had more trouble disregarding what every reader of the book could not help noticing: the Book of Mormon was a complex story. In 1833 the editor of the *Painesville Telegraph,* E. D. Howe, one of Mormonism's most devoted critics, and an excommunicated Mormon named Philastus Hurlbut teamed up to write an exposé and thought they had stumbled across the answer. While gathering material, Hurlbut learned that some residents of Conneaut, Ohio, saw in the Book of Mormon resemblances to a manuscript written by Solomon Spalding, a former resident of their town. When interviewed, they swore that the Spalding story told of lost tribes of Israel moving from Jerusalem to America led by characters named Nephi and Lehi. One deponent remembered the names of Moroni and Zarahemla. Hurlbut pursued Spalding's widow to Massachusetts and eventually located a manuscript that told of a migration to America, but the migrants were Romans and the story bore slight resemblance to the Book of Mormon. Hurlbut concluded there must have been another manuscript. Piecing together one surmise after another, he and Howe eventually decided that Sidney Rigdon had obtained Spalding's now lost manuscript while in Pittsburgh, where

Spalding had submitted his work to a publisher. Rigdon transformed the novel into the Book of Mormon by adding the religious parts. Believing the Palmyra critics' characterization of Joseph as a lazy ignoramus, Howe and Spalding were sure "that there had been, from the beginning of the imposture, a more talented knave behind the curtain. . . ." Sidney Rigdon, a formidable preacher, a colleague of Alexander Campbell's, and a close student of the Bible, was the only one qualified for the task. "If there was a man in the world that could successfully spread and give a name to the vagaries of the Smiths, it was Rigdon." He was "the Iago, the prime mover of the whole conspiracy." Somehow or other Rigdon conveyed the manuscript to Smith without being detected, and then pretended to be converted when the missionaries brought the Book of Mormon to Kirtland in 1830.[35]

The critics thus explained the Book of Mormon by handling it piecemeal, perceiving a portion at a time, accounting for that, and then struggling to comprehend more as ingenuity enabled them to construct more elaborate explanations. The most surprising fact to the Palmyra townspeople was that Joseph, the supposedly lazy son of a money digger, should even pretend to write a book. Cole took care of that fact with Walters's recitations from Cicero's *Orations.* The letter from Palmyra to Painesville (perhaps written by Cole in a sober mood) saw the book as a copy of the Bible and credited a group of Joseph's cronies with originating the "gold bible." Campbell, while still calling Joseph ignorant, at least acknowledged the Book of Mormon's treatment of theological issues and gave it credit for attempting to "decide every question" troubling New York for the past ten years. Campbell made it strictly a local production, a reflection of Joseph's knowledge and ignorance. Campbell prepared the way for Howe and Hurlbut, who added recognition of narrative complexity. They solved the problem of the involved theology and the intricate narrative by specifying two authors, one a theologian and the other a novelist.

Although built on slight evidence and an abundance of speculation, the Howe-Hurlbut hypothesis, because it encompassed more of the actual content of the book than any of its predecessors, remained the standard explanation of non-Mormon critics well into the twentieth century.[36] The fact that Howe and Hurlbut contradicted Alexander Campbell was overlooked. Anti-Mormon writers felt no obligation to explain why the learned Bible student Rigdon would make all the elementary theological blunders Campbell identified, or why Rigdon's grammar should be so faulty. The view that Joseph wrote the book out of his own experience was cast aside until the Spalding theory failed and a revival of Campbell's environmentalist hypothesis became necessary once again.

Perhaps the most serious failing in all the critiques of the Book of Mormon was an inability to deal with text in any detail. Howe and

Hurlbut acknowledged the story by hypothesizing a novelist as co-author but did not discuss the story itself. Campbell referred to the Book of Mormon positions on theological issues but failed to say what they were or how they related to religion of the time. Cole saw similarities to the Bible but made no actual comparisons. The outsiders' yearning to find some rational explanation caused them to hurry their work. Their aim was always to explain away the Book of Mormon rather than understand it. Failing to ground their views in the actual contents of the books, the critiques did not do justice to the work's actual complexity, and their conclusions were unstable, even ephemeral.[37]

THE NEW CRITICS

In recent decades the environmentalist explanation of the Book of Mormon has replaced the Spalding hypothesis among non-Mormon scholars. In 1902 I. Woodbridge Riley, a Yale Ph.D. and the author of *The Founder of Mormonism,* pointed out the many flaws in the Spalding theory. To fill the vacuum left by the old ideas, Alexander Campbell's 1831 analysis gradually came to be favored once again. All but a few critics have dropped Spalding and Rigdon and credited Joseph Smith with authorship, as did Campbell. According to the environmentalists, Joseph absorbed images, attitudes, and conceptions from upstate New York rural culture and wove them into the Book of Mormon story.

While the work of these scholars has illuminated the Book of Mormon's relationship with American culture, the analysis of contemporary environmentalists suffers from the same shortcomings as the work of their predecessors. The determination to explain the Book of Mormon's origins (and to explain away the angel stories) has limited the capacity to understand the book on its own terms. The presumed cultural influences — anti-Masonry, republicanism, the theories of Indian origins, and romantic nationalism, for example — do roughly resemble certain elements in the Book of Mormon, but the environmental theories leave too many other elements unexplained.

Alexander Campbell first cited anti-Masonry as one of the elements of New York culture thought to be an influence on the Book of Mormon. Campbell thought that a certain group of Book of Mormon people called Gadiantons, who "began to bind themselves in secret oaths to aid one another in all things, good or evil," were a reflection of Masonry.[38]

Western New Yorkers had particular reason to respond to the sinister Gadianton bands because of the furor caused by the famous Morgan case. William Morgan, a renegade Mason who had published Masonic secrets in the years immediately preceding publication of the Book of Mormon, was mysteriously abducted from jail in Canandaigua in September, 1826, and never heard from again. Popular opinion blamed the kidnapping on the Masons. Trials held in January, 1827, brought light sentences to the defendants, although they pled guilty to a conspiracy "to seize, carry off, and hold" the victim. The mercy shown the conspirators angered many who followed the trial. They attributed the result to Masonic influence on the bench and in the jury. Pamphlets reviewing the abduction and trial began to appear in large numbers. A corpse that washed ashore from Lake Ontario in October, 1827, was first thought to be Morgan, though later identified as a drowning victim. Strangely the furor did not die down. From October, 1826, through the middle of 1831, eighteen trials of Masonic conspirators took place in five western counties, and in the fall of 1827 fifteen candidates were elected to the state legislature on anti-Masonic principles. Anti-Masonry soon became a national political force. In the 1828 presidential election much was made of the facts that John Quincy Adams was not a Mason and Andrew Jackson was. Anti-Masonic parties sprang up in Pennsylvania, Massachusetts, Connecticut, Maine, Vermont, Ohio, Indiana, and Michigan. In 1830 and 1831 the Anti-Masonic party held national conventions and in 1832 ran a presidential candidate, William Wirt of Maryland. John Quincy Adams ran for the governorship of Massachusetts in 1833 on an Anti-Masonic ticket.[39]

The interest in Masonry provided a large market for anti-Masonic books and audiences for speakers who traveled from town to town to divulge Masonic secrets. The pamphlets rehearsed in great detail the lengthy Masonic initiation rites, elucidating the initiations into each of the degrees and going on to describe the specialized orders in Masonry's many branches. Besides playing to the public's fascination with hidden rituals, the anti-Masonic literature dwelt on a phrase in the rites pledging initiates to protect their Masonic brothers in difficulty whether they were "right or wrong." Above all else the exposés emphasized the threat of death to any who divulged Masonic secrets. Morgan's abduction proved the oaths were deadly serious. How could the nation be safe when thousands of Masons, many in positions of great influence, were bound to shield their brothers from prosecution no matter what the offense, and to destroy any who divulged the secrets?

The association of Gadianton bands and Masonry arose from a few obvious similarities that Campbell might have noticed in a single reading of the Book of Mormon. The members of the Gadianton bands took oaths to conceal one another's crimes, they identified each other with signs and passwords, and they conspired to subvert government. All these understandably sounded to Campbell like an anti-Masonic view of Masonry. Expanding on his insight, an early twentieth-century psychologist thought the similarities in the names Mormon and Morgan proved conclusively that only a western New Yorker, saturated with anti-Masonry, could have composed the Book of Mormon and only between 1826 and 1834 when anti-Masonry was at its peak.[40] Joseph Smith's later initiation into the Masons when a lodge was organized in Nauvoo in 1842 seems to confirm the idea of a fascination with Masonry, even though in Nauvoo Joseph was for the Masons instead of against them.

What the critics neglect in their preoccupation with American influences is the broader picture of Gadianton growth in Book of Mormon society, raising the question if concentration on the resemblances alone is an adequate method of interpreting the bands. The groups labeled by Mormon as Gadiantons were not one continuing society, like the Masons, but five distinct combinations that sprang up among the Nephites and Jaredites. Three of the five bands took shape in the eighty-five years between 52 B.C. and the coming of Christ in 33 A.D., during a period of severe social and political instability. The original band came into being around 52 B.C. and lasted until 17 B.C. The immediate occasion for its formation was competition among the three sons of a chief judge for succession to their father's office. The supporters of one of the defeated sons refused to accept the voice of the people and conspired with one Kishkumen to assassinate Pahoran, the successful son. The conspirators "entered into a covenant, yea, swearing by their everlasting Maker, that they would tell no man that Kishkumen murdered Pahoran." Gadianton rose to influence among this group because he was "exceeding expert in many words, and also in his craft, to carry on the secret work of murder and of robbery. . . ." Gadianton aspired to the judgment seat himself and promised his followers "power and authority" in return for their support.[41]

A subsequent group of Gadiantons was a collection of Lamanites and Nephite dissenters. Around 12 B.C. they infested mountain hideaways, descending to plunder and murder and then retreating again. Nephite dissenters continued to join them until they became "an exceeding great band of robbers." These roving bands were powerful enough to withstand "the whole armies of the Nephites," and did "cause great fear to come unto the people upon all the face of the land." The Gadiantons laid cities to waste and were presumptuous enough to demand that one of the chief judges relinquish the government to them. Not until the Nephites scorched the earth and relinquished their land could they defeat the Gadiantons. Without farms to plunder, the robbers lost their strength, and around 21 A.D. they suffered defeat.[42]

One can see why Alexander Campbell thought he saw Masons in the Book of Mormon. Conditioned by anti-Masonic rhetoric, he understandably reacted to familiar elements in the story, but readers approaching from another perspective might have noted quite different aspects of the Gadianton bands. They could with equal ease be perceived as modern terrorist guerrillas, dissenters at war with the old order, penetrating villages on the margins of official control, undermining from within, and attacking openly when they had strength. Viewed in context, the Masonic-like oaths and covenants were secondary to direct attacks on government through assassinations and military raids. ·

The similarities noted by the critics, rather than constituting an explanation of the Gadianton bands, speak more for the difficulties the Book of Mormon presented to American readers. Only limited portions were intelligible as expressions of American culture. Critics concentrated on selected proof texts and neglected the context.[43] Their method necessarily obscured differences between American and Book of Mormon culture. In the supposed anti-Masonic passages in the Book of Mormon, nothing was said about Masonic degrees or elaborate initiation rituals. Anti-Masonic books went on endlessly with all the details of how one passed form degree to degree, while acceptance of a simple oath of secrecy and allegiance admitted a person to the Gadianton bands. Nor did the Gadiantons connect with Solomon's temple, the Masonic craft, or Hiram, builder of the great temple. Perhaps most important, the crucial event in the anti-Masonic campaign, the murder of the Masonic traitor William Morgan in 1826, had no equivalent in the Book of Mormon.[44]

The differences may explain why critics in Joseph Smith's own day made so little of anti-Masonry in the Book of Mormon. In his 1831 critique Alexander Campbell only mentioned Masonry and passed on. Subsequent 1830s critics neglected the point entirely, since they credited Solomon Spalding with authorship. Alexander Campbell himself in time subscribed to the Spalding theory and dropped the point about Masonry.[45]

Likewise, converts paid no attention to anti-Masonry. With the Anti-Masonic party growing rapidly after 1829 in New England, New York, and Ohio, Mormon converts might be expected to join the campaign to rid the nation of secret combinations. Insofar as early Mormons had political preferences, they likely were anti-Masons, but these sentiments were entirely overshadowed. Lucy Mack Smith said nothing about Masonry, Morgan, or anti-Masonry in her autobiography. Joseph was equally neglectful. At the height of the anti-Masonic excitement from 1829 to 1833, Masonry was scarcely mentioned among the Mormons. The people who knew anti-Masonry and the Book of Mormon in the 1830s made less of the connection than critics today.[46]

Book of Mormon republicanism was another item briefly noted by Alexander Campbell and expanded by later scholars. Midway in their history the Nephites ended monarchy and instituted a government based on the "voice of the people." To signify the importance of the change, they numbered their years from what was called the "reign of the judges," until the birth of Christ established a still more fundamental baseline for their calendar. Lehi seemed to associate democracy with the very nature of the American continents when he declared that "this land shall be a land of liberty unto the Gentiles, and there shall be no kings upon the land. . . ." "He that raiseth up a king against me shall perish, for I, the Lord, the king of heaven, will be their king. . . ." These were presumably reassuring words for a newly minted republic, one of a tiny handful among the formidable monarchies of the earth.[47]

And yet the reign of the judges in the Book of Mormon bears little resemblance to nineteenth-century American republicanism. Nephite culture was never republican insofar as the Book of Mormon describes government. The first prophet, Nephi, allowed himself to be made a king and established a line of kings that lasted 500 years. Around 92 B.C. King Mosiah gave up his throne and established a system of judges chosen by the voice of the people, but the resulting government was a far cry from the American pattern. The chief judge, by democratic standards, was more king than president, as suggested by the Book of Mormon phase "the reign of the judges." After the first judge, whose name was Alma, was proclaimed by the voice of the people, he enjoyed life tenure. When he chose to resign because of internal difficulties, he selected his own successor, who was the founder of a dynasty of judges. In the next succession the judgeship passed to the chief judge's son and thence, according to his "right," as the book says, to the successive sons of the judges. The "voice of the people" entered only marginally into the appointment of an officer who essentially enjoyed life tenure and hereditary succession.[48]

Furthermore all of the constitutional checks on Nephite rulers, whether kings or judges, are missing. The standard three branches of government do not appear. The chief judge was judge, executive, and legislator combined. In wartime he raised men, armed them, and collected provisions. His titles were interchangeable: chief judge and governor. He was also lawmaker, for no conventional legislature can be found in the Book of Mormon. In the early part of the book the law was presented as traditional, handed down from the fathers as "given them by the hand of the Lord," and "acknowledged by this people" to make it binding. Later, the chief judge assumed the power of proclaiming or at least elaborating laws. Alma gave his successor Nephihah the "power to enact laws according to the laws which had been given." Any major constitutional changes, such as a return to formal kingship, required approval of the people, but day-to-day legislation, so far as the record speaks, was the prerogative of the chief judge. Perhaps most extraordinary by American standards, nothing was made of taxation by a popular assembly. Oppressive kings overtaxed the people, but the remedy never lay in a representative body of any kind. The maxim "no taxation without representation" had no standing in Nephite consciousness.[49]

Mormons themselves have mistaken the reign of judges for republicanism. In one edition of the Book of Mormon a twentieth-century editor's chapter heading to Mosiah 29, where Mosiah established judgeships, says the king "recommends representative form of government." The preconceptions of the modern age led Mormons as well as critics to see things in the Book of Mormon that are not there. It has been difficult for Mormon and non-Mormon alike to grasp the real intellectual problem of the Book of Mormon, briefly summed up by one of Joseph Smith's non-Mormon contemporaries in a New York magazine in the early 1840s. Speaking of the Book of Mormon, one "Josephine" observed that "the style is a close imitation of the scriptural, and is remarkably free from any allusions that might betray a knowledge of the present political or social state of the world. The writer lives in the whole strength of his imagination in the age he portrays."[50] That the Book of Mormon portrays another world in many ways alien to our own is the hardest point for modern readers to deal with.

The critics cannot be faulted for saying that the Book of Mormon was a history of the Indians. The book obviously was that, and early Mormons told the world it was. Lucy Smith wrote to her sister-in-law in January, 1829, over a year before publication of the Book of Mormon, and described it as a record "placed in the earth many hundred years ago by the forefathers of our Indians." Samuel Smith asked the innkeeper at the end of the first day of missionary work in June, 1830, "if he did not wish to purchase a history of the origin of the Indians." Five months later the four missionaries to the Indians presented the Book of Mormon in Ohio as "an account of their origin, and a prophecy of their final conversion to Christianity. . . ." In 1831 Lucy Smith, on her way to visit her brother Stephen Mack's family in Detroit, told a fellow passenger that the Book of Mormon was "a record of the origin of the Aborigines of America."[51]

The missionaries had good reason to cast the Book of Mormon in that light. Settlers in New York and Ohio had a natural curiosity about Indians. The Palmyra newspapers occasionally ran items about Indians and Indian ruins in the miscellaneous information section. The Manchester rental library purchased Josiah Priest's *The Wonder of Nature and Providence,* which included materials on the Hebraic origins of the Indians. Priest, a popularizer rather than a student of Indian origins, wrote another such volume for publication in 1833. *American Antiquities and Discoveries in the West,* which sold 22,000 copies in thirty months. The mysterious mounds of Ohio provoked a steady stream of speculation about the cultures that created them. Samuel Smith probably hoped that the innkeeper would read the Book of Mormon out of curiosity if nothing else.[52]

Writers could not agree among themselves on where the Indians came from. Priest's popular 1833 volume speculated that Noah's Ark came to rest in America, and that Polynesians, Egyptians, Greeks, Romans, Scandinavians, Jews, Welsh, Scots, and Chinese migrated to America and contributed to Indian stock. His eclecticism satisfied the public, which apparently was willing to accept supposition in lieu of an authoritative explanation. Scholars could offer nothing better. In 1875 a conference of the world's experts broke up in confusion over attempts to sort out the evidence.[53]

The Book of Mormon offered as reasonable an explanation as any for the time. From the seventeenth century on, ministers in Europe and America had argued that the Indians were Israelites on the grounds of similarities in Hebrew and Indian culture. Increase Mather, Samuel Sewall, Samuel Willard, Jonathan Edwards, and Ezra Stiles had published such opinions, borrowing in part from European sources such as Thomas Thorowgood to prove their point. The idea received fresh impetus from James Adair's *The History of the American Indians,* published in London in 1775. Adair lived for forty years among the Indians as a trader before retiring to write his observations. Excited by Adair's evidence, Elias Boudinot, founder and first president of the American Bible Society, introduced a wide American audience to the theory of Israelite origins in his *Star in the West,* which appeared in 1816. Spurred by his work, other authors began combing accounts of Indian life in search of evidence. Ethan Smith, a minister in Poultney, Vermont, in *View of the Hebrews,* published in 1823, reviewed the findings of Adair and Boudinot and added evidence from many other sources. The reviews of *View of the Hebrews* (and presumably the sales) warranted an enlarged second edition in 1825. Josiah Priest, a man with his eye on the main chance, further complimented Smith by plagiarizing scores of pages in his own *Wonder of Nature and Providence.*[54]

From one perspective, the Book of Mormon was one more account of Israel in America. But it would be a mistake to see the book as an imitation of these earlier works. Nor is there evidence of heavy borrowing from *View of the Hebrews,* as some critics have said. Comparison of the two works reveals too many fundamental differences.[55]

Ethan Smith's reconstruction of Indian history had one purpose: to identify Indians with the lost ten tribes. The full title of Smith's book was *View of the Hebrews: or, The Tribes of Israel in America.* He derived his inspiration from Elias Boudinot's *A Star in the West: A Humble Attempt to Discover the Long Lost Tribes of Israel, Preparatory to Their Return to Their Beloved City, Jerusalem.* The argument turned heavily on a few biblical passages purportedly written about the tribes. Amos 8:11, 12, for example, was believed to describe their migration in prophesying of a people who would "wander from sea to sea, and from the north even to the east. . . ." Smith conjectured that the ten tribes had moved northward from Assyria, where they had been taken captive, and then east to the ocean. The words "sea to sea" meant the Mediterranean and the Pacific. The tribes crossed to North America, possibly via the Bering Straits, and moved south to fill both American continents. Ethan Smith argued that all of the lost tribes remained together because the Bible spoke of dispersed Judah and the "outcasts" of Israel. "It inevitably follows," he insisted, "that the ten tribes of Israel must now have somewhere on the earth a distinct existence in an outcast state."[56]

Ethan Smith believed that God kept the American continents vacant as a reservoir for the tribes during their long apostasy. Smith had little to say about their history in America, except that a civilized group built the well-known mounds and fortifications before extermination by a degenerate branch. For the most part God paid no heed to the tribes in their American home. Their original religion steadily deteriorated until only fragments remained to recall the savages' biblical origins. In Ethan Smith's view, investigators understandably found only traces of Mosaic religion. When the time for the fulfillment of God's ancient covenant with Israel arrived, the Indians would convert to Christ and a number of them would return to their ancient promised land.[57]

The excitement in Ethan Smith's book lay in the light it shed on an old puzzle — where were the lost ten tribes, that mysterious group who dropped out of history after their captivity in Assyria? And on this point the Book of Mormon was a disappointment. Lehi and his family were not the ten tribes. Lehi left for the new world 125 years after the Assyrian captivity and from Jerusalem, not Assyria. His people were never identified as the lost tribes. The ten tribes were mentioned, as Parley Pratt noted, by the Savior when he said he would visit them after he left the Nephites, but nothing was said of an American home for the tribes. They were another group, located in another part of the world. The Indians by the Book of Mormon account, rather than being the other half of ancient

Israel, were descendants of a tiny band that slipped out of Jerusalem long after the ten tribes had disappeared.[58]

Moreover, the Book of Mormon version of Indian origins contradicted much of Ethan Smith's scriptural evidence. One of the key proof texts in Ethan Smith's treatise did not work for the Book of Mormon. Lehi went south, not north, as Amos 8 prescribed, and stayed by the Red Sea before launching into the Indian Ocean rather than traveling from sea to sea. Nor were the cultural similarities of Indians and Hebrews entirely relevant. Ethan Smith piled up proofs of Indian practice of Mosaic ritual and law. Book of Mormon peoples abided by the Mosaic law until the coming of Christ, but Mormon buried that fact as if it were of little importance. Nephite prophets taught Christ and the resurrection. Sacrifices, feasts, temple worship, all the material evidence in *View of the Hebrews* received scant attention amidst the outpouring of sermons on salvation through Christ. After the appearance of the Savior the Mosaic law was abandoned altogether and presumably sifted out of Nephite culture. Almost everything Ethan Smith worked so industriously to prove, the Book of Mormon disproved or disregarded.

The critics have mistakenly searched too hard for specific parallels in the Book of Mormon and *View of the Hebrews,* while neglecting the moral purpose of Ethan Smith's work. Before he was historian or anthropologist, Smith was a preacher. The burden of his message was that the Indians were Israel, a branch of God's chosen people. The great promises made to them in the ancient covenants were soon to be fulfilled. The point for modern Americans was to pay attention to this benighted people. As a reviewer expressed it, the moral of the book was "the weight of obligation which now rests on Gentile Christians and eminently on American Christians to extend the gospel to the Jews."[59]

If we are to ask where the Book of Mormon converged with the American culture of the 1830s, the theme of Israel's restoration is a better contact point than Ethan Smith's theory about the lost tribes. Smith attached the Indians to the destiny of the Jews to make proselyting among the tribes an aspect of the promised conversion of all Israel, and so did the Book of Mormon.

In this effort, Ethan Smith worked in a well-established tradition. The association of Jews and Indians went back at least as far as the sixteenth century. Elizabethan divines came to believe that the future of the Jews was foretold in Romans 11 and Revelations 16:12, as well as in Isaiah and Ezekiel. A number of seventeenth-century Puritans urged Parliament to readmit Jews to England (they had been expelled in 1290 by royal decree) so as to facilitate their conversion. At the same moment, the great seventeenth-century Amsterdam rabbi Manasseh Ben Israel petitioned Parliament for readmission for his own reason: to complete the dispersion of Israel through the entire world. The Bible prophesied that the Jews would be scattered into every land, and presumably the return to Palestine would not begin until the dispersion was complete. Ben Israel's comprehensive view of Israel's history encompassed America and the Indians as well. His conviction that Israel must be dispersed to the four corners of the globe required that he identify the Indians as among the chosen people. He published his views in 1650, in *Hope of Israel*, which became a touchstone for subsequent investigators. His Puritan allies in the movement to readmit Jews to England shared his belief. Thomas Thorowgood wrote *The Jews in America*, and Increase Mather interspersed sermons on Indian origins with tracts on Jewish conversion.[60]

The French Revolution at the end of the eighteenth century set off another wave of speculation about Israel's return. Napoleon, the antichrist of the era, startled millennialists when he convened a Jewish Sanhedrin in Paris in 1807. Speculation ran wild, especially among those who interpreted prophecy to say that the Jews would ally with the antichrist just prior to their break with evil and their conversion to Christ. As the fury of the revolution mounted, religious leaders in England and America began to make specific preparations. The pastor of the Presbyterian Church in Elizabethtown, New Jersey, David Austin, broke with the church in 1791 and constructed houses for the Jews whom he believed would soon need shelter en route to the Holy Land. In 1809 Joseph S.F.C. Frey, a converted Jew, formed the London Society for Promoting Christianity among the Jews. In 1820, after migration to New York City, Frey organized the American Society for Meliorating the Condition of the Jews. Within four years the society claimed 200 auxiliaries and a circulation of 20,000 for its paper *Israel's Advocate*. By the mid-1820s the restoration of the Jews was a major question for Christians attempting serious explication of the millennial calendar.[61]

When Joseph Frey wanted assistance with a plan to organize a refuge for ostracized Jewish converts, he went to Elias Boudinot, the author of *Star in the West*, the 1816 volume on Indians as Israelites, and probably the most distinguished Christian layman in America. As president of the American Bible Society, Boudinot approved the scheme for a refuge and recommended a revival of the society for evangelizing Jews. In his will Boudinot left a tract of land to start a Jewish colony. Probably through Boudinot, Frey met Ethan Smith. In the second edition of *View of the Hebrews*, Smith announced that "the Rev. Mr. Frey, the celebrated Jewish preacher, and Agent for the American Meliorating Society, upon reading the *View of the Hebrews*, and warmly approving the sentiment in it that the American Indians are the ten tribes, informed the writer of these sheets, that he owned a pamphlet, written by the Earl of Crawford and Linsey, entitled, 'The Ten Tribes.' " Apparently Frey had long taken an interest in the Indians, for he remembered that Crawford, a British army officer in the Revolution, had argued that the Indians were descendants of the ten tribes. Later in life Frey tried his own hand at proving that the Indians were the lost tribes of Israel.[62]

The nineteenth century, like the seventeenth, saw a blending of Jewish and Christian interest in the return of the Jews and the conversion of Indians. Mordecai Noah, a New York promoter and publicist, petitioned the New York assembly in 1820 to permit him to purchase Grand Island in the Niagara River near Buffalo as a gathering place for the Jews preceding their return. Despite the annoyance and embarrassment of many American Jews, Noah bravely renamed the island Ararat, proclaimed himself "Governor and Judge of Israel," and dedicated Grand Island in an extravagant ceremony in 1825. In the spirit of Manasseh Ben Israel, Noah invited the Indian tribes of America, as remnants of the lost ten tribes, to join their Jewish brethren on the island.[63]

The dedication on the title page of the Book of Mormon struck a familiar note in 1830. The record was "to show unto the remnant of the House of Israel what great things the Lord hath done for their fathers; and that they may know the covenants of the Lord, that they are not cast off forever — And also to the convincing of the Jew and Gentile that Jesus is the Christ, the Eternal God, manifesting himself unto all nations." Like Ethan Smith's *View of the Hebrews*, the Book of Mormon directed its readers to attend to lost Israel, whether Jew or Indian. The descendants of Lehi were not the lost ten tribes, as Indians were conventionally thought to be, but they were part of the diaspora. Jacob, Nephi's brother, spoke of many groups whom "the Lord God has led away from time to time from the house of Israel," now scattered on "the isles of the sea." "Yea, the more part of all the tribes have been led away," Nephi said, "and they are scattered to and fro upon the isles of the sea; and whither they are none of us knoweth, save that we know that they have been led away." Lehi was of the tribe of Joseph through his son Manasseh, and America, Lehi's promised land, was the isle to which God led him. The Book of Mormon's mission was to convert the Indian fragment of Israel along with all the other dispersed remnants, including Jews and the lost tribes. Many Americans besides Ethan Smith understood that mission and could believe in it. Here the book and its American environment did come together.[64]

Despite the convergence, the potential alliance of Mormons with other advocates of the Jews and of Indian Israel never became a reality. The reason was that Mormons and a Congregational minister like Ethan Smith could never agree on the role of the gentile Christian church. The

Book of Mormon made very clear that every church in the last day would fall into apostasy, carried away by pride and lost in a tangle of false teachings. "They have all gone astray save it be a few, who are the humble followers of Christ; nevertheless, they are led, that in many instances they do err because they are taught by the precepts of men." Rather than a moment of triumph for gentile Christianity, Israel's restoration was an hour of judgment. The gentiles' last act in the closing hour of their dispensation was to bring forward the Book of Mormon to Lamanites and Jews. The restoration of the Book of Mormon was actually a watershed in sacred history, when Israel was to be restored, and the gentiles, who had abused the Christian Gospel, were rejected. In their apostate condition the gentiles needed the Book of Mormon as much as Israel. The book was a test and separation. If the gentiles believed, they would join Israel and "be a blessed people upon the promised land forever. . . ." If they turned away, they would be scourged, driven, and cast off. In either event the last days belonged to Israel. The early Mormons could not join forces with the gentile Christian churches to convert Israel, for Christians in Mormon eyes, were as benighted as the Jews.[65]

The Book of Mormon perspective on the Christian churches connects with one other hypothesis about cultural influences on the book: the belief that it enshrined "the romantic nationalism of the new republic and the optimism and expectation that characterized the third decade of the nineteenth century. . . ." The American land was given an honored place in Book of Mormon sacred history; American civilization was not. The false teachers in the churches, the Book of Mormon said of modern times, "rob the poor because of their fine sanctuaries; they rob the poor because of their fine clothing; and they persecute the meek and the poor in heart, because in their pride they are puffed up." The Book of Mormon, Moroni wrote, would come to light in a day when "there shall be great pollutions upon the face of the earth; there shall be murders, and robbing, and lying, and deceiving, and whoredoms, and all manner of abominations. . . ." Mormons showed more affinity for premillennialist disillusionment with contemporary society and the belief that "the deterioration in religion and culture had reached crisis proportions" than for American optimism and romantic nationalism.[66]

The same pessimism darkened the Smith family's private views of the world. Father Smith's dream of the contemporary religious situation presented a picture of dead fallen timber in a landscape dreary, silent, and devoid of life. In keeping with their reservations, half the family stayed away from church altogether, and the others followed their mother into

Presbyterianism only ofter holding back for nearly twenty years. Joseph, Jr., wrote to his St. Lawrence County cousins before translating the Book of Mormon to tell them "that the sword of vengeance of the Almighty hung over this generation and except they repent and obeyed the Gospel, and turned from their wicked ways, humbling themselves before the Lord, it would fall upon the wicked, and sweep them from the earth. . . ." The lessons Lucy learned from the Book to Mormon, as she wrote her brother Solomon in 1831, were "that the eyes of the whole world are blinded; that the churches have all become corrupt, yea every church upon the face of the earth; that the Gospel of Christ is nowhere preached."[67]

Similar disillusionment had overtaken the men who were attracted to the Prophet. Martin Harris told Charles Anthon during the consultation concerning the characters that the Book of Mormon would "produce an entire change in the world and save it from ruin." After the translation was completed, Oliver Cowdery wrote Joseph that "some times I feel almost as though I could quit time and fly away and be at rest in the Bosom of my Redeemer for the many deep feelings of sorrow and the many long struglings in prayr of sorrow for the Sins of my fellow beings. . . ." Mormon optimism arose not from romantic hope for Amercia but from the faith grounded in the Book of Mormon that God would redeem the land from the evil that prevailed there.[68]

BELIEVERS

While Cole, Campbell, Howe, and Hurlbut worked at discrediting the Book of Mormon, a few people believed in it. Roughly a hundred individuals were baptized in New York by the end of 1830, and as many more again in Ohio. The converts read the Book of Mormon with great interest. Thomas Marsh, a resident of Charlestown, Massachusetts, visiting in nearby Lyons, heard of the "Golden Book" while it was still in press and, "highly pleased" with the report of Oliver Cowdery and Martin Harris, took home sixteen pages of proof to study with his family. Marsh soon joined the church and moved west. The Smith cousins in St. Lawrence County were likewise immediately attracted. George A. Smith and his mother spent all one Saturday and Sunday poring over the Book of Mormon. George noted down objections as he read, but when he defended the volume against detractors, he found that he answered all of his own questions. Parley Pratt said that when the Book of Mormon first fell into his hands, he "read all day; eating was a burden, I had no desire for food; sleep was a burden when the night came, for I preferred reading to sleep."[69]

Unfortunately, very few said what it was in the book that caught their attention and finally convinced them. Parley Pratt said that "as I read, the spirit of the Lord was upon me, and I knew and comprehended that the book was true, as plainly and manifestly as a man comprehends and knows that he exists." Ezra Thayer heard Hyrum Smith preach at a meeting in the yard of the Smith house. After the meeting Hyrum handed Thayer a copy of the Book of Mormon. "I said, let me see it. I then opened the book, and I received a shock with such exquisite joy that no pen can write and no tongue can express." All this without reading a word. When he opened the book again, he felt "a double portion of the Spirit." "I did not know whether I was in the world or not. I felt as though I was truly in heaven." A copy of the Book of Mormon came to Jared Carter through the brother of a convert. "After reading a while in the Book of Mormon and praying earnestly to the Lord that he would show me the truth of the Book I became immediately convinced that it was a revelation of God and it had such an influence on my mind that I had no mind to pursue my business. . . ."[70]

The experience of reading the book transcended the specific contents. Samuel Smith, who carried books to some of the towns around Palmyra shortly after publication, made no arguments on its behalf. When he gave a copy to the wife of John P. Greene, a Methodist preacher in Bloomington, Samuel explained "the most profitable manner of reading the book . . . which was to ask God, when she read it, for a testimony of the truth of what she had read, and she would receive the Spirit of God, which would enable her to discern the things of God." Mr. and Mrs. Greene followed his directions and soon joined the church, followed not long thereafter by Mrs. Greene's brothers, Phineas and Brigham Young. From all reports the converts seem to have acted on their spiritual feelings more than their sympathy with specific ideas.[71]

It is no easier to deduce the appeal of the Book of Mormon from the influence it exercised in the church after its organization in 1830. A rapid adoption of certain Book of Mormon teachings would suggest what early Mormons valued most. But, strange to say, the book had far less apparent influence than one would expect, given Joseph Smith's investment of effort in the translation. A few things are clear about the Book of Mormon's role. Early Mormon preachers cited Book of Mormon texts in their sermons, stimulated perhaps by passages in the Doctrine and Covenants where the modern church was admonished to "become even as Nephi of old," or to "beware of pride, lest ye become as the Nephites of old." Parley Pratt remembered speaking "the word of God with power, reasoning out of the Scriptures and the Book of Mormon" a week after his baptism. The early revelations repeatedly characterized the Book of Mormon as containing "the fulness of the gospel of Jesus Christ." It was a book to be laid alongside the Bible. "The Book of Mormon and the holy scriptures are given of me," a revelation said, "for your instruction."[72]

On the other hand, the Book of Mormon did not become a handbook for doctrine and ecclesiastical practice. It was not as if a new truth had been laid out in the teachings of the ancient Nephites and the modern church was to pore over the record to extract policy and teachings. From the outset doctrine came day by day in revelations to Joseph Smith. Those revelations comprised the backbone of belief, the doctrine and covenants for the church. The teachings of the Book of Mormon were never repudiated, nor did it fail to inspire and instruct its readers. The modern Saints avoided infant baptism just as Mormon had instructed the church in the fourth century. The sacrament prayers in the Book of Mormon were repeated word for word in the modern church. But most of the applicable Book of Mormon doctrines and principles were revealed anew to Joseph Smith, and derived their authority from the modern revelation as much as from the Book of Mormon. After establishing a principle of the forgiveness of enemies, one revelation declared, "Behold, this is the law I gave unto my servant Nephi, and thy fathers, Joseph, and Jacob, and Isaac, and Abraham, and all mine ancient prophets and apostles." The Book of Mormon citation confirmed modern revelations just like a biblical reference.[73]

Alexander Campbell thought the Book of Mormon was Joseph Smith's attempt to decide "all the great controversies," but neither Joseph nor the early Mormons used the book that way. Mormons were much more likely to seek revelation through their Prophet. Despite the effort that went into the translation, Joseph Smith did not make the book the foundation of the church. The Book of Mormon was more like another book of scripture that, as one revelation said, did "throw greater views upon my gospel."[74]

When converts said little, and the church as a body did not conspicuously adopt distinctive Book of Mormon teachings, how is the appeal of the Book of Mormon to be understood?[75] Judging from the recorded responses, we must be prepared to believe that the very idea of a new revelation inspired people. They touched the book, and the realization came over them that God had spoken again. Apart from any specific content, the discovery of additional scripture in itself inspired faith in people who were looking for more certain evidence of God in their lives.

CHAPTER V

THE CHURCH OF CHRIST

Sometime in the early spring of 1830 Joseph Knight came over to Harmony from Colesville, picked up Joseph Smith at his cabin on the Hale property, and drove him to Manchester where the elder Smiths were living with Hyrum. On the way Joseph told Knight "there must be a church formed." Knight said he was not told the day when the church was to be organized, but Joseph did have a precise date in mind. He had made the long journey to Palmyra twice the previous winter, to stop Abner Cole's plagiarism and to keep Grandin at work on the Book of Mormon, but returned both times to Harmony without forming a church. Organization had to await the arrival of April 6, the date given by revelation, probably as far back as the summer of 1829.[1]

The group that met at the Whitmer house in Fayette on Tuesday, April 6, consisted of six elders and about fifty others from Colesville, Manchester, and the Fayette area. The official organizers for legal purposes were Joseph Smith, Jr., Oliver Cowdery, Hyrum Smith, Peter Whitmer, Jr., Samuel H. Smith, and David Whitmer. Joseph's first act after opening the meeting with "solemn prayer" was to ask if the brethren accepted Joseph and Oliver as teachers and whether the brethren wanted to organize as a church. After receiving unanimous approval, Joseph ordained Oliver an elder, and Oliver ordained Joseph. They blessed bread and broke it with the brethren, and blessed wine and drank it. Then Oliver and Joseph laid hands on the members present to give the Holy Ghost and confirm them. The Holy Ghost came over them and some prophesied while others praised the Lord and rejoiced. Joseph Knight reported that "Joseph gave them instructions how to Bild up the Church and exorted them to Be faithful in all things for this is the work of God." Joseph and Oliver ordained some of the brethren to priesthood offices "as the Spirit manifested unto us," and "after a happy time spent in witnessing and feeling for ourselves the powers and blessings of the Holy Ghost," they dismissed.[2]

Besides its significance for the band of believers, the organization of the church was a momentous event in the private history of the Smith family. Lucy had looked for a church since the time of her illness in Randolph. Joseph, Sr., attended with her for short stretches from time to time, but always gave up in disgust after a few Sundays. Finally in Palmyra, perhaps under revival influence, Lucy joined the Presbyterians and by so doing divided the family. Hyrum, Samuel, and Sophronia went with her; Joseph, Sr., Alvin, and Joseph, Jr., stayed away. Joseph, Sr., had no heart for churches or ministers. His visionary dreams depicted the religious world as a desolate barren field covered with dead fallen timber and devoid of animal or vegetable life. The intimation of Lucy's minister, the Reverend Benjamin Stockton, that Alvin had gone to hell because of his refusal to attend church confirmed Joseph Sr.'s convictions about clerical hypocrisy. Lucy said her husband thought "no order or class of religionists" understood the Kingdom of God. And yet his religious dreams suggest how in his subconscious he also longed for a church. He dreamed of people going to judgment on their way to the meetinghouse. When he arrived too late, he "was almost in a state of total despair." After satisfying the porter of his faith in Christ, Joseph, Sr., to his great relief, was permitted to enter the building — but only in a dream.[3]

In the evening after the organization of the church, Martin Harris, Orrin and Sarah Rockwell, Lucy Smith, and Joseph Smith, Sr., were baptized in a small stream. Lucy said that Joseph, Jr., his eyes filled with tears, grasped his father's hand as he came from the water. "Oh, my God! have I lived to see my own father baptized into the true church of Jesus Christ!" Joseph Knight remembered how Joseph, Jr., after the baptism "bast out with greaf and Joy and seamed as tho the world Could not hold him. He went out into the Lot and appeared to want to git out of site of every Body and would sob and Crie and seamed to Be so full that he could not live." Knight and Oliver Cowdery went after Joseph and finally brought him back to the house. "He was the most wrot upon that I ever saw any man," Knight recalled. "His joy seemed to Be full."[4]

The record does not clearly tell when Joseph first realized he was to organize a church. The revelation of error in all churches when he was fourteen implied the need for a true church. In his later years Joseph said that he learned then "that the fullness of the gospel should at some future time be made known unto me." Oliver Cowdery said in 1834 that Moroni told Joseph that he was later to receive the priesthood, baptize, and bestow the Holy Ghost. But after receiving the plates, amidst his poverty and the harassment of neighbors, Joseph seemed to have been solely preoccupied with translating the Book of Mormon, as if that were his only goal. The first written revelation in the late summer of 1828 spoke of "the works, and the designs, and the purposes of God," and of "the work of the Lord," but specified only the conversion of "the Nephites, and the Jacobites, and the Josephites, and the Zoramites." One could think of Joseph Smith as a John Wesley or George Whitefield carrying forward a certain well-focused mission within Christianity without a separate church organization.[5]

That was not to be. A revelation given in March, 1829, before the arrival of Oliver Cowdery, when only a few pages of the Book of Mormon were in manuscript, described this generation as the time of "the rising up and the coming forth of my church out of the wilderness." Through that spring the orientation of the revelations shifted away from the Book of Mormon toward the conversion of souls. In May a revelation directly announced that "if this generation harden not their hearts, I will establish my church among them." The Book of Mormon became less an end in itself and more a means of bringing people to repentance. Through the account of the Nephites and Lamanites the Lord would "bring to light their marvelous works, which they did in my name; yea, and I will also bring to light my gospel which was ministered unto them. . . ." The aim was to gather the Lord's people "as a hen gathereth her chickens under her wings, if they will not harden their hearts." "Yea, if they will come, they may, and partake of the waters of life freely." That spring the revelations to individuals—Hyrum, Joseph Knight, David Whitmer, John Whitmer, and Peter Whitmer, Sr.—all emphasized teaching the Gospel rather than proclaiming the Book of Mormon. "And now, behold, I say unto you, that the thing which will be of the most worth unto you will be to declare repentance unto this people, that you may bring souls unto me, that you may rest with them in the kingdom of my Father."[6]

The church that was foreshadowed was to give that urge full expression. It was not narrowly conceived as a mechanism for spreading the Book of Mormon or converting the Indians; rather, it was to call men back to Christ in the full power of the Gospel. A revelation to David Whitmer and Oliver Cowdery in June, 1829, expressed the thrust of the work and the message:

Remember the worth of souls is great in the sight of God; for, behold, the Lord your Redeemer suffered death in the flesh; wherefore he suffered the pain of all men, that all men might repent and come unto him. And he hath risen again from the dead, that he might bring all men unto him, on conditions of repentance. And how great is his joy in the soul that repenteth! Wherefore, you are called to cry repentance unto this people. And if it so be that you should labor all your days in crying repentance unto this people, and bring, save it be one soul unto me, how great shall be your joy with him in the kingdom of my Father!⁷

The formation of a church called upon abilities in Joseph he had never before manifest. He had to appoint leaders and organize people under them. Considering his lack of experience, the new church came into being with remarkably little confusion. The form of church organization had been the most hotly contested issue of the English Reformation of the seventeenth century. The choices of the parties were memorialized in the names by which they came to be known — Congregational, Presbyterian, and Episcopal — and the debates continued into the nineteenth century as an aspect of denominational competition. In naming officers and distributing authority, Joseph inevitably awakened old antagonisms, but the opposition he met was surprisingly mild.

The traditional dispute over ecclesiastical authority was embodied in the words "congregational" and "episcopal." In the Roman church and subsequently in the Church of England, each bishop (*episcopus*) held authority in direct descent from Peter the apostle, and hence had the right to govern the church. Bishops ordained all priests and appointed them to their parishes. The Congregationalists, by contrast, believed that elders and bishops in the New Testament received their appointments from their congregations. Although ordination may have come under the hands of previously ordained pastors, a minister had no authority apart from a specific congregation. At the congregational end of the spectrum power lay with the people, and at the episcopal end with the bishops. In between, the Presbyterians, in a mixed form of government, authorized regional presbyteries, composed of the clergy and elected elders from each congregation, to assign pastors to their parishes.

The revolution against monarchy and the establishment of republicanism in the United States created an atmosphere more congenial to congregational democracy than to episcopal hierarchy. No denomination suffered more from the pressure of the democratic spirit than the Methodists, the group that originally attracted Joseph Smith more than any other. John Wesley, the movement's founder, deeply aristocratic in bearing and spirit himself, had no sympathy for democracy in church government. "As long as I live," he wrote in 1790, "the people shall have no share in choosing either stewards or leaders among the Methodists." "We are no republicans and never intend to be." And yet by 1830 local exhorters were demanding representation in the General Conference (where only ordained elders had a seat), and traveling elders were insisting on the right to elect their presiding elders (appointed by the bishop). An independent reform journal, *The Mutual Rights of Ministers and Members of the Methodist*

Episcopal Church, appeared in the 1820s to work "for the recovery of mutual rights of ministers and members of the Church of Christ from the usurpation and tyranny . . . of hierarchies. . . ." Forced at last to choose between loyalty to traditional Methodism and their democratic principles, the reformers in November, 1830, formed the Methodist Protestant church. Its constitution made no provision for bishops or presiding elders and granted equal representation to lay members in annual and general conferences. With 5,000 members at its inception, increasing to 118,000 by 1880, the democratic branch of Methodism remained independent until it reunited with the Methodist Episcopal church in 1939.[8]

Whatever Joseph did, he would be working against the democratic pressures that divided the Methodists and worked to dissolve hierarchies in every church. He would have to step carefully to avoid the pitfalls. The offices mentioned in the Book of Mormon suggested a general pattern to follow. Elders, priests, and teachers were the common officers in the Nephite churches. Elders were the highest of the three, with authority to administer bread and wine in remembrance of Christ's flesh and blood, baptize, and bestow the Holy Ghost by laying on hands. Priests exercised similar powers, save they could not bestow the Holy Ghost. Before the visit of Christ, a high priest presided over the church as a whole; after the Savior came, the twelve disciples governed.[9]

The revelation on church organization to Joseph built on the Book of Mormon pattern, with deacons added to assist the teachers. Elders were empowered to baptize, administer the sacrament, bestow the Holy Ghost, ordain other priesthood officers, take the lead in meetings, and bless children. Priests had the same duties save for bestowing the Holy Ghost, blessing children, and ordaining elders. Teachers and deacons were assistants to the priests without any ordinance powers, charged primarily to "watch over the church always, and be with and strengthen them."[10]

The collection of offices was arranged in graded order. Elders were to take charge in meetings, and in their absence, first priests and then teachers. Although priests could ordain priests, teachers, and deacons, only elders could issue a license authorizing each ordained person "to perform the duty of his calling." Elders also met in quarterly conferences "to do whatever church business is necessary to be done at the time," reminiscent of the Methodist Annual Conference of Elders. At the head stood Joseph and Oliver, the First and Second Elders respectively.[11]

Although no more than a bare outline of church government, the revelation on priesthood offices made abundantly clear that the new church was not to be radically democratic in the congregational vein. The congregations of Saints had only a slight role in the selection of their own officers.[12] On the day of church organization Joseph asked if the assembled people accepted Oliver and himself as their teachers, but only later were the members formally given the right to consent to officers nominated by the priesthood leaders. At first power lay primarily with the elders.

On the other hand, neither Joseph and Oliver nor the elders made any attempt to monopolize authority. David Whitmer said six men had been ordained elders by August, 1829, and ordinations flowed readily from Joseph's hands thereafter. Although never formally enunciated, the policy of ordaining every worthy male member quickly took effect in practice. A Book of Mormon principle facilitated this practice. "All their priests and teachers should labor with their own hands for their support," Alma and Mosiah had taught. "When the priests left their labor to impart the word of God unto the people, the people also left their labors to hear the word of God. And when the priest had imparted unto them the word of God they all returned again diligently unto their labors. . . ." The purpose was explicitly democratic: "the priest, not esteeming himself above his hearers, for the preacher was no better than the hearer, neither was the teacher any better than the learner; and thus they were all equal. . . ." Among Joseph's followers the principle of equality never had to be em-phasized, for they were all common men when they began. But the prohibition on payment to the clergy prevented distinctions from arising and eliminated a common cause of jealousy between laity and clergy. Most important, because elders and priests received no remuneration for their labors, the authority of the priesthood could be liberally distributed without arousing expectations of support or putting excessive demands on the members.[13]

Joseph and Oliver had no special authority bestowed upon them. In the table of organization they appeared as the first among equals. Besides being First and Second Elders, they were soon designated apostles, but a revelation of the previous June had foreshadowed twelve apostles to be identified by Oliver Cowdery and David Whitmer and "to go into all the world to preach my gospel unto every creature." If authority was to be concentrated, the new church was to be apostolic rather than episcopal, but Joseph and Oliver were the first apostles, not the only ones.[14]

Far more important than any constitutional powers was a designation for Joseph revealed on the day of the church's organization: "Behold there shall be a record kept among you; and in it thou shalt be called a seer, a translator, a prophet, an apostle of Jesus Christ, an elder of the church through the will of God the Father, and the grace of your Lord Jesus Christ. . . ." From the time of the discovery of the seerstone through the completion of the translation, Joseph's influence had always sprung from his followers' faith in his supernatural powers. The revelation told the church, "Thou shalt give heed unto all his words and commandments which he shall give unto you as he receiveth them, walking in all holiness before me. . . ." Those words merely codified what was fact already. People followed Joseph Smith because, as the revelation said, they received his word "as if from mine own mouth." The authority of the church was charismatic in the technical sense, based on a gift of divine power in the leader. Apart from any constitutional authority, Joseph led the church because he was the Lord's prophet.[15]

CONVERSIONS

On the first Sunday after the church organization, Oliver Cowdery preached and a half-dozen people were baptized. Oliver baptized another eight in Seneca Lake the next Sunday. In the month of April at least twenty-three people were baptized, possibly two or three more.[16]

The first baptized members were Joseph's family and close friends: Oliver Cowdery, Martin Harris, the Whitmers, the Smiths. But almost at once strangers began gravitating toward Joseph. Thomas Marsh, who had heard of the "gold bible" while visiting in Lyons, was at age twenty-nine a disillusioned Methodist and a seeker. After his discussions with Oliver and Martin, Marsh returned to Charlestown, Massachusetts, to tell his wife and family. He corresponded with Joseph and Oliver over the next year and in September, 1830, moved to Palmyra. David Whitmer baptized Marsh and Oliver ordained him an elder. His family accompanied hm to Palmyra but did not come into the church. A revelation through Joseph assured him that "I will bless you and your family, yea, your little ones; and the day cometh that they will believe and know the truth and be one with you in my church."[17]

Solomon Chamberlain, a Lyons resident, heard of the Book of Mormon in 1829 when a journey to upper Canada brought him within a mile of the Smith house. He had long believed that "there was no people on the earth that was right, and that faith was gone from the earth, excepting a few and that all Churches were corrupt." The Lord had showed him in vision in 1816 a church to come raised up "after the Apostolic order," with "the same powers, and gifts that were in the days of Christ." When Chamberlain called on the Smiths, his first question was, "Is there any one here that believes in visions or revelations?" When Hyrum replied, "Yes, we are a visionary house," Chamberlain gave him a pamphlet to read aloud to Joseph, Sr., and a few of the Whitmers who were present. Hyrum broke down crying as he read, and passed the pamphlet to Christian Whitmer. After elaborating on his vision of an apostolic church, Chamberlain said, "If you are a visionary house I wish you would make known some of your discoveries, for I think I can bear them." Hyrum gave

Chamberlain sixty-four pages of proof of the Book of Mormon to take into Canada. As soon as the Book of Mormon was published, Chamberlain toured with eight or ten copies for a little over a week. A conference of reformed Methodists, the denomination he was most closely connected with, scorned him, but a Free Will Baptist church was more receptive. Soon after the organization of the church, Joseph baptized Chamberlain and his wife in Seneca Lake.[18]

Parley Pratt was living on a farm he had opened in Ohio, about thirty miles from Cleveland, when he fell under the influence of Sidney Rigdon, a reformed Baptist and follower of Alexander Campbell and Walter Scott, the restorationist. Pratt liked Rigdon's preaching because he taught the "ancient gospel" as Pratt understood it — faith in Christ, repentance toward God, baptism, and the promise of the Holy Ghost. All Rigdon and Scott lacked in Pratt's eyes was "the authority to minister in holy things — the apostleship, the power which should accompany the form." Pratt joined the little society formed in his neighborhood and took his turn preaching. A year later, in August, 1830, he was moved to sell his farm and with his wife head east along the Erie Canal on an indefinite preaching mission. An inner prompting caused him to leave the canal boat at Newark and head into the country. Like Chamberlain and Marsh, he heard of the Book of Mormon by chance and visited Hyrum Smith. In their all-night talk Pratt told of his misgivings concerning the lack of "a commissioned priesthood, or apostleship to minister in the ordinances of God." After reading the Book of Mormon and duly weighing all he had heard, Pratt was convinced "that this was a new *dispensation* or *commission*, in fulfilment of prophecy, and for the restoration of Israel, and to prepare the way before the second coming of the Lord." He and Hyrum walked the twenty-five miles to the Whitmers, and around September 1 Oliver baptized him in Seneca Lake. The same evening hands were laid on his head for the gift of the Holy Ghost and Parley was ordained an elder. "I now felt," he said, "that I had authority in the ministry."[19]

Besides welcoming people like Marsh, Chamberlain, and Pratt who turned up in the Smith dooryard, Joseph commissioned missionaries to spread word of the Book of Mormon. Soon after the organization he directed Samuel to take books to Livonia, a day's journey away, to sell if possible. Samuel was turned out at five different places on his first day, June 30, including the inn where he had planned to stay the night. He washed his feet in a brook as a testimony against the innkeeper and slept under an apple tree. A poor widow took an interest in the book but was too poor to purchase a copy. At Bloomington a Methodist preacher, John P. Greene, somewhat gingerly agreed to take around a subscription paper on his next circuit for a book he believed to be nothing more than a "nonsensical fable." When Samuel, along with Lucy and Joseph Smith, Sr., returned in two weeks, no copies had been sold. Not until the late fall did Mrs. Greene finally read the book and take an interest. When Samuel presented her with a copy "she burst into tears," he reported, "and requested me to pray with her." He instructed her to pray for a testimony of the truth as she read, and left. Both Greenes soon were baptized. (The fame of Samuel's mission rests both on its being among the first and on the conversions of Mrs. Greene's brothers: Phineas, Brigham, and Joseph Young, and with them Heber C. Kimball.)[20]

Although Samuel Smith's mission and Parley Pratt's conversion are still legendary among Mormons, neither missions nor chance encounters like Pratt's brought the greatest number of people into the church during the early months. Before the Kirtland mission belief in the Book of Mormon spread mainly along family lines. Not just brothers and sisters but cousins, in-laws, and uncles listened and believed. Five Whitmer children and three of their spouses were baptized in the first few months, besides the parents. Eleven Smiths, six Jollys, and five Rockwells joined in the same period. The most remarkable collection of kin was the offspring and relatives of Joseph Knight, Sr., and his wife Polly Peck Knight, the Colesville family that had befriended Joseph ever since he dug Spanish treasure for Josiah Stowell. Two of Polly Knight's brothers and a sister, their spouses, and a sister-in-law accepted the Book of Mormon and were baptized. Five of the Knight children, four of them with spouses, joined, plus Joseph Knight's sister, Mary Knight Slade and five of her children. Altogether twenty-eight people came into the church through the Knight-Peck connection in the first few months, forming the core of the Colesville branch. The Knights and the other four families accounted for sixty baptisms in the first nine months.[21]

Almira Mack, the daughter of Lucy's much-admired brother Stephen, visited the Smiths in May, 1830, and accepted the new faith. The Smiths made plans immediately to tell others of their kin about the church. In January, 1829, a year before the publication of the Book of Mormon, Lucy had written her husband's sister, Martha Pierce, who had married and remained in Royalton when the other Smiths migrated to New York. Lucy wrote, she said, "to soften your heart that you may seek for a witness of the truth of this work. . . ." Two years later she wrote a long letter to her brother Solomon Mack and he subsequently joined. In 1831 she went to Michigan, where she converted the widow of her brother Stephen.

Joseph Smith, Sr., and young Don Carlos Smith, still a boy of fourteen, set out in August, 1830, for Stockholm, St. Lawrence County, New York, the stronghold of the Smiths. The Smiths had written to the family in the fall of 1828 about Joseph Jr.'s revelations. Jesse Smith, the prickly eldest son, scoffed at Joseph Jr.'s pretensions. It irritated Jesse, as he wrote to Hyrum, that "your good, pious, and Methodistical Uncle Asael induced his father to give credit to your tale of nonsense." But the other St. Lawrence Smiths listened with interest to Joseph, Sr., and Don Carlos. Father Asael, eighty-seven and about to die, read the Book of Mormon nearly through without the aid of glasses. He said "he always knew that God was going to raise up some branch of his family to be a great benefit to mankind."[22]

With the exception of young Asael, the brothers were at first skeptical, but they wanted to hear all they could from Joseph. Jesse's efforts to seal him off from the rest of the family were to no avail. Silas threatened to throw Jesse out of the house if he continued to insult Joseph. John kept him overnight at his house by a trick and heard the story. Joseph stayed one night with his sisters, giving him time to talk to them. By the time he left Stockholm, the family had copies of the Book of Mormon and knew about the church. John was baptized in 1832, and Silas, Asael, and their mother, Mary Duty Smith, soon followed. Jesse was the only one of the living brothers not to join. Even he felt the tug of the powerful clan ties. When Joseph left Stockholm, he gave Jesse his hand and bade him farewell. "Farewell, Jo, for ever," Jesse stiffly replied. "I am afraid," Joseph replied, "it will be for ever, unless you repent." This was too much even for Jesse. He broke into tears and the two silently parted.[23]

Conversion altered the lives of the believers in conventional and in extraordinary ways. Faith in Joseph and the Book of Mormon evoked the traditional Christian urge to renounce one's sins. W. W. Phelps, the editor of the *Ontario Phoenix*, which he had published in Canandaigua since 1828, had a copy of the Book of Mormon within two weeks of its publication and believed it at once. When he visited the Prophet on December 24, 1830, the account Joseph gave of himself aroused in Phelps his "first determination to quit the folly of my way." After his conversion in Kirtland, Sidney Rigdon rose to speak in the Methodist chapel, "*apparently* much affected and deeply impressed. He seemed exceedingly humble, confessed the sins of his former life, his great pride, ambition, vain glory, etc., etc." Like Phelps and Rigdon, William Smith at his conversion "felt willing to forsake the world, the flesh, and the devil, and go down into the waters of baptism, and take upon me the name of Jesus Christ. . . ."[24]

But, in addition, Mormonism imparted a new perspective on the world and called forth new life plans. William Smith said he "became awakened to the necessity of embracing the plans of salvation, and of the necessity of publishing a knowledge of Jesus Christ and his gospel among all nations, kindreds, tongues and people; that the nations afar off might hear of his glory and learn of his fame. . . ." He saw from the start that the necessity of publishing the Gospel was a personal imperative. "I began to think it was my duty to preach the gospel and warn the nations of the earth of the great things about to take place." As men joined the church, they were almost immediately ordained and many of them sent off to preach. Personal conversion and purification were joined with a call to take a public role. Following his baptism, William Smith entertained solemn thoughts "concerning the work of the last days, and the great responsibility under which I had just been laid, to live soberly, righteously, and godly before the world, in order that the Lord might be glorified and honored through me." Besides being a faith and an ethic, Mormonism was a work.[25]

It is marvelous to think now of this tiny handful of New York farmers and artisans setting out to fill the earth with the Gospel. They began their work like the first apostles in a world that had never heard of Christianity, virtually without allies or fellow workers. In April someone applied for membership without rebaptism, and Joseph was told by revelation that "all old covenants have I caused to be done away in this thing; and this is a new and an everlasting covenant, even that which was from the beginning. Wherefore, although a man should be baptized a hundred times it availeth him nothing. . . ." The older Christian churches were without authority, their works were dead, and the Mormons were alone.[26]

No single teaching caused the early missionaries more trouble than the requirement of rebaptism, with its implication of universal Christian apostasy. Sidney Rigdon felt a terrible shock in Kirtland when the missionaries told him of the clean break he must make with his past. After Rigdon joined the church, Thomas Campbell, his former associate, prepared to debate him on this very point, as one of Mormonism's offenses against Christianity. The missionaries themselves made as little of rebaptism as possible. The revelations told them "of tenets thou shalt not talk, but thou shalt declare repentance and faith on the Savior, and remission of sins by baptism, and by fire, yea, even the Holy Ghost." Moreover they were to declare the glad tidings "with all humility, trusting in me, reviling not against revilers." And yet the hard fact could not be blunted. They alone among all Christians had the truth. A traveling preacher who met the Whitmers in March, 1830, came away with the impression that any who failed to believe the Book of Mormon "would be given up and lost forever."[27]

While the missionary work went forward, Joseph continued to shuttle among the various clusters of believers. He and Emma still lived in the cabin in Harmony near Isaac Hale, and the elder Smiths with Hyrum in Manchester. Around the Whitmers in Fayette clustered a group of sympathetic family members and friends, and another had formed around the Joseph and Polly Knight family in Colesville. In the latter part of April

Joseph Smith visited his old friend in Colesville, who had given him employment in 1826 and befriended him through the translation of the plates. Joseph characterized Knight as a Universalist; he spoke of himself as a "Restorationar," one who wished to restore the doctrines and practices of the New Testament church and eliminate all else. Neighbors and family members met to hear Joseph's teachings and pray for "wisdom to understand the truth."[28]

At their meetings the little group "got into the habit of praying Much," and Joseph Smith once asked Newel Knight, Joseph Knight's son, to pray. Newel begged off, saying he would rather pray alone in the woods. When he tried it the next morning, however, he was no more able to pray than in public. On his return home his appearance worried his wife and she sent for the Prophet. Joseph found him "suffering very much in his mind, and his body acted upon in a very strange manner; his visage and limbs distorted and twisted in every shape and appearance possible to imagine; and finally he was caught up off the floor of the apartment, and tossed about most fearfully."[29]

Joseph looked on aghast, along with eight or nine others who had collected in the house, until he finally caught Newel by the hand. Newel pled with Joseph to cast out the devil, and Joseph said, "If you know that I can, it shall be done." Almost unconsciously Joseph rebuked the devil, and Newel spoke out immediately that he saw the devil leave. Newel's body relaxed and he could be laid on his bed. He later reported that "the visions of heaven were opened to my view." Entirely absorbed in his contemplations, he was unaware of what was happening until he "felt some weight pressing upon my shoulder and the side of my head," and found "that the Spirit of the Lord had actually caught me up off the floor, and that my shoulder and head were pressing against the beams." Joseph marked the casting out of the devil as "the first miracle" done in the church, commenting that "it was done not by man, nor by the power of man, but it was done by God, and by the power of godliness. . . ." Those who witnessed the scene were of course impressed, and most finally joined the church. Newel visited the Whitmers in Fayette in the last week in May, and David Whitmer baptized him.[30]

Even writing eight years later, Joseph could not hide the pleasure in this miracle. He never was one to enlarge on the sensational, but manifestations of extraordinary powers confirmed his understanding of the church. As in the days of the first apostles, it was to teach the simple principles of the Christian Gospel—faith, repentance, baptism, the gift of the Holy Ghost—and to enjoy divine gifts as the Lord chose to reward the faith of the Saints.

DOCTRINE

By these means the Gospel was to spread through the earth. Ideally the missionaries would not enter into denominational competition. They would not revile against revilers or match tenet against tenet, only teach the truth of Christ and baptize those who believed. Of course that was not to be. Thomas Campbell challenged Sidgney Rigdon less than two months after Sidney's conversion. From the beginning Mormons were forced to defend themselves, and that meant elaborating doctrines and the simple first principles. Questions of doctrine inevitably arose within the church as well, and the members came to Joseph for answers. Stroke by stroke the new church defined its teachings on issues that troubled believers.

Martin Harris had raised questions from the beginning. In early April, 1830, before the organization, when Joseph Smith and Joseph Knight came across him in the road carrying a bundle of books, Martin asked once more for a revelation. He awoke that night at the Smith house and complained of a weight on his chest. "I felt some thing as Big as a great Dog sprang upon my Brest." In the morning Martin again demanded a commandment. Later in the day Joseph and Oliver received the revelation that is now numbered 19 in the Doctrine and Covenants.[31]

The revelation told Martin to repent, not to covet his neighbor's wife, nor to seek his neighbor's life. In direct answer to his request, he was commanded not to "covet thine own property, but impart it freely to the printing of the Book of Mormon. . . ." The revelation also spoke on a doctrinal point that may have been bothering him. One of the queries discussed locally in print, and probably in churchyards, was the duration of divine punishment. The growing emphasis on God's goodness in the early nineteenth century called into question the justice of unending punishment for sinners as taught by traditional Calvinism. In answer to the question, the revelation observed that "it is not written that there shall be no end to this torment, but it is written *endless torment.*" "For, behold, I am endless, and the punishment which is given from my hand is endless punishment, for Endless is my name. Wherefore — Eternal punishment is God's punishment." Sinners did not suffer endlessly; they suffered God's punishment.[32]

As commonly happened when Joseph spoke for the Lord, the revelation did not stop with a simple answer to Martin's question, or with a commandment to finance the Book of Mormon, or even with an explanation of eternal punishment. As if to warn Martin that God's punishment was not to be taken lightly even if it did not endure forever, the revelation measured the dimensions of divine wrath. "Repent lest I smite you by the rod of my mouth, and by my wrath, and by my anger, and your sufferings be sore — how sore you know not, how exquisite you know not, yea, how hard to bear you know not."

Then, rising above the specifics of Martin's situation, the revelation drew a picture of Jesus' suffering.

For behold, I, God, have suffered these things for all, that they might not suffer if they would repent; but if they would not repent they must suffer even as I; Which suffering caused myself, even God, the greatest of all, to tremble because of pain, and to bleed at every pore, and to suffer both body and spirit — and would that I might not drink the bitter cup, and shrink — Nevertheless, glory be to the Father, and I partook and finished my preparation unto the children of men.

Coming back to Martin, the revelation made its application: "Wherefore, I command you again to repent, lest I humble you with my almighty power; and that you confess your sins, lest you suffer these punishments of which I have spoken, of which in the smallest, yea, even in the least degree you have tasted at the time I withdrew my Spirit." The taste of punishment probably alluded to Martin's anguish when he lost the 116 pages of manuscript and suffered the pains of hell for it.[33]

For the most part doctrine accumulated piecemeal in the fashion of the revelation to Martin. The Saints learned what to teach from studying the Book of Mormon and by garnering a point here and there from revelations addressed to specific circumstances. In the spring of 1830, however, Joseph and Oliver prepared for the use of the missionaries and for the guidance of the church a summary of principles and practices. The information that went into section 20 as it now appears in the Doctrine and Covenants had come to Joseph and Oliver over the previous year. The precise date of church organization had been given in June, 1829. A revelation to Oliver dated 1829, and still today in manuscript form only, contains directions about ordinations, the sacrament, and baptism that were carried over into section 20. Other doctrines may have been forming in Joseph's mind as he brought the new church into existence.[34]

Section 20 was probably not written in its present form until after April 6, 1830. For one thing, the organization is spoken of in the past tense: "It being regularly organized and established agreeable to the laws of our country. . . ." In the Book of Commandments, the revelation's first printed form, it was dated June, 1830. Since it was presented to the conference held on June 9 for approval, the formulation must have taken place between April 6 and June 9.[35]

The revelation differs from its predecessors in not speaking in the first person in the voice of the Lord. The opening sentence obscures who is speaking by omitting a predicate altogether, and the next few sentences merely describe events without revealing the identity of the spokesman. In verse 17, however, the nature of the composition is made clear: "For the Lord God has spoken it; and we, the elders of the church, have heard and bear witness to the words of the glorious Majesty on high. . . ." The words were a statement from the elders of the church. From verses 16 through 36 the statement is in the form of a testimony of the two elders who witnessed the words of God, Joseph and Oliver. From verse 37 to the end more straightforward directions are given but never in the voice of God. Section 20 compares to the later revelations, which took the form of letters from Joseph to the Saints, in being a record of what the Prophet had learned from the Lord, spoken in Joseph's own voice.

Before there was a book of Doctrine and Covenants to define church beliefs, this statement, joined later by section 42, "the law," represented what the church stood for. The 1829 revelation to Oliver Cowdery was called "articles of the Church of Christ," and the version of section 20 printed in the Kirtland edition of the *Evening and Morning Star* was referred to as "articles and covenants." In editions of the Doctrine and Covenants published between 1835 and 1869 the current section 20 was printed just after the preface as some indication of its pre-eminence.[36]

Section 20, in keeping with its name, "articles and covenants," resembled the confessions of faith of Christian denominations, both in the form of the language and the topics covered: the fall, the nature of man, the atonement, resurrections, redemption, justification, and sanctification. From time to time parts were added and subtracted as thought necessary to complete the statement. Section 22 was part of section 20 in some early versions; verses 66 and 67 on the privileges of priesthood offices were added as the organizational structure grew. After acceptance by the June 9 conference, missionaries often carried personal copies for teaching prospective members.[37]

The articles defined the Mormon position on a few controversial issues without becoming argumentative. The question of infant baptism was resolved with the provision that "no one can be received into the church of Christ unless he has arrived unto the years of accountability before God, and is capable of repentance." The Calvinist principle of irresistible grace was struck down in favor of the idea that "there is a possibility that man may fall from grace and depart from the living God," in harmony with the emphasis in the Book of Mormon on human freedom and responsibility.[38]

For the most part, however, the articles made no effort to distinguish the new church from other denominations. The purpose seems to have been just the opposite, to identify the new organization as a respectable Christian church, holding to the established principles of the Gospel. The radical aspect of Mormonism, the new revelations to Joseph Smith, were not slighted. The main outline of Joseph's experiences was briefly summarized, including the ministration "by an holy angel, whose countenance was as lightning, and whose garments were pure and white above all other whiteness," but the First Vision was mentioned only as the time when "it was truly manifested unto this first elder that he had received a remission of his sins. . . ." Joseph's visions were not flaunted before the world. They were simply acknowledged as part of the church's history.[39]

The articles dealt in passing with the charge that Joseph's revelations added to the Bible, contrary to the warning in Revelations 22 not to add to the words of the book. The statement said that the church's beliefs were true "according to the revelations of John, neither adding to, nor diminishing from the prophecy of his book, the holy scriptures, or the revelations of God which shall come hereafter by the gift and power of the Holy Ghost, the voice of God, or the ministering of angels." The current revelations were a continuation of the ancient scriptures. John's statement was interpreted to mean that men were not to add to or diminish the revelations of God, whether given in ancient or modern times.[40]

As further reassurance to investigators, the statement of doctrine in verses 16 to 36 used familiar language from the traditional creeds and reaffirmed standard Christian beliefs. The formulation of church procedures was conventional. Elders, priests, teachers, and deacons were well-known church officers. There were to be conferences and sacraments. Members were admitted in much the traditional way, by baptism of believing and repentant converts. The wayward were to be dismissed and their names blotted out. The articles presented the church as no cult or sect with eccentric beliefs or bizarre forms of worship, but as a church among churches, stable, disciplined, and orthodox.

Joseph came back from Colesville and Harmony to Fayette in May apparently mainly to hold a conference in accord with the provisions in "the Church articles and covenants." According to the meeting's minutes, the "Elders of the Church" held the conference, after the manner of the Methodists whose elders were the sole participants in quarterly conferences. But there were only seven elders present among the thirty members. Others who were only "anxious to learn" joined in as well. The "articles and covenants" were read and "received by unanimous voice of the whole congregation, consisting of most of the male members of the Church." The official business included confirmation of newly baptized members, ordination of priests, and the issuance of licenses. The license to Joseph Smith, Sr., said, "Liberty Power and Authority Given to Joseph Smith sen. signifying and Proving that he is a Priest of this Church of Christ established and regularly Organized in these last days A D 1830 on the 6th day of April. . . ." Joseph Smith, Jr., and Oliver Cowdery signed as First and Second Elders. Licenses were issued to elders, priests, and teachers.[41]

The official minutes kept by Oliver Cowdery recorded these formalities and noted briefly the form of worship. Joseph read Ezekiel 14, prayed, and exhorted the members. At the end prayer was offered "by all the brethren present, and dismissed by Brother Oliver Cowdery." The staid depiction in the minutes and in the articles and covenants was, of course, only part of the story. Visitation of divine power played a much larger role in the faith and worship of the Saints than the official documents revealed. Joseph remembered that "the Holy Ghost was poured out upon us in a miraculous manner" at the conference. "Many of our number prophesied, whilst others had the heavens opened to their view. . . ." Some were so overcome they had to be laid on beds, among them Newel Knight, who said "he saw heaven opened, and beheld the Lord Jesus Christ, seated at the right hand of the majesty on high." Joseph said that in a vision of the future Newel "saw there represented the great work which through my instrumentality was yet to be accomplished." Joseph long remembered the excitement of those early days and the visionary experiences of the first converts.

To find ourselves engaged in the very same order of things as observed by the holy Apostles of old, to realize the importance and solemnity of such proceedings; and to witness and feel with our natural senses, the like glorious manifestations of the powers of the Priesthood, the gifts and blessings of the Holy Ghost, and the goodness and condescension of a merciful God unto such as obey the everlasting Gospel of our Lord Jesus Christ, combined to create within us sensations of rapturous gratitude, and inspire us with fresh zeal and energy in the cause of truth.

To the members themselves the new church was much more than another church among churches.[42]

TRIALS

After the conference Joseph returned to Harmony, and then with Emma, Oliver, and David and John Whitmer set out again to visit Joseph Knight in Colesville. By late June a number of Knight family members were ready to join the church. On Saturday afternoon, June 26, they dammed a small stream to make a pond for baptisms and appointed a meeting for the Sabbath. Not everyone who came was friendly. Animosity had built up in Colesville along with the Knights' interest. Saturday night the dam was torn out, and unfriendly faces were among the group that heard Oliver and others preach on Sunday.[43]

Joseph's very success among the Knights was one of the causes of opposition. He frightened the community when their neighbors and kins-men became his followers. Not just mobs but preachers and town leaders felt they had to intervene. The Presbyterian minister in Colesville, the Reverend Mr. Shearer, got involved with Emily Coburn, the sister of Newel Knight's wife, Sally. Emily, who was still a minor living with her brother Esick in Sandford, near Colesville, had visited Sally Knight to dissuade her from believing in Joseph Smith and the Book of Mormon and instead became interested herself. Emily attended the Sunday meeting at Newel Knight's. After the meeting she was told her brother wished to see her in a patch of woods a little distance from the house. Esick asked why Emily had not come back to Sandford, and while she was explaining, Shearer came up and took her by the hand. To her annoyance, he refused to let go despite her objections. By then Sally Knight and a group of Mormons joined the group, Sally wrenched Emily's hand away from Shearer and left with Emily, while Esick Coburn and Shearer tried to deal with the Knight men.[44]

Shearer and Esick were not easily defeated. They obtained from Em-ily's father, Amariah Coburn, a power of attorney and took Emily by force of law. She was returned to her brother's house in Sandford and disciplined by the Presbyterian Church in Sandford where apparently Shearer also had responsibilities. In the long run, Emily had her way. Within a few months of the confrontation at the Knights she was baptized.[45] Shearer wrote up the story for the Home Missionary Society. His chief complaint against the Mormons was their claim to be the exclusive Church of Christ, but clearly far more serious was the anguish and anger of families like Emily's who saw brothers and sisters and children seemingly carried away by an exotic deception.[46]

The Mormons put the dam back in place early Monday morning and held their baptism later that day. Oliver Cowdery baptized Joseph and Polly Knight along with eleven others in the Knight connection, plus Levi Hall and Emma Smith. On their way back the party met a collection of the Knights' neighbors who scoffed at the new Mormons and asked if they had been washing sheep. About fifty men surrounded Joseph Knight's house, Joseph Smith said, "raging with anger, and apparently determined to commit violence upon us." When Joseph left for Newel's house to escape the taunts and threats, they followed along, hovering on the verge of a physical attack. Joseph parried their demeaning questions and tried to disregard the insults.[47]

A meeting had been set for the evening to confirm the newly baptized members, but before they got started a constable from South Bainbridge, Ebenezer Hatch, delivered a warrant for Joseph's arrest. Doctor A. W. Benton of Chenango County, whom Joseph Knight called a "catspaw" of a group of vagabonds, brought charges against Joseph as a disorderly person. Hatch, who turned out to be sympathetic to Joseph, told him the mob actually wanted to get him into their hands. By setting out smartly, the two got away from the group of toughs surrounding the constable's wagon. On the way to South Bainbridge a wheel came off and the mob nearly caught up, but, working fast, Joseph and the constable replaced it and drove on. Hatch lodged Joseph in a tavern in South Bainbridge and slept all night with his feet against the door and his musket by his side to prevent intrusions.[48]

Joseph appeared the next morning at ten before Justice Joseph Chamberlain of Chenango County. The exact nature of the charges is not entirely clear. Joseph Smith said it was for "setting the country in an uproar by preaching the Book of Mormon," which was his most recent offense. Joseph Knight said Benton swore out the warrant against the Prophet for "pertending to see under ground," thus going back to the old money-digging business of the 1826 trial. The fact that Josiah Stowell, Joseph's employer in the silver mine venture, was called to testify suggests that the accusers wished to reopen the case. Benton himself said Joseph Smith was brought to trial "in order to check the progress of the delusion, and open the eyes and understanding of those who blindly followed." From that perspective money digging and the Book of Mormon flowed together and were part of the same fraudulent scheme. As Benton said in a report to the *Evangelical Magazine and Gospel Advocate* the next year, "the Book of Mormon was brought to light by the same magic power by which he pretended to . . . discover hidden treasure."[49]

The accusers could not fault Joseph Smith for making converts like Emily Coburn or Sally Knight, probably the real reason for local outrage. Instead they focused on attempts to defraud through claims to supernatural powers, an illegal act under New York law. The prosecution called Josiah Stowell and tried to get him to say that Joseph told Stowell "that an angel had appeared unto him and authorized him to get the horse from you." Stowell flatly denied the accusation and claimed that Joseph had paid for the horse. Though Stowell only held Joseph's note, he was "ready to let him have another horse on the same terms." Similarly Jonathan Thompson was asked if Joseph had gotten a yoke of oxen by claiming a revelation. Thompson also said he was paid. Stowell's two daughters, who had kept company with Joseph at one time, were given a chance to report misconduct but cleared him entirely.[50]

In all, twelve witnesses were called. Two attorneys, Seymour and Burch, handled the prosecution, and Joseph Knight hired attorneys for the Prophet. Knight first engaged an acquaintance, James Davidson. When

Davidson surveyed the situation at the courtroom, he said "it looked like a sqaley Day" and advised hiring John Reid, a local man noted for his speaking ability. Both were farmers with experience in the law. Reid later said that Joseph "was well known for truth and uprightness; that he moved in the first circles of the community, and he was often spoken of as a young man of intelligence and good morals. . . ." Reid thought bigots among the sectarian churches were responsible for bringing charges. The hearing dragged on until midnight, when Chamberlain, whom Reid considered a man of "discernment," acquitted Joseph and discharged him.[51]

Joseph no sooner heard the verdict than a constable from Broome County served a warrant on him for virtually the same crimes. This time he received rougher treatment. Besides heaping abuse on Joseph, the constable hurried him off, after a long day in court without food, on a fifteen-mile journey through the night without a pause for a meal. The constable offered no protection from the tavern haunters who ridiculed the Prophet when the two of them finally stopped for the night. Although close to home by this time, Joseph was refused the privilege of spending the night with his wife. After a dinner of crusts and water, Joseph was put next to the wall and the constable lay close against him to prevent escape.[52]

At ten the next morning Joseph was in court again, this time before three justices who formed a court of special sessions with the power to expel him from the county. Seymour and Burch again ran the prosecution, calling up another flock of witnesses. Newel Knight was interrogated about his healing, and Seymour rehearsed the old money-digging charges. Reid said witnesses were examined until 2 A.M. and the case argued for another two hours. The three justices again acquitted Joseph and discharged him. Reid and Davidson presented the case so well that most of the onlookers were won over, including the constable, who apologized for his bad treatment. He warned Joseph that his enemies had not given up, and planned to tar and feather him. The constable took Joseph out a back door, and he made his way to Emma's sister's house where his wife awaited him. The next day Joseph and Emma were safely home in Harmony.[53]

Joseph and Oliver tried to steal back to Colesville a few days later to complete the confirmations which the trials had interrupted, but their enemies were too alert. They no sooner arrived at the Knights' than the mob began to gather. The Knights had suffered along with Joseph. On the night of the trial their wagons were turned over and some of them sunk in the water. Rails were piled against the doors and chains sunk in the stream. The mob was keeping an eye on the Knight house and spotted Joseph and Oliver. There was no time for a meeting or even refreshments.[54] They had to flee immediately.

Joseph said they traveled all night, "except a short time during which we were forced to rest ourselves under a large tree by the wayside, sleeping and watching alternately." It may have been on this occasion that Peter, James, and John appeared to Joseph and, as a later revelation said, "ordained you and confirmed you to be apostles, and special witnesses of my name, and bear the keys of your ministry and of the same things which I revealed unto them. . . ." Erastus Snow later said that Peter, James, and John appeared to Joseph "at a period when they were being pursued by their enemies and they had to travel all night, and in the dawn of the coming day when they were weary and worn who should appear to them but Peter, James and John, for the purpose of conferring upon them the Apostleship, the keys of which they themselves had held while upon the earth, which had been bestowed, upon them by the Savior." Addison Everett wrote to Oliver Huntington about an overheard conversation between Hyrum and Joseph wherein Joseph spoke of a trial involving Mr. Reid. In trying to escape the mob, "Joseph and Oliver went to the woods in a few rods, it being night, and they traveled until Oliver was exhausted and Joseph almost carried him through mud and water. They traveled all night and just at the break of day Olive[r] gave out entirely and exclaimed 'O! Lord! How long Brother Joseph have we got to endure this thing,' Brother Joseph said that at that very time Peter, James and John came to them and Ordained them to the Apostleship."[55]

The divine visitation lifted their spirits without alleviating the pressures on Joseph and the small band of believers. Although a score or more converts had been baptized since the organization of the church, the Momons and particularly Joseph met hostility, ridicule, and threats of violence on every hand. Emma, in the way of wives, suffered indirectly from the persecution heaped upon her husband. Apart from the harassment, life had been hard for her. Three and a half years of marriage had afforded her few moments of uninterrupted domestic peace. She had nearly perished herself when her first-born son died in childbirth in June, 1828. Joseph had been gone from home more than half of the time since the winter of 1830, seeing to the publication of the Book of Mormon, organizing the church, preaching, and baptizing. She accompanied him sometimes, but on her most recent trip to Colesville she had seen her husband arrested and tried twice, and a mob try to tar and feather him. In July, 1830, when Joseph and Oliver fled home to Harmony from Colesville, she was pregnant—with twins, as it turned out.

In July, after his return from Colesville, Joseph received a pair of domestic revelations to help him set his personal affairs in order: section 25 in the current Doctrine and Covenants to Emma, and section 24 to Oliver and himself. Emma's revelation admonished her to "murmur not because of the things which thou has not seen," implying a deficiency in her faith, but she was a believer. She had permitted Oliver Cowdery to baptize her at Colesville in late June and she was soon to be confirmed. Long after Joseph was dead and she was remarried, Emma held on to her conviction of the Book of Mormon's authenticity. She knew Joseph could not have written the book himself. The revelation for her envisioned a substantial role in the church besides being wife to Joseph. She was to be "ordained under his hand to expound scriptures, and to exhort the church. . . ." Emma may have had literary inclinations, for the revelation also said that "thy time shall be given to writing, and to learning much." Her first assignment was "to make a selection of sacred hymns," a task completed in 1835 when the first Mormon hymnal was published.[56]

Like her father, Isaac, Emma worried about Joseph as a provider. The revelation told her to "lay aside the things of this world, and seek for the things of a better," and promised "an inheritance in Zion." But promises did not feed the household or provide for security in future years. Joseph's revelation made very clear that his support was to come from the church. "In temporal labors thou shalt not have strength, for this is not thy calling," it said. He was to "continue in calling upon God in my name, and writing the things which shall be given thee by the Comforter, and expounding all scriptures unto the church." He was to confirm the churches in "Colesville, Fayette, and Manchester, and they shall support thee. . . ." Joseph was to derive his support like the itinerant Methodist preachers. "Thou shalt take no purse nor scrip, neither staves, neither two coats, for the church shall give unto thee in the very hour what thou needest for food and for raiment, and for shoes and for money, and for scrip." He was not to abandon farming altogether: the revelations commanded him to sow his fields, and in late August Joseph paid $200 to Isaac Hale for the thirteen acres along the Susquehannah that Isaac had lent them. But even as he made the purchase, Joseph knew his work was not to be on the land.[57]

The hostility of the past month, the most severe he had known, weighed on Joseph's spirit as much as Emma's. She was told in her revelation that her calling was to "be for a comfort unto my servant, Joseph Smith, Jun., thy husband, in his afflictions, with consoling words, in the spirit of meekness." Joseph needed her love. He also took comfort in the revelations and the signs of divine approval of his work. Although admonished at the time to "require not miracles," he later remembered that, "notwithstanding all the rage of our enemies, we had much consolation, and many things occurred to strengthen our faith and cheer our hearts." What he had in mind specifically was a dream of Sally Knight that foretold his second visit to Colesville in July. He clung to these little signs for confidence "that eventually we should come off victorious, if we only continued faithful to Him who had called us forth from darkness into the marvelous light. . . ." Joseph was long grateful that "the Lord who well knew our infantile and delicate situation, vouchsafed for us a supply of strength. . . . " A revelation "was a precious morsel" of life-giving bread.[58]

The revelations gave no assurance that his troubles would soon end. He was told to "be patient in afflictions, for thou shalt have many. . . ." On the other hand, he was not required to bear ridicule and abuse without redress. "Whosoever shall lay their hands upon you by violence, ye shall command to be smitten in my name; and behold, I will smite them according to your words, in mine own due time." When a place failed to receive the Prophet, he was to "leave a cursing instead of a blessing, by casting off the dust of your feet against them as a testimony." Nothing in Joseph's temperament or in the revelations encouraged the church to cultivate martyrdom. Though powerless, they were not supine. They were to resist oppression as best they could, if only by casting off the dust of their feet as a testimony against their enemies. The revelation promised Joseph that "whosoever shall go to law with thee shall be cursed by the law."[59]

The Knights' unfailing friendship buoyed up Joseph and Emma through the rough seas of the summer. Sally and Newel visited them in early August at Harmony, and the four of them with John Whitmer held a service together. Neither Sally nor Emma had been confirmed because of the mob's intervention in Colesville. While Joseph was going to obtain wine for the sacrament, a heavenly messenger stopped him and com-manded him not to buy wine or strong drink of his enemies. They were to use new-made wine of their own manufacture. They complied, partook of the sacrament, and confirmed the two sisters. Joseph remembered that they "spent the evening in a glorious manner. The Spirit of the Lord was poured out upon us, we praised the Lord God, and rejoiced exceedingly." The damage done in early July was soon repaired, and the Smiths' ship sailed on.[60]

Meanwhile the Colesville members still awaited Joseph's return to be confirmed in the church. He set August 21 as the day for a meeting, but was delayed while awaiting the arrival of friends from Fayette and Manchester. By August 29 Hyrum and David Whitmer had gotten to Harmony and were able to accompany Joseph and John Whitmer on the treacherous trip. Joseph said they all "called upon our Heavenly Father, in mighty prayer," to open the way. His enemies had advertised a $5 reward to anyone who reported Joseph Smith's entrance into the town. On the way the party of Mormons came upon a road crew that included some of Joseph's bitterest enemies. To his amazement, "they looked earnest[ly] at us, but not knowing us, we passed on without interruption." That night they confirmed the Colesville members, partook of the sacrament, "and held a happy meeting, having much reason to rejoice in the God of our salvation. . . ." The next morning the Mormons slipped away without being detected and arrived home without mishap.[61]

Harmony was not to remain home for long. Relations with Isaac Hale were deteriorating even before the trip to Colesville for the confirmation meeting. He was Joseph's sole protection in Harmony against growing resentment among the neighbors, and they saw to it that Isaac heard every rumor. Isaac Hale's brother-in-law, Nathaniel Lewis, a leader among the Methodists, was a particularly determined enemy who prided himself on his attempts to trip up the Prophet. In August someone got to Isaac and turned him against his son-in-law. The Hales precipitously lost faith in Mormon doctrine and in Joseph. Within a few years they published affidavits maligning his character and presenting him as a money digger. Without Isaac's protection Joseph and Emma were defenseless. They went through with the purchase of Isaac's thirteen-acre farm on August 25 but were already making plans to leave. Peter Whitmer, Sr., once again offered his house as a refuge, and in the last week of August Newel Knight moved Joseph and Emma in a wagon to Fayette.[62]

Joseph's presence was needed in Fayette for other reasons. Through the summer Oliver Cowdery and the Whitmer family began to conceive of themselves as independent authorities with the right to correct Joseph and receive revelation. Oliver had witnessed at least three major revelations with Joseph and been granted the title of Second Elder in the articles and covenants. Perhaps he thought it his prerogative and duty to object when he detected errors. Oliver moved from Harmony to Fayette in July, leaving John Whitmer to work with Joseph on the compilation of the revelations. Shortly after Oliver's arrival at the Whitmers', he wrote Joseph about a mistake in the articles and covenants. The objectionable passage was the present verse 37 of section 20 regarding the qualifications for baptism: "And truly manifest by their works that they have received of the Spirit of Christ unto a remission of their sins." Possibly Oliver felt that the requirement to prove the reception of the Spirit verged dangerously close to the traditional Puritan practice of insisting on evidence of grace before granting church membership. Since ordinarily the minister evaluated candidates, he exercised great power over admissions. Oliver saw in those words the seeds of priestcraft.[63]

Joseph wrote Oliver at once asking "by what authority he took upon him to command me to alter or erase, to add to or diminish from, a revelation or commandment from Almighty God." Rather than risk a misunderstanding, Joseph made a special trip to Fayette to straighten out the matter. Oliver had the whole Whitmer family on his side, and Joseph was hard-pressed to convince them they were wrong. "It was not without both labor and perseverance that I could prevail with any of them to reason calmly on the subject." Christian Whitmer came over to Joseph's point of view first and gradually the others were persuaded. Joseph believed the error had "its rise in presumption and rash judgment," and from the experience they were all to learn "the necessity of humility and meekness before the Lord, that he might teach us of his ways. . . ."[64]

The Fayette group still had more to learn. When Joseph arrived in September, the Whitmers and Oliver were studying the revelations of Hiram Page. Page, the husband of David Whitmer's sister Catherine, had a "roll of papers," as Newell Knight reported it, full of revelations through a stone. Joseph had put aside his seerstone after completing the Book of Mormon translation, and David Whitmer later thought this a big mistake. Late in life he said that only the seerstone revelations received through June, 1829, were trustworthy. Perhaps he believed Page because he took up use of a stone when Joseph had stopped.[65]

Joseph had suppressed the previous criticism of his revelation by force of argument. This time he "thought it wisdom not to do much more than to converse with the brethren on the subject," and wait for the conference scheduled for September 26. Joseph recognized the danger of competing revelations. Newel Knight, who came up for the conference, found Joseph "in great distress of mind." The two of them occupied the same room before the conference, and Newel said "the greater part of the night was spent in prayer and supplication." Rather than face the brethren individually and risk another outburst later, Joseph turned to the church to settle the matter for good. During the conference meeting the stone was discussed at great length. Joseph brought a new revelation dealing with Hiram Page to the session, but it was not by sheer revelatory power that Joseph prevailed. The major point he made was that Page's revelations "were entirely at variance with the order of God's house, as laid down in the New Testament, as well as in our late revelations." He turned the question into a constitutional issue: did Hiram Page have the authority to promulgate revelation? The new revelation emphasized that the reception of revelation for the church had "not been appointed unto him, neither shall anything be appointed unto any of this church contrary to the church covenants." The articles and covenants adopted at the previous conference now proved their usefulness. They laid out procedures and leadership structure that inhibited erratic claims to authority and revelation, which were the downfall of other charismatic religious groups. "For all things must be done in order," the revelation insisted, "and by common consent in the church, by the prayer of faith." Joseph had Oliver read the articles and covenants to the conference, and then Joseph himself explained their meaning. After the investigation "Brother Joseph Smith, Jr., was appointed by the voice of the conference to receive and write Revelations and Commandments for this Church."[66]

The conference established Joseph's authority as the head of the church. A revelation received on the day of organization had designated him as "a seer, a translator, a prophet, an apostle of Jesus Christ. . . ." The Page incident clarified the rights of that office, particularly in relation to Oliver, the Second Elder and in many instances a co-revelator with Joseph. Joseph was Moses, to "receive commandments and revelations in this church." Oliver was Aaron, "to declare faithfully the commandment and the revelations . . . unto the church." Oliver might speak authoritatively but was not to "write by way of commandment, but by wisdom." The Prophet alone was to inscribe scripture. To leave no question, Oliver was bluntly told not to "command him who is at thy head, and at the head of the church . . . ," for only Joseph had the "keys of the mysteries, and the revelations."[67]

Although not yet twenty-four, Joseph showed his capacity to take command and to exercise the power of his office even with his closest comrades. The church as a whole honored him for it. Newel Knight said of the conference that "it was wonderful to witness the wisdom that Joseph displayed on this occasion, for truly God gave unto him great wisdom and power, and it seems to me, even now, that none who saw him administer righteousness under such trying circumstances, could doubt that the Lord was with him, as he acted." The revelations directed Oliver to tell Hiram Page that he had been deceived, and by the end of the investigation "Brother Page, as well as the whole Church who were present, renounced the said stone, and all things connected therewith, much to our mutual satisfaction and happiness."[68]

GATHERING

As was frequently true in subsequent years, Joseph did not take his triumph at the conference as an occasion to slow down for a time. The conference revelations marked the beginning of a major new initiative: missionary work to the Indians. Oliver received a commission to go to the Lamanites in the same revelation that directed him to subordinate himself to Joseph. Soon after, Peter Whitmer was told to join Oliver, so that the conference was able to engage in "singing and prayer in behalf of Brother Oliver Cowdery and Peter Whitmer, Jr., who were previously appointed to go the Lamanites." In October Parley Pratt and Ziba Peterson were added to the party. The revelations firmly placed Oliver at the head, since "none have I appointed to be his counselor over him in the church, concerning church matters, except it is his brother, Joseph Smith, Jun." The three others solemnly covenanted to "assist him faithfully in this thing, by giving heed unto all his words and advice." As a precaution, the whole group was also admonished to "give heed to that which is written, and pretend to no other revelation. . . ." Emma and the other sisters made clothing for the men, and in late October they set out for the West and Indian territory.[69]

The Book of Mormon gave the missionaries ample reason for making the long trip to the Missouri. The book's main purpose was to recover the lost remnant of ancient Israel. The revelations spurred Joseph to translate the plates, that "through the testimony of their fathers," the knowledge of Christ would reach the "Lamanites, and the Lemuelites, and the Ishmaelites, who dwindled in unbelief." As it took shape in the fall of 1830, however, the mission to the Lamanites came to be seen as a piece of a larger plan. In the solemn covenant that Oliver Cowdery signed on October 17, he promised to teach the Indians and "to rear up a pillar as a witness where the Temple of God shall be built, in the glorious New Jerusalem." Oliver was to locate a site for the holy city prophesied in both the biblical book of Revelations and the Book of Mormon, and the identification of that place affected the whole world, not just the Indians.[70]

The idea of a New Jerusalem came from John the Revelator, who saw "the holy city, new Jerusalem, coming down from God out of heaven, prepared as a bride adorned for her husband." The Book of Mormon added specificity to the brief Bible reference. Ether, the Book of Mormon prophet, looking beyond the days of Christ's mortal life on earth, "spake concerning a New Jerusalem upon this land," meaning America. Oliver Cowdery's call to an Indian mission brought the holy city still closer to home when it said that the city of Zion "shall be on the borders of the Lamanites." The elders at the September conference knew that the border of Indian territory lay along the western edge of Missouri, where the federal government was forcibly moving eastern states' Indians.[71]

Both John and Ether described a city descending from heaven after the earth had been entirely renewed, but Ether's comment about a New Jerusalem to "be built upon this land" implied a humanly constructed city as well. The remnant of Joseph in America shall "build up a holy city unto the Lord, like unto the Jerusalem of old." During his American visit the resurrected Christ described a future time when the remnant of Jacob and converted gentiles would "build a city, which shall be called the New Jerusalem," a place where all of the Lord's scattered people could gather. Oliver went to the Missouri to mark the spot where an actual city could go up.[72]

These references assumed more importance because of another revelation given to Joseph Smith just before the September conference. The revelation described in gruesome detail the calamities to come upon the earth before Christ's Second Coming: a plague of flies, maggots, flesh falling from people's bones and eyes from their sockets, signs in the heavens, a destructive hailstorm, and devouring fire. In the meantime, the revelation said, the church's job was to find the righteous and bring them to safety. "And ye are called to bring to pass the gathering of mine elect; for mine elect hear my voice and harden not their hearts; wherefore the decree hath gone forth from the Father that they shall be gathered in unto one place upon the face of this land, to prepare their hearts and be prepared in all things against the day when tribulation and desolation are sent forth upon the wicked." The New Jerusalem was to be a refuge against the coming terrors. The conversion of the Indians, the building of the New Jerusalem, and the gathering of the elect all flowed together into a single plan to prepare the world for the Savior's Second Coming.[73]

Circumstances prepared the Saints to study this revelation carefully. Interest in the millennium reached a high point among British and American Christians between 1828 and 1832. Conferences, sermons, books, plans, and reforms of every sort were oriented around the biblical prophecies of a reign of righteousness. Millennial speculation, however, did not all forecast the same schedule of events. Later students have divided the writings of this period into premillennial and postmillennial with reference to the item when the Second Coming was to occur. The premillennialists located Christ's return before the thousand years of peace and the postmillennialists after the millennium. The difference in scheduling affected the basic outlook of the two groups. The premillennialists emphasized cataclysmic destruction of the wicked and thus, by inference, the impotence of human institutions, even the church, to improve society or halt the course of wickedness. The postmillennialists believed the world would move gradually into righteousness and peace through missionary work, reform, and the expansion of the Christian church. God's power worked through human institutions to establish a millennial society.[74]

The early Mormon view of the millennium cut across this division. The September revelation explicitly said that Christ was to return before the millennium. Vivid descriptions of the calamities awaiting the wicked also put Mormons on the premillennial side. And yet the building of a New Jerusalem, an actual society for the righteous, and the great stress on human effort, tinged Mormonism with postmillennialism. Converts were not to be passive onlookers while the powers of heaven cleansed the earth. There was a definite work for the infant church to accomplish.

This millennial perspective affected the life of every convert. From the beginning Joseph's revelations had stressed the work awaiting each one. The revelations at the September conference defined much more precisely what the work was to be. The people of the earth, the Indians especially but not exclusively, were to be taught faith and repentance, and gathered to the city of Zion, where they could weather the tribulations and prepare themselves for the Second Coming. Although not until the next winter were the details clarified, already there was a clear hint of a holy society that was to grow until it filled the earth.[75]

The individual revelations received after the fall conference interwove this new perspective into the calls to the work. Parley Pratt's brother Orson, who had been converted by his brother in Canaan, New York, was told to "lift up your voice as with the sound of a trump, both long and loud, and cry repentance unto a crooked and perverse generation, preparing the way of the Lord for his second coming." Ezra Thayre and Northrop Sweet were informed that the Lord would "gather mine elect from the four quarters of the earth, even as many as will believe in me." When they were told to "thrust in your sickles, and reap with all your might, mind, and strength," the words were the same as in earlier calls, but now gathering and the Second Coming deepened the purpose. Sidney Rigdon learned that "the poor and the meek shall have the gospel preached unto them, and they shall be looking forth for the time of my coming, for it is nigh at hand—." The obscurity and ignorance of church members was part of the plan. "Wherefore," the revelation to Rigdon said, "I call upon the weak things of the world, those who are unlearned and despised, to thrash the nations by the power of my Spirit. . . ."[76]

The revelation on the premillennial gathering threw into question the routine activities of everyday life. Were the Mormons to stay in New York or were they soon to be gathered elsewhere? What would be required in preparation for the Second Coming? Through the fall of 1830, while Oliver and the Lamanite missionaries explored the Indian territory for the site of the temple and the city of Zion, every plan for the future was tentative. Joseph and Emma labored under a double uncertainty. Besides awaiting light on a gathering place, they were without a house or a farm in New York. Hostility in Harmony made return there unlikely in the near future, although they held on to their house and thirteen acres until June 28, 1833, when it was finally sold. The elder Smiths were unable to support them, for they were living with Hyrum and in flux themselves. In the fall Joseph received a revelation that Hyrum's life was in danger and that he and Jerusha should move from Manchester to Colesville. In early October they moved in with Newel and Sally Knight, and Hyrum took over leadership of the Colesville church. By October 14 he was preaching at a meeting held at Hezekiah Peck's. Joseph also urged his father to leave Manchester for the same reason—to avoid harassment from the local people. A revelation said that Joseph, Sr., was to move to Waterloo near the Whitmers, the one locality where Mormons were still welcome.[77]

The day after Hyrum left for Colesville, Lucy and Joseph, Sr., and their daughter Lucy found themselves alone. Don Carlos, Catherine, and William were away, and Samuel had taken another missionary tour to see John Greene and his wife. The neighbors began to call through the day asking for Hyrum, and that night Joseph, Sr., fell ill. Around ten o'clock the next morning a Quaker gentleman came to speak with Joseph, Sr. The Quaker had purchased Joseph Sr.'s note for $14 and wanted to collect. The possessor of a note of indebtedness had the right to collect when he chose, but because of the shortage of currency, debts were ordinarily collected at times when cash was available and after fair warning. Joseph offered to pay $6 on the spot and asked for a little time. The gentleman was adamant and threatened prosecution. Finally the point came clear. As Lucy remembered the conversation, he said, "If thou dost not pay me immediately, thou shalt go forthwith to the jail, unless . . . thou will burn up those Books of Mormon; but if thou wilt burn them up, then I will forgive thee the whole debt." Lucy offered her gold beads, to no avail. The gentleman beckoned a constable who had been waiting outside, and Joseph was carried off without even a moment to finish his porridge.[78]

Lucy applied the next morning for papers that would release Joseph, Sr., from jail to the prison yard, where at least he could work to repay the debt. On her return a young man inquired after Hyrum to collect a debt on behalf of Dr. McIntyre. Lucy arranged for corn and beans to be carted to the doctor's house for payment the next day. The following night, after the account had been erased, while she was home alone with her nine-year-old daughter, Lucy was once again accosted for the McIntyre debt. A rap came at the door, and a stranger asked for Hyrum. He was soon followed by a second, third, and fourth. Claiming a search warrant, they threatened to take some corn they found above Hyrum's room. While they were searching, Lucy happened to glance out the window and nearly fainted at what she saw. "As far as I could see by the light of two candles and a pair of carriage lamps, the heads of men appeared in every direction, some on foot, some on horseback, and the rest in wagons." Lucy stepped aside for a moment to pray, when to her great relief William bounded into the room. Ever impulsive, William took in the situation at a glance and sprang up the stairs brandishing a handspike. He chased the four strangers outside and confronted the crowd. At his appearance the lights were extinguished, and in an instant the mob disappeared.[79]

Samuel came in late that night aching from a heavy cold and a twenty-one-mile walk since sunset. On hearing the news, he agreed to go the next day to his father in the Canandaigua jail. He found Joseph, Sr., in a sorry state. Debtors were expected to provide their own keep while imprisoned, and Joseph had eaten only a small basin of weak broth in three days. Samuel bought food and arranged for his father's release to the jail yard. Joseph obtained employment with a cooper and in thirty days repaid the debt and earned enough to bring home extra clothing for the family. On Sundays he preached the Gospel and converted two persons whom he baptized after his release. In late October or early November he was reunited with his family.[80]

In his father's absence, Samuel took over the responsibility for moving the family to Waterloo. They moved into the house of one Kellog, located between Waterloo and Seneca Falls, although actually within the boundaries of Seneca Falls. The neighbors welcomed them with food and visits. The contrast with the animosity in Manchester touched Lucy. The Smiths were soon holding evening meetings for singing and prayer which a dozen or more people attended.[81] Joseph and Emma soon followed the elder Smiths to Waterloo. Joseph and Emma had stayed with the Whitmers for the September conference and then spent time in Manchester while the elder Smiths were there. Joseph meanwhile had preached in various places. They were not to remain in Waterloo for long. It was but another temporary stopping place. Forces were gathering that would uproot them entirely.[82]

News came first from an unexpected quarter. En route to Indian territory, the Lamanite missionaries paused in northeast Ohio to bring word of the Book of Mormon to Sidney Rigdon, Parley Pratts's associate in the Campbellite movement. Rigdon and over a hundred of his followers in Mentor, Painesville, and Kirtland had accepted the Gospel and been baptized. On December 10 Rigdon and Edward Partridge from Painesville arrived in Waterloo in the middle of a meeting at Joseph Smith Sr.'s house. Partridge, who had withheld judgment until he met the Prophet, was baptized the next day.[83]

In many respects Rigdon was the most auspicious of the converts to Mormonism to that point. Although reared on a farm in central Pennsylvania, Rigdon qualified as a Baptist minister in 1819, when he was twenty-six, by dint of self-education. He preached in Trumbull County, Ohio, and in Pittsburgh until 1824, when he broke with the Baptists over the doctrine of infant damnation. While he worked as a tanner for two years with his brother-in-law, Rigdon was discussing religion with Alexander Campbell and Walter Scott, two independent and vigorous young men who wished to restore the Christian church to its original purity and sought to eliminate every belief and form of worship that was not mentioned in the New Testament. In 1826 Rigdon moved to Bainbridge, Ohio, where he preached the doctrines he had developed in discussions with

Campbell and Scott. Scott meanwhile was preaching what he called the "restored gospel" in nearby New Lisbon, Ohio, with great success. In the course of a thirty-year ministry he was said to have converted a thousand souls a year. Attracted by similar doctrines, people in Mentor, Ohio, asked Rigdon to preach, and although he refused a salary, they began a house for him. He was preaching in a number of nearby towns when Parley Pratt fell under Rigdon's influence and set out on the fateful mission to New York in the summer of 1830 that brought Pratt into contact with the Book of Mormon.[84]

Campbell and Rigdon had a falling out in August, 1830, over Rigdon's organization of a communal society. In October Parley Pratt presented Rigdon with a copy of the Book of Mormon. The doctrines of a literal gathering and an imminent millennium impressed him. He could not believe that a twenty-five-year-old could have written the book. After two weeks of close study he accepted baptism at Pratt's hands. His Mentor congregation was furious and refused him the house that had just been completed. Sidney moved to Hiram and formed a little church of Mormon converts. In the late fall he and Edward Partridge, a prosperous hatter and one of Rigdon's followers, determined to meet Joseph Smith in person.[85]

David Whitmer offered the view of one New York Mormon with regard to Rigdon: "Rigdon was a thorough Bible scholar, a man of fine education, and a powerful orator." He had qualities none of them could match, including Joseph. Resentment and jealousy tinged Whitmer's comments. He later observed that Rigdon "soon worked himself deep into Brother Joseph's affections, and had more influence over him than any other man living." "Brother Joseph rejoiced believing that the Lord had sent to him this great and mighty man Sydney Rigdon, to help him in the work."[86]

But as noteworthy as the awe and envy of the rustic converts was the confidence with which Joseph dealt with a man thirteen years his senior and far his superior in education. Rigdon received a revelation and call like so many of Joseph's associates in which Sidney was told "thou wast sent forth, even as John, to prepare the way before me, and before Elijah which should come, and thou knewest it not." The role of the Prophet and, by implication, their relationship was succinctly stated: "I have sent forth the fulness of my gospel by the hand of my servant Joseph; and in weakness have I blessed him." Rigdon's superior learning was of secondary importance, for to Joseph had been given "the keys of the mystery of those things which have been sealed, even things which were from the foundation of the world. . . ." Sidney was to "watch over him that his faith fail not," and to "write for him; and the scriptures shall be given, even as they are in mine own bosom to the salvation of mine own elect. . . ." Joseph was the revelator and Sidney the scribe, support, and spokesman who was to "preach my gospel and call on the holy prophets to prove his words, as they shall be given him."[87]

In the early winter Joseph and Sidney toured the church centers in New York, preaching as they went. Wherever he spoke—Fayette, Canandaigua, Palmyra, or Colesville—Sidney made an impression. Emily Coburn said that, when Sidney came to Colesville, "we did not class him as a Mormon, as we were informed that he was a Baptist minister, from Paynesville, Ohio." At Palmyra "the people stood trembling and amazed, so powerful were his words, and some obeyed. . . ." But no amount of learning or eloquence could prevail against the fixed opinions of the people. In Colesville, despite the respect temporarily afforded him, "it was all in vain," John Whitmer said. The enemies of the Prophet threatened to kill both Joseph and Sidney. Sidney "was too smart for them therefore they wanted to trouble him."[88]

The reaction in Colesville and elsewhere confirmed the wisdom of a revelation received just before Joseph and Sidney left on their preaching tour, commanding them to "go to the Ohio." In fact, the entire church was to move, awaiting the time when Oliver Cowdery returned from the Lamanites with word about the site for the city of Zion in the West. John Whitmer was sent ahead with a letter of introduction to the Ohio Mormons, while Joseph made preparations to leave.[89]

The quarterly conference met as scheduled at Peter Whitmer's in Fayette on January 2, 1831. The usual business was conducted, but a further revelation about the move to Ohio pre-empted everyone's attention. The revelation explained that one reason for going, as everyone knew, was "that the enemy in the secret chambers seeketh your lives." The other reason was to begin the gathering. "And that ye might escape the power of the enemy and be gathered unto me a righteous people, without spot and blameless—wherefore, for this cause I gave unto you the commandment that ye should go to the Ohio. . . ." The members interpreted this to mean that they were now "to begin the gathering of Israel." The revelation contained hints of a new society to be founded. "There I will give unto you my law; and there you shall be endowed with power from on high." "Hear my voice and follow me," they were promised, "and you shall be a free people, and ye shall have no laws but my laws when I come, for I am your lawgiver, and what can stay my hand." From their base in Ohio, missionaries would "go forth among all nations" and "Israel shall be saved, and I will lead them whithersoever I will. . . ."[90]

Quick sale of property to effect a sudden move inevitably meant poor prices and substantial losses. The revelation foresaw the difficulty. "And they that have farms that cannot be sold, let them be left or rented as seemeth them good." The members were reminded that "the riches of the earth are mine to give," and told that the Lord would give them "greater riches, even a land of promise, a land flowing with milk and honey, upon which there shall be no curse when the Lord cometh. . . ." Meanwhile they were not to forget the poor. Men should be appointed to "look to the poor and the needy, and administer to their relief that they shall not suffer; and send them forth to the place which I have commanded them." The church was to "beware of pride" as the Lord subsequently blessed them with riches, "lest ye become as the Nephites of old."[91]

The revelation closed with an admonition to each one to "go to with his might, with the labor of his hand, to prepare and accomplish the things which I have commanded." By the last week of January the advance party was ready for departure. Sidney Rigdon delivered a parting sermon from the courthouse steps in Waterloo to the populace at large, warning them to flee from the wrath to come. Joseph traveled with Emma and Joseph Knight in a sleigh provided by Joseph Knight, Jr. By the first week in February the Prophet was in Kirtland.[92]

Through the winter and early spring a few members made their way west to Kirtland in small parties. Joseph asked that Hyrum and Joseph Smith, Sr., come as soon as they could. Samuel, Sophronia, and Catherine Smith went ahead of their parents. Orson Pratt and Emily Coburn were there by early spring. The rest sold their property as they could and waited for the ice to break. In late April the Colesville members, under the supervision of Newel Knight and Joseph Knight, Jr., loaded themselves and their belongings into oxen-drawn covered wagons and headed for Ithaca. At the foot of Lake Cayuga they transferred everything to a boat for the trip to the head of the lake, where they changed to a canal boat. The Cayuga and Seneca Canal connected the lake with the Erie Canal. By May 1 they were all in Buffalo.[93]

Lucy Smith put a party of fifty aboard a canal boat from a dock not far from her front door. The Smith house fronted on the Cayuga and Seneca Canal. Thomas Marsh led another party of about thirty Waterloo Saints. They left around May 3 or 4 and reached Buffalo by May 8.[94] Heavy ice on Lake Erie blocked further passage of both Colesville and Waterloo Saints. While the others marked time, Lucy loaded her party onto a steamboat and told them all to pray for clear water. A crack appeared in the ice, the captain cast loose, and the boat scraped through as the ice closed behind them. She reached Fairport, just eleven miles from Kirtland, about May 11. The others arrived three days later, after the ice had cleared.[95]

A Palmyra group of about fifty, including Martin Harris, set out for Kirtland in mid-May. That was the end of the large migrations. By June,

1831, the bulk of the first year's converts had left New York. Missionaries criss-crossed back through the state in subsequent years, teaching their kinsmen and preaching publicly when they could obtain a platform. Brigham Young and Heber Kimball would be baptized in New York in 1832. But New York would never again be Mormon headquarters. The Hill Cumorah, the place of the First Vision, the Smith farmhouse, the Peter Whitmer farm — all were left behind, their importance for the founding of the church sacrificed for the moment to the demands of expanding it. The truly sacred places lay to the west, at the sites for the city of Zion and the temple. The Mormons left New York to escape their enemies, but still more in search of the designated places where under the inspiration of God they could build Zion and plant their families in a promised land.[96]

CHAPTER VI

THE RESTORATION
OF ALL THINGS

Joseph Smith was scarcely twenty-five when he and Emma arrived in Kirtland in early February, 1831. They had been married four years and a week. Emma was pregnant with twins, a boy and a girl. In April they would be born and die within three hours.

Joseph entered a new world when he stepped out of the sleigh in Kirtland. He strode into the store of Newell K. Whitney and Sidney Gilbert on Main Street and into the midst of friends. Whitney and Gilbert were two of nearly a hundred converts who awaited Joseph's arrival. The Smiths' poverty and the stories of money digging receded into the background in the face of his following in Kirtland. "I am Joseph the Prophet," he told Newell Whitney as they shook hands.[1] Although the editor of the *Painesville Telegraph* would diligently import all of the Palmyra gossip, Joseph Smith's role as Prophet, the leader of a church and people, would henceforth predominate, even in the public mind.

In the week that Joseph and Emma arrived, Thomas Campbell sent a letter to Sidney Ridgon, long considered by Campbell "not only as a courteous and benevolent friend, but as a beloved brother and fellow-laborer in the gospel." "Alas! how changed, how fallen!" Campbell wrote. He addressed Rigdon "as the professed disciple and public teacher of the infernal book of Mormon," challenging him to debate the proposition of the "all-sufficiency and the alone-sufficiency of the Holy Scriptures of the Old and New Testaments, vulgarly called the Bible, to make every intelligent believer wise to salvation. . . ."[2]

The debate with Thomas Campbell never occurred in public, but it must have repeatedly taken place privately as former followers of Sidney Rigdon made choices for themselves. A Disciple who lived through the period said the nearby church at Mentor where Sidney Rigdon preached "was shaken as by a tempest under the outbreak of Mormonism." For some like Parley Pratt, Mormonism added an element missing from the Disciples' gospel — divine authority — and they believed Joseph Smith. Others held to the established Disciple principle that before faith must come a well-authenticated testimony of a divine miracle. To pray for faith was to tempt God. A contemporary Disciple observed "that when the Mormon preacher approached a disciple, with the proposition to pray for a sign, or evidence of the truth of his system, he was met with an intelligent refusal. . . ." Such Disciples dismissed Mormonism as "pretentious visions," in "nowise superior to those of the first Shakers, Jemima Wilkinson, the French Prophets, etc."[3]

The stir Mormonism caused among the followers of Campbell and Rigdon informs us, in the absence of direct accounts, how Mormonism probably appeared to prospective converts. The rapid conversion of Sidney Rigdon and many of his followers in Kirtland suggests that Mormon missionaries taught a familiar Gospel. Judging from later accounts and sermons, Mormons concentrated on the same simple New Testament principles that distinguished Disciple preaching. In 1830 Mormonism probably was closer to the Campbellite and related movements than to any other Christian group. At the same time, Mormonism offended Disciples, who associated it with Jemima Wilkinson and the French Prophets more than the New Testament. The opposing responses suggest that Mormonism, while resembling the primitive Gospel movement in some respects, went beyond it in others. A comparison brings into focus what Mormonism had become by the time Joseph Smith and his followers left New York in 1831.[4]

The founders of the Disciples movement were Alexander Campbell and his father, Thomas Campbell. Alexander Campbell arrived in the United States in 1809 from Scotland following his father, who came in 1807. Both men desired to unite the diverse Christian denominations on the basis of a rigorous adherence to New Testament teachings.

In 1808 Thomas Campbell broke with the Presbyterians and formed a Christian association for study and worship. His followers' search of the scriptures soon persuaded them that immersion was the only authorized mode of baptism, and by 1813 the Campbellites applied for admission to a Baptist association. The Baptists accepted them even though the Campbells refused to acknowledge the validity of any of the traditional confessions of faith on the grounds that the New Testament was their sole guide. In 1824 Alexander Campbell published a series of thirty-two essays entitled *A Restoration of the Ancient Order of Things* to show that a radical commitment to New Testament doctrines and practices would bring the millennium.[5]

By 1827 seventeen Baptist churches in northeast Ohio and western Pennsylvania, grouped into the Mahoning Association, worshipped under the influence of Alexander Campbell. Although confident that they had found the truth, the churches were small and not growing. When fourteen of the churches gave their annual reports in 1827, the net gain for all of them was only sixteen members. The total membership was around 500. Campbell appealed to his friend Walter Scott, then the principal of an academy in nearby Steubenville, to become a traveling evangelist in the Mahoning Association. Under the pressure of this assignment, Scott struggled to pull together the Disciples' preaching in a form that would appeal and convert. The result was a summary of the scriptural order for the conversion of sinners which he later called "The Gospel Restored": (1) faith; (2) repentance; (3) baptism; (4) remissions of sins; (5) the Holy Spirit; (6) eternal life through patient continuance in well doing.[6]

Though simple, the effect on audiences was sensational. A prominent Presbyterian in New Lisbon who happened into a meeting and caught the end of Scott's sermon immediately presented himself for baptism. Scores of baptisms followed, and the revival spread. Sidney Rigdon visited Scott in March, 1828, and adopted Scott's method with similar results. Twenty-one persons came forward to be baptized on Rigdon's first attempt in Mentor. Within a short time fifty were added to his congregation there, and a new congregation was formed in Kirtland. By the end of the year the Disciples measured their increase in the hundreds, and the Mahoning Association doubled in size.[7]

The simple principles most emphasized by Scott—faith, repentance, and baptism for the remission of sins—resembled closely the teaching of the Mormon missionaries, but they had a different significance for the Disciples. Walter Scott considered them to be a breathtaking discovery because he and the Campbells were struggling to free themselves from Calvinistic evangelism. The key question for Calvinists of this generation was, when was faith real and when was forgiveness granted? The evangelical denominations—Congregationalists, Presbyterians, Methodists, and Baptists—believed that only grace could implant faith and signify forgiveness. The true convert passed through a tortuous "experience" in which he suffered painful guilt before relief came with an infusion of divine grace. Before a person could have confidence in the remission of his sins and even gain admission to the church, he or she must relate such an experience.

The Campbells objected to this strenuous psychological ordeal and tried to reduce conversion to a simpler order. Walter Scott relied on the sermon of Peter in Acts 2:38 for this "plan of salvation." There the scripture said that repentant believers were to be baptized for remission of sins.

Rather than pass through an experience, Christians needed only to believe in Christ, repent, and be baptized. Baptism assumed great importance, for it signaled the remission of sins without the anguish of a revival conversion. As one disciple said, the Calvinist method of conversion "led the soul through 'much tribulation' of darkness and uncertainty, to a faint and flickering hope," while the New Testament process of conversion asked people only to believe, repent, and be baptized. The Disciples reached the vast numbers who had failed under evangelical preaching to experience the proper "states of mind and frames of feeling," and who rejoiced to receive assurance of salvation through obedience to a simple scriptural Gospel that they were able of their own volition to obey.[8]

Sidney Rigdon and the members of his congregations in Kirtland and Hiram were not required to abandon any of their basic principles to accept Mormonism, but while the teachings were the same, the revelations to Joseph Smith showed no signs of the Disciples' struggle against Calvinist evangelism. Converts may have come to Mormonism as an alternative to evangelical conversion, just as they flocked to Walter Scott, but the Mormon revelations did not make the sharp distinctions of the Disciple preachers. A revelation of March, 1830, had instructed the elders to "declare repentance and faith on the Savior, and remission of sins by baptism, and by fire, yea, even the Holy Ghost."[9] Disciples would have objected to remission of sins by baptism *and* by fire, for introducing the Holy Ghost implied the necessity of an experience. The Mormons were less sensitive to that implication simply because they were less preoccupied with revivalist conversion.

The point where the two groups did converge was best described by the Disciples' phrase, "the restoration of the ancient order of things." Both groups believed in an apostasy from Christianity, necessitating a restoration of the doctrine and practices of New Testament Christianity. Mormons may have borrowed the word "restoration," used in this sense, from the Disciples. In the revelations given through 1830 the word "restoration" referred mainly to the restoration of Israel to a knowledge of the ancient covenants and to the favor of the Lord. Later on Mormons used the word to mean the restoration of the church of the New Testament, just as the Disciples did. When he wrote his history in 1838, Joseph spoke of the church's great happiness at the first conference in June, 1830, "to find ourselves engaged in the very same order of things as observed by the holy Apostles of old. . . ."[10]

But a word in common could not conceal the fundamental differences between Mormon and Campbellite teachings. No one at the time dwelt on the similarities, much less acted on them. The followers of Campbell separated themselves from the Baptists in 1830 and reached out to like-minded groups across the country to form a new church. The Christian churches of Kentucky, followers of Barton Stone, and the scattered primitive Gospel congregations in New England gravitated toward the emerging Disciples movement on the principle of a rigorous restoration of New Testament beliefs. The Mormons were never considered as potential allies, nor would Joseph Smith have given a moment's thought to amalgamation with the Campbellites when the various groups came together in 1832.

The most basic modes of understanding created a gulf between them. When Alexander Campbell pulled his teachings together into a treatise in 1835, he explained how he had arrived at his principles: "The object of this volume is to place before the community in a plain, definite and perspicuous style, the *capital principles* which have been elicited, argued out, developed, and sustained in a controversy of *twenty-five years,* by the tongues and pens of those who rallied under the banner of the Bible alone."[11] Joseph Smith had not "elicited, argued out, developed and sustained" his teachings. Mormon principles came by revelation. The only significant controversy in the church to that point was over who received revelation. Campbell repudiated not only Joseph Smith's revelations but the very idea of revelation in modern times. As Thomas Campbell claimed in his February letter to Sidney Rigdon, the Campbellites faith rested on "the all-sufficiency and the alone-sufficiency of the Holy Scriptures."[12] Joseph Smith went too far when he sought to restore not just the teachings but the methods of the New Testament. Campbell believed Christians were to follow the apostles and prophets, not to be apostles and prophets. He put a distance between himself and the Bible. Campbellites objected, for example, to the Mormon ordinance of laying on of hands for the gift of the Holy Ghost. The apostles admittedly practiced it, but Campbell thought only the apostles had the authority. Mormons claimed to have apostolic authority and confidently bestowed the Holy Ghost through the laying on of hands. The ethos of Mormonism was epitomized in the enlargement of the Campbellite word "restoration" into the phrase "the restoration of all things."

The major works of Alexander Campbell and Joseph Smith reflected the differences in their ways of learning. In 1835 Campbell published *The Christian System* and subsequently issued three more editions that grew at last to a volume of 354 pages. Chapter One was entitled "The Universe," and from there Campbell went through "The Bible," "God," "Man as He Was," "Man as He Is," and so on. The Bible alone, for all Campbell's protestations, was not sufficient to systematize and interpret the true meaning of the Gospel without a commentary. Joseph Smith's Doctrine and Covenants, the compilation of his revelations, totaled finally 133 sections in the modern edition, some 250 pages. Each of the revelations was given on a specific occasion, most addressed to an issue of the moment. They are a combination of commandments, rebukes, instructions, apocalyptic visions, history, comfort, and encouragement, anything but a systematic treatise building from basic principles. In its miscellaneous, occasional, unsystematic nature, the Doctrine and Covenants was more like the Bible itself than a theological treatise.

Campbell's *Christian System* reveals how fully he was a child of the Enlightenment, ordering, rationalizing, systematizing. A modern scholar has made a whole book out of Campbell's Enlightenment-inspired attacks on ecclesiastical tyranny and his rationalist defenses of Christianity. In the same spirit Walter Scott the evangelist taught that Christian preachers were to evoke faith in their hearers by presentation of the "evidences" for Christ's divine mission. Like all Christian rationalists, Campbell thought the attestation of miracles lay at the very foundation of belief. But in conformity with rationalist taste, he also repudiated current miracles. Supernatural manifestations of divine power were temporary gifts to the infant church to get it on its feet. In its maturity Christians needed no further evidence. Campbell was as skeptical as the most jaundiced deist about spiritual gifts. He dismissed them all as superstitions, with a vehemence offensive to some of his Baptist associates, who protested that he seemed to foreclose all operations of the Holy Spirit after the apostolic age.[13]

The power of Enlightenment skepticism had far less influence on Joseph Smith, perhaps at first because rationalism had not penetrated Smith family culture very deeply. The Prophet showed no sign of wavering when exposed to the scorn of Palmyra's rationalist editors and to the criticism of Campbell himself. Joseph told of the visits of angels, of direct inspiration, of a voice in the chamber of Father Whitmer, without embarrassment. He prized the Urim and Thummim and the seerstone, never repudiating them even when the major charge against him was that he used magic to find buried money. His world was not created by Enlightenment rationalism with its deathly aversion to superstition. The Prophet brought into modern America elements of a more ancient culture in which the sacred and the profane intermingled and the Saints enjoyed supernatural gifts and powers as the frequent blessing of an interested God.

In 1828 Campbell published a Bible based on the translation of George Campbell, James McKnight, and Phillip Doddridge, with such emendations as replacing the word "baptism" with "immersion" (John the Baptist became John the Immerser). Alexander Campbell wrote a preface and added 100 pages of critical notes and appendices. Joseph Smith also had reason to feel the need of an improved Bible. The prophet Nephi in the Book of Mormon saw that the original Bible had "many plain and precious things taken away" as it passed through the hands of the "great and abominable church." As early as October, 1830, just after the memorable Fayette conference, Joseph undertook a revision. A portion of this new "translation" dated before October 21, 1830, covers Genesis 1:1 through 5:28. But Joseph Smith was not preparing scholarly notes and appendices or retranslating from the ancient languages as Campbell was. He made changes in the wording of the scriptures themselves, based not on his learning but on revelation.[14]

Joseph Smith's patient attention to the Old Testament text reflected another difference. Campbell sharply separated the Mosaic and the Christian dispensations. The Christian Gospel was a new institution, not an extension of Old Testament law. Modern Christians were to emulate the new order that began with the birth of the Savior. In contrast, Joseph Smith nearly obliterated the line between New and Old Testaments. In the opening pages of the Book of Mormon, set in 600 B.C., the prophet Lehi beheld a vision of Christ coming to earth. Nephi saw Mary in Nazareth and the birth of Jesus, and from there on the pre-Christian Book of Mormon prophets invariably bore testimony "that Jesus is the Christ, the Eternal God, manifesting himself unto all nations."[15]

By the same token, in the Mormon scheme the prophets of the Old Testament possessed keys and powers still useful in modern times. Later Joseph Smith was to receive ordinations from Moses and Elijah, and the Priesthood of Melchizedek was traced back to the time of Abraham. The restoration of all things included the divine works of all the dispensations preceding Christ.

Joseph's attention to the Old Testament text was an aspect of his interest in the entire span of sacred history and his desire to encompass the whole of it within the restored gospel. In his vision of the Gospel kingdom, ancient and modern were to freely intermingle. In a sense, Joseph Smith transported his followers back beyond enlightenment and medieval times, disregarded the classical age, and joined modern Mormons to the world of ancient Israel and the still more distant past of the Bible patriarchs.

The reunion with the deep past was accomplished by the revival of stories and visions of ancient prophets whose lives thereby entered the moral imaginations of nineteenth-century Saints as models and archetypes. The revision of the Bible provided occasions to recover and revivify the prophets' experiences. Most of Joseph Smith's alterations were words and phrases, but in certain passages entire incidents or long prophecies were added.

Joseph's attention was first turned to the Old Testament in June, 1830. Sometime near the first conference, while wading through "trials and tribulations" as he later reported, "the Lord, who well knew our infantile and delicate situation, vouchsafed for us a supply of strength . . . of which the following was a precious morsel." What followed were "the words of God, which he spake unto Moses at a time when Moses was caught up into an exceedingly high mountain, and he saw God face to face, and he talked with him. . . ."[16] The vision told of Moses's confrontation with Satan and instruction from God wherein the purpose of creation was unfolded. "For behold, this is my work and my glory— to bring to pass the immortality and eternal life of man."[17]

The June revelation was the length of a single long Bible chapter, but it was only an introduction. In the late summer or fall of 1830 Joseph Smith received a continuation that flowed into the familiar. "I am the Beginning and the End, the Almighty God, by mine Only Begotten I created these things; yea, in the beginning I created the heaven, and the earth upon which thou standest. And the earth was without form, and void." The remainder of the revelation continued Genesis as found in the Bible from the creation and fall through the early patriarchs down to Noah before the flood. The final words of the Book of Moses, as it was later called, corresponded to Genesis 6:13.[18]

For the most part Joseph's revised version followed the Bible text with changes in words and phrases only. The most elaborate extension dealt with the life of Enoch, an Old Testament figure who was to loom large in Mormon thinking. In the Bible Genesis Enoch's name occurs in a genealogy as the seventh from Adam and the father of Methusaleh. He is distinguished there for having "walked with God: and he was not; for God took him." He is mentioned briefly in Hebrews and Jude, but what piqued the curiosity of the early converts was the "lost book" of the Bible attributed to Enoch, of which they apparently had knowledge. Commenting on this interest, Joseph wrote in his history that "to the joy of the little flock . . . did the Lord reveal the following doings of olden times, from the prophecy of Enoch."[19]

According to Joseph Smith's revelation, Enoch was a seer and a preacher so powerful that, when he spoke, "the earth trembled, and the mountains fled . . . and the roar of the lions was heard out of the wilderness; and all nations feared greatly." Enoch collected a people and built a city called Zion. Enlarging on a mere hint in the Bible, Joseph Smith's account said that Enoch's whole city was taken up into heaven. It was not to remain there always. Enoch looked down through time to the day when his city would descend again to unite with another Zion, called the New Jerusalem, built by a people gathered from all the earth.[20]

The sacred history of the past at that point flowed into the Mormon present. Soon after Joseph Smith received the vision, Oliver Cowdery trudged through the snow to Missouri to find the place for the holy city, the New Jerusalem, where Enoch and modern Mormons were to be united. In time an economic system for equalizing property and eliminating poverty was revealed and called the Order of Enoch. The Zion of Enoch was to be restored in the present, and the two holy cities were destined to become one.[21]

When Joseph Smith set out to revise the Old Testament in the fall of 1830, he absorbed most of these revelations on Moses into his text of Genesis. Oliver Cowdery recopied part of the initial transcription in October before he left for the West, dividing it into chapters, and John Whitmer kept working on it through October and November. But despite the preparations, the revised version of the Bible never reached print in Joseph Smith's lifetime, thus delaying the appearance of the Prophecy of Enoch in its entirety. It finally appeared in the *Times and Seasons* in Nauvoo in 1843, as part of Joseph Smith's serialized history of the church. In 1851 Franklin D. Richards published the words of Moses and the Prophecy of Enoch in England, and in 1880 they were officially accepted as scripture by the church in Utah.[22]

The delay in publication was not an indication of the marginality of the Moses and Enoch revelations in Mormon belief. Joseph's comments in his history and the eagerness of the Missouri Mormons to publish these revelations in the early numbers of their newspaper speak for the interest of the church, as do the frequent references to Enoch's city and his economic order in other revelations and sermons.

The greatest error would be to mistake these narratives from ancient times as mere objects of curiosity, revealing a Mormon taste for the mysteries of antiquity. The two revelations mark another significant difference from the Campbellites. Just such stories as these anchored Mormon belief. The emphasis of the Campbellites was on distilling the essence of the Gospel from the scriptures, turning Bible stories and preachments into an orderly set of principles. Joseph Smith's revelations, on the other hand, made new sacred narratives that were themselves the foundation of belief. The visions of Enoch and Moses were added to similar visions of Nephi and Ether in the Book of Mormon. The Book of Mormon throughout is composed of happenings wherein God directed, reproved, punished, and redeemed his people. To all these were added Joseph Smith's own experiences, the discovery and translation of the Book of Mormon, the First Vision, the restoration of the priesthoods, and a series of visions and revelations thereafter.

These stories of sacred occurrences formed the substance of Mormon belief as early as 1830. What distinguished Mormonism was not so much the Gospel Mormons taught, which in many respects resembled other

Christians' teachings, but what they believed had happened—to Joseph Smith, to Book of Mormon characters, and to Moses and Enoch. Mormons ever afterward were unable to take much interest in formal theology or systematizing treatises like Campbell's. No such attempts achieved the place in Mormon faith that creeds assumed in other churches. The core of Mormon belief was a conviction about actual events. The test of faith was not adherence to a certain confession of faith but belief that Christ was resurrected, that Joseph Smith saw God, that the Book of Mormon was true history, and that Peter, James, and John restored the apostleship. Mormonism was history, not philosophy.

The result has been a seeming contradiction, noted recently by a modern anthropologist. Mormons believe "their doctrine is already centralized, clearly defined, and easily identified," and at the same time "at the heart of Mormonism is a continous revision of meaning by the individual believer," adapting doctrine to his or her individual circumstances.[23] The sacred stories of Enoch, Moses, Nephi, Mormon, and Joseph Smith envelop Mormons in the realities of divine power and the redemption of Christ, without confining them to the specific formulation of a historic creed. From the stories they distill inspiration and direction, but in manifold forms adaptable to the varied circumstances of modern life and the diversity of personalities. The general meaning of the events has always been unmistakable to the Saints; God has restored His Kingdom to prepare the world for the return of the Savior. But in detail, as applied to individuals, the stories continuously unfold new meanings.

In the final analysis, the power of Joseph Smith to breathe new life into the ancient sacred stories, and to make a sacred story out of his own life, was the source of his extraordinary influence. The strength of the church, the vigor of the Mormon missionary movement, and the staying power of the Latter-day Saints from 1830 to the present rest on belief in the reality of those events.

A NOTE ON SOURCES AND AUTHORITIES

Writings on Mormon history, as has often been noted, suffer from a division between the works of believers and nonbelievers.[1] Readers of this book will recognize at once that the author is a Mormon while Thomas O'Dea or David Brion Davis is not. This division burdens the reader who must always be conscious of the historian's own attitude toward Mormonism. But partisanship has its benefits too. The most important is the industry and thoroughness of researchers on Mormon topics simply because more than the satisfaction of curiosity is at issue. Thanks to the intensity of the students of Mormonism, we know more about the Joseph Smith, Sr., family than any other poor farmers of the nineteenth century. Efforts have been made to recover every act, every word. The Smiths themselves kept records, their friends ransacked their memories for scraps to include in reminiscences, and the enemies of Joseph Smith solicited gossip from everyone who had known the family. Modern researchers have analyzed all of this and added to it information from tax lists, court records, land title files, and all the other sources of modern social history. Though it was not their purpose, the defenders and the critics have told us more about life course and mentality among the poor in nineteenth-century rural society than can be learned from the study of any other American family.

The sources have been assembled and analyzed in four works on which this history is largely based: Richard L. Anderson, *Joseph Smith's New England Heritage* (1971), tracks Joseph Smith's Mack and Smith parents and grandparents across New England; Milton Backman, *Joseph Smith's First Vision* (1971), covers the settlement of the Smith family in Palmyra and Manchester, New York, through the time of Joseph Smith's 1820 vision; Larry C. Porter, "A Study of the Origins of the Church of Jesus Christ of Latter-day Saints in the States of New York and Pennsylvania, 1816-1831" (1971), emphasizes places, structures, and early converts but tells much more; and finally Francis W. Kirkham assembled two volumes of source material in *A New Witness for Christ in America* (1959, 1967). Kirkham's central concern was to vindicate Joseph Smith's account of the discovery and translation of the Book of Mormon, but to achieve that end he collected and reproduced long excerpts from virtually all of the nineteenth-century sources, Mormon and anti-Mormon.

Both the Smiths and the Macks wrote about their lives, some of them even before Joseph Smith became prominent. The most complete narratives are Lucy Mack Smith's *Biographical Sketches of Joseph Smith, the Prophet* (1853), and Joseph Smith, Jr., *History of the Church,* 7 vols. (1932-51). Lucy Smith's account is now augmented by an early manuscript version. Solomon Mack, Lucy's father, and Asael Smith, Joseph Smith Sr.'s father, also wrote. William Smith, Joseph Jr.'s somewhat truculent brother, and his uncle John Smith and cousin George A. Smith each recounted experiences from the early days before the church came into being.[2]

Among Joseph's close associates, Oliver Cowdery composed a series of formal and at times pretentious letters for the *Latter-day Saints' Messenger and Advocate* in Kirtland in 1834 and 1835. The letters are most valuable for Cowdery's personal recollections, but he attempted to incorporate information from others including Joseph Smith himself. The most extensive account from Martin Harris, not a literary person, was an interview in *Tiffany's Monthly* in 1859, which was used by the editor, a Spiritualist, to sustain his thesis that Joseph Smith was under the influence of low-grade, malicious spirits. David Whitmer issued a number of statements over his long life, both to confirm his early testimony and to justify his separation. *An Address to All Believers* (1887), the most detailed, was moved more by the latter spirit. Its theme was Joseph's fallibility and his gradual departure from the true sources of inspiration after April, 1830, as he fell under the influence of Sidney Rigdon. The most candid and revealing of the reminiscences is the unpolished but vivid recollection of Joseph Knight, Joseph Smith's Colesville friend. Although a believer and admirer, Knight's very simplicity and faith enabled him to tell what he knew, oblivious to the requirements of Joseph Smith's office or the need to defend the Prophet. Knight's son Joseph also recorded a much briefer collection of incidents from the early period.[3]

None of the early critics of the Mormons were as candid as Knight. Joseph Smith aroused anger and anxiety from the beginning, and everyone from newspaper editors to next-door neighbors felt obliged to denounce him. The newspapers scoffed at the Book of Mormon as a patent fraud months before it was published. Philastus Hurlbut, an excommunicated Mormon, and E. D. Howe, the Painesville, Ohio, editor who found that the Mormons made good copy, collected statements from the neighbors in 1833 and published them in *Mormonism Unvailed* (1834); they were equally scornful. The affidavits have been challenged for their authenticity because of Hurlbut's and Howe's undisguised animosity, but while questionable in detail, there is little reason to believe the neighbors felt otherwise. Isaac Hale published a statement independently of Hurlbut and Howe in the *Susquehannah Register,* and subsequently two one-time Palmyrans, Pomeroy Tucker and Orasmus Turner, who claimed to know the Smiths, wrote books in the same vein.[4] Public opinion seems to have crystalized by the time the Church of Christ was organized, and only a few lone voices dared credit the Smiths with any degree of veracity or character. For that very reason the accusations of indolence, superstition, and intemperance must be read as expressions of the anxieties troubling New York villagers as much as factual descriptions of Joseph Smith's family.[5]

The Howe-Hurlbut volume effectively stopped the development of Mormon studies by providing an explanation of Joseph Smith and the Book of Mormon so in keeping with nineteenth-century prejudices that no further investigation was required. Joseph Smith was categorized as a charlatan prophet, a nineteenth-century Muhammad who collected followers from among the ignorant and superstitious all for his own gain.[6] Even sophisticated opinion required no more. In Roget's original *Thesaurus* in 1852 the Book of Mormon appeared along with the Koran, Vedas, and Zendavesta under the heading of "pseudo-revelation." The theory of the Book of Mormon as Sidney Rigdon's plagiarization of Solomon Spalding's novel completed the picture. Anti-Mormon scholarship was satisfied to elaborate this interpretive line, and Mormon scholarship after telling Joseph Smith's story did little more than react to the criticism.

The beginning of the modern non-Mormon view dates from I. Woodbridge Riley's Yale Ph.D. dissertation in history, published as *The Founder of Mormonism: A Psychological Study of Joseph Smith, Jr.* (1902). Riley's scorn not just for Joseph Smith but for all religion mars the work for modern readers, and his reliance on the obsolete physiological psychology of Krafft-Ebing detracts from the book's persuasiveness. But *The Founder of Mormonism* is nonetheless the most original and important non-Mormon work of the twentieth century. Riley's greatest achievement was to break with the Spalding theory of the Book of Mormon, which he analyzed at length and destroyed. The removal of one of the pillars of the skeptical interpretation compelled Riley to seek an alternative, which he accomplished with great imagination. He revived Alexander Campbell's short-lived belief that contemporary cultural influences accounted for the Book of Mormon, and identified the nineteenth-century themes in the volume: anti-Catholicism, anti-Masonry, fear of infidelity, and curiosity about Indian origins. Riley was the first to suggest Ethan Smith's *View of the Hebrews* (1823) and Josiah Priest's *Wonders of Nature and Providence* (1825) as sources for the Book of Mormon. He also saw that the emerging science of psychology might throw light on Joseph Smith, and ingeniously applied what was at hand. Following Krafft-Ebing, Riley reached the conclusion that "the psychiatric definition of the epileptic fits the prophet to a dot" (p. 74).[7]

The Spalding theory persisted in the major works on Mormonism in the early twentieth century in spite of Riley's arguments. William A. Linn's *Story of the Mormons* (1902) repeated and extended the older view. Eventually George B. Arbaugh in *Revelation in Mormonism: Its Character and Changing Forms* (1932) followed Riley's lead, as did Fawn Brodie in *No Man Knows My History* (1945). As notable for its journalistic brilliance as for its scholarship, *No Man Knows My History* presented Riley's arguments and findings in a form more palatable to twentieth-century tastes. Krafft-Ebing was laid aside for a less rigorous but more straightforward view of Joseph Smith as an ingenious myth maker, absorbing ideas from his cultural environment. Brodie argued that Joseph Smith wrote the Book of Mormon himself because he was the kind of person able to write such books. In the appendix to a later edition of *No Man Knows My History*, Brodie offered a psychoanalytic interpretation of his character.[8]

No major changes comparable to Riley's innovations have altered the Mormons' view of their own origins. Mormon authors basically tell the story as

Joseph Smith told it.[9] Even so well-informed a book as Donna Hill's *Joseph Smith, the First Mormon* (1977), while adding details and making minor adjustments, attempts nothing fundamentally new. Mormon research in the early period has tended to be motivated by challenges from critics and to concentrate on specific questions: Was there a revival in the Palmyra area in 1820? Did Joseph Smith tell about the First Vision before 1838? Was he tried for money digging in 1826? How did he translate the golden plates? When was the Melchizedek Priesthood restored? Mormons have felt little incentive to strive for a deeper understanding in cultural and social terms when they believe Joseph Smith himself disclosed the deepest meaning of his own work in religious terms.

In recent years a few scholars have attempted a broader social interpretation of Mormon origins. Whitney R. Cross in *The Burned-Over District* (1950), Thomas F. O'Dea in *The Mormons* (1957), and David Brion Davis in "The New England Origins of Mormonism," *New England Quarterly,* 26 (June, 1953):147-60, set the pace. Cross associated Mormonism with the epidemic of New York religious innovations and reform movements in the second quarter of the nineteenth century and explained them all as a Yankee-Puritan response to conditions in a society just past the pioneering period. Davis highlighted the Puritan connections. O'Dea's most significant ideas dealt with the formation of Mormon group identity, but his somewhat unfocused comments on the Book of Mormon suggested an array of possible cultural influences acting on the book.

The most significant work has been accomplished by Marvin Hill, Mario DePillis, and Jan Shipps. Hill has associated the early Mormons with the amorphous Christian primitivism movement of the early nineteenth century. The primitivists were noted for their rejection of contemporary religious culture and a yearning for return to the purity of early Christianity. Hill identifies both common attitudes and actual persons moving from Christian primitivist groups into the Mormon movement. His ideas are consonant with the argument of Mario DePillis with regard to the Mormon quest for authority in a world disordered culturally and socially by rapid change. Hill emphasizes the anti-pluralist attitude of the Mormons in their insistence on their being one true church.[10]

The most imaginative innovation of recent years is found in the work of Jan Shipps, *Mormonism: The Story of a New Religious Tradition* (1985). Benefiting from the perspective of such historians of religion as Mircea Eliade, Shipps argues that Joseph Smith's revelations provided the cultural impetus for a new religious tradition, detached from Catholicism and Protestantism. Mormons departed from the Christian tradition as Christianity itself departed from Judaism. Neither Christianity nor Mormonism repudiated the scriptural past. Both attempted to assimilate, fulfill, and indeed to recapitulate sacred history. But in each case new revelations put the past in a new light and set believers on a new course. Shipps's work breaks the deadlock between believers and skeptics, and offers a perspective on Mormon beginnings that may provide a meeting ground for those Mormon and non-Mormon scholars who are willing to accept her broad view of world religion and world culture.

NOTES

The following frequently cited works appear in the notes only as shortened references.

Anderson, Richard Lloyd. *Joseph Smith's New England Heritage: Influences of Grandfathers Solomon Mack and Asael Smith.* Salt Lake City: Deseret Book Co., 1971.

Backman, Milton V., Jr. *Joseph Smith's First Vision: The First Vision in Its Historical Context.* Salt Lake City: Bookcraft, Inc., 1971.

The Book of Mormon. Tr. Joseph Smith, Jr. Rev. ed. Salt Lake City: Church of Jesus Christ of Latter-day Saints, 1981. Citations are to individual books of the Book of Mormon.

The Doctrine and Covenants of the Church of Jesus Christ of Latter-day Saints. Rev. ed. Salt Lake City: Church of Jesus Christ of Latter-day Saints, 1981.

Jessee, Dean. "Joseph Knight's Recollection of Early Mormon History." *B.Y.U. Studies,* 17 (Autumn, 1976):29-39.

Journal History of the Church of Jesus Christ of Latter-day Saints. Church Archives, Historical Departments, Church of Jesus Christ of Latter-day Saints, Salt Lake City. Abbreviated to Church Archives.

Kirkham, Francis W. *A New Witness for Christ in America: The Book of Mormon.* Vol. 1, 4th ed.; vol. 2, rev. ed. Salt Lake City: Utah Printing Co., 1967, 1959.

Latter-day Saints' Messenger and Advocate (Kirtland, Ohio). Cited as *Messenger and Advocate.*

Porter, Larry C. "A Study of the Origins of the Church of Jesus Christ of Latter-day Saints in the States of New York and Pennsylvania, 1816-1831." Ph.D. diss., Brigham Young University, 1971.

Smith, Joseph. *History of the Church of Jesus Christ of Latter-day Saints.* Ed. B. H. Roberts. 7 vols. Salt Lake City: Church of Jesus Christ of Latter-day Saints, 1932-51.

Smith, Lucy. *Biographical Sketches of Joseph Smith, the Prophet, and His Progenitors for Many Generations.* London and Liverpool: Published for Orson Pratt by S. W. Richards, 1853; reprint ed., New York: Arno Press and the New York Times, 1969.

————. Preliminary Manuscript of *Biographical Sketches of Joseph Smith,* typescript, Church Archives. Pagination through p. 115 was assigned to a photocopy of the typescript. Richard L. Anderson of Brigham Young University is preparing an edition of the Preliminary Manuscript.

Smith, William. *William Smith on Mormonism. . . .* Lamoni, Iowa: Printed at Herald Steam Book and Job Office, 1883.

INTRODUCTION

1. Backman, *Joseph Smith's First Vision,* p. 176.

2. For the general religious ferment within which Mormonism arose, see Gordon S. Wood, "Evangelical America and Early Mormonism," *New York History,* 61 (Oct., 1980):359-86.

3. Backman, *Joseph Smith's First Vision,* p. 177.

4. Albert Post, *Popular Free Thought in America, 1825-1850* (New York: Columbia University Press, 1943), pp. 131-37.

I. THE JOSEPH SMITH FAMILY

1. Lucy Smith, *Biographical Sketches,* p. 279.

2. Ibid.

3. Lucy Smith, Preliminary Manuscript, p. 1.

4. Martha Jane Knowlton Coray, a Nauvoo schoolteacher, recorded Lucy Smith's narrative in a series of notebooks from which a preliminary manuscript was prepared. Coray and Lucy Smith further revised the manuscript, and Orson Pratt published it in Liverpool in 1853 with Lucy Smith's permission. Brigham Young appointed a committee to correct inaccuracies and make other editorial changes. This version was finally published as *History of the Prophet Joseph Smith,* revised by George A. Smith and Elias Smith (Salt Lake City: Improvement Era, 1902). A later edition based on the 1902 edition was published as *History of Joseph Smith by His Mother, Lucy Mack Smith,* with notes and comments by Preston Nibley (Salt Lake City: Bookcraft, 1958). For a discussion of the history of the manuscript and the significance of the revisions in the 1902 edition, see Jan Shipps, "The Prophet, His Mother, and Early Mormonism: Mother Smith's History as a Passageway to Understanding," mimeograph, Church Archives. The version cited throughout is a reprint of the 1853 edition, supplemented by references to the Preliminary Manuscript.

5. Lucy Smith, *Biographical Sketches,* p. 281.

6. Ibid., p. 56.

7. Ibid., pp. 279, 281.

8. Ibid., p. 15.

9. Ibid., p. 33.

10. Solomon Mack gave his birthday as Sept. 26, 1735. Solomon Mack, *A Narrative of the Life of Solomon Mack* (Windsor, Vt., [1811]), p. 5. Lucy Mack Smith gave the same date. Lucy Smith, *Biographical Sketches,* p. 15. The vital

records of Lyme, Conn., show Sept. 15, 1732. For a discussion of the point, see Anderson, *Joseph Smith's New England Heritage,* p. 162. For John Mack and the Lyme economy, see Jackson Turner Main, "The Economic and Social Structure of Early Lyme," in *A Lyme Miscellany,* ed. George J. Willauer, Jr. (Middletown, Conn.: Wesleyan University Press, 1977), pp. 31, 36. Main calculates that John Mack doubled the value of the estate left by his father.

11. The prose portions of Solomon Mack's *Narrative* are conveniently reprinted with excellent notation in Anderson, *Joseph Smith's New England Heritage,* pp. 34-58. All future references are to this edition. Solomon Mack's early life is described on pp. 35-36.

12. Solomon Mack, *Narrative,* p. 41; Anderson, *Joseph Smith's New England Heritage,* p. 31.

13. Anderson, *Joseph Smith's New England Heritage,* pp. 7-10, 162, 26. The average Lyme farm consisted of about 100 acres. Main, "Early Lyme," p. 34.

14. In his 1811 pamphlet Solomon implied that he made the money for his Granville land after his discharge from the army. Lucy excerpted a passage from an earlier and more coherent journal that says he used his war earnings to pay for the land. Solomon Mack, *Narrative,* p. 40; Lucy Smith, *Biographical Sketches,* p. 18.

15. A Marlow deed of 1773 calls him "Solomon Mack of Marlow," but his son Solomon, Jr., was born in Gilsum in 1773. Anderson, *Joseph Smith's New England Heritage,* pp. 10, 12, 165. For conditions in Gilsum and for Mack involvement in settlement, see Silvanus Hayward, *History of the Town of Gilsum, New Hampshire from 1752 to 1879* (Manchester, N.H.: Printed for the author by John B. Clarke, 1881), pp. 17-30, 136, 172, 204, 206, 208.

16. Solomon Mack, *Narrative,* pp. 40-42. His *Narrative* indicates (p. 42) that Solomon may not have lost his Granville holdings entirely until around 1777.

17. Lucy gives 1776 as the year of her birth in *Biographical Sketches* (p. 36), but Gilsum town records say 1775. Anderson, *Joseph Smith's New England Heritage,* p. 182.

18. The population profile is taken from census figures in Hayward, *Gilsum,* pp. 35, 146.

19. Lucy Smith, *Biographical Sketches,* p. 35; Hayward, *Gilsum,* pp. 146-47. There were fifty-nine polls in 1793, which would include all who had earnings. There is a possibility that Gilsum fudged on the downward side in its report on land, animals, and people, since the legislature based the tax load on such returns. Deacon Hayward remembered sixty-seven houses with families in 1794, which would have produced more than the fifty-nine polls in the 1793 census.

20. Solomon Mack, *Narrative,* p. 41.

21. Ibid. Solomon said he carried the army baggage to Skenesborough, now Whitehall, N.Y. Anderson, *Joseph Smith's New England Heritage,* pp. 165-66.

22. Solomon Mack, *Narrative,* pp. 42-43. On Solomon's fits, see I. Woodbridge Riley, *The Founder of Mormonism: A Psychological Study of Joseph*

Smith, Jr. (New York: Dodd, Mead, 1902), pp. 39-76, and Anderson, *Joseph Smith's New England Heritage*, pp. 13-14, 166.

23. Solomon Mack, *Narrative*, p. 42; Anderson, *Joseph Smith's New England Heritage*, pp. 18, 170, 184, 185; Lucy Smith, Preliminary Manuscript, p. 19.

24. Solomon Mack, *Narrative*, pp. 45-49 (quotation from p. 49). McCurdy was from a New Hampshire town that originally was part of Gilsum. Solomon gives the name as Cordy, but probate records say McCurdy or McCordy. Anderson, *Joseph Smith's New England Heritage*, p. 172. Solomon had been in debt to John McCurdy, one of the richest men in Connecticut who died in 1786 with an estate valued at £37,118. Private debts owed to him came to £6,249. Main, "Early Lyme," pp. 42, 45.

25. Solomon Mack, *Narrative*, p. 49; Anderson, *Joseph Smith's New England Heritage*, pp. 19, 21, 67; Lucy Smith, Preliminary Manuscript, p. 14.

26. Solomon Mack, *Narrative*, p. 52; Lucy Smith, Preliminary Manuscript, p. 10; Lucy Smith, *Biographical Sketches*, p. 36.

27. Lucy Smith, *Biographical Sketches*, p. 36.

28. Ibid., pp. 23-29 (quotation from p. 29). The friends listed in a few lines of the Preliminary Manuscript are omitted from the published version. Preliminary Manuscript, p. 19. Richard Anderson collates the various accounts of the sickness of the two sisters in *Joseph Smith's New England Heritage*, pp. 74-87.

29. Lucy Smith, *Biographical Sketches*, pp. 36-37.

30. Hayward, *Gilsum*, pp. 110-11, 104.

31. Solomon Mack, *Narrative*, pp. 52, 54, 57; Lucy Smith, *Biographical Sketches*, p. 19; Lucy Smith, Preliminary Manuscript, p. 35.

32. Lucy Smith, *Biographical Sketches*, pp. 53, 21, 24-29.

33. Ibid., p. 25.

34. Jason Mack removed permanently to Nova Scotia only after Solomon accompanied him there. Solomon's brother Samuel preceded them both. Stephen's move to Detroit and Lucy's to New York were the only truly independent excursions beyond the family circle. Ibid., pp. 30-33; Lucy Smith, Preliminary Manuscript, pp. 14-15.

35. Lucy Smith, *Biographical Sketches*, pp. 30-33, 189; Anderson, *Joseph Smith's New England Heritage*, pp. 28, 180.

36. Lucy Smith, Preliminary Manuscript, p. 102; Lucy Smith, *Biographical Sketches*, p. 37; Porter, "Study of Origins," p. 10.

37. The standard works on the Smith ancestry are Mary Audentia Smith Anderson, *Ancestry and Posterity of Joseph Smith and Emma Hale* ... (Independence, Mo.: Herald Publishing House, 1929), and Joseph F. Smith, Jr., "Asahel Smith of Topsfield, with Some Account of the Smith Family," *Historical Collections of the Topsfield Historical Society*, 8 (1902):87-101. For Samuel Smith, see Anderson, *Joseph Smith's New England Heritage*, pp. 89, 187-89. The obituary appeared in *Salem* (Mass.) *Gazette*, Nov. 22, 1785. Samuel Smith earned the honors he received. An extensive comparison of election patterns in eighteenth-century Massachusetts shows that sons of entrenched aristocratic families were usually elected to major town offices in their twenties. Ordinary men who won

the respect of the town through prudence and proven competence were ordinarily elected to the office of selectman in their early forties. Samuel Smith was chosen moderator, his first major office, in 1758 at age forty-four. Edward M. Cook, Jr., *The Fathers of the Towns: Leadership and Community Structure in Eighteenth-Century New England* (Baltimore: Johns Hopkins University Press, 1976). On the town of Topsfield, see the sketch by Donald Q. Cannon, "Topsfield, Massachusetts: Ancestral Home of the Prophet Joseph Smith," *B.Y.U. Studies,* 14 (Autumn, 1973):56-76.

38. Anderson, *Joseph Smith's New England Heritage,* pp. 91, 92, 193-94.

39. Ibid., pp. 92-94, 193-94.

40. Ibid., pp. 94-95.

41. A discussion of private debt in a New England community is found in Charles S. Grant, *Democracy in the Connecticut Frontier Town of Kent* (New York: Columbia University Press, 1961), pp. 66-82. In nearby Ipswich before the Revolution, the average number of debts owed at death in Chebaco parish was thirty-three. In that period it was unusual for an estate to collapse into insolvency. In the 1780s the economy was badly depressed, and debts owed an estate were harder to collect. Christopher M. Jedrey, *The World of John Cleaveland: Family and Community in Eighteenth-Century New England* (New York: W. W. Norton, 1979), pp. 91-92. See also Peter J. Coleman, *Debtors and Creditors in America: Insolvency, Imprisonment for Debt, and Bankruptcy, 1607-1900* (Madison: University of Wisconsin Press, 1974).

42. Anderson, *Joseph Smith's New England Heritage,* pp. 95-97. The quotation is from John Smith's History, written July 20, 1839, and reproduced, with some omissions, in ibid., pp. 147-54 (quotation from p. 148).

43. Anderson, *Joseph Smith's New England Heritage,* pp. 190, 196, 204.

44. Porter, "Study of Origins," p. 11; Anderson, *Joseph Smith's New England Heritage,* pp. 100, 151-53.

45. Population figures are given in Walter Hill Crockett, *Vermont: The Green Mountain State,* 4 vols. (New York: Century History Co., 1921), 2:499; Hamilton Child, *Gazeteer of Orange County, Vt., 1762-1888* (Syracuse, N.Y.: Syracuse Journal Co., 1888), pp. 472, 535.

46. Samuel Williams, *The Natural and Civil History of Vermont* (Walpole, N.H.: Isaiah Thomas and David Carlisle, 1794), p. 318.

47. Crockett, *Vermont,* 2:511.

48. Anderson, *Joseph Smith's New England Heritage,* pp. 102, 110, 118, 152.

49. Ibid., p. 109. Tunbridge was organized as a town on Mar. 21, 1786, and sent a representative to the legislature the following year. Child, *Orange County,* pp. 473, 478.

50. The complete heading of the letter is: "A few words of advice, which I leave to you, my dear wife and children, whom I expect ere long to leave." The holograph is in the Church Archives. The document was published by Joseph Field Smith in "Asahel Smith of Topsfield." The best modern edition is

in Anderson, *Joseph Smith's New England Heritage,* pp. 124-29. Citations are to this edition. Quotations are on pp. 124, 127, 126.

51. Anderson, *Joseph Smith's New England Heritage,* pp. 95, 195, 203; Asael Smith, "A few words of advice," pp. 124, 127.

52. Asael Smith, "A few words of advice," pp. 126-27.

53. Ibid., pp. 127-28.

54. Anderson, *Joseph Smith's New England Heritage,* pp. 111, 153, 212-14.

55. Ibid., pp. 111-16, 211-17. Of the thirteen members of the Asael Smith family, seven accepted the Mormon faith, three died before they had an opportunity, and three rejected it. John Smith, who was baptized in 1832, was the first to join the church.

56. Ibid., pp. 91-92, 188-89, 207.

57. Asael Smith, "A few words of advice," p. 124.

58. For a description of eighteen-century rationalist Christianity in New England, see Conrad Wright, *The Beginnings of Unitarianism in America* (Boston: Starr King Press, 1955).

59. Joseph Henry Allen and Richard Eddy, *A History of the Unitarians and Universalists in the United States* (New York: Scribner, 1903). The Arminians had no patience with Murray. Wright, *Beginnings,* p. 189.

60. Asael Smith, "A few words of advice," pp. 125-26.

61. David M. Ludlum, *Social Ferment in Vermont, 1791-1850* (New York: Columbia University Press, 1939), pp. 29-34 (quotations on pp. 29, 34).

62. Anderson, *Joseph Smith's New England Heritage,* pp. 106, 207-8. A majority of the inhabitants of Montpelier were said to be Universalist before 1809. Ludlum, *Social Ferment,* p. 34. A more lasting Universalist society came into being in Tunbridge in 1837. Child, *Orange County,* p. 492.

63. Ludlum, *Social Ferment,* pp. 28-30, 41-43, 47-48 (quotations from pp. 30, 43). Nathan Perkins published the narrative of his trip in 1789, and Thomas Robbins did the same in 1796.

64. Lucy Smith, *Biographical Sketches,* pp. 154-57; Anderson, *Joseph Smith's New England Heritage,* p. 105. A daughter-in-law of Asael's said he renounced Universalism on his deathbed. Anderson, *Joseph Smith's New England Heritage,* p. 215.

65. Lucy Smith, *Biographical Sketches,* p. 45; Anderson, *Joseph Smith's New England Heritage,* p. 118. Evidence for a son prior to Alvin is found in Patriarchal Blessing Book, Book A, Dec. 9, 1834, Church Archives. Addressing the Smith family, Joseph Smith, Sr., speaks of "three seats" vacated by death: "The Lord in his just providence has taken from me at an untimely birth a son. . . . My next son, Alvin . . . was taken. . . ." I am grateful to Richard Anderson for this reference. The Smiths also lost Ephraim in 1810. Larry Porter found Lucy Smith's 1799 date for Alvin's birth in conflict with the 1798 date in the Tunbridge vital records. Porter, "Study of Origins," p. 14.

66. Lucy Smith, *Biographical Sketches,* p. 45; Child, *Orange County,* pp. 343, 535; Crockett, *Vermont,* 2:502-3, 513, 521. The mercantile business fre-

quently attracted ambitious men of small fortunes. Robert Gross, *The Minutemen and Their World* (New York: Hill and Wang, 1976), pp. 91-92.

67. Lucy Smith, *Biographical Sketches*, p. 49; Daniel Boorstin, *The Americans: The National Experience* (New York: Random House, 1965), pp. 7-8.

68. Lucy Smith, *Biographical Sketches*, pp. 49-51. Travel time from central Vermont to New York City around 1800 was approximately six days. Allen Pred, *Spatial Dynamics of U.S. Urban-Industrial Growth, 1800-1914* (Cambridge: M.I.T. Press, 1966), p. 177.

69. Lucy Smith, Preliminary Manuscript, p. 26; Lucy Smith, *Biographical Sketches*, p. 51. Larry Porter suggests the possibility that the farm was sold in the family. In June, 1803, Asael Smith mortgaged two of his lots to Thomas Emerson of Topsfield for $700, which may have provided him cash to make the purchase. Porter, "Study of Origins," pp. 17-18.

70. The Smiths' Tunbridge property was immediately adjacent to the Royalton line. Porter, "Study of Origins," pp. 11-12. For the moves of a family of comparable economic circumstances, see the case of Ezekiel Brown, told in Gross, *Minutemen*, p. 90.

71. Porter, "Study of Origins," p. 17; Lucy Smith, *Biographical Sketches*, pp. 49-51; Anderson, *Joseph Smith's New England Heritage*, pp. 174-75; Archibald F. Bennett, "Solomon Mack and His Family," *Improvement Era*, 59 (Jan., 1956):36.

72. Lucy Smith, *Biographical Sketches*, p. 56. Porter has assembled evidence that the attending doctor was Joseph Adam Denison of Bethel, Vt., a community twelve miles northwest of Sharon. "Study of Origins," pp. 19-20n.

73. Lucy Smith, *Biographical Sketches*, pp. 40-41. Solomon Mack was having trouble holding on to the farm. There is evidence of a second mortgage in 1807, and he lost the farm to the previous owner in 1811. Solomon received $500 for the land, which had been priced at $800 when he purchased it, an indication that he had not paid in full when it was deeded back. Anderson, *Joseph Smith's New England Heritage*, pp. 175-76.

74. Donna Hill, *Joseph Smith, the First Mormon* (Garden City, N.Y.: Doubleday, 1977), p. 35; Lucy Smith, Preliminary Manuscript, pp. 26-27; Frederick Chase, *A History of Dartmouth College and the Town of Hanover, New Hampshire (to 1815)* (Brattleboro, Vt.: Vermont Printing Co., 1928), pp. 634-35. Catherine was born July 28, 1812. Lucy Smith, *Biographical Sketches*, p. 41.

75. Lucy Smith, *Biographical Sketches*, p. 60.

76. Joseph A. Gallup, *Sketches of Epidemic Diseases in the State of Vermont from Its First Settlement to 1815* (Boston: T. B. Wait and Sons, 1815); Lucy Smith, *Biographical Sketches*, pp. 59-61.

77. Lucy Smith, *Biographical Sketches*, pp. 62-66; Lucy Smith, Preliminary Manuscript, p. 30; Joseph Smith, Manuscript History of the Church, Book A-1, Note A, p. 131, Church Archives. For a technical description of the infection and the operation, and for the history of Dr. Nathan Smith, see LeRoy S. Wirthlin, "Nathan Smith (1762-1828): Surgical Consultant to Joseph Smith," *B.Y.U. Studies*, 17 (Spring, 1977):319-38, and "Joseph Smith's Boyhood Operation: An 1813 Surgical Success," *B.Y.U. Studies*, 21 (Spring, 1981):131-54.

78. Lucy Smith, *Biographical Sketches*, p. 65.

79. Joseph Smith, Manuscript History, Book A-1, pp. 131-32; Lucy Smith, *Biographical Sketches*, p. 65.

80. Lucy Smith, *Biographical Sketches*, pp. 63-64.

81. Ibid., p. 64.

82. Lucy Smith, Preliminary Manuscript, p. 31.

83. Lucy Smith, *Biographical Sketches*, pp. 61, 63.

84. Ibid., pp. 64-65.

85. Ibid., pp. 54-55.

86. Ibid., pp. 70, 183-84.

87. Ibid., p. 63.

88. Ibid., p. 46.

89. Ibid.

90. Charles A. Johnson, *The Frontier Camp Meeting: Religion's Harvest Time* (Dallas: Southern Methodist University Press, 1955); William G. McLoughlin, *Modern Revivalism: Charles Grandison Finney to Billy Graham* (New York: Ronald Press, 1959); Richard L. Bushman, *From Puritan to Yankee: Character and the Social Order in Connecticut, 1690-1765* (Cambridge, Mass.: Harvard University Press, 1967), chaps. 12, 13; Alan Heimert, *Religion and the American Mind: From the Great Awakening to the Revolution* (Cambridge, Mass.: Harvard University Press, 1966); George M. Marsden, *The Evangelical Mind and the New School Presbyterian Experience* (New Haven, Conn: Yale University Press, 1970).

91. Lucy Smith, *Biographical Sketches*, pp. 37, 47.

92. Ibid., pp. 47-48; Lucy Smith, Preliminary Manuscript, pp. 5, 23.

93. Lucy Smith, Preliminary Manuscript, unnumbered page near the end; Lucy Smith, *Biographical Sketches*, p. 54.

94. Solomon Mack, *Narrative*, p. 57; Lucy Smith, *Biographical Sketches*, pp. 56, 60-61.

95. Lucy Smith, *Biographical Sketches*, pp. 57-58.

96. *William Smith on Mormonism*, p. 6; interview with William Smith, Bradtville, Wis., Nov., 1893, printed in *Salt Lake City Deseret News*, Jan. 20, 1894, in Kirkham, *New Witness for Christ*, 1:44.

97. Lucy Smith, Preliminary Manuscript, p. 33.

98. Anderson, *Joseph Smith's New England Heritage*, p. 213.

99. Lucy Smith, *Biographical Sketches*, p. 66; David M. Ludlum, *The History of American Weather: Early American Winters, 1604-1820* (Boston: American Meteorological Society, 1966), pp. 190-94; Child, *Orange County*, p. 535; Lewis D. Stilwell, *Migration from Vermont* (Montpelier: Vermont Historical Society, 1948), pp. 125-39, 151. The unseasonably cold weather across North America and northern Europe in 1816 is generally attributed to the volcanic explosion of Tambora on Sumbawa in 1815, which blew fifteen cubic kilometers of volcanic ash and pulverized rock into the atmosphere. John D. Post, *The Last Great Subsistence Crisis in the Western World* (Baltimore: Johns Hopkins University Press, 1977).

100. Many Vermonters on their way to New York took the St. Lawrence turnpike from Plattsburgh to Carthage, opened in 1812 and 1813. Stilwell, *Migration,* p. 139. Judging from the $150 debt that Lucy paid at the last minute, the Smith debts could easily have amounted to $200 or $300. Lucy Smith, Preliminary Manuscript, p. 34.

101. Lucy Smith, *Biographical Sketches,* p. 67; Stilwell, *Migration,* p. 135; Lucy Smith, Preliminary Manuscript, p. 34.

102. Lucy Smith, Preliminary Manuscript, pp. 34-35; Lucy Smith, *Biographical Sketches,* pp. 67-68; Joseph Smith, Manuscript History, Book A-1, pp. 131-32.

103. Lucy Smith, *Biographical Sketches,* pp. 68-69. Lydia Mack was injured when the sleigh in which she was riding overturned. She died in 1818. Joseph Smith, Manuscript History, Book A-1, pp. 131-32; Anderson, *Joseph Smith's New England Heritage,* p. 25.

104. The accounts of Joseph, Jr., and Lucy differ slightly on details of the journey. Lucy says she paid Howard; Joseph says his father gave Howard the money. Joseph says the incident with the wagon took place in Utica; Lucy, who presumably had a more accurate sense of location than her ten-year-old son, said it occurred twenty miles west of Utica. Lucy Smith, Preliminary Manuscript, p. 36; Lucy Smith, *Biographical Sketches,* p. 69; Joseph Smith, Manuscript History, Book A-1, pp. 131-32.

105. Joseph Smith, Manuscript History, Book A-1, pp. 131-32.

106. Lucy Smith, *Biographical Sketches,* p. 70; Lucy Smith, Preliminary Manuscript, p. 36; Joseph Smith, Manuscript History, Book A-1, pp. 131-32.

II. THE FIRST VISIONS

1. For the settlement of the Massachusetts–New York boundary dispute, see Thomas C. Cochran, *New York in the Confederation* (Port Washington, N.Y.: I. J. Friedman, 1970; first published 1932). A briefer, more recent account is Ray Allen Billington, *Westward Expansion: A History of the American Frontier,* 2d ed. (New York: Macmillan, 1960), pp. 251-59.

2. Backman has assembled much useful information about Palmyra and Manchester in *Joseph Smith's First Vision.* The federal census figures are on p. 45.

3. Neil Adams McNall, *An Agricultural History of the Genesee Valley, 1790-1860* (Philadelphia: University of Pennsylvania Press, 1952), pp. 70, 96-98.

4. Horatio Gates Spafford, *A Gazeteer of the State of New-York* (Albany: B. D. Packard, 1824), p. 80; Horatio Gates Spafford, *A Gazeteer of the State of New-York* (Albany: H. C. Southwick, 1813), p. 152; Backman, *Joseph Smith's First Vision,* p. 27.

5. Backman, *Joseph Smith's First Vision,* p. 32; Spafford, *Gazeteer* (1813), p. 7; Spafford, *Gazeteer* (1824), p. 80.

6. Backman, *Joseph Smith's First Vision,* p. 33.

7. Ronald E. Shaw, *Erie Water West: A History of the Erie Canal, 1772-*

1864 (Lexington: University of Kentucky Press, 1966), p. 130; Nathan Miller, *The Enterprise of a Free People: Aspects of Economic Development in New York State during the Canal Period, 1792-1838* (Ithaca, N.Y.: Published for the American Historical Association by Cornell University Press, 1962), p. 94.

8. Spafford, *Gazeteer* (1824), pp. 400-401; Backman, *Joseph Smith's First Vision*, p. 45.

9. Spafford, *Gazeteer* (1824), pp. 400-401.

10. Blake McKelvey, *Rochester: The Water-Power City, 1812-1854* (Cambridge, Mass.: Harvard University Press, 1954), pp. 71, 100; McNall, *Genesee Valley*, p. 100; Whitney R. Cross, *The Burned-Over District: The Social and Intellectual History of Enthusiastic Religion in Western New York, 1800-1850* (Ithaca, N.Y.: Cornell University Press, 1950), p. 70. In 1827 Rochester had eight newspapers. McKelvey, *Rochester*, p. 151.

11. McKelvey, *Rochester*, pp. 72, 75, 76; Shaw, *Erie Water*, p. 240; Spafford, *Gazeteer* (1824), p. 484.

12. Backman, *Joseph Smith's First Vision*, p. 30.

13. Lucy Smith, *Biographical Sketches*, p. 70; Pomeroy Tucker, *Origin, Rise, and Progress of Mormonism* (New York: D. Appleton and Co., 1867), p. 12. Wheat harvesters made $1.50 a day in the Genesee Valley. McNall, *Genesee Valley*, p. 112.

14. Larry Porter presents evidence for the purchase of a farm in 1818 and the construction of a cabin 8,778 feet south of Main Street in Palmyra as determined by a road survey. "Study of Origins," pp. 40-42. The price is indeterminate because the terms of the purchase agreement are unknown. Annual payments of $100 were completed in 1825, but the amount of down payment is unknown. Recognizing the poverty of most settlers, land agents required very little; 5 percent of the purchase price was common. McNall, *Genesee Valley*, p. 41. The draft manuscript of Lucy Smith's *Biographical Sketches* implies that the first payment was made before the Smiths began working the farm; the published version leaves the impression they raised the money while they worked the farm. Preliminary Manuscript, p. 37; *Biographical Sketches*, p. 70. The descent of the property from Phelps and Gorham to the Smiths is traced in Backman, *Joseph Smith's First Vision*, pp. 41, 43.

15. Porter, "Study of Origins," pp. 39-44. Porter suggests that the misplacement of the farm house was a simple mistake attributable to faulty surveying. For descriptions of the house, see Tucker, *Origin*, p. 13; Lucy Smith, *Biographical Sketches*, p. 71.

16. David M. Ellis, *Landlords and Farmers in the Hudson-Mohawk Region, 1790-1850* (Ithaca, N.Y.: Cornell University Press, 1946), pp. 40, 73, 101; Lucy Smith, *Biographical Sketches*, p. 70. Orasmus Turner recalled only a small spot near the Smith house cleared of underbrush in 1819 or 1820. *History of the Pioneer Settlement of Phelps and Gorham's Purchase, and Morris' Reserve* (Rochester, N.Y.: William Allington, 1851), pp. 212-13; see also Tucker, *Origin*, p. 13.

17. Spafford, *Gazeteer* (1824), pp. 400-401; Ellis, *Landlords and Farmers*, pp. 75-76, 91, 101, 102, 113; Tucker, *Origin*, p. 14. Lucy later said they made 1,000

pounds of maple sugar a year. Preliminary Manuscript, p. 39. In New England
a twenty-to-thirty-acre farm left little market surplus after feeding a family of
six, but the new soil of New York yielded much larger harvests. Robert A. Gross,
The Minutemen and Their World (New York: Hill and Wang, 1976), pp. 85-
86; Ellis, *Landlords and Farmers*, pp. 105-7.

   18. Lucy Smith, *Biographical Sketches*, pp. 70-71; Tucker, *Origin*, p. 14;
Kirtland Letter Book, 1829-35, pp. 1-2, Church Archives, cited in Backman,
Joseph Smith's First Vision, p. 44. Lucy Smith's Preliminary Manuscript, p. 37,
says Alvin returned home "with the necessary amount of money for all except
the last payment." It is unlikely that he could have earned the required amount
in a single year. The more modest statement in the published version seems
closer to the truth.

   19. Lucy Smith, Preliminary Manuscript, p. 38; Lucy Smith, *Biographical
Sketches*, p. 71. In the Preliminary Manuscript, pp. 38-39, Lucy relates an incident
that took place soon after the purchase of land. The story reveals something of
Lucy Smith's perspective on her life and her place in society.

> A friend of mine having invited several of her associates to take tea with
> her one afternoon, sent an urgent request for me also to call on her with
> the rest. The lady's invited were some wealthy merchants' wives and the
> minister's lady. We spent the time quite pleasantly, each seeming to enjoy
> those reciprocal feelings which renders the society of our friends delightful
> to us. When tea was served up we were passing some good-natured remarks
> upon each other when one lady observed, "Well I declare Mrs. [Smith]
> ought not to live in that log house of hers any longer. She deserves a better
> fate, and I say she must have a new house." "So she should," says another,
> "for she is so kind to everyone, she ought to have the best of everything."
> "Ladies," said I, "thank you for your compliments, but you are quite mis-
> taken. I will show you that I am the wealthiest woman that sits at this
> table." "Well," said they, "now make that appear." "Now mark," answered
> I to them. "I have never prayed for riches of the world, as perhaps you
> have, but I have always desired that God would enable me to use enough
> wisdom and forbearance in my family to set good precepts and example
> before my children, whose lives I always besaught the Lord to share, as
> also to secure the confidence and affection of my husband that we acting
> togather in the education and instruction of our children, that we might
> in our old age reap the reward of circumspection joined with parental
> tenderness, viz. the pleasure of seeing our children dignify their Father's
> name by an upright and honorable course of conduct in after life. I have
> been gratified so far in all this and more. I have, tis true, suffered many
> disagreeable disappointments in life with regard to property, but I now find
> myself very comfortably situated to what any of you are. What we have
> has not been obtained at the expense of the comfort of any human being.
> We owe no man. We never distressed any man, which circumstance almost
> invariably attends the mercantile life. So I have no reason to envy those
> who are engaged. Beside there is none present who have this kind of wealth
> that have not lately met with a loss of chi[l]dren or othe[r] friends (which
> really was the case). And now, as for Mrs [   ], the minister's lady, I ask
> you how many nights of the week you are kept awake with anxiety about

your sons who are in habitual attendance on the grog shop and gambling house?" They all said with a look that showed conviction, "Mrs. S[mith], you have established the fact." Reader, I merely relate this that you may draw a moral therefrom that may be useful to you.

20. Lucy Smith, *Biographical Sketches,* pp. 72, 56. For the Book of Mormon comparisons, see I Nephi 8 and 11, and *Biographical Sketches,* pp. 58-59; II Nephi 33:10-15, and *Biographical Sketches,* pp. 281-82. For the relationship of Joseph Smith Sr.'s dreams and the dreams of Nephi and Lehi in the Book of Mormon, see Hal Hougey, *The Truth about the "Lehi Tree-of-Life" Stone* (Concord, Calif.: Pacific Publishing Co., 1963), and C. Wilfred Griggs, "The Book of Mormon as an Ancient Book," *B.Y.U. Studies,* 22 (Summer, 1982):259-78.

21. Lucy Smith, *Biographical Sketches,* pp. 70-71.

22. Ibid., pp. 72, 58.

23. Ibid., p. 74.

24. Milton Backman estimates the Presbyterian membership in Palmyra village at sixty-five, and the Society of Friends at thirty. The Macedon Baptists listed 146 members. Backman, *Joseph Smith's First Vision,* pp. 61-71.

25. James H. Hotchkin, *A History of the Purchase and Settlement of Western New York, and of the Rise, Progress, and Present State of the Presbyterian Church in That Section* (New York: M. W. Dodd, Brick Church Chapel, 1848), p. 122.

26. Ibid., pp. 74, 378.

27. Ibid., p. 74.

28. Backman, *Joseph Smith's First Vision,* pp. 5, 67.

29. Hotchkin, *History,* p. 378; Lucy Smith, *Biographical Sketches,* p. 72.

30. The quotations are from Kirtland Letter Book, 1829-35, which contains (pp. 1-6) the earliest recorded account of Joseph Smith's First Vision, written most probably in 1832. The statement has been reprinted in full with editorial comment and with subsequent accounts in Dean C. Jessee, "The Early Accounts of Joseph Smith's First Vision," *B.Y.U. Studies,* 9 (1969):275-94. The 1832 statement and the other accounts are conveniently reprinted in Backman, *Joseph Smith's First Vision,* pp. 155-77. References to the 1832 statement, "A History of the life of Joseph Smith, Jr.," are to the Backman edition. Quotations in the text are on p. 155.

31. Milton Backman, in *Joseph Smith's First Vision,* pp. 79-89, has assembled the evidence on religious revivals in the Palmyra area. The Reverend Wesley P. Walters of the United Presbyterian Church in Marissa, Ill., has questioned the occurrence of a revival in Palmyra in 1819-20. Mr. Walters finds a number of inconsistencies in the various narratives of this period, but his major finding is the paucity of evidence for membership increases in Palmyra churches. He believes that Joseph Smith actually had an 1823-24 revival in mind and mistakenly assigned it to 1819-20. His argument rests mainly on the assertion that Joseph Smith's account could only have referred to revivals in Palmyra village and not to religious awakenings in nearby towns. Wesley P. Walters "New Light on Mormon Origins from the Palmyra Revival," *Dialogue,* 4 (Spring, 1969):60-81. See also "A Reply to Dr. Bushman," pp. 94-100, and "Joseph Smith's First

Vision Story Revisited," *Journal of Pastoral Practice,* 4 (1980). Besides the material compiled by Milton Backman, the issue of an 1820 revival is treated in Richard L. Anderson, "Circumstantial Confirmation of the First Vision through Reminiscences," *B.Y.U. Studies,* 9 (Spring, 1969):373-404; Larry C. Porter, "Reverend George Lane — Good 'Gifts,' Much 'Grace,' and Marked 'Usefulness,'" *B.Y.U. Studies,* 9 (Spring, 1969):321-40; Peter Crawley, "A Comment on Joseph Smith's Account of His First Vision and the 1820 Revival," *Dialogue,* 6 (Spring, 1971):106-7. Attempting to sum up the controversy for an audience of non-Mormon scholars, Marvin Hill said that "the point made by Walters that the revival must have come in 1823 or 1824 does not bear up under scrutiny." "Secular or Sectarian History? A Critique of *No Man Knows My History,*" *Church History,* 43 (Mar., 1974):83. Subsequently Hill concluded that the great revival referred to likely did occur in 1824, but that lesser religious excitements had influenced Joseph Smith in 1819 and 1820. Marvin Hill, "The First Vision Controversy: A Critique and Reconciliation," *Dialogue,* 15 (Summer, 1982):31-46. The quotation from Joseph Smith is in Joseph Smith, *History of the Church,* 1:2. The quotation from Backman is in Backman, *Joseph Smith's First Vision,* p. 82.

32. In recounting her baptism around 1803, Lucy Smith by implication suggested a date for her membership in the Presbyterian church in Palmyra. She had searched for a minister who would baptize her without the requirement of commitment to one church. She found such a man, who left her "free in regard to joining any religious denomination." After this, she says, "I stepped forward and yielded obedience to this ordinance; after which I continued to read the Bible as formerly until my eldest son had attained his twenty-second year." *Biographical Sketches,* pp. 48-49. Alvin was twenty-two in 1820. Unfortunately, the Presbyterian records that could confirm this date are lost. In an 1893 interview William Smith said that Hyrum, Samuel, and Catherine were Presbyterians, but since Catherine was only eight in 1820, and Sophronia, whom Joseph named, was seventeen, Sophronia was more likely to be the sister who joined. Interview with William Smith, Nov., 1893, *Deseret News* (Salt Lake City), Jan. 20, 1894, reprinted in Kirkham, *New Witness,* 1:44; Joseph Smith, *History of the Church,* 1:3. Later Western Presbyterian Church records mention Lucy, Hyrum, and Samuel, but neither Catherine nor Sophronia. Sophronia meanwhile had married and possibly transferred her membership. Porter, "Study of Origins," pp. 45-46. All the circumstantial evidence notwithstanding, the date of Lucy Smith's engagement to Presbyterianism remains a matter of debate. It is possible to argue plausibly that she did not join until later Palmyra revivals in 1824. Hill, "First Vision Controversy," pp. 39-42.

33. Tucker, *Origin,* p. 28; Turner, *History,* p. 214; Backman, *Joseph Smith's First Vision,* p. 177. On the careers of Pomeroy Tucker and Orasmus Turner, see Anderson, "Circumstantial Confirmation," p. 377.

34. Joseph Smith, *History of the Church,* 1:3.

35. Lucy Smith, *Biographical Sketches,* pp. 73, 84; Turner, *History,* pp. 213-14; John Alonzo Clark, *Gleanings by the Way* (Philadelphia: W. J. and J. K. Simon, 1842), p. 225; Joseph Smith, "History of the life of Joseph Smith, Jr.," p.

156. Pomeroy Tucker says that as Joseph grew up, he "learned to read comprehensively," including the Bible and works of fiction. *Origin,* p. 17. On the literary environment of Palmyra and Manchester, see Robert Paul, "Joseph Smith and the Manchester (New York) Library," *B.Y.U. Studies,* 22 (Summer, 1982):333-56.

36. Joseph Smith, "History of the life of Joseph Smith, Jr.," p. 156.

37. Turner, *History,* p. 214; Oliver Cowdery to W. W. Phelps, *Messenger and Advocate,* Feb. 1, 1835, p. 78; Joseph Smith, "History of the life of Joseph Smith, Jr.," pp. 156-57.

38. Joseph Smith, *History of the Church,* 1:3-4.

39. Ibid.

40. William Smith dates the revival as 1822 and 1823 and gives Joseph's age as seventeen, but William also dates the Smith move to the Manchester farm as 1821, three years later than the actual occurrence. William's chronology (he was eight in 1819) seems to have been off by three years all along the line. *William Smith on Mormonism,* p. 5; cf. Anderson, "Circumstantial Confirmation," pp. 398-401. On the location of the vision, see a newspaper interview with Joseph Smith first published in the *New York Spectator,* Sept. 23, 1843, and reprinted in Backman, *Joseph Smith's First Vision,* p. 176.

41. For a discussion of the place of the First Vision in Mormon theology, see James B. Allen, "The Significance of Joseph Smith's First Vision in Mormon Thought," *Dialogue,* 1 (Autumn, 1966):29-45, and "The Emergence of a Fundamental: The Expanding Role of Joseph Smith's First Vision in Mormon Thought," *Journal of Mormon History,* 7 (1980):43-61; Marvin Hill, "On the First Vision and Its Import in the Shaping of Early Mormonism," *Dialogue,* 12 (Spring, 1979):90-99.

42. Joseph Smith, "History of the life of Joseph Smith, Jr.," pp. 155, 157.

43. Ibid., pp. 156-57.

44. Ibid., p. 157; Jessee, "Early Accounts," pp. 283-87. On the import of the changes, see Neal E. Lambert and Richard H. Cracroft, "Literary Form and Historical Understanding: Joseph Smith's First Vision," *Journal of Mormon History,* 7 (1980):31-42, and, from another perspective, Richard P. Howard, "An Analysis of Six Contemporary Accounts Touching Joseph Smith's First Vision," *Restoration Studies,* 1:95-117.

45. The quotations are from an interview with Robert Matthias, who called himself "Joshua the Jewish Minister," recorded in Manuscript History, Nov. 9, 1835, pp. 120-22. The account is reprinted in Jessee, "Early Accounts," pp. 284-85, and Backman, *Joseph Smith's First Vision,* pp. 158-59.

46. Joseph Smith, *History of the Church,* 1:5.

47. Backman, *Joseph Smith's First Vision,* p. 159; Joseph Smith, *History of the Church,* 1:5-6.

48. Joseph Smith, *History of the Church,* 1:6. For another young convert who desired to conceal his religious experience, see James Mitchell, ed., *The Life and Times of Levi Scott, D.D.* (New York: Phillips and Hunt; Cincinnati: Cranston and Stowe, 1885), p. 38.

49. In the Preliminary Manuscript Lucy described a family conversation

about the confusions in the churches. Joseph said little but appeared to be thinking deeply. "After we ceased conversation he went to bed and was pondering in his mind which of the churches were the true one. But he had not laid there long till he saw a bright light enter the room where he lay. He looked up and saw an angel of the Lord standing by him. The angel spoke: 'I perceive that you are enquiring in your mind which is the true church. There is not a true church on earth, no not one, and has not been since Peter took the keys of the Melchesidec Priesthood after the order of God into the Kingdom of Heaven. The churches that are now upon the earth are all man made churches' " (p. 40). William Smith said Joseph prayed in the woods where an angel appeared and told him the churches were in error. The use of the word "angel" instead of "the Lord" may not be significant, for Joseph himself at one point referred to the heavenly messengers in the grove as angels, but William goes on to say the angel told Joseph of the plates. *William Smith on Mormonism,* pp. 8-9; Backman, *Joseph Smith's First Vision,* p. 159. Pomeroy Tucker said an angel appeared to Joseph after he prayed "alone in the wilderness" and told him that "all the religious denominations were believing in false doctrines." Tucker distinguished this visitation from a subsequent angel who told Joseph of the plates. Tucker, *Origin,* p. 28.

50. Joseph Smith, *History of the Church,* 1:6; *Wayne Sentinel* (Palmyra), Oct. 22, 1823; John Samuel Thompson, *Christian Guide* (Utica, N.Y.: A. G. Danby, 1826), p. 71: "The Spiritual Travels of Nathan Cole," ed. Michael Crawford, *William and Mary Quarterly,* 3d ser., 33 (Jan., 1976):96.

51. *Connecticut Evangelical Magazine,* 5 (1805):349; Joseph Smith, *History of the Church,* 1:6-7. The New England divines Joseph Bellamy and Samuel Hopkins both argued against personal revelations. Joseph Bellamy, *True Religion Delineated . . .* (Boston: S. Kneeland, 1750), p. 92; Samuel Hopkins, *The System of Doctrines . . . ,* 2 vols. (Boston: Isaiah Thomas and Ebenezer T. Andrews, 1793), 1:603-4. The announcement of a general apostasy among the churches would have been familiar to the Methodist preacher. That was the common message of the visions; see, for example, *The Sense of the United Non-conforming Ministers* (London, 1693), p. 6. I am indebted to Michael Crawford for this reference. Asa Wild carried the same information away from his vision. Cf. Elias Smith, *The Life, Conversion, Preaching . . . of Elias Smith* (Portsmouth, N.H.: Beck and Foster, 1816). Marvin Hill enlarges on the belief in apostasy among a number of lay Christians in the early nineteenth century, in "Role of Christian Primitivism in the Origin and Development of the Mormon Kingdom, 1830-1844" (Ph.D. diss., University of Chicago, 1968). See also Marvin Hill, "The Shaping of the Mormon Mind in New England and New York," *B.Y.U. Studies,* 9 (Spring, 1969):351-72.

52. Joseph Smith, "1838 Recital of the First Vision," in Backman, *Joseph Smith's First Vision,* pp. 164-65. Cf. Joseph Smith, *History of the Church,* 1:6-8.

53. Joseph Smith, *History of the Church,* 1:9; *William Smith on Mormonism,* pp. 9-10, 104; Joseph Smith, "History of the life of Joseph Smith, Jr.," p.

156; Richard L. Anderson, "Joseph Smith's New York Reputation Reappraised," *B.Y.U. Studies,* 10 (Spring, 1970):306. For places where Joseph might have worked while away from home, see Porter, "Study of Origins," p. 279.

54. Lucy Smith, Preliminary Manuscript, p. 48; Joseph Smith, *History of the Church,* 5:126-27.

55. Lucy Smith, *Biographical Sketches,* pp. 86-87; Lucy Smith, Preliminary Manuscript, p. 40. Probably because the Smiths lost the farm and house, they were remembered as good workers but poor. Backman, *Joseph Smith's First Vision,* p. 119. The vicissitudes of life seem to have weighed heavily on Joseph, Sr. In a patriarchal blessing given to Hyrum, Dec. 9, 1834, Joseph, Sr., commended Hyrum for the respect he paid his father despite difficulties: "Though he has been out of the way through wine, thou has never forsaken him nor laughed him to scorn." Hyrum Smith Papers, Church Archives. Since there is no evidence of intemperance after the organization of the church, Joseph, Sr., likely referred to a time before 1826 when Hyrum married and left home. For a hostile assessment of Joseph, Sr., see Turner, *History,* p. 213.

56. Joseph Smith, *History of the Church,* 1:9. The only other evidence of persecution are a reminiscence by Thomas H. Taylor of Manchester about Joseph being ducked in a pond for teaching what he believed, and an inexplicable attempt on his life recorded by Lucy Smith. She said an unknown attacker took a shot a Joseph one day as he entered the yard. The times of both incidents are uncertain. Backman, *Joseph Smith's First Vision,* p. 119; Lucy Smith, *Biographical Sketches,* p. 73.

57. Joseph Smith, *History of the Church,* 1:10, 9; Joseph Smith, Manuscript History, Book A-1, Note C, p. 135. A young Methodist convert of the same period regretted the time when after his conversion he became "fond of fun and frolic." Mitchell, *Levi Scott,* p. 32.

58. Joseph Smith, *History of the Church,* 1:11. The frame house remained unfinished in 1823, and unless some family members slept there to relieve congestion, Joseph received Moroni in the cabin. Porter, "Study of Origins," pp. 76-77. In 1835 Oliver Cowdery commented that Joseph prayed when "slumber had spread her refreshing hand over others beside him. . . ." *Messenger and Advocate,* Feb., 1835.

59. Joseph Smith, *History of the Church,* 1:11-12. Joseph said nothing about forgiveness of sins in his 1838 account, but Oliver Cowdery mentioned this personal message twice in his 1835 letters. *Messenger and Advocate,* Feb., July, 1835. In her Preliminary Manuscript Lucy Smith connected the visit of Moroni with the declaration that "there is not a true church on the earth." William Smith did the same. But the retelling of the events long after the fact does not necessarily imply that the two Smiths understood in 1832 that the Christian churches were apostate. Lucy remained an active member of the Presbyterian church until 1828 and took an interest in an itinerant preacher in Palmyra in the 1824 revivals. Lucy Smith, Preliminary Manuscript, p. 40; *William Smith on Mormonism,* pp. 8-9; Lucy Smith, *Biographical Sketches,* pp. 90-91.

60. Joseph Smith, *History of the Church,* 1:12.

61. Ibid., 1:12-13.

62. Ibid., 1:13-14.

63. Lucy Smith, *Biographical Sketches*, pp. 81, 82; Joseph Smith, *History of the Church*, 1:14-15.

64. *Messenger and Advocate*, July, Oct., 1835; Joseph Smith, *History of the Church*, 1:15-16. In the Preliminary Manuscript, p. 44, Lucy Smith mentioned four pillars of cement.

65. Joseph Smith, *History of the Church*, 1:14, 16; Lucy Smith, *Biographical Sketches*, p. 83. In the Preliminary Manuscript Lucy Smith said that as Joseph lifted the plates out of the box, "the thought flashed across his mind that there might be something more in the box that would be a benefit to him in a pecuniary point of view. In the excitement of the moment he laid the record down in order to cover up the box least some one should come along and take away whatever else might be deposited there." When he turned, the plates were gone. He prayed to the Lord to know why, and the angel appeared. His mistake was to lay down the record when he had been commanded not to let the plates out of his hands until they were safely at his father's house. Joseph opened the box again and saw the plates inside, but when he tried to take them, he was thrown to the ground (pp. 44, 45). In the published version Lucy Smith assigned this experience to 1824 on the second visit to the hill. *Biographical Sketches*, p. 85. Joseph Knight told much the same story as Lucy Smith, probably because he heard it from her. Jessee, "Joseph Knight's Recollection," p. 31. Oliver Cowdery said Joseph reflected on the value of the plates going to the hill, and tried unsuccessfully three times to take them out of the box. Each time he suffered an enervating shock. When Joseph asked why, the angel appeared and revealed "the prince of darkness, surrounded by his innumerable train of associates." Then in an extensive vision the true purpose of the plates was revealed, and Moroni admonished Joseph to resist the power of the evil one. *Messenger and Advocate*, Oct., 1835.

66. *William Smith on Mormonism*, pp. 9-10; Lucy Smith, *Biographical Sketches*, p. 84. In Lucy Smith's Preliminary Manuscript and in William Smith's account, Joseph went to the hill a day or more after Moroni's visit. On at least one intervening evening the family gathered around to hear him tell about the angel's visit. Lucy Smith, Preliminary Manuscript, pp. 42-44.

67. Lucy Smith, *Biographical Sketches*, p. 87. Dr. Gain Robinson, a friend of the family and owner of a drug store, recorded a visit to the Smith cabin on Nov. 19. Robinson was an uncle and mentor of McIntyre. Porter, "Study of Origins," pp. 73-75.

68. Lucy Smith, *Biographical Sketches*, p. 88.

69. Ibid., p. 89; Joseph Smith, *History of the Church*, 5:126-27; 2:380-81.

70. Lucy Smith, *Biographical Sketches*, p. 90.

71. Lucy Smith and Joseph Smith, Jr., placed Alvin's death in 1824, but this article and his gravestone in the John Swift Memorial Cemetery in Palmyra definitely establish 1823 as the correct year of his death. Porter, "Study of Origins," pp. 73-76.

72. Lucy Smith, *Biographical Sketches,* pp. 90-91; Walters, "New Light."

73. Lucy Smith, *Biographical Sketches,* p. 91. Hyrum married Jerusha Barden in Manchester. Lucy Smith, *Biographical Sketches,* p. 40.

74. Lucy Smith, *Biographical Sketches,* pp. 92-93; *Amboy Journal,* Apr. 30, 1897. Josiah Stowell may have had a cousin in Palmyra, Simpson Stowell. Porter, "Study of Origins," p. 123.

75. Ellis, *Landlords and Farmers,* pp. 123, 125, 126; McKelvey, *Rochester,* pp. 82, 87, 165; McNall, *Genesee Valley,* pp. 36, 39, 42; Turner, *Origin,* p. 31. Land prices dropped in 1819 along with farm products. The Smiths bought their land one year too soon. McNall, *Genesee Valley,* p. 39.

76. Lucy Smith, *Biographical Sketches,* pp. 91, 94; McNall, *Genesee Valley,* p. 40.

77. Lucy Smith, *Biographical Sketches,* p. 95; *William Smith on Mormonism,* pp. 12-13. The years 1824 and 1825 were especially hard in New York and Pennsylvania. In some places land could be purchased for the cost of the improvements. Ellis, *Landlords and Farmers,* pp. 125-26.

78. Lucy Smith, *Biographical Sketches,* pp. 94-95; McNall, *Genesee Valley,* p. 43.

79. Lucy Smith, *Biographical Sketches,* p. 96. Lucy Smith's story contains some puzzles. It is not clear why Stoddard asked the Smiths to raise the money instead of the land agent simply returning Stoddard's payment, or why Hyrum would even consider such a proposition, since it amounted to paying for the farm twice.

80. Lucy Smith, *Biographical Sketches,* pp. 96-98; Porter, "Study of Origins," pp. 106-10. In Jan., 1829, Lucy Smith told her sister-in-law in Vermont that the farm had been sold for $700, and they must leave it in the spring. This account of the loss of the farm, which covered up the anguish the Smiths had felt at their failure to make the payment, suggests that either at the time of Durfee's purchase or later the Smiths were compensated for their labors. Lucy may have been unfair to the carpenter Calvin Stoddard. He probably was the same Calvin Stoddard to marry Lucy's daughter Sophronia on Dec. 2, 1827. Lucy Smith to Martha Pierce, Royalton, Vt., Jan. 23, 1829, Church Archives; Lucy Smith, *Biographical Sketches,* p. 40.

81. Lucy Smith, *Biographical Sketches,* pp. 98, 129; Porter, "Study of Origins," pp. 108-9; *William Smith on Mormonism,* p. 14. Lucy said Durfee took six months' labor of fifteen-year-old Samuel as one year's rent. Preliminary Manuscript, pp. 58-59.

82. Lucy Smith, *Biographical Sketches,* p. 40. Lucy Smith said Joseph, Jr., wished to marry Emma Hale in Dec., 1825, which would have been less than one month after he met her. Lucy was putting the house in order to receive the bride when Stoddard ordered the family out. Preliminary Manuscript, pp. 52-53.

83. For the holdings and biographies of Stowell and Knight, see Porter, "Study of Origins," pp. 174-79, 181-85.

84. "Joseph Knight's Incidents of History from 1827 to 1844," compiled by

Thomas Bullock from loose sheets in Joseph Knight Jr.'s possession, Aug. 16, 1862, Church Archives; Lucy Smith, *Biographical Sketches,* pp. 91-92; Joseph Smith, *History of the Church,* 1:17; Porter, "Study of Origins," pp. 105, 124-25. Lucy Smith said Stowell learned about the mine from an old document that fell into his hands. *Biographical Sketches,* p. 91; see also *Messenger and Advocate,* Oct., 1835. An account in the *Amboy Journal,* Mar. 30, 1897, claimed that a woman named Odle told William Hale, a distant relative of Isaac's, about the treasure. Martin Harris said Joseph and his father were part of a company to dig for treasure. *Tiffany's Monthly,* 5 (May, 1859):164. Larry Porter has identified the signatories to the agreement, all of whom lived in the vicinity. Porter, "Study of Origins," pp. 125-26. Emily C. Blackburn, the author of *The History of Susquehannah County,* published in 1873, gave directions to the place where the digging purportedly went on. The biggest of the five holes was twenty feet deep and 150 feet in circumference. Larry C. Porter visited the site on Aug. 27, 1968, and Mar. 20, 1970, and reported "definite disturbances of the earth" in the place that Mrs. Blackburn described. Porter, "Study of Origins," p. 127.

85. Lucy Smith, *Biographical Sketches,* pp. 91-92. Willard Chase claimed that he found the stone. E. D. Howe, *Mormonism Unvailed* (Painesville, Ohio: By the author, 1834), pp. 240-41. B. H. Roberts says the stone was found in the well of Clark Chase, as does Pomeroy Tucker. B. H. Roberts, *A Comprehensive History of the Church of Jesus Christ of Latter-day Saints,* 6 vols. (Salt Lake City: Published by the Church, Deseret News Press, 1930), 1:129; Tucker, *Origin,* p. 19; cf. John A. Widtsoe, *Joseph Smith: Seeker after Truth, Prophet of God* (Salt Lake City: Deseret News Press, 1951), pp. 260-67. Martin Harris said the well was Mason Chase's. *Tiffany's Monthly,* 5:169.

86. Emma Bidamon, Nauvoo, to Mrs. Pilgrim, Mar. 27, 1870, Library of the Reorganized Church of Jesus Christ of Latter Day Saints, Independence, Mo. I am indebted to Richard L. Anderson for this reference. *Latter-day Saints' Millennial Star,* 26:119; Roberts, *Comprehensive History,* 6:230. See also *Tiffany's Monthly,* 5:163-70; Oliver Cowdery, *Defence in a Rehearsal of My Grounds for Separating Myself from the Latter-day Saints* (Norton, Ohio: Pressley's Job Office, 1839), pp. 2-3; David Whitmer, *An Address to All Believers in Christ* (Richmond, Mo.: By the author, 1887), p. 12; Edward Stevenson, *Reminiscences of Joseph, the Prophet, and the Coming Forth of the Book of Mormon* (Salt Lake City: By the author, 1893), pp. 10-19, 30. Pomeroy Tucker said the stone was white and glassy rather than dark. *Origin,* p. 19. For a Book of Mormon prophecy of the seerstone, see Alma 27:33.

In an 1856 entry in his journal Hosea Stout reported Brigham Young as saying that Joseph Smith had found the gold plates by means of a seerstone. Juanita Brooks, ed., *On the Mormon Frontier: The Diary of Hosea Stout, 1844-1861,* 2 vols. (Salt Lake City: University of Utah Press and Utah State Historical Society, 1964), 2:593. Martin Harris was reported by the editor of *Tiffany's Monthly* as saying that Joseph found the plates "by looking in the stone found in the well of Mason Chase. The family had likewise told me the same thing."

Tiffany's Monthly, 5:169; see also, Turner, *Origin,* p. 216; Howe, *Mormonism Unvailed,* pp. 246, 252; Henry Harris affidavit in Kirkham, *New Witness,* 1:133.

87. *Tiffany's Monthly* 5:164 (Martin Harris); Howe, *Mormonism Unvailed,* p. 263 (Isaac Hale); Tucker, *Origin,* pp. 19-20. The purported 1826 court record has Joseph say that "while at Palmyra he had frequently ascertained . . . where lost property was, of various kinds; that he has occasionally been in the habit of looking through this stone to find lost property for three years. . . ." Phillip Schaff, ed., *A Religious Encyclopedia,* 3 vols. (New York: Funk and Wagnalls, 1882-84), 2 (1883):1576-77, commonly referred to as *Schaff-Herzog Encyclopedia of Religious Knowledge.* In the *Tiffany's Monthly* interview Martin Harris supposedly said that Joseph found a pin in a pile of shavings with the aid of the stone. The most comprehensive account of the seerstone is Richard Van Wagoner and Steve Walker, "Joseph Smith: The Gift of Seeing," *Dialogue,* 22 (Summer, 1982):48-68.

88. Fawn Brodie, *No Man Knows My History: The Life of Joseph Smith the Mormon Prophet* (New York: Alfred A. Knopf, 1945), pp. 18-21, 29-31.

89. Howe, *Mormonism Unvailed,* pp. 240-41; Tucker, *Origin,* p. 19; William H. Kelley, "The Hill Cumorah . . . The Stories of Hurlbut, Howe, Tucker, etc. from Late Interviews," *Saints Herald* (Plano, Iowa), 28 (June 1, 1881):167, cited in Anderson, "Joseph Smith's New York Reputation," pp. 296-97; *Naked Truths about Mormonism,* Apr., 1888 (interview with Caroline Rockwell Smith), cited in Anderson, "Joseph Smith's New York Reputation," p. 300; Lucy Smith, *Biographical Sketches,* pp. 102, 109. For another Palmyra seerstone, see *Wayne Sentinel,* Dec. 27, 1825.

90. Howe, *Mormonism Unvailed,* pp. 238-39, 232-33; *Naked Truths,* Apr., Jan., 1888; Kelley, "The Hill Cumorah," p. 167, in Anderson, "Joseph Smith's New York Reputation," p. 307; "W. D. Purple MD: Greene, 1877," photocopy, Church Archives.

91. *Rochester Gem,* May 15, 1830; *New York Folklore Quarterly,* 1:20; 2:174-81; 3:252-53; 13:215-17; Richard Mercer Dorson, *Jonathan Draws the Long Bow* (Cambridge, Mass.: Harvard University Press, 1946), pp. 115, 119, 179, 180, 182; Barnes Frisbie, *The History of Middletown, Vermont in Three Discourses* (Rutland, Vt.: Tuttle and Co., 1867), pp. 44-65. For further evidence of treasure seeking and stone looking, see *Lyons* (N.Y.) *Advertizer,* Aug. 29, 1827; *Palmyra Reflector,* Feb. 1, 1831; *Ontario* (N.Y.) *Depository,* Feb. 9, 1825; *Wayne Sentinel* (Palmyra), Oct. 29, 1823, Feb. 16, Mar. 2, Dec. 27, 1825; *Norwich* (N.Y.) *Journal,* July 2, 1828; *Tiffany's Monthly,* 5:165; Josiah Priest, *The Wonders of Nature and Providence* (Albany, N.Y.: J. Priest, 1825), pp. 562-63; Rhamanthus M. Stocker, *Centennial History of Susquehannah County, Pennsylvania* (Philadelphia: R. T. Peck and Co., 1887), Appendix by J. B. Buck. In a series on the Book of Mormon published in Feb., 1831, the editor of the Palmyra *Reflector* observed that from "time immemorial" people had believed in spirits guarding treasure, and that it was a common belief in New York. "It may not be amiss in this place to mention that the MANIA of money-digging soon began rapidly to diffuse itself through many parts of this country; men and women without distinction

of age or sex became marvelous wise in the occult sciences, many dreamed, and others saw visions disclosing to them deep in the bowels of the earth, rich and shining treasures, and to facilitate those mighty mining operations (money was usually if not always sought after in the night time,) divers devices and implements were invented. . . ." See also Jerald and Sandra Tanner, *Joseph Smith and Money Digging* (Salt Lake City: Modern Microfilm Co., 1970).

92. David Mays, ed., *Disappointment, or the Force of Credulity* (Gainesville: University Presses of Florida, 1976), p. 41; Keith Thomas, *Religion and the Decline of Magic* (New York: Scribner's, 1971), p. 236 and passim. See also Herbert Leventhal, *In the Shadow of the Enlightenment: Occultism and Renaissance Science in Eighteenth-Century America* (New York: New York University Press, 1976), and Jon Butler, "Magic, Astrology, and the Early American Religious Heritage," *American Historical Review*, 84 (Apr., 1979):317-46. One Eli Yarnall, who was born in Chester County, Pa., and moved to Philadelphia in the eighteenth century, was reputed to have exercised the gift of second sight at age seven. His mother would not permit him to "divine for money" lest he lose the gift, which she considered heaven-sent. John Fanning Watson, *Annals of Philadelphia*, 3 vols. (Philadelphia: Edwin S. Stuart, 1884), 1:272-73. Besides seeking treasure, Goodwin Wharton joined forces with John Wildman, the former Leveller, to find the Urim and Thummim from the breastplate of the High Priest of the Temple. Thomas, *Religion and the Decline of Magic*, p. 236.

93. Howe, *Mormonism Unvailed*, pp. 238, 232-33. Hurlbut himself may have injected some of the excuses into the affidavits to polish up the respectability of his informants.

94. Anderson, "Joseph Smith's New York Reputation," p. 296; Kirkham, *New Witness*, 2:363.

95. Lucy Smith, Preliminary Manuscript, p. 40.

96. Howe, *Mormonism Unvailed*, pp. 232-34, 238, 239, 242, 251-53; *Tiffany's Monthly*, 5:164. *Tiffany's Monthly* was a spiritualist journal that was willing to admit supernatural influence in Joseph Smith's revelations, but attributed them to "a band of spirits, of not very exalted character." In *Tiffany's* view Joseph Smith was a sincere but misled medium. *Tiffany's Monthly*, 5:119. The editor was inclined, therefore, to make the most of the money-digging exploits as evidence of the debased spirits at work on the Smith family. The *Tiffany's* interview with Martin Harris has him say that the company of money diggers consisted of Josiah Stowell, Mr. Beeman, Samuel Lawrence, George Proper, Joseph Smith, Jr., his father, and Hyrum Smith. They dug in Palmyra and in Pennsylvania. William Stafford's affidavit said the family claimed that, by looking in his stone, Joseph "could see all things within and under the earth." Joseph Capron claimed "the family of Smiths held Joseph, Jr. in high estimation on account of some supernatural power, which he was supposed to possess." Howe, *Mormonism Unvailed*, pp. 237-38, 259. Richard Anderson concluded that if the Smiths were involved in money digging, "they participated in a passing cultural phenomenon, shared widely by people of known honesty. However, the supernaturalism presented in early Mormon sources is restrained, qualitatively distinct

from the magical superstitions of the money digging stories." Anderson, "Joseph Smith's New York Reputation," p. 302. For a partly humorous dissection of the money-digging charges against the Smiths, see Hugh Nibley, *The Myth Makers* (Salt Lake City: Bookcraft, 1961), pp. 89-190.

97. Joseph Smith, *History of the Church,* 1:14; *Messenger and Advocate,* Oct., 1835; Lucy Smith, Preliminary Manuscript, pp. 41-42.

98. *Tiffany's Monthly,* 5:169.

99. Philastus Hurlbut recorded the affidavits of William Stafford and Peter Ingersoll in Dec., 1833. Howe, *Mormonism Unvailed,* pp. 232-33, 238-39. William H. Kelley, an apostle of the Reorganized Latter Day Saint Church, returned much later to interview Palmyra residents, among them John Stafford, and published the results in 1883. Cited in Anderson, "Joseph Smith's New York Reputation," p. 307.

100. The Palmyra *Reflector* articles wished to imply Joseph Jr.'s involvement with money diggers, but the editor avoided a direct accusation. Feb. 11 and 14, 1831, reprinted in Kirkham, *New Witness,* 2:68-72. Lucy Smith, *Biographical Sketches,* p. 92. In the *Elders Journal* for 1838, published in Far West, the question was asked, "Was not Joseph Smith a money-digger?" "Yes, but it was never a very profitable job for him as he only got fourteen dollars a month for it." Joseph Smith, *History of the Church,* 3:29. The reference is apparently to Joseph's work with Stowell in Harmony.

101. Howe, *Mormonism Unvailed,* pp. 263, 268. Isaac Hale said Joseph, Jr., was "very saucy and insolent to his father."

102. Oliver Cowdery said that while Joseph was in the Bainbridge area and before he received the plates, an "officious person complained of him as a disorderly person," but he was "honorably acquitted." *Messenger and Advocate,* Oct., 1835. For the evidence for a trial, see Wesley P. Walters, "Joseph Smith's Bainbridge, N.Y., Court Trials," *Westminster Theological Journal,* 36 (Winter, 1974):123-55, and Wesley P. Walters, "From Occult to Cult with Joseph Smith, Jr.," *Journal of Pastoral Theology,* 1 (Summer, 1977):121-31. For an analysis of the contradictions in the various transcripts of the trial and of the questionable circumstances under which some of the supporting evidence was discoverd, see Marvin S. Hill, "Joseph Smith and the 1826 Trial: New Evidence and New Difficulties," *B.Y.U. Studies,* 12 (Winter, 1972):223-33. Cf. Brodie, *No Man,* pp. 20-31; Jerald and Sandra Tanner, *Joseph Smith's 1826 Trial* (Salt Lake City: Modern Microfilm Co., 1971). F. L. Stewart is conducting research that calls into question the purported trial documents. She finds contradictions between the supposed record and the forms required by New York statute.

103. Three accounts of the trial are known to exist: one by A. W. Benton, a physician living in South Bainbridge who published a brief account in the *Evangelical Magazine and Gospel Advocate,* Apr. 9, 1831; a second by W. D. Purple, another physician present at the trial, in the *Chenango Union* (Norwich, N.Y.), May 3, 1877; and a third, presumably an actual trial record torn from the book of the presiding justice of the peace, Albert Neely, and published first in *Fraser's Magazine,* Feb., 1873, and subsequently in the article on Mormonism

by the Episcopal bishop of Utah, Daniel S. Tuttle, in Schaff, *Religious Encyclopedia,* 2:1576. All three of the accounts are reprinted conveniently in Kirkham, *New Witness,* 2:359-68, 467. The quotation above is at 2:361.

104. Walters, "Joseph Smith's Bainbridge Court Trials," p. 146; Kirkham, *New Witness,* 2:364. Purple was properly disdainful, as an enlightened physician was obligated to be. Kirkham, *New Witness,* 2:362-68.

105. Kirkham, *New Witness,* 2:360

106. Ibid., 2:360-61 366; Howe, *Mormonism Unvailed,* p. 257. The trial record published in *Fraser's Magazine* said that Joseph spent only a small part of his time in money digging. Joseph did not deny the power to find treasure with the stone, and may have sought a hidden cache of gold and silver in Salem in 1836, but after 1826 his father's preoccupation with gold digging abated and Joseph was no longer pressed to use the stone for that purpose. *Doctrine and Covenants* 111; Brodie, *No Man,* pp. 192-93. In Nauvoo an English convert gave a pair of seerstones used by church members in England to George A. Smith. George Smith showed the stones to Joseph, "who pronounced them Urim and Thummim — as good as ever was upon the earth — but he said, 'They have been consecrated to devils.' " Wardle Mace Journal, p. 66, Church Archives.

107. Kirkham, *New Witness,* 2:360. Porter summarizes the evidence of Joseph's school attendance in Chenango County and possibly Broome County in "Study of Origins," pp. 174, 184-85. For his involvement in wool carding, see Emily M. Austin, *Mormonism, or Life among the Mormons* (Wisconsin: M. J. Cantwell, 1882), p. 32.

108. Joseph Knight, Jr., "Incidents"; Joseph Smith, *History of the Church,* 1:94; Josiah Stowell, Jr., New York, to J. S. Fullmer, Cambria, Luzerne County, Pa., Feb. 17, 1843, Church Archives.

109. Joseph Knight Jr.'s account gives Nov., 1827, rather than 1826 as the date of Joseph's arrival back in Colesville, but since Knight's date conflicts with the well-documented chain of events following Sept. 23, 1827, it seems best to assume that Knight was off by a year. Joseph Knight, "Incidents."

110. Lucy Smith, *Biographical Sketches,* p. 93; Joseph Smith, *History of the Church,* 1:90-91. The best summary of the Hale family's history is Porter, "Study of Origins," pp. 114-21, 125, 128. The Hales later publicly repudiated Joseph Smith. *Susquehannah Register* (Montrose, Pa.), May 1, 1834; Howe, *Mormonism Unvailed,* p. 263.

111. *Saints Herald,* Oct. 1, 1879, cited in Porter, "Study of Origins," p. 187; Joseph Smith, *History of the Church,* 1:17; Walters, "From Occult to Cult," p. 123. Emily Coburn said that Emma taught school before she married. Porter, "Study of Origins," p. 194; for further details on the circumstances of the marriage, see pp. 188-95. Isaac Hale said Joseph carried Emma off, but Emma herself told the story differently. Howe, *Mormonism Unvailed,* p. 263. Martin Harris may have provided Joseph with a new suit for courting. Donna Hill, *Joseph Smith, the First Mormon* (Garden City, N.Y.: Doubleday, 1977), p. 69.

The most authoritative study of Joseph Smith's appearance is Ephraim Hatch, "What Did Joseph Smith Look Like," *Ensign,* 11 (Mar., 1981):65-73. Hatch summarizes his findings based on verbal descriptions as follows: "People say that he was a good-looking man, at least six feet tall, with a youthful appearance. He weighed between 180 and 212 pounds. He had a broad, muscular chest and shoulders which, in later years were slightly rounded. He had small hands, large feet, and long legs. His head was large, oblong oval in shape. His hair was fine, not curly, and light brown, changing to auburn in later years. His eyes, light hazel or blue, were set far apart deep in the head, and were shaded by long, thick lashes and bushy brows. His nose was long and prominent. His face had a pleasant expression with an unconscious smile. His upper lip was full and a little protruding. His chin was broad and square with very little beard. His forehead was sloping and unfurrowed. His complexion was light, sometimes called pale. He was usually well-dressed, generally in black with a white necktie." Hatch concludes that the most authoritative portrait was a full-length profile done in Nauvoo in 1842, probably by Sutcliffe Maudsley, a British convert. The background of the portrait is described in Lavina Fielding Anderson, "139-Year-Old Portraits of Joseph and Emma Smith," *Ensign,* 11 (Mar., 1981):62-64.

112. Joseph Smith, *History of the Church,* 1:17; Howe, *Mormonism Unvailed,* p. 263. Peter Ingersoll transported the Smiths to Harmony and later claimed that in the conversation with Isaac Hale Joseph acknowledged that "he could not see in a stone now, nor never could." Howe, *Mormonism Unvailed,* p. 234. Isaac Hale's account is more to be trusted in view of the fact that Joseph never repudiated the powers of the stone on any other occasion.

113. Howe, *Mormonism Unvailed,* p. 235.

114. Lucy Smith, Preliminary Manuscript, p. 42; Lucy Smith, *Biographical Sketches,* p. 73.

115. *Painesville* (Ohio) *Telegraph,* Mar. 22, 1831. See Nibley, *Myth Makers,* pp. 182-83, 190, for the tendency of Joseph Smith's contemporaries to attach qualities to him rather than seeing him for what he was.

116. Lucy Smith, *Biographical Sketches,* pp. 98-99.

117. Ibid., p. 99.

III. TRANSLATION

1. Jessee, "Joseph Knight's Recollection," pp. 32-33; Lucy Smith, *Biographical Sketches,* p. 99. Joseph Knight and Willard Chase both said Samuel Lawrence had gone to the Hill Cumorah at one time. "Recollection," p. 4; E. D. Howe, *Mormonism Unvailed* (Painesville, Ohio: By the author, 1834), p. 243. Martin Harris was reputed to have said that Lawrence was a member of the money-digging company with which the Smiths were associated. *Tiffany's Monthly,* 5:164. Knight recalled Joseph instructing his father to tell Lawrence that if he showed up at the hill, Joseph would "thrash the stumps with him." Jessee, "Joseph Knight's Recollection," p. 33.

2. Lucy Smith, *Biographical Sketches,* p. 100.

3. Ibid., pp. 99-101.

4. Ibid., p. 101, Lucy Smith, Preliminary Manuscript, pp. 61-62; Jessee,

"Joseph Knight's Recollection," p. 33. A description attributed to Martin Harris added that the glasses were about two inches in diameter, perfectly round, and 5/8 of an inch thick at the center, thinning at the edges. *Tiffany's Monthly,* 5:164-65; *Millennial Star,* 44:87; cf. *William Smith on Mormonism,* p. 12.

5. Lucy Smith, *Biographical Sketches,* pp. 101-2, 104. Martin Harris said the plates were first hidden in a hollow oak tree top. *Tiffany's Monthly,* 5:165; cf. Howe, *Mormonism Unvailed,* p. 246. Willard Chase said Joseph asked him to make a box. Howe, *Mormonism Unvailed,* p. 245.

6. Brigham Young went on to say, "When Joseph obtained the treasure, the priests, the deacons, and religionists of every grade, went hand in hand with the fortune teller, and with every wicked person, to get it out of his hands, and to accomplish this, a part of them came out and persecuted him." *Journal of Discourses,* 26 vols. (London: Latter-day Saints' Book Depot, 1855-86), 2:180-81.

7. Lucy Smith, *Biographical Sketches,* pp. 102-3; Lucy Smith, Preliminary Manuscript, p. 63.

8. Lucy Smith, *Biographical Sketches,* pp. 104-5; *Tiffany's Monthly,* 5:166. Willard Chase said Joseph told him the plates weighed between forty and sixty pounds. Howe, *Mormonism Unvailed,* pp. 245-46.

9. Lucy Smith, *Biographical Sketches,* p. 106.

10. Ibid., pp. 106, 108; Jessee, "Joseph Knight's Recollection," pp. 33-34.

11. *Tiffany's Monthly,* 5:167; Jessee, "Joseph Knight's Recollection," pp. 33-34; *Kansas City Daily Journal,* June 5, 1881, cited in Porter, "Study of Origins," p. 235. Willard Chase later claimed he was promised "a share in the book" in return for making a box for the plates. Howe, *Mormonism Unvailed,* p. 245.

12. Lucy Smith, *Biographical Sketches,* pp. 108-9; *Tiffany's Monthly,* 5:167.

13. For background on Martin Harris, see Richard L. Anderson, "Martin Harris, the Honorable New York Farmer," *Improvement Era,* 72 (Feb., 1969):18-21; Backman, *Joseph Smith's First Vision,* pp. 14-15; John Alonzo Clark, *Gleanings by the Way* (Philadelphia: W. J. and J. K. Simon, 1842), p. 223; Stanley B. Kimball, "The Anthon Transcript: People, Primary Sources, and Problems," *B.Y.U. Studies,* 10 (Spring, 1970):326-28; Wayne Cutler Gunnell, "Martin Harris, Witness and Benefactor to the Book of Mormon" (M.A. thesis, Brigham Young University, 1971).

14. *Tiffany's Monthly,* 5:164, 166-67; Howe, *Mormonism Unvailed,* p. 255; Lucy Smith, *Biographical Sketches,* pp. 110-11.

15. Lucy Smith, *Biographical Sketches,* pp. 111-12; *Tiffany's Monthly,* 5:167. Martin Harris said his wife and daughter returned from the visit to the Smiths with a report of having hefted the plates in their box. *Tiffany's Monthly,* 5:168.

16. *Tiffany's Monthly,* 5:168-70. There is some evidence that Martin and two others went to Hill Cumorah to look for more treasure but succeeded only in finding a stone box. "We got excited about it and dug quite carefully around it, and we were ready to take it up, but behold by some unseen power, it slipped back into the hill." Interview with Ole Jensen, July, 1875, cited in Donna Hill, *Joseph Smith, the First Mormon* (Garden City, N.Y.: Doubleday, 1977), p. 66. David Whitmer talked to Palmyra people who said they knew Joseph had the

plates because they "saw the place in the hill that he took them out of, just as he described it to us before he obtained them." *Kansas City Daily Journal,* June 5, 1881, cited in Porter, "Study of Origins," p. 235.

17. *Tiffany's Monthly,* 5:170.

18. Lucy Smith, *Biographical Sketches,* p. 113; Lucy Smith, Preliminary Manuscript, p. 73; *Tiffany's Monthly,* 5:170. Peter Ingersoll said Joseph asked him for a loan, with Alva Hale promising security. Howe, *Mormonism Unvailed,* p. 236.

19. Lucy Smith, *Biographical Sketches,* p. 113; *Tiffany's Monthly,* 5:170. Joseph Knight said Emma wished to return to her family in Harmony because she was feeling unwell. Jessee, "Joseph Knight's Recollection," p. 34.

20. Howe, *Mormonism Unvailed,* p. 264; Jessee, "Joseph Knight's Recollection," p. 34. For the history of the house where Joseph and Emma lived, see Porter, "Study of Origins," pp. 133-37.

21. Joseph Smith, *History of the Church,* 1:12, 19; *Doctrine and Covenants,* section 9, verses 7-8 (henceforth cited as 9:7-8); Lucy Smith, Preliminary Manuscript, p. 70; Jessee, "Joseph Knight's Recollection," p. 34.

22. Joseph Smith Letter Books, p. 5, Church Archives, quoted in Hill, *Joseph Smith,* p. 75; Lucy Smith, *Biographical Sketches,* pp. 113-14.

23. Jessee, "Joseph Knight's Recollection," p. 34; Lucy Smith, Preliminary Manuscript, p. 70; Lucy Smith, *Biographical Sketches,* pp. 113-14; Fayette Lapham, "Interview with the Father of Joseph Smith . . . ," *Historical Magazine* (1870), reprinted in Kirkham, *New Witness,* 2:387; Joseph Smith, *History of the Church,* 1:19. John Clark, who says Martin called on him before setting out for the East, reported that he went "in quest of some interpreter who should be able to decipher the mysterious characters of the golden Bible." Kirkham, *New Witness,* 1:417.

24. Kimball, "Anthon Transcript," pp. 328-29, 334; Joseph Smith, *History of the Church,* 1:20.

25. Kimball, "Anthon Transcript," pp. 336-37.

26. The 1834 Anthon letter first appeared in Howe, *Mormonism Unvailed,* pp. 269-72, and the 1841 letter in Clark, *Gleanings,* chap. 22. Both are reprinted in Kirkham, *New Witness,* 1:414-21.

27. Kirkham, *New Witness,* 1:416-18. Two versions of the Anthon Transcript were published in 1844. David Whitmer's grandson donated a copy to the RLDS Church in 1903. David Whitmer earlier claimed that Martin Harris gave him the original. Kimball, "Anthon Transcript," pp. 346-49. In Apr., 1980, the original was found sealed between the pages of a Smith family Bible. Daniel W. Bachman, "Sealed in a Book: Preliminary Observations on the Newly Found 'Anthon Transcript,' " *B.Y.U. Studies,* 20 (Spring, 1980):321-45. See also Edward H. Ashment, "The Book of Mormon and the Anthon Transcript: An Interim Report," *Sunstone,* 5 (May-June, 1980):29-31. On the authenticity of the characters, see Ariel L. Crowley, "The Anthon Transcript: An Evidence for the Truth of the Prophet's Account of the Origin of the Book of Mormon," *Improvement Era,* 45 (1942):14-15, 58-60, 76-80, 124-25, 150-51, 182-83.

28. Joseph Smith, *History of the Church*, 1:20. Ariel Crowley has identified transcript characters that somewhat resemble Chaldaic, Arabic, and Assyriac and could have led Anthon to his opinion. "Anthon Transcript," p. 76. One difficulty with the Harris story is that the characters on the Anthon Transcript are still undecipherable. Either Anthon was bluffing or Harris was mixed up.

29. Joseph Smith, *History of the Church*, 1:20. Harris says he subsequently went to Mitchill, who confirmed Anthon's judgment; Anthon said Harris arrived with a note from Mitchill. Kirkham, *New Witness*, 1:415, 418.

30. Joseph Smith Letter Book, p. 5, quoted in Hill, *Joseph Smith*, pp. 77-78. Joseph Smith wrote a note on the back of the Anthon Transcript about the fulfillment of the prophecy: "These caractors were dilligently coppied by my own hand from the plates of gold and given to Martin Harris who took them to New York Citty but the learned could not translate it because the Lord would not open it to them in fulfillment of the propscy of Isaih written in the 29th chapter and 11th verse." Dean Jessee, judging from the similarity of the ink in the note and in the characters, believes that the note was written soon after the characters. Bachman, "Sealed in a Book," pp. 330, 344.

31. Jessee, "Joseph Knight's Recollection," p. 35. In his Feb., 1835, letter on Joseph Smith in the *Messenger and Advocate*, Oliver Cowdery said the angel told Joseph that "the scriptures must be fulfilled before it is translated, which says that the words of a book, which were sealed, were presented to the learned; for thus has God determined to leave men without excuse. . . ." Orson Pratt said Martin Harris had no knowledge of Isaiah 29 before he went to New York City. *Journal of Discourses*, 2:288. Before his death Martin Harris is reported to have said the same thing. Anthony Metcalf, *Ten Years before the Mast* (Milad, Idaho: By the author, 1888), p. 71.

32. *Rochester* (N.Y.) *Advertiser and Telegraph*, Aug. 31, 1829, reprinted from the *Palmyra Freeman*, Aug., 1829. The *Painesville* (Ohio) *Telegraph* picked up the story Sept. 22, 1829. W. W. Phelps's letter of Jan. 15, 1831, addressed to E. D. Howe, appeared in *Mormonism Unvailed*, p. 273. 1836 is the first missionary reference cited by Robert N. Hullinger, *Mormon Answer to Skepticism: Why Joseph Smith Wrote the Book of Mormon* (St. Louis: Clayton Publishing House, 1980), p. 94. James McChesney tells of a Mormon sermon on Isaiah 29 preached in Brooklyn in that year in *An Antidote to Mormonism* (New York: By the author, 1838), p. 21.

33. Lucy Smith, *Biographical Sketches*, p. 115; Kimball, "Anthon Transcript," pp. 330, 343; Pomeroy Tucker, *Origin, Rise and Progress of Mormonsim* (New York: D. Appleton and Co., 1867), p. 42; Clark, *Gleanings*, pp. 229-30. When James Gordon Bennett of the *New York Morning Courier and Enquirer* interviewed Charles Butler, the Geneva banker to whom Martin Harris applied for a loan to subsidize printing of the Book of Mormon, Butler recalled Martin saying the professor at Columbia thought the characters "very curious but admitted that he could not decypher them." Leonard J. Arrington, "James Gordon Bennett's 1831 Report on 'The Mormonites,' " *B.Y.U. Studies*, 10 (Spring, 1970):362.

34. Lucy Smith, *Biographical Sketches*, pp. 114-15.

35. Jessee, "Joseph Knight's Recollection," p. 34; Lucy Smith, *Biographical Sketches*, pp. 116-17.

36. Joseph Smith, *History of the Church*, 1:20-21; *Millennial Star*, 44 (1881):78-79, 86-87, quoted in Paul R. Cheesman, *The Keystone of Mormonism: Little Known Truths about the Book of Mormon* (Salt Lake City: Deseret Book Co., 1973), pp. 40-41.

37. Lucy Smith, Preliminary Manuscript, p. 77; Joseph Smith, *History of the Church*, 1:21; cf. *Doctrine and Covenants* 5:1.

38. Lucy Smith, *Biographical Sketches*, p. 118; Porter, "Study of Origins," p. 146. On the baby's name, see Lavina Fielding Anderson, "139-Year-Old Portraits of Joseph and Emma Smith," *Ensign*, 11 (Mar., 1981):64.

39. Lucy Smith, *Biographical Sketches*, pp. 118-20. Geneva was about twenty miles from the Smith farm and a likely stopping place.

40. Ibid., pp. 120-21.

41. Ibid., pp. 121-23. Some Palmyrans believed that Mrs. Harris burned the manuscript. Tucker, *Origin*, pp. 45-46. Lucy Smith implied divine retribution when she reported that a dense fog covered Martin Harris's fields and blighted his wheat on the day he discovered the loss.

42. Lucy Smith, *Biographical Sketches*, pp. 121-22. The crisis gives some idea of the family's involvement in Joseph's work. They all were watching and hoping. Lucy's concern went back to the years when Joseph was trying to get the plates, and she felt he was not precise in his obedience. She noted the small errors Joseph made, such as laying the plates down when he took them from the stone box on the second visit instead of holding them until he got home. When Joseph went for the plates in 1827, Lucy "spent the night in prayer and supplication to God, for the anxiety of my mind would not permit me to sleep." That morning her "heart fluttered at every footstep," fearing "lest Joseph might meet with a second disappointment." She trembled as he entered, "lest all might be lost in consequence of some failure in keeping the commandments of God. . . ." Father Smith cautioned the family against taking chances with the plates, reminding them "that for a small thing, Esau lost his birthright and his blessing. It may be so with Joseph." The loss of the 116 pages renewed the family's fear. Lucy Smith, *Biographical Sketches*, pp. 83, 86, 100, 101, 103; see also Preliminary Manuscript, p. 82.

43. *Doctrine and Covenants* 3:4, 11.

44. Joseph Smith, *History of the Church*, 1:21-22; Lucy Smith, *Biographical Sketches*, p. 125.

45. *Doctrine and Covenants* 3:1-3, 5-8.

46. Ibid., 3:9-10.

47. Joseph Smith, *History of the Church*, 1:104; see also Richard P. Howard, *Restoration Scriptures: A Study of Their Textual Development* (Independence, Mo.: Herald Publishing House, 1969), pp. 196-97.

48. *Doctrine and Covenants* 3:1, 4.

49. Ibid. 3:16, 19, 20. The fulfillment of ancient covenants was a major

theme in Oliver Cowdery's account of Moroni's instructions in 1823. *Messenger and Advocate,* Feb., July, Oct., 1835.

While the revelation put beyond question Joseph's Christian orientation, it also made clear that he had laid aside evangelical modes of thinking — the preoccupation with personal sin and the yearning for grace and salvation. The revelation said nothing about conviction of sin and humiliation, the standard evangelical themes. The question for Joseph was not so much relief from sin as eligibility to aid in the work of God among the remnants of the ancient tribes. The revelation's most comforting note was the assurance that, if he repented, "thou art still chosen, and art again called to the work. . . ." *Doctrine and Covenants* 3:10.

50. *Amboy Journal,* Mar. 30, 1897. I am indebted to Linda Newell and Valerie Avery for this reference.

51. Lucy Smith, *Biographical Sketches,* pp. 125-26. David Whitmer said Moroni did not return the Urim and Thummim in September, and instead gave Joseph a seerstone that was used for the remaining translation. *Chicago Inter-Ocean,* Oct. 17, 1886; "Question asked of David Whitmer at his home in Richmond Ray County Mo Jan 14-1885 relating to the Book of Mormon and the History of the Church of Jesus Christ of LDS by Z. H. Gurley," Church Archives. *Historical Record,* p. 623, a monthly periodical of church history published between 1882 and 1890, confirmed Whitmer's story. Of the translation process, Emma said, "The first that my husband translated was translated by the use of the Urim and Thummim, and that was the part that Martin Harris lost, after that he used a small stone, not exactly black, but was rather a dark color." Emma Smith Letter Collection, Reorganized Church of Jesus Christ of Latter Day Saints Archives, cited by James E. Lancaster, "By the Gift and Power of God: The Method of Translation of the Book of Mormon," *Saints Herald,* Nov. 15, 1962, p. 15. These references were provided by Richard Van Wagonen and Steve Walker.

52. Jessee, "Joseph Knight's Recollection," pp. 35-36; Joseph Smith, *History of the Church,* 1:28; Lucy Smith, *Biographical Sketches,* p. 126.

53. Lucy Smith, *Biographical Sketches,* pp. 124, 127; Lucy Smith to Mary Pierce, Royalton, Vt., Jan. 23, 1829, Church Archives. In the letter Lucy said William was living with a joiner in Canandaigua that winter, trying his hand at a trade.

54. Jessee, "Joseph Knight's Recollection," pp. 35, 36; *Doctrine and Covenants* 4. Virtually all of the language of section 4 comes from the Bible: verse 1, Isaiah 29:14; verse 2, Mark 12:30, Luke 10:27, 1 Cor. 1:8; verse 4, John 4:35, 36; verse 5, 1 Cor. 13:13; verse 6, 2 Peter 1:5-7; verse 7, Matt. 7:7, 8, Luke 18:1, James 1:5. On the complexities of Joseph Smith Sr.'s second trip to Harmony, see Dean Jessee, "Lucy Mack Smith's 1829 Letter to Mary Smith Pierce," *B.Y.U. Studies,* 22 (Fall, 1982):457-58.

55. Porter, "Study of Origins," pp. 151-53; Lucy Smith, *Biographical Sketches,* p. 124. Emma gave the information in an interview Feb. 4-10, 1879, with her son, Joseph Smith III, published in *Saints Herald* (Plano, Iowa), Oct. 1, 1879, pp. 289-90.

56. *Messenger and Advocate,* Oct., 1834; Lucy Smith, *Biographical Sketches,* pp. 128-29.

57. Information on Oliver Cowdery may be found in Stanley P. Gunn, *Oliver Cowdery, Second Elder and Scribe* (Salt Lake City: Bookcraft, Inc., 1962); Richard L. Anderson, "The Second Witness of Priesthood Restoration," *Improvement Era,* 82 (Sept., 1968):15-24. Oliver Cowdery was a third cousin of Lucy Smith.

58. Lucy Smith, *Biographical Sketches,* pp. 128-30.

59. *Messenger and Advocate,* Oct., 1834; Joseph Smith, *History of the Church,* 1:32; Clark, *Gleanings,* p. 230; *Saints Herald,* May 19, 1888, quoted in Cheesman, *Keystone,* p. 42. Tucker, *Origin,* p. 36, said a blanket hung between Oliver and Joseph.

60. The description of translation comes from Emma Smith, Oliver Cowdery, David Whitmer, Martin Harris, and William Smith. *Saints Herald,* Oct. 1, 1879, May 19, 1888; Oliver Cowdery, *Defence in a Rehearsal of My Grounds for Separating Myself from the Latter Day Saints* (Norton, Ohio: Pressley's Job Office, 1839), p. 22; [David Whitmer], *An Address to All Believers in Christ* (Richmond, Mo.: David Whitmer, 1887), pp. 12, 30; Clark, *Gleanings,* p. 240; *Millennial Star,* 44:78-79, 86-87; *William Smith on Mormonism,* p. 11. Many of the relevant statements are quoted in Cheesman, *Keystone,* pp. 40-43. For further discussion of the translation process, see B. H. Roberts, "Translation of the Book of Mormon," *Improvement Era,* Apr., May, July, 1906, and Lancaster, "By the Gift and Power of God." The most comprehensive account is Richard Van Wagoner and Steve Walker, "Joseph Smith: 'The Gift of Seeing,' " *Dialogue,* 22 (Summer, 1982):48-68. Richard Howard has pointed out that early newspaper accounts of the translation make no mention of the Urim and Thummim. The first was in the *Evening and Morning Star* (Independence, Mo.), Jan., 1833. Previously the instrument was called "interpreters." Howard, *Restoration Scriptures,* p. 207.

61. *Messenger and Advocate,* Oct., 1834. In a pamphlet purportedly published at Norton, Ohio, in 1839, after his alienation from Joseph Smith, Cowdery supposedly said, "I have sometimes had seasons of skepticism in which I did seriously wonder whether the Prophet and I were men in our sober senses when he would be translating from plates through 'the Urimn and Thummimn' and the plates not be in sight at all." *Defence,* p. 22. The pamphlet is called in question because the only source is a reprint by a fervent anti-Mormon, R. B. Neal, in 1906. No original is known to exist, and there is no evidence for a printing establishment in Norton, Ohio, in 1839. Anderson, "Second Witness," pp. 15-24.

62. *Doctrine and Covenants* 6:14, 22-23; Joseph Smith, *History of the Church,* 1:35.

63. *Book of Commandments for the Government of the Church of Christ* (Zion [Independence, Mo.]: W. W. Phelps, 1833; reprinted, Independence, Mo.: Board of Publication, Church of Christ Temple Lot, n.d.), section 7, verse 3 (hereafter cited as 7:3); *Doctrine and Covenants* 8:6, 6:10, 7, 12, 11, 13; cf. Exodus 7, Numbers 17, Hebrews 9:4.

64. *Doctrine and Covenants* 3:11; 6:25-28; see also 5:4, 31.

65. Joseph Smith, *History of the Church,* 1:36; *Doctrine and Covenants* 8:1-4.

66. *Doctrine and Covenants* 9:8, 11, 1, 2. Oliver helped Joseph translate the Book of Abraham. Joseph Smith, *History of the Church,* 2:236, 286; *Messenger and Advocate,* Dec., 1835.

67. *Doctrine and Covenants* 10:14, 18, 31, 39-42. The order of translation has been established through analysis of the handwriting of the original manuscript. The bulk of the writing in the fragments of I Nephi that have been saved is in the hand of Oliver Cowdery, with a number of passages in a hand that most resembles John Whitmer's. Oliver's is the first hand to appear, writing I Nephi 2:2-23. There is no evidence of Emma Smith's hand as would be expected had Joseph begun with I Nephi after the loss of the first 116 pages. Joseph did not meet John Whitmer until after June 1, 1829, when Joseph and Oliver moved to Fayette from Harmony. Thus it is unlikely that Emma and Joseph began work on I Nephi in the winter of 1829 when they resumed translating. It also appears that the Book of Mosiah in the current Book of Mormon is not complete. It begins abruptly without the introduction that Mormon affixed to all the other books he abridged. Possibly the first pages of Mosiah were among the 116 lost. The handwriting analysis was accomplished by Dean Jessee and presented in "The Original Book of Mormon Manuscript," *B.Y.U. Studies,* 10 (Spring, 1970):269-78.

The order of translation in turn bears on the date of section 10 in the *Doctrine and Covenants,* currently dated "summer 1828." The manuscript version of the *History of the Church* gives May, 1829, for the date of section 10. The *Book of Commandments,* the first printed version of the *Doctrine and Covenants,* dated the section May, 1829, as well. A later editor changed the date to summer, 1828, because the directions for translating I Nephi are in that section. The revelation would have lost its point by May, 1829, if Joseph had begun the translation of I Nephi three months previously. On the other hand, if Joseph had not translated I Nephi by May because he had started with Mosiah when he resumed work after the loss of the 116 pages, section 10 was relevant in May.

In conjunction with the dating change of section 10, the text of the manuscript was also altered. Insertions and interpositions in the manuscript in another hand changed the words so as to fit section 10 into the chronology where the later editor believed it rightfully belonged. With the information provided by Dean Jessee's analysis, confidence is restored in the original manuscript and dating. The emendations in the Manuscript *History of the Church* are in vol. A-1, p. 11. For further information on the editorial background of *History of the Church,* see Dean Jessee, "The Writing of Joseph Smith's History," *B.Y.U. Studies,* 11 (Summer, 1971):439-73.

Lucy Smith gave a brief idea of the contents of the lost manuscript in a letter to her sister-in-law, Mary Pierce, written in Jan., 1829, before I Nephi was translated.

I now come. to say something of the record it was placed in the earth many hundred years ago by the forefathers of our Indians, they descended from a prophet of the Lord whose name was Lehi he fled from Jerusalem with his family and also his wife's brother's family a few days before Nebuchadnezzar besieged the City and layed it in ashes, for although Lehi prophesied unto the Jews in the name of the Lord that they must repent of their sins, yet they would not, neither would they believe the wonders which were shown to him in dreams concerning Christ that he should be Crucified, therefore God commanded the people of Lehi to get out of Jerusalem and flee into the wilderness and at length they were directed to enter upon the Land of America: now a part of the people of Lehi whose head was named Laman (a son of Lehi) became savage and they sought to exterminate their more virtuous brethreren [sic] who were called the people of Nephi therefore God cast off the people of Laman and he cursed them with a dark skin but the people of Nephi he preserved and prospered so long as they obeyed his commandments, and they were not unskilled workmen having a knowledge of the arts together with the sciences. but they had among them that same secret society which had brought Jerusalem and the whole nation of the Jews to destruction; and after many years they became the more wicked than their accursed bretheren, and God seeing that they would not repent of the evil he visited them with extinction.

Lucy Smith's account suggests a few of the additional facts in the earlier version, such as Ishmael being the brother of Lehi's wife, Sariah, and the presence in Jerusalem of secret societies like those that later infiltrated Nephite government. Lucy Smith to Mary Pierce, Royalton, Vt., Jan. 23, 1829, Church Archives.

68. Lucy Smith, *Biographical Sketches,* pp. 132-35; *Doctrine and Covenants* 10:20-29, 31-34. At one point Lucy Smith said Mrs. Harris instigated the suit in Aug., 1829; at another she says Joseph moved to Fayette "about the time of the trial," which would be June, 1829. The August date is inconsistent with other events, for Lucy says that Mrs. Harris's action was brought on by news of Joseph's great success in translating and receiving revelations in Harmony. The Harrises knew of this success at least by June when Joseph moved to Fayette and Martin visited him there, and probably much earlier.

69. Jessee, "Joseph Knight's Recollection," p.36; Joseph Smith, *History of the Church,* 1:47, 48. Because Knight was "very anxious to know his duty as to this work," Joseph Smith inquired and received a revelation on his friend's behalf. In words reminiscent of the revelation to Joseph, Sr., Knight was told to "give heed with your might, and then you are called." *Doctrine and Covenants* 12:9.

70. *Messenger and Advocate,* Oct., 1834; Joseph Smith, *History of the Church,* 1:35, 36. The relevant passages in the *Book of Mormon* are Alma 45:18; III Nephi 1:3; 28:7, 38.

71. *Messenger and Advocate,* Oct., 1834; Joseph Smith, *History of the Church,* 1:39-41; *Doctrine and Covenants* 13. Lucy Smith said that "one morning they sat down to their work, as usual, and the first thing which presented itself through the Urim and Thummim, was a commandment for Joseph and Oliver

to repair to the water, and attend to the ordinance of Baptism." *Biographical Sketches,* p. 131.

72. Joseph Smith, *History of the Church,* 1:42-43.

73. Ibid., 1:44; Lucy Smith, *Biographical Sketches,* p. 131.

74. *Doctrine and Covenants* 11:12-16; Joseph Smith, *History of the Church,* 1:51.

75. Joseph Smith, *History of the Church,* 1:44.

76. Porter, "Study of Origins," pp. 164, 223, 225, 235-36; Joseph Smith, *History of the Church,* 1:48; Lucy Smith, *Biographical Sketches,* p. 137.

77. Porter, "Study of Origins," pp. 236-37; Lucy Smith, *Biographical Sketches,* pp. 136-37. David Whitmer said it took two and a half days to drive from Fayette to Harmony. David Whitmer told about his first encounter with the gold plates and Oliver Cowdery in an interview in the *Kansas City Daily Journal,* June 5, 1881. He related the small miracles connected with the journey in an interview with James Hart printed in the *Deseret Evening News* (Salt Lake City), Mar. 25, 1884, and with Orson Pratt and Joseph F. Smith in the same newspaper Nov. 16, 1878.

78. *Deseret Evening News,* Nov. 16, 1878; Joseph Smith, *History of the Church,* 1:48-49. Lucy Smith said that Joseph was directed to let the angel carry the plates to Fayette. After Joseph got to the Whitmers, "the angel would meet him in the garden, and deliver them up again into his hands." Lucy Smith, *Biographical Sketches,* p. 137.

79. Porter, "Study of Origins," pp. 224-28, 230.

80. Ibid., pp. 229-30.

81. *Deseret Evening News,* Nov. 16, 1878; *Doctrine and Covenants* 14, 15, 16; Joseph Smith *History of the Church,* 1:51.

82. *Deseret Evening News,* Mar. 25, 1884; Porter, "Study of Origins," p. 238; Jessee, "Book of Mormon Manuscripts," pp. 273, 276-77; Joseph Smith, *History of the Church,* 1:49.

83. David Whitmer, *Address to All Believers,* p. 30; statement to William H. Kelley and G. A. Blakesless, Sept. 15, 1882, quoted in Roberts, *Comprehensive History,* 1:130-31.

84. Joseph Smith, *History of the Church,* 1:51.

85. *Doctrine and Covenants* 5:7.

86. Ibid. 5:2, 10, 11, 13, 24.

87. In his history Joseph referred to the two passages in the probable order of translation, first Ether and then II Nephi. He did not mention II Nephi 27:12, perhaps because they were not that far along. Joseph Smith, *History of the Church,* 1:52. The Book of Mormon quotation is from II Nephi 27:12.

88. Joseph Smith, *History of the Church,* 1:53; *Doctrine and Covenants* 17. Lucy Smith remembered Martin accompanying her and her husband on the trip to the Whitmers'. *Biographical Sketches,* p. 138.

89. Lucy Smith, *Biographical Sketches,* p. 138.

90. David Whitmer gave an account of the vision in *Kansas City Daily*

Journal, June 5, 1881, and *Saints Herald,* Mar. 1, 1882. Joseph Smith's account is in *History of the Church,* 1:54-55.

91. Joseph Smith, *History of the Church,* 1:55.

92. Lucy Smith also remembered Martin Harris as saying, "I have also looked upon the plates and handled them with my hands. . . ." The written testimony of the three witnesses makes no mention of handling the plates. Preliminary Manuscript, p. 104.

93. Lucy Smith, *Biographical Sketches,* p. 139.

94. Joseph Smith, *History of the Church,* 1:56; Hill, *Joseph Smith,* pp. 90-94. For the later lives of the three men, see Richard L. Anderson, *Investigating the Book of Mormon Witnesses* (Salt Lake City: Deseret Book, 1981).

95. Joseph makes no mention of a visit to Palmyra between the experiences of the three and the eight witnesses. He places the visit later. *History of the Church,* 1:57, 71. The Smiths were about to be forced to leave their rented farm in Feb., 1829, when Oliver first came to live with them. *William Smith on Mormonism,* p. 14; Porter, "Study on Origins," pp. 108-9; Lucy Smith, *Biographical Sketches,* p. 129.

96. Joseph Smith, *History of the Church,* 1:57-58. Lucy Smith said Joseph had previously learned that one of the ancient Nephites would bring the plates to the Smith place of worship. For further information on this group, see Richard L. Anderson, "Five Who Handled the Plates," *Improvement Era,* 72 (July, 1969):39ff.

97. David Whitmer said the translation was completed around July 1, 1829. *Kansas City Daily Journal,* June 5, 1881. Lucy Smith placed completion prior to the vision of the three witnesses, which would have been near the middle of June. *Biographical Sketches,* p. 138; cf. Whitmer, *Address to All Believers,* p. 30.

98. Joseph Smith, *History of the Church,* 1:60-61; *Doctrine and Covenants* 128:21. David Whitmer claimed that he and at least five others were ordained elders by Aug., 1829: Joseph Smith, Oliver Cowdery, Peter Whitmer, Samuel H. Smith, and Hyrum Smith. *Address to All Believers,* p. 32.

99. Joseph Smith, *History of the Church,* 1:58, 71; Porter, "Study of Origins," pp. 86-87; Tucker, *Origin,* pp. 51-53. Lucy Smith said that a gang of Palmyra toughs planned to stop Joseph from signing the agreement, but he walked unharmed between them as they lined the fence along his route. Lucy Smith, *Biographial Sketches,* pp. 141-43.

100. Tucker, *Origin,* p. 54. Tucker said Joseph Smith applied unsuccessfully to George Crane, a Quaker living in Macedon, for funding. Lucy Smith understood that Martin Harris contracted for half the costs and Joseph and Hyrum for the other half. *Biographical Sketches,* p. 142. The Harris mortgage is dated Aug. 25, 1829. Porter, "Study of Origins," p. 88.

101. Lucy Smith, *Biographical Sketches,* pp. 142-43; Tucker, *Origin,* p. 53; Thomas Gregg, *Prophet of Palmyra* (New York: J. B. Alden, 1890), pp. 39-43; John H. Gilbert to James T. Cobb, Palmyra, Feb. 10, 1879, quoted in Porter, "Study of Origins," pp. 88-89; Oliver Cowdery, Manchester, to Joseph Smith, Jr., Dec. 28, and Nov. 6 1829, Joseph Smith Collection, Box 2, Folder 1, Church

Archives. In the Nov. 25, 1830, issue of the *Cleveland Herald* the editor reported knowing Oliver Cowdery as a "dabbler in the art of Printing" seven or eight years earlier. In the Nov. 6, 1829, letter to Joseph, Oliver reported a brief delay while Grandin waited for additional type. The Book of Mormon job may have exceeded Grandin's normal capacities.

102. Joseph Smith, Harmony, to Oliver Cowdery, Oct. 22, 1829, Joseph Smith Collection. Lucy Smith implies that Joseph returned to Harmony immediately after contracting with Grandin, which would have been in late June or July, but in addition to Joseph's own word in the above letter, Pomeroy Tucker and Stephen Harding say they saw him in the printing office after work on the Book of Mormon began. Lucy Smith, *Biographical Sketches*, p. 142; Tucker, *Origin*, p. 56; Gregg, *Prophet of Palmyra*, pp. 280-84.

103. Russell R. Rich, "The Dogberry Papers and the Book of Mormon," *B.Y.U.Studies*, 10 (Spring, 1970):316-17. Lucy Smith identifies Dogberry as Abner Cole. *Biographical Sketches*, p. 148.

104. Lucy Smith, *Biographical Sketches*, p. 149; Oliver Cowdery to Joseph Smith, Jr., Dec. 28, 1829.

105. Lucy Smith, *Biographical Sketches*, pp. 149-50; Rich, "Dogberry Papers," pp. 317-18. Dogberry's subsequent paper, the *Liberal Advocate*, is described in Joseph W. Barnes, "Obediah Dogberry: Rochester Freethinker," *Rochester History*, 36 (July, 1974):1-23.

106. Rich, "Dogberry Papers," p. 316; Lucy Smith, *Biographical Sketches*, pp. 143-44, 146-47; Backman, *Joseph Smith's First Vision*, pp. 182-83.

107. Cole's comments in the Palmyra *Reflector* are reprinted in Kirkham, *New Witness*, 2:29-30, 36-37. On Luther Howard, see Rich, "Dogberry Papers," p. 320. Lucy Smith said Cole peddled his papers ten or twenty miles into the country. *Biographical Sketches*, p. 149.

108. Oliver Cowdery to Joseph Smith, Nov. 6, 1829; Lucy Smith, *Biographical Sketches*, pp. 150-51.

109. The agreement is in the Joseph Smith, Sr., file, Church Archives, according to Hill, *Joseph Smith*, p. 97. On the Toronto trip, see David Whitmer, *Address to All Believers*, pp. 30-31; Oliver Cowdery, *Defence*. Lucy Smith, *Biographical Sketches*, p. 151. This may have been the time when Martin Harris requested a $1,300 loan from Charles Butler of the New York Life Insurance and Trust Company of Geneva, N.Y. Butler told Harris that publishing a bible was improper business for a farmer. Butler dated Harris's visit in 1831 or 1832, an error unless Martin went to Butler in the spring of 1831 as the note to Grandin fell due. Charles Butler Papers, Library of Congress. The 1832 date is eliminated because James Gordon Bennett interviewed Butler in the summer of 1831 and Harris had made his application before that time. Arrington, "Bennett's 1831 Report," p. 355. See also Hill, *Joseph Smith*, p. 95.

110. Grandin announced in the Mar. 19 issue that the *Book of Mormon* would be ready in the coming week.

111. Jessee, "Joseph Knight's Recollection," pp. 36-37; *Doctrine and Cov-*

enants 19:26, 35. On poor sales, see Lucy Smith, *Biographical Sketches,* p. 152; Tucker, *Origin,* p. 60.

112. Francis Kirkham has compiled a great many of the news articles on Mormonism in *New Witness,* 2:28-50. The articles noted by Kirkham (plus one additional essay in the *Painesville Telegraph*) appeared in the following order: *Wayne Sentinel,* June 26, 1829; *Rochester Advertiser,* Aug. 21, 1829; *Palmyra Reflector,* Sept. 2, 1829; *Rochester Gem,* Sept. 5, 1829; *Palmyra Reflector,* Sept. 16, 1829; *Painesville Telegraph,* Sept. 22, 1829; *Palmyra Reflector,* Oct. 7, Dec. 9, 1829, Jan. 2, Feb. 27, 1830; *Wayne Sentinel,* Mar. 19 and 26, 1830; *Rochester Republican,* Mar. 30, 1830; *Rochester Daily Advertiser,* Apr. 2, 1830; *Palmyra Reflector,* Apr. 19, May 1, 1830; *Horn of the Green Mountains* (Manchester, Vt.), May 4, 1830; *Rochester Gem,* May 15, 1830. The Bennett quote is from Arrington, "Bennett's 1831 Report," p. 357.

113. Reprinted in Kirkham, *New Witness,* 2:30, 31.

114. Ibid., 2:31-32, 40-41, 47-48.

115. *The Book of Mormon* (Palmyra, N.Y.: E. B. Grandin for the author, 1830), pp. v, vi.

116. *Book of Mormon* (1830), p. vi.

IV. THE BOOK OF MORMON

1. Mormon 2:1; 1:15. On Mormon's years, see Mormon 2:2; 8:1-5.

2. Mormon 2:13, 15, 8, 18.

3. Alma 50:20. Lehi first enunciated this promise, and subsequent prophets repeated it, using almost identical words and referring to them as the words the Lord spoke to Lehi. II Nephi 1:9, 10, 20, 32; 3:2; 4:4; Jarom 9; Omni 6; Mosiah 2:22, 31; Alma 9:13; 36:1, 30; 37:13; 38:1; 45:6-8; 48:15.

4. II Nephi 5:21.

5. II Nephi 5:25.

6. Mormon 5:17-18.

7. Mormon 6:4, 6.

8. Mormon 6:7-22.

9. Mormon 8:2-6.

10. Mosiah 8:7-19; 28:11-17. In an editorial aside Mormon commented that the account on the twenty-four gold plates would "be written hereafter; for behold, it is expedient that all people should know the things which are written in this account." Mosiah 28:19. Moroni may have translated the Book of Ether to comply with his father's request.

11. Ether 13:13-18; 15:34.

12. Ether 1:34; 2:13, 16-17; 3:1, 8, 25; 15:33; Moroni 9:23.

13. Ether 4:4-7; 5:1.

14. Moroni 1:1-4; 10:32; Joseph Smith, *History of the Church,* 1:11.

15. *Book of Mormon* (1830), pp. 531-34. On the structure of the book, see John A. Tvedtnes, "Composition and History of the Book of Mormon," *New Era,* Sept., 1974, pp. 41-43.

16. In their wordprint analysis of Book of Mormon authors, Wayne Larsen, Alvin C. Rencher, and Tim Layton observe that the authorship or source shifts approximately 2,000 times in the text of the Book of Mormon. "Who Wrote the Book of Mormon? An Analysis of Wordprints," *B.Y.U. Studies*, 20 (Spring, 1980):229.

17. For efforts in the direction of a literary analysis, see Douglas Wilson, "Prospects for the Study of the Book of Mormon as a Work of American Literature," *Dialogue*, 3 (Spring, 1968):29-41; John W. Welch, "Chiasmus in the Book of Mormon," *B.Y.U. Studies*, 10 (Autumn, 1969):69-84; Stan Larson, "Textual Variants in Book of Mormon Scholarship," *Dialogue*, 10 (Autumn, 1977):8-30; Noel B. Reynolds, "Nephi's Outline," *B.Y.U. Studies*, 20 (Winter, 1980):131-49; Steven C. Walker, "More Than Meets the Eye: Concentration in the Book of Mormon," *B.Y.U. Studies*, 20 (Winter, 1980):199-205. No one has exceeded Hugh Nibley's appreciation of the complexity of the Book of Mormon. See *Lehi in the Desert and the World of the Jaredites* (Salt Lake City: Bookcraft, 1952); *An Approach to the Book of Mormon*, 2d ed. (Salt Lake City: Deseret Book Co., 1964); and *Since Cumorah: The Book of Mormon in the Modern World* (Salt Lake City: Deseret Book Co., 1967). A recent collection of essays that shows the difficulty of explaining the Book of Mormon as Joseph Smith's production is Noel B. Reynolds, ed., *Book of Mormon Authorship: New Light on Ancient Origins* (Provo, Utah: Religious Studies Center, Brigham Young University, 1982).

18. Joseph Smith, *History of the Church*, 1:84. Kirkham reprints the Palmyra *Reflector* articles in *New Witness*, 2:53, 54. Most of the early newspaper articles on Mormonism can be most conveniently consulted in the same volume.

19. Kirkham, *New Witness*, 2:53, 56.

20. Ibid., 2:42-43, 89-94. Professor Milton Backman of Brigham Young University has made photocopies of articles on Mormonism in the *Painesville* (Ohio) *Telegraph* and other early Ohio newspapers and deposited them in the Brigham Young University Library.

21. Kirkham, *New Witness*, 2:64-65.

22. Ibid., 2:60-62, 65-66, 70, 93, 95; Alexander Campbell, *Delusions: An Analysis of the Book of Mormon* (Boston: Benjamin H. Greene, 1832), pp. 5-6. On Cole as a promulgator of skepticism, see Joseph W. Banner, "Obediah Dogberry: Rochester Free-thinker," *Rochester History*, 36 (July, 1974):1-24.

23. Kirkham, *New Witness*, 2:66, 71; cf. 73, 76.

24. Ibid., 2:68. By the same token, Palmyra residents claimed the believers in Mormonism were "generally of the dregs of community, and the most unlettered people than can be found anywhere." Ibid., 2:98. In Ohio the Mormon missionaries' labors were "principally blest," according to the *Cleveland Herald* of Nov. 25, 1830, "among the superstitious and ignorant or hypocritical. . . ."

25. Nov. 30, Dec. 7, 1830, Feb. 15, 1831, in Kirkham, *New Witness*, 2:43, 45, 85. Thomas Campbell argued that God provided New Testament missionaries with "such potent and evincive arguments, both prophetic and miraculous, as no candid inquirer could mistake, without abandoning both his senses and his reason." Kirkham, *New Witness*, 2:90; cf. Campbell, *Delusions*, p. 15.

The Book of Mormon actually threatened the Bible, unless faith in the Bible could be clearly distinguished from superstitious belief in the Book of Mormon. The Reverend John A. Clark, a local Episcopal priest and acquaintance of Martin Harris, thought this was "one of the most pernicious features of this Historical Romance, — that it claims for itself an entire equality in point of divine authority with the sacred canon. It is not only calculated to deceive and delude the credulous, and marvel loving, but to strengthen the cause of infidelity." John A. Clark, *Gleanings by the Way* (Philadelphia and New York: W. J. and J. K. Simon and Robert Carter, 1842), p. 282.

The Book of Mormon eventually spawned a series of volumes dealing with evidences for it, modeled after the apologies for the Bible: Charles Thompson, *Evidences in Proof of the Book of Mormon* (Batavia, N.Y.: D. D. Waite, 1841); *The External Evidences of the Book of Mormon, Examined* (London: Briscoe, n.d.); J. H. Flanigan, *Mormonism Triumphant: A Reply to Palmer's Internal Evidence against the Book of Mormon* (Liverpool: R. James, 1849); and the culminating work in this genre, B. H. Roberts, *New Witness for God,* 2d ed. (Salt Lake City: Deseret News, 1911).

26. William Paley, *The Works of William Paley,* 5 vols. (Boston and Newport, R.I.: J. Belcher, and Rousmaniere and Barber, 1810-12), 2:65, 66, 207. This analysis is elaborated more fully in Richard L. Bushman, *Joseph Smith and Skepticism* (Provo, Utah: Brigham Young University Press, 1974).

27. Kirkham, *New Witness,* 2:73.

28. *Doctrine and Covenants* 24:13; 63:8-9, 11-12; Campbell, *Delusions,* p. 15. The story of the First Vision and of the visitation of Moroni as composed in 1838 showed more signs of acknowledging the arguments of the rationalists. Joseph presented himself as an innocent boy who met intense persecution and yet clung to his faith because he "had actually seen a light, and in the midst of that light I saw two Personages, and they did in reality speak to me. . . ." The point was that he had no other reason for believing except the miracle, and he persisted despite the persecution. Joseph Smith, *History of the Church,* 1:7-8; Bushman, *Joseph Smith and Skepticism,* p. 7. A visitor to the Whitmers in Mar., 1830, left with the impression that they said "twelve apostles were to be appointed, who would soon confirm their mission with miracles. . . ." David Marks, *The Life of David Marks to the 26th Year of His Age* (Limerick, Me.: The Morning Star, 1831), p. 340.

29. Kirkham, *New Witness,* 1:163; cf. Clark, *Gleanings,* p. 241.

30. Kirkham, *New Witness,* 2:73-74, 53, 98; see also p. 51.

31. Ibid., 2:98. The editors of the *Cleveland Herald* (Nov. 25, 1830) and the *Painesville Telegraph* (Mar. 22, 1831) appear to have accepted the idea that the Book of Mormon was "chiefly garbled from the Old and New Testaments."

32. Kirkham, *New Witness,* 2:91.

33. Campbell, *Delusions,* pp. 11, 13, 15.

34. Ibid., pp. 15, 13, 7, 11-12.

35. E. D. Howe, *Mormonism Unvailed* (Painesville, Ohio: By the author, 1834), pp. 278, 100, 289-90. Sidney Rigdon was suspected of complicity in the

production of the Book of Mormon by the summer of 1831. James Gordon Bennett, who interviewed people concerning Mormonism in that summer, published this hypothesis in the *New York Morning Courier and Enquirer,* Aug. 31, 1831, and the *Hillsborough* (Ohio) *Gazette* of Oct. 29, 1831, stated that "there is no doubt but the ex-parson from Ohio is the author of the book which was recently printed in Palmyra, and passes for the new Bible." On Bennett, see Leonard J. Arrington, "James Gordon Bennett's 1831 Report on 'The Mor-monites,' " *B.Y.U. Studies,* 10 (Spring, 1970):353-74.

I. Woodbridge Riley was the first non-Mormon to publish a refutation of the Spalding hypothesis; it appeared in his Yale Ph.D. thesis and in *The Founder of Mormonism: A Psychological Study of Joseph Smith, Jr.* (New York: Dodd, Mead, 1902), pp. 369-95. Further arguments were presented in Fawn M. Brodie, *No Man Knows My History: The Life of Joseph Smith the Mormon Prophet* (New York: Alfred A. Knopf, 1945), pp. 419-33. The most definitive discussion is Lester E. Bush, Jr., "The Spalding Theory Then and Now," *Dialogue,* 10 (Autumn, 1977):40-69. According to Orasmus Turner, the people of Palmyra did not accept the Spalding hypothesis. *History of the Pioneer Settlement of Phelps and Gorham's Purchase* (Rochester, N.Y.: William Alling, 1851), p. 214; cf. Clark, *Gleanings,* pp. 240-41, 268.

36. Bush, "Spalding Theory," pp. 55-57.

37. Alexander Campbell himself changed his opinion on the authorship of the Book of Mormon, and accepted the Spalding-Rigdon hypothesis despite the contradictions with his own 1831 analysis. *Millennial Harbinger,* 3d ser., 1 (Jan., 1844):38; 4th ser., 6 (Dec., 1856):698.

38. Campbell, *Delusions,* p. 9. Robert N. Hullinger has argued that the Book of Mormon was intended to discredit corrupt modern Masonry, but that Joseph Smith drew heavily on Masonic lore and symbols. *Mormon Answer to Skepticism: Why Joseph Smith Wrote the Book of Mormon* (St. Louis: Clayton Publishing House, 1980), pp. 100-119.

39. The most complete studies of anti-Masonry are Charles McCarthy, "The Anti-Masonic Party: A Study of Political Anti-Masonry in the United States, 1827-1840," American Historical Association, *Annual Report, 1902* (Washington, D.C., 1903), vol. 1, and William Preston Vaughan, *The Antimasonic Party in the United States, 1826-1843* (Lexington: University Press of Kentucky, 1983). For the early stages of the movement, see Ronald P. Formisano and Kathleen Smith Kutolowski, "Antimasonry and Masonry: The Genesis of Protest, 1826-1827," *American Quarterly,* 29 (Summer, 1977): 139-65. See also Whitney R. Cross, *The Burned-Over District: The Social and Intellectual History of Enthusiastic Religion in Western New York, 1800-1850* (Ithaca, N.Y.: Cornell University Press, 1950; paperback ed., New York: Harper Torchbooks, 1965), pp. 113-25.

William Morgan, an indigent stonemanson and one-time member of the lodge in LeRoy, had joined with others to found a lodge in Batavia, N.Y., thirty miles southwest of Rochester. The other organizers, apparently doubtful of his character, left his name off the application and went ahead without him. Presumably angered by this rejection, Morgan conspired with a Batavia printer, David Miller, to publish a book exposing Masonic secrets, *Illustration of Masonry by One of the Fraternity Who Has Devoted Thirty Years to the Subject.* Miller was threatened and an attempt was made to burn his shop. Morgan was arrested on charges of petty theft and jailed in Canandaigua for failure to pay a debt of $3. On Sept. 12, 1826, a group of men came to the jail, paid the debt, and carried Morgan off in a carriage. Later depositions proved that Masons had kidnapped him and driven him with fresh relays of horses across the Canadian border and then back to Fort Niagara. At that point Morgan dropped out of sight forever.

40. Walter F. Prince, "Psychological Tests for the Authorship of the Book of Mormon," *American Journal of Psychology,* 27 (July, 1917):373-95, and "A Footnote: Authorship of the Book of Mormon," *American Journal of Psychology,* 30 (Oct., 1919):427-28. Another non-Mormon critic was unable to place much credence in Prince's analysis. Theodore Schroeder observed of Prince's tests of Book of Mormon authorship that "to me they seem not at all rigorous nor a valid test of anything, and not even an important contribution to any problem except perhaps to the psychology of Dr. Prince." "Authorship of the Book of Mormon," *American Journal of Psychology,* 30 (Jan., 1919):66-72.

41. Helaman 1:11; 2:4, 5.

42. Helaman 11:24-26, 32; III Nephi 2:11-12; 3:1-9; 4:1-14; 27.

43. The best non-Mormon explication of the Book of Mormon is Thomas F. O'Dea, *The Mormons* (Chicago: University of Chicago Press, 1957), chap. 2, followed in a more hostile spirit by Riley, *Founder of Mormonism,* pp. 77-138.

44. William Morgan himself set the pattern for anti-Masonic literature in *Illustrations of Masonry,* 3d ed. (New York: Printed for the author, 1827). Twelve editions were brought out in Rochester in 1827. Blake McKelvey, *Rochester: The Water-Power City, 1812-1854* (Cambridge, Mass.: Harvard University Press, 1945), pp. 154-55. For guides to the literature, see Formisano and Kutolowski, "Antimasonry and Masonry," n. 8, and Milton W. Hamilton, "Antimasonic Newspapers, 1826-1834," *Papers of the Bibliographical Society of America,* 32 (1938):74ff.

45. See note 37.

46. The *Painesville Telegraph* reported on Mar. 22, 1831, that one Billy Perkins said that Mormonism was the anti-Masonic religion "because *all* who have embraced it are antimasons." The editor, himself an anti-Mason, reminded Perkins that the Mormon bible was printed in a Masonic printing office under a Masonic injunction of secrecy. The exchange probably represented a gambit of the Masonic and Anti-Masonic parties around Painesville to discredit one another by associating the Mormons with their opponents.

47. Campbell, *Delusions,* p. 13; Mosiah 29; Alma 1:11; II Nephi 10:11, 14. For an explication of apparent republicanism in the Book of Mormon, see O'Dea, *The Mormons,* pp. 32-33, 268, nn. 19-21. The incongruities are enlarged upon in Richard L. Bushman, "The Book of Mormon and the American Revolution," *B.Y.U. Studies,* 17 (Autumn, 1976):3-20.

48. II Nephi 5:18; 6:2; Jacob 1:9; Alma 4:16; 50:39; Helaman 1:13. See also Omni 12; Mosiah 7:9; 19:26; 23:6.

49. Mosiah 29:13-25; Alma 1:14; 2:2-7; 4:16; 46:34; 50:1-7; 60:1-9; III Nephi 3:1.

50. The article entitled "The Book of Mormon" appeared in the magazine *New Yorker* and was reprinted in *Times and Seasons*, Feb. 1, 1841. "One of the Greatest Literacy Curiosities of the Day," *Dialogue*, 12 (Spring, 1979):100-101.

51. Lucy Smith to Mary Pierce, Royalton, Vt., Jan. 23, 1829, Church Archives; Lucy Smith, *Biographical Sketches*, pp. 152, 186; *Painesville Telegraph*, Feb. 15, 1831; Parley P. Pratt, ed., *Autobiography of Parley Parker Pratt*, 5th ed. (Salt Lake City: Deseret Book Co., 1961), p. 59.

52. *Palmyra Register*, Jan. 28, 1818, May 26, June 2, 1819; *Western Farmer*, Sept. 18, 1821; *Palmyra Herald*, Nov. 14, July 24, Oct. 30, 1822, Feb. 19, 1823; *Wayne Sentinel*, Nov. 3, 1824, Oct. 11, 1825, July 24, 1829; Manchester rental library, accession number 208; Robert Silverberg, *Mound Builders of Ancient America: The Archaeology of a Myth* (Greenwich, Conn.: New York Graphic Society, 1968), p. 83. The fullest compilation of sources on the Indians is Hullinger, *Mormon Answer*, pp. 48-64.

53. Silverberg, *Mound Builders*, pp. 82-89; Robert Wauchope, *Lost Tribes and Sunken Continents: Myth and Method in the Study of American Indians* (Chicago: University of Chicago Press, 1962), pp. 97-102. A writer scornful of the idea of a Hebrew connection said the clergy mainly propagated this notion. James Buchanan, *Sketches, etc., of the North American Indians* (New York, 1824).

54. Ethan Smith, *View of the Hebrews: Or, the Tribes of Israel in America*, 2d ed., enl. (Poultney, Vt.: Smith and Shute, 1825), pp. v-viii. A photomechanical reprint of the 1825 edition has been produced by Modern Microfilm Co., Salt Lake City, Utah. On popular and scientific theories of Indian origins, see, besides Silverberg, *Mound Builders*, and Wauchope, *Lost Tribes*, Lee E. Huddleston, *Origins of the American Indians: European Concepts, 1492-1729* (Austin: Published for the Institute of Latin American Studies by the University of Texas Press, [1967]); Peter Toon, ed., *Puritans, the Millennium and the Future of Israel: Puritan Eschatology 1600 to 1660* (Cambridge, England: Clarke, [1970]), pp. 117-21; Roy Harvey Pearce, *Savagism and Civilization: A Study of the Indian and the American Mind* (Baltimore: Johns Hopkins University Press, 1967); Justin Winsor, "The Progress of Opinion Respecting the Origins and Antiquity of Man in America," in *Narrative and Critical History of America*, 8 vols. (Boston: Houghton Mifflin, 1884-89), 1:369-412; cf. 1:115-16. According to Winsor, the most commonly held opinion was that the Indians were Tartars who sailed from Kamachatka to Alaska and drifted down the coast.

On Adair, see *Dictionary of American Biography*, ed. Allen Johnson and Dumas Malone, 10 vols. (New York: Charles Scribner's Sons, 1964), 1:33-34. On Boudinot, see Elias Boudinot, *The Life, Public Services, Addresses, and Letters of Elias Boudinot* (Boston and New York: DaCapa Press, 1971; reprint of 1896 ed.); George Adams Boyd, *Elias Boudinot, Patriot and Statesman 1740-1821*

(Princeton, N.J.: Princeton University Press, 1952). Boudinot spoke at the City Hotel in Palmyra in 1820. Hullinger, *Mormon Answer*, p. 58. On Ethan Smith, see William B. Sprague, *Annals of the American Pulpit*, 9 vols. (New York: R. Couter, 1857-69). On Josiah Priest, see Winthrop Hillyer Duncan, "Josiah Priest, Historian of the American Frontier," *American Antiquarian Society Proceedings*, 44 (1935):45-102.

55. On the comparison of *View of the Hebrews* and the Book of Mormon, see Riley, *Founder of Mormonism*, pp. 126-28 (Riley emphasized the parallels with Priest, *Wonder of Nature*, but Priest plagiarized virtually all of his material word for word from *View of the Hebrews*); Brodie, *No Man*, pp. 45-49; Mervin B. Hogan, " 'A Parallel': A Matter of Chance versus Coincidence," reprinted in the Modern Microfilm edition of *View of the Hebrews*, from *Rocky Mountain Mason*, Jan., 1956; Charles A. Davies, " 'View of the Hebrews' and the Book of Mormon," *Saints Herald* (Plano, Iowa), Aug. 1, 1962; Robert N. Hullinger, "The Lost Tribes of Israel and the Book of Mormon," *Lutheran Quarterly*, 22 (Aug., 1970):319-29; Spencer J. Palmer and William L. Knecht, "View of the Hebrews: Substitute for Inspiration?" *B.Y.U. Studies*, 5 (Winter, 1964):105-15; Roy E. Weldon, "Masonry and Ethan Smith's 'A View of the Hebrews,' " *Saints Herald*, 119 (Sept., 1972):26-28.

56. Ethan Smith, *View of the Hebrews*, pp. 70-83 (quotation on p. 73).

57. Ibid., pp. 73, 82-83, 172-73.

58. Pratt, *Autobiography*, p. 38. In his 1816 treatise on the lost tribes, Elias Boudinot commented that "every serious reader, who takes the divine scriptures for his rule of conduct, must believe that these people of God are yet in being in our world, however unknown at present to the nations. . . . God has preserved a majority of his people Israel in some unknown part of the world, for the advancement of his own glory." *Star in the West*, p. 49. Wherever word of the Book of Mormon spread, people assumed it told of the ten tribes. After visiting the Whitmers in Mar., 1830, David Marks, an itinerant preacher, wrote that the Book of Mormon was "a history of the ten tribes of Israel which were lost." Marks, *Life*, p. 340. Writing in 1867, Pomeroy Tucker, the Palmyra printer who knew Joseph Smith, said the plates contained a record of "the long-lost tribes of Israel." *Origin, Rise and Progress of Mormonism* (New York: D. Appleton and Co., 1867), p. 29. See also nn. 62 and 63. By contrast, when Lucy Smith wrote her sister-in-law in Vermont, hoping to persuade her to believe, Lucy mentioned Indians but not a word about the lost ten tribes. Lucy Smith to Mary Pierce, Royalton, Vt., Jan. 23, 1829, Church Archives.

59. Ethan Smith, *View of the Hebrews*, p. vi. Smith and Boudinot had exactly the same purpose in mind. Boudinot's views of Israel's future, including the ten tribes, was that "they are to be converted to the faith of Christ, and instructed in their glorious prerogatives, and prepared and assisted to return to their own land and their ancient city, even the city of Zion. . . ." "Who knows but God has raised up these United States in these latter days, for the very purpose of accomplishing his will in bringing his beloved people to their own land." *Star in the West*, p. 297. Hullinger in *Mormon Answer*, p. 58, argues

that Ethan Smith's primary purpose was to refute skeptics by giving evidence of a second people whom God had preserved through the ages along with the Jews. This viewpoint, in my opinion, underestimates the force of Christian preoccupation with the coming millennium and makes primary what was secondary.

60. On the movement to restore Jews to England, see Peter Toon, "Puritan Eschatology," in Toon, *Puritans, the Millennium and the Future of Israel*, pp. 115-27. On Manasseh Ben Israel, see Lynn Glaser, *Indians or Jews? An Introduction to a Reprint of Manasseh Ben Israel's The Hope of Israel* (Gilroy, Calif.: Roy V. Boswell, c. 1973). Increase Mather's sermons on the conversion of the Jews include *The Mystery of Israel's Salvation* (1669), *Strange Doctrine* (1708), *Faith and Fervency* (1710), and *Five Sermons* (1719). In 1621 William Gouge, an influential Presbyterian minister, published a tract by Sir Henry Finch, sergeant at law, called *The Calling of the Jews: A Present to Judah and the Children of Israel that Joyned with Him and to Joseph (The Valiant Tribes of Ephraim) and All the House of Israel that Joyned with Him*. Toon, *Puritans, the Millennium and the Future of Israel*, p. 32.

61. Nahum Sokolow, *History of Zionism, 1600-1918* (New York: Ktav Publishing House, 1969), pp. 80-82; LeRoy Edwin Froom, *The Prophetic Faith of Our Fathers: The Historical Development of Prophetic Interpretation*, 4 vols. (Washington, D.C.: Review and Herald, 1946-54), 3:239-40; Ernest R. Sandeen, *The Roots of Fundamentalism: British and American Millenarianism, 1800-1930* (Chicago: University of Chicago Press, 1970), pp. 20, 55; Lee M. Friedman, *The American Society for Meliorating the Condition of the Jews and Joseph S. C. F. Frey Its Missionary* (Boston: no pub., 1925), p. 12; Aaron Bancroft, *Discourse Delivered before the Worcester Auxiliary Society Meliorating the Condition of the Jews* (Worcester: W. Manning, 1824); George L. Berlin, "Joseph S. C. F. Frey, the Jews, and Early Nineteenth-Century Millenarianism," *Journal of the Early Republic*, 1 (Spring, 1981):27-49.

62. Friedman, *American Society*, pp. 7-10; Ethan Smith, *View of the Hebrews*, p. 118. The pamphlet Frey referred to was Charles Crawford, *Essay upon the Propagation of the Gospel, in Which There Are Facts to Prove That Many of the Indians in America Are Descended from the Ten Tribes* (Philadelphia: J. Gales, 1799; 2d ed., James Humphreys, 1801). Other Englishmen evinced the same interest: Israel Worsley, *A View of the American Indians . . . Shewing Them to Be the Descendants of the Ten Tribes of Israel* (London: Printed for the author by R. Hunter, 1828); Barbara Allan Simon, *Ten Tribes of Israel Historically Identified with the Aborigines of the Western Hemisphere* (London: R. B. Seeley, 1836). For Frey's writings on Indians as the lost ten tribes, see Berlin, "Joseph S. F. C. Frey," pp. 41-43.

63. Lewis F. Allen, "Founding of the City of Ararat on Grand Island by Mordecai M. Noah," *Publications of the Buffalo Historical Society*, 1 (1879):303-28. For local coverage of Noah, see *Wayne Sentinel*, Sept. 27, 1823, Oct. 4, 11, 1825. See also Isaac Goldberg, *Major Noah: American-Jewish Pioneer* (Philadelphia: Jewish Publication Society of America, 1936), p. 148. The most recent

biography of Noah is Jonathan D. Sarna, *Jacksonian Jew: The Two Worlds of Mordecai Noah* (New York: Holmes and Meier, 1981). Noah published his views on Indian origins in *Discourse on the Evidences of American Indians Being the Descendants of the Ten Tribes of Israel* (New York: James Van Norden, 1837).

64. II Nephi 10:22; I Nephi 22:4; 5:14-16; Alma 10:3; 46:23. See also II Nephi 6:5; Jacob 5; III Nephi 15:15; 16:1-4; 17:4; *Doctrine and Covenants* 35:25; 38:33; 39:11.

65. II Nephi 28:11-14; I Nephi 14:2. See also I Nephi 13:5-7, 9, 26, 28, 40-41; 14:7, 11; II Nephi 10:18-19; 28:6, 14; III Nephi 16; 21; 26:20-21; 28:3-4.

66. O'Dea, *The Mormons,* p. 26; II Nephi 28:11-14; Mormon 8:31; Sandeen, *Roots of Fundamentalism,* pp. 13, 22; Marvin Hill, "The Shaping of the Mormon Mind in New England and New York," *B.Y.U. Studies,* 9 (Spring, 1969):354. See also *Doctrine and Covenants* 35:7.

67. Lucy Smith, *Biographical Sketches,* p. 57; George A. Smith, History, cited in Donna Hill, *Joseph Smith, the First Mormon* (Garden City, N.Y.: Doubleday, 1977), pp. 83-84; Lucy Smith to Solomon Mack, Jan 6, 1831, Church Archives.

68. Kirkham, *New Witness,* 1:415; Oliver Cowdery, Manchester, to Joseph Smith, Dec. 28, 1829, Joseph Smith Collection, Box 2, Fd. 1, Church Archives.

69. Porter, "Study of Origins," pp. 94-96; Pratt, *Autobiography,* p. 37.

70. Pratt, *Autobiography,* p. 37; Porter, "Study of Origins," pp. 99, 207.

71. Lucy Smith, *Biographical Sketches,* pp. 166-67; Joseph Smith, *History of the Church,* 1:296-97. For Sidney Ridgon's conversion, see Hill, *Joseph Smith,* p. 122.

72. *Doctine and Covenants* 33:8; 38:39; 20:9; 33:16; Pratt, *Autobiography,* p. 42. See also *Doctrine and Covenant* 10:45; 19:26; 27:5; 42:12.

73. On infant baptism, see Moroni 8:5-24; *Doctrine and Covenants* 68:25. For sacrament prayers, see Moroni 4:3; 5:2; *Doctrine and Covenants* 20:77, 79. The quotation is at *Doctrine and Covenants* 98:32.

74. Campbell, *Delusions,* p. 13; *Doctrine and Covenants* 10:45.

75. For discussions of the Book of Mormon's appeal, see O'Dea *The Mormons,* chap. 2; Marvin Hill, "The Role of Christian Primitivism in the Origin and Development of the Mormon Kingdom, 1830-1844" (Ph.D. diss., University of Chicago, 1968), pp. 111-20. For the appeal of Mormonism generally, see Leonard J. Arrington and Davis Bitton, *The Mormon Experience: A History of the Latter-day Saints* (New York: Alfred A. Knopf, 1969), pp. 20-43.

76. Moroni 10:4.

V. THE CHURCH OF CHRIST

1. Jessee, "Joseph Knight's Recollection," pp. 36-37; Joseph Smith, *History of the Church,* 1:64-65.

2. David Whitmer is the only one to report attendees other than the six elders. He says about twenty were from Colesville, fifteen from Manchester, and twenty from the Fayette area. Journal of Edward Stevenson, Jan. 2, 1887, mi-

crofilm, Church Archives, cited in Porter, "Study of Origins," p. 249. A list of possible attendees along with those known to be there is given in "Lord Chose Organization Date," *Church News*, 50 (Jan. 5, 1980):3. The names of the organizers are known from a statement submitted by Joseph Knight, Jr., Aug. 11, 1862, at Salt Lake City. Joseph Knight was not present himself, but obtained the list from Oliver Cowdery. David Whitmer gave Edward Stevenson a similar list in 1887, except that Whitmer substituted John Whitmer for Samuel Smith. Joseph Smith, *History of the Church*, 1:76; Joseph Knight File, Church Archives; Journal of Edward Stevenson, Jan. 2, 1887. For a full discussion, see Porter, "Study of Origins," p. 249n, and Richard L. Anderson, "Who Were the Six Who Organized the Church on 6 April 1830?" *Ensign*, 10 (June, 1980):44-45. The order of events is described in Joseph Smith, *History of the Church*, 1:77-79. Joseph Knight said that Joseph Smith received the revelation recorded in *Doctrine and Covenants* 21 on the day of organization. Jessee, "Joseph Knight's Recollection," p. 37.

3. Lucy Smith, *Biographical Sketches*, pp. 57, 72; William Smith, in an interview by E. C. Briggs, *Deseret News* (Salt Lake City), Jan. 20, 1894, cited in Donna Hill, *Joseph Smith, the First Mormon* (Garden City, N.Y.: Doubleday, 1977), p. 60n17.

4. Jessee, "Joseph Knight's Recollection," p. 37; Joseph Smith, *History of the Church*, 1:79; Lucy Smith, *Biographical Sketches*, p. 151. Lucy Smith said the baptism occurred in the morning, but Joseph Knight and Joseph Smith, Jr., place it after the organizational meeting.

5. Joseph Smith, *History of the Church*, 4:536; *Doctrine and Covenants* 3:1, 9, 17. Oliver Cowdery said in 1835 that Moroni told Joseph that he was later to receive the priesthood, baptize, and bestow the Holy Ghost. *Messenger and Advocate*, Oct., 1835.

6. *Doctrine and Covenants* 5:14; 10:53, 61, 62; 16:6. See also 14:8; 15:6; 18:41.

7. Ibid. 18:10-15. As one measure of the impact of this revelation, Oliver echoed these words in a letter to Hyrum Smith, June 14, 1829. Joseph Smith Collection, Box 2, Fd. 1, Church Archives.

8. The story of the schism is told in Douglas R. Chandler, "The Formation of the Methodist Protestant Church," in Emory Stevens Bucks, ed., *The History of American Methodism*, 3 vols. (Nashville, Tenn.: Abingdon Press, 1964), 1:636-83 (quotations on pp. 636, 652). Solomon Chamberlain met Brigham and Phineas Young at a conference of reformed Methodists in 1830. Solomon Chamberlain, "A Short Sketch of the Life of Solomon Chamberlain," cited in Porter, "Study of Origins," p. 94.

9. On elders, priests, and teachers, see Alma 6:1; Moroni 2:2; 3:1; 4:1. On the high priest, see Mosiah 29:42; Alma 4:18; 26:7. On the twelve disciples, see III Nephi 12:1; 19:4-6; 27:1-3; IV Nephi 14; Moroni 2.

10. *Doctrine and Covenants* 20:38-46, 48, 57, 70.

11. *Doctrine and Covenants* 20:45, 49, 56, 62, 64. The right of a conference to issue a license was added to 20:64 later. *A Book of Commandments for the*

Government of the Church of Christ (Zion [Independence, Mo.]: W. W. Phelps and Co., 1833; reprinted, Independence, Mo.: Church of Christ, Temple Lot, [n.d.]), 24:44. The elders in conference were to receive the names of new members from the various churches. *Doctrine and Covenants* 20:81, 82.

12. The provision for a sustaining vote, *Doctrine and Covenants* 20:65, was a later addition. See *Book of Commandments* 24:44, 45, where the present verses 62-67 of section 20 are omitted or worded differently.

13. David Whitmer, *An Address to All Believers in Christ* (Richmond, Mo.: By the author, 1887), p. 32; Mosiah 27:5; Alma 1:26.

14. *Doctrine and Covenants* 18:28, 37. David Whitmer said that Joseph and Oliver exercised even less authority prior to Apr. 6, 1830. Whitmer claimed that Joseph assumed the title of "Prophet Seer and Revelator" because "some of the brethren began to think that the Church should have a leader, just like the children of Israel wanting a king." *Address to All Believers*, p. 33.

15. *Doctrine and Covenants* 21:1, 4-5. Even in the disillusionment of his later years, David Whitmer remembered that "we had all confidence in Brother Joseph, thinking that as God has given him so great a gift as to translate the Book of Mormon, that everything he would do must be right." *Address to All Believers*, p. 34. For a moment in Apr., 1830, Joseph may have felt that he was not in need of great authority or even of the divine gift any longer. Long after the event David Whitmer remembered Joseph handing the seerstone to Oliver Cowdery and telling Oliver and David "that he was through with it, and he did not use the stone any more. He said he was through the work that God had given him the gift to perform, except to preach the gospel." *Address to All Believers*, p. 32. If the memory was accurate, Joseph did not labor under the illusion for long.

16. Joseph Smith, *History of the Church*, 1:81; Porter, "Study of Origins," pp. 259-60.

17. Joseph Smith, *History of the Church*, 1:117; "History of Thomas Baldwin Marsh," *Deseret News* (Salt Lake City), Mar. 24, 1858, cited in Porter, "Study of Origins," pp. 94-95; *Doctrine and Covenants* 31:2. Oliver Cowdery wrote to Joseph Smith, Nov. 6, 1829, that a Marsh letter of Oct. 29 reported no success in interesting others in Charlestown. Joseph Smith Collection, Box 2, Fd. 1.

18. Chamberlain, "Short Sketch," quoted in Porter, "Study of Origins," pp. 92-93, 360-62. Porter reproduces the entire "Short Sketch" in Appendix D.

19. Parley P. Pratt, ed., *Autobiography of Parley Parker Pratt*, 5th ed. (Salt Lake City: Deseret Book Co., 1961), pp. 31, 38, 42.

20. Lucy Smith, *Biographical Sketches*, pp. 151-53, 166-67.

21. The definitive discussion of the early converts is Porter, "Study of Origins," pp. 92-101, 198-217, 259-68.

22. Ibid., p. 261; Lucy Smith to Martha Pierce, Royalton, Vt., Jan. 23, 1829, Church Archives; Lucy Smith to Solomon Mack, Jan. 6, 1831, Church Archives; *Mormon Literature*, pp. 543-45; Anderson, *Joseph Smith's New England Heritage*, pp. 111-13. On the background of Lucy Smith's letter and for an accurate transcription, see Dean Jessee, "Lucy Mack Smith's 1829 Letter to Mary Smith

Pierce," *B.Y.U. Studies,* 22 (Fall, 1982):455-65. John Smith later wrote, "We had always been accustomed to being treated with much harshness by our brother. . . ." Lucy Smith, *Biographical Sketches,* p. 155.

23. Anderson, *Joseph Smith's New England Heritage,* p. 113; Lucy Smith, *Biographical Sketches,* p. 156.

24. Porter, "Study of Origins," p. 102; *Painesville* (Ohio) *Telegraph,* Feb. 15, 1831; *William Smith on Mormonism,* p. 15.

25. *William Smith on Mormonism,* pp. 15-16.

26. *Doctrine and Covenants* 22:1-2. "From this time I could behold the situation of the world," William Smith remembered of his conversion, "and the Spirit taught me that the harvest was great and the laborers were few." *William Smith on Mormonism,* p. 16.

27. *Painesville* (Ohio) *Telegraph,* Feb. 15, 1831; *Doctrine and Covenants* 19:30-31; David Marks, *The Life of David Marks to the 26th Year of His Age* (Limerick, Me.: The Morning Star, 1831), p. 340.

28. Jessee, "Joseph Knight's Recollection," p. 37; Joseph Smith, *History of the Church,* 1:84. Hyrum had purchased an eighty-acre farm adjacent to the Smith property and erected a log house there. *William Smith on Mormonism,* p. 14. For the timing of the move of Joseph Smith, Sr., and Lucy Smith, see Porter, "Study of Origins," pp. 107-8.

29. Joseph Smith, *History of the Church,* 1:82.

30. Ibid., 1:83-84. William Smith's date of the miracle, June 10, conflicts with the well-attested conference on June 9 in Fayette, *William Smith on Mormonism,* p. 10.

31. Jessee, "Joseph Knight's Recollection," p. 37.

32. *Doctrine and Covenants* 19:6, 10, 11, 26; J. Sellar, *Sermons on the Doctrine of Everlasting Punishment* (Canandaigua, N.Y., 1828).

33. *Doctrine and Covenants* 19:15-20.

34. Robert J. Woodford, "The Historical Development of the Doctrine of Covenants" (Ph.D. diss., Brigham Young University, 1974), pp. 287-90. Joseph himself spoke as if section 20 had been given in advance of the organization of the church. *History of the Church,* 1:64.

35. *Doctrine and Covenants* 20:1; *Book of Commandments* 24. Most editions of the *Doctrine and Covenants* give no date for section 20. Woodford, "Historical Development," p. 286.

36. Woodford, "Historical Development," p. 299.

37. For a compilation of religious creeds, see Philip Schaff, *The Creed of Christendom,* vol. 3: *Evangelical Protestant Creeds,* 4th ed., rev. and enl. (Grand Rapids, Mich.: Baker, 1966), and Williston Walker, *The Creeds and Platforms of Congregationalism* (Boston: Pilgrim Press, 1960; reprint of 1893 ed.). The best analysis of the history and uses of section 20 is Woodford, "Historical Development," pp. 286-93, 299-301.

38. *Doctrine and Covenants* 20:71, 32.

39. Ibid. 20:6, 5.

40. Ibid. 20:35.

41. Journal History, June 9, 1830, Joseph Smith Collection, Box 5, Fd. 15,

Ms d 155. According to the Journal History, Samuel Smith was ordained an elder and Joseph Smith, Sr., and Hyrum Smith were ordained priests.

42. Porter, "Study of Origins," pp. 273-74; Joseph Smith, *History of the Church*, 1:84-86.

43. Joseph Smith, *History of the Church*, 1:86-87.

44. Porter, "Study of Origins," pp. 199-200.

45. Emily Coburn's own account differs in a few details from Joseph Smith's version. Emily M. Austin, *Mormonism; or Life among the Mormons* (Wisconsin: M. J. Cantwell, 1882); Joseph Smith, *History of the Church*, 1:87; Porter, "Study of Origins," pp. 199-201.

46. Hill, *Joseph Smith*, pp. 110-11.

47. Joseph Smith, *History of the Church*, 1:88; Porter, "Study of Origins," pp. 202-3; "Joseph Knight's Incidents," Church Archives.

48. Wesley P. Walters, "Joseph Smith's Bainbridge, N.Y., Court Trials," *Westminster Theological Journal*, 36 (Winter, 1974):124; Joseph Smith, *History of the Church*, 1:88-89; Jessee, "Joseph Knight's Recollection," p. 38.

49. Joseph Smith, *History of the Church*, 1:88, 95; Hill, *Joseph Smith*, p. 113. There is an unexplained contradiction in the records as to the day of the trial. By Joseph's account, the South Bainbridge trial began Tuesday, June 29. Chamberlain's bill for trying Joseph showed Thursday, July 1. Both Joseph Smith and Joseph Knight said the trial occurred the day after the arrest, and Ebenezer Hatch's bill charged the county only for keeping him twenty-four hours. Two days are unaccounted for. Walters, "Bainbridge, N.Y., Court Trials," pp. 124-25; Jessee, "Joseph Knight's Recollection," p. 38; Joseph Smith, *History of the Church*, 1:88-89.

50. Jessee, "Joseph Knight's Recollection," p. 38; Joseph Smith, *History of the Church*, 1:90.

51. Walters, "Bainbridge, N.Y., Court Trials," p. 125; Joseph Smith, *History of the Church*, 1:94-95.

52. Joseph Smith, *History of the Church*, 1:91.

53. Ibid., 1:95-96.

54. Ibid., 1:97; "Joseph Knight's Incidents."

55. Joseph Smith, *History of the Church*, 1:97; *Doctrine and Covenants* 27:12; *Journal of Discourses*, 26 vols. (London: Latter-day Saints' Book Depot, 1855-86), 23:183; Addison Everett to Oliver B. Huntington, St. George, Utah, Feb. 17, 1881, cited in Oliver Boardman Huntington Journal, no. 14, Jan. 31, 1881, Brigham Young University Library, Provo, Utah.

The exact time of the visit of Peter, James, and John has always been a puzzle in Mormon history. Neither Joseph nor any of the other early chroniclers mentioned the event in their histories. It is usually assumed that the visitation must have occurred after the appearance of John the Baptist on May 15, 1829, and before the organization of the church on Apr. 6, 1830. Larry C. Porter has placed the visit of Peter, James, and John in late May or early June, 1829. "Dating the Melchizedek Priesthood," *Ensign*, 9 (June, 1979):5-10. See also B. H. Roberts's note in Joseph Smith, *History of the Church*, 1:40-41n.

There are, however, problems with this sequence. No mention is made in the records of a visit to Colesville in June, 1829, or of persecution there, or of a trial involving Mr. Reid, conditions associated with the visit by Snow and Everett. Moreover, Joseph and Oliver were at the peak of their translation activity in that month, besides moving to Fayette, leaving them little time to spare. On the other hand, the visit to Colesville, the trial, and the assistance of Mr. Reid are all well-attested occurrences in the summer of 1830. Moreover, Joseph inserted the first reference to Peter, James, and John in a revelation dated Aug. 1830. That is why in the text above the visit of Peter, James, and John is assigned to the summer of 1830. But the difficulties with both of the proposed dates — summer 1829 or summer 1830 — means that we will not know for certain until more information is uncovered.

It should be noted that one witness of Oliver Cowdery's return to the church in 1848 reported that he said, "I was also present with Joseph when the Melchisedek Priesthood was conferred by the holy angels of God, which we then conferred on each other, by the will and commandment of God." The fact that the *Deseret News* in reprinting the journal in 1859 miscopied the plural "angels" and made it "angel," and that no one else made much of Cowdery's testimony until later, suggest that the question of Melchisedek Priesthood restoration was not of notable importance at that time. Richard L. Anderson, "Reuben Miller, Recorder of Oliver Cowdery's Reaffirmations," *B.Y.U. Studies,* 8 (Spring, 1968):277-78, 282-85. For the various accounts of priesthood restoration, see Richard L. Anderson, "The Second Witness of Priesthood Restoration," *Improvement Era* (Sept., 1968), pp. 15-20.

56. *Doctrine and Covenants* 25:4, 7-8, 11.

57. Ibid. 25:10, 2; 24:9, 5, 3, 18; Joseph Smith Collection, Ms d 155, Box 6, Fd. 3, Church Archives. Larry Porter presents evidence from the federal census that a boy between ten and fifteen was living with Joseph and Emma that summer and attending school. "Study of Origins," pp. 167-68.

58. *Doctrine and Covenants* 25:5; Joseph Smith, *History of the Church,* 1:101, 98.

59. *Doctrine and Covenants* 24:8, 15-17.

60. Joseph Smith, *History of the Church,* 1:106, 108; *Doctrine and Covenants* 27:3, 4.

61. Joseph Smith, *History of the Church,* 1:108-9. Newel Knight records a derivative version in "Journal of Newel Knight," *Scraps of Biography, Tenth Book of the Faith Promoting Series* (Salt Lake City: Deseret Book Co., 1883), pp. 63-64.

62. Porter, "Study of Origins," pp. 169-70; Joseph Smith, *History of the Church,* pp. 108-9.

63. Joseph Smith, *History of the Church,* 1:104-5; Porter, "Study of Origins," p. 167.

64. Joseph Smith, *History of the Church,* 1:105.

65. Newel Knight, "Journal," pp. 64-65; Joseph Smith, *History of the*

Church, 1:109-10; Whitmer, *Address to All Believers,* pp. 31-36, 42, 49, 53, 55, 58.

66. Joseph Smith, *History of the Church,* 1:110, 115; *Doctrine and Covenants* 28:12-13; Newel Knight, "Journal," p. 65; Journal History, Sept. 26, 1830.

67. *Doctrine and Covenants* 21:1; 28:2-3, 5-7.

68. Newel Knight, "Journal," pp. 64-65; *Doctrine and Covenants* 28:11; Joseph Smith, *History of the Church,* 1:115.

69. *Doctrine and Covenants* 28:8; 30:7; 32:4; Journal History, Sept. 26, 1830; Pratt, *Autobiography,* p. 47; Lucy Smith, *Biographical Sketches,* p. 169. The covenant was published by Ezra Booth in one of a series of letters in the *Ravenna* (Ohio) *Star,* Dec. 8, 1831, microfilm, Brigham Young University Library, Provo, Utah.

70. *Doctrine and Covenants* 3:16-18; *Ravenna Star,* Dec. 8, 1831.

71. Revelation 21:2; Ether 3:4; *Doctrine and Covenants* 28:9.

72. Revelation 3:12; 21:1, 2; Ether 3:4-6; 13:8-10.

73. *Doctrine and Covenants* 29:7-8, 14-21.

74. Ernest R. Sandeen, *The Roots of Fundamentalism: British and American Millenarianism, 1800-1930* (Chicago: University of Chicago Press, 1970), pp. 12-14, 23.

75. Part of Hiram Page's appeal was that his revelations told about "the upbuilding of Zion." Joseph Smith, *History of the Church,* 1:109.

76. Ibid., 1:127; *Doctrine and Covenants* 34:6; 33:6-7; 35:15, 13.

77. Porter, "Study of Origins," pp. 109, 293; Lucy Smith, *Biographical Sketches,* pp. 159, 171; Hill, *Joseph Smith,* p. 118.

78. Lucy Smith, *Biographical Sketches,* pp. 160-61.

79. Ibid., pp. 163-64.

80. Ibid., pp. 165, 170. Larry Porter calculates that the thirty days' imprisonment extended either from Thursday, Sept. 30, to Oct. 29, or from Oct. 7 to Nov. 5. Lucy placed Joseph Smith Sr.'s arrival in Waterloo during Edward Partridge's visit, which would be after Dec. 10. *Biographical Sketches,* p. 170.

81. Lucy Smith, *Biographical Sketches,* pp. 167-68. Larry Porter has connected the names of various individuals mentioned by Lucy Smith with names in the Seneca Falls census for 1830. Local tradition holds that the Smiths lived there in a neighborhood known as Kingdom. "Study of Origins," pp. 269-73.

82. Lucy Smith, *Biographical Sketches,* pp. 158, 168-69; Jessee, "Joseph Knight's Recollection," p. 38.

83. Lucy Smith, *Biographical Sketches,* p. 170; Joseph Smith, *History of the Church,* 1:129n.

84. John Wickliffe Rigdon, "The Life and Testimony of Sidney Rigdon," ed. Karl Keller, *Dialogue,* 1 (Winter, 1966):18-25; Daryl Chase, "Sidney Rigdon, Early Mormon" (M.A. thesis, University of Chicago, 1931).

85. Joseph Smith, *History of the Church,* 1:128-29; Hill, *Joseph Smith,* pp. 120-22.

86. Whitmer, *Address to All Believers,* p. 35.

87. *Doctrine and Covenants* 35:4, 17-20, 23.

88. Porter, "Study of Origins," pp. 287-89; Jessee, "Joseph Knight's Recollection," p. 38.

89. *Doctrine and Covenants* 37:1, 3; Porter, "Study of Origins," pp. 291-92. Lucy Smith placed John Whitmer's departure for Kirtland in the late fall of 1829 before the Indian missionaries left Kirtland. *Biographical Sketches,* pp. 169-70. The *Painesville Telegraph* reported the arrival of Whitmer in the week prior to the paper's issue of Jan. 18, 1831.

90. Joseph Smith, *History of the Church,* 1:140; *Doctrine and Covenants* 38:28, 31-33, 22; Porter, "Study of Origins," pp. 275, 296. Lucy wrote her brother Solomon Mack on Jan. 6, 1831, that God "has now made a new and everlasting covenant, and all that will hear His voice and enter, He says they shall be gathered together into a land of promise and He himself will come and reign on earth with them a thousand years." Church Archives.

91. *Doctrine and Covenants* 38:37, 18, 35, 39. John Whitmer said some of the Saints doubted the revelation to move to Ohio, thinking that Joseph "invented it himself to deceive the people that in the end he might get gain." Porter, "Study of Origins," p. 311.

92. *Doctrine and Covenants* 38:40; Porter, "Study of Origins," pp. 289-90; Jessee, "Joseph Knight's Recollection," p. 38. Lucy Smith says Ezra Thayer and Newel Knight also accompanied the first group, but Newel Knight led the Colesville Mormons to Ohio later in the spring. *Biographical Sketches,* p. 171. Joseph speaks loosely of traveling to Ohio with Sidney Rigdon and Edward Partridge, but the two groups arrived a few days apart, Sidney on Feb. 1, 1831, and Joseph a few days later. Joseph Smith, *History of the Church,* 1:145; Porter, "Study of Origins," p. 291; *Doctrine and Covenants* 35:22.

93. The Colesville members left their homes on Apr. 19 or 21 and departed Ithaca on Apr. 25, 1931. Porter, "Study of Origins," pp. 297-98, 302-7, 314. Larry C. Porter and Jan Shipps, eds., "The Colesville New York 'Exodus' Seen from Two Documentary Perspectives," *New York History,* 62 (Apr., 1981):201-11.

94. Lucy Smith, *Biographical Sketches,* pp. 172-73; Porter, "Study of Origins," pp. 316-17.

95. Lucy Smith, *Biographical Sketches,* pp. 176-83; Porter "Study of Origins," pp. 308, 319-20.

96. Porter, "Study of Origins," pp. 321-22.

VI. THE RESTORATION OF ALL THINGS

1. Joseph Smith, *History of the Church,* 1:146.

2. A. S. Hayden, *Early History of the Disciples in the Western Reserve, Ohio* (Cincinnati: Chase and Hall, 1875; reprinted, New York: Arno Press and the New York Times, 1972), pp. 217-18.

3. Ibid., pp. 195, 216, 219. For bibliography on the encounter of Mormons and Disciples of Christ, see Hans Rollmann, "The Early Baptist Career of Sidney Rigdon in Warren, Ohio," *B.Y.U. Studies,* 21 (Winter, 1981):37.

4. Marvin S. Hill, "The Role of Christian Primitivism in the Origin and

Development of the Mormon Kingdom, 1830-1844" (Ph.D. diss., University of Chicago, 1968); Peter Crawley, "The Passage of Mormon Primitivism," *Dialogue,* 13 (Winter, 1980):26-37.

5. Robert Frederick West, *Alexander Campbell and Natural Religion* (New Haven, Conn.: Yale University Press, 1948), pp. 172-73.

6. Winfred E. Garrison and Alfred T. DeGroot, *The Disciples of Christ: A History* (St. Louis: Christian Board of Publication, 1948), pp. 185, 188; Hayden, *Early History of the Disciples,* p. 71. Alexander Campbell thought the name "Gospel Restored" was pretentious. Garrison and DeGroot, *Disciples of Christ,* p. 188.

7. Hayden, *Early History of the Disciples,* pp. 192-94; Garrison and DeGroot, *Disciples of Christ,* p. 188.

8. Hayden, *Early History of the Disciples,* pp. 69-71, 76-77.

9. *Doctrine and Covenants* 19:31. Lucy Smith showed an awareness of the issue in a letter to her brother Solomon Mack, Jan. 6, 1831, when she wrote that after the day of Pentecost Peter did not tell his hearers "to go away and mourn over their sins weeks and months, and receive a remission of them and then come and be baptized, but he told them first to repent and be baptized, and the promise was that they should receive a remission of their sins and the gift of the Holy Ghost. . . ." Church Archives. For the interest of Mormon converts in primitive Christianity, see Hill, "Role of Christian Primitivism," pp. 57-59. See also Nathan O. Hatch, "The Christian Movement and the Demand for a Theology of the People," *Journal of American History,* 67 (Dec., 1980):545-67.

10. II Nephi 3:24; 9:2; 10:2; 25:17; 30:5; Helaman 15:11; Mormon 9:36; Joseph Smith, *History of the Church,* 1:85, 79.

11. Alexander Campbell, *The Christian System, in Reference to the Union of Christians, and a Restoration of Primitive Christianity, as Plead in the Current Reformation* (Cincinnati: H. S. Bosworth, 1866; reprinted, New York: Arno Press and the New York Times, 1969), p. 8.

12. Hayden, *Early History of the Disciples,* p. 218.

13. West, *Alexander Campbell and Natural Religion,* pp. 136-44; Garrison and DeGroot, *Disciples of Christ,* pp. 183-84.

14. Garrison and DeGroot, *Disciples of Christ,* pp. 196-97; I Nephi 13:28; Richard P. Howard, *Restoration Scriptures: A Study of Their Textual Development* (Independence, Mo.: Herald Publishing House, 1969), pp. 70-81; Robert J. Matthews, *"A Plainer Translation": Joseph Smith's Revision of the Bible: A History and Commentary* (Provo: Brigham Young University Press, 1969), pp. 56-72; *Doctrine and Covenants* 37:1; Joseph Smith, *History of the Church,* 1:170, 130-32.

15. I Nephi 1:9-11; 11:13-21, quotation on title page.

16. Joseph Smith, *History of the Church,* 1:98; *The Pearl of Great Price: A Selection from the Revelations, Translations, and Narrations of Joseph Smith* (Salt Lake City: Church of Christ of Latter-day Saints, 1978), Moses 1:1, 2.

17. Moses 1:37-39.

18. Moses 1:40; 2:1-2. Chapters 2-8 of the current Book of Moses are traditionally dated Dec., 1830. Joseph Smith himself never gave a precise date, but the original manuscript in Oliver Cowdery's and John Whitmer's hands for Moses 1-5:43, dated before Oct. 21, 1830, suggests that part of these revelations came earlier. Oliver Cowdery left New York for Missouri on Oct. 15. The remainder, recorded mainly in Nov. and Dec. 1830, is in John Whitmer's and Sidney Rigdon's hands. Howard, *Restoration Scriptures,* pp. 74, 78-79, 170; Matthews, *"A Plainer Translation,"* pp. 67-72.

19. Genesis 5:18-24; Hebrews 11:5; Jude 14; Joseph Smith, *History of the Church,* 1:132-33.

20. Moses 6:35, 38; 7; Hebrews 11:5.

21. The June revelation of the words of Moses instructed the Prophet to "show them not unto any except them that believe," as if the narrative was for the comfort and illumination of the little church only. The second installment of the revelation was addressed to the elders of the Church of Christ, again with the caution to show only to believers. Yet the revelation was sufficiently public for E. D. Howe to learn of it soon after John Whitmer arrived in Ohio in Jan., 1831; excerpts from the Prophecy of Enoch and the revision of Genesis appeared in the Mormon *Evening and Morning Star* in Missouri in 1832 and 1833. Moses 1:42; 5:32; *Painesville Telegraph,* Jan. 18, 1831; James R. Clark, *The Story of the Pearl of Great Price* (Salt Lake City: Bookcraft, 1955), pp. 28, 187.

22. Howard, *Restoration Scriptures,* pp. 78-80; Clark, *Story of the Pearl of Great Price,* p. 187. The Reorganized Latter Day Saint Church published the June revelation on Moses as section 22 of their Doctrine and Covenants in 1864, and the remainder in the Inspired Version of the Bible in 1867. Howard, *Restoration Scriptures,* p. 73.

23. Mark P. Leone, *Roots of Modern Mormonisn* (Cambridge, Mass.: Harvard University Press, 1979), pp. 171-72.

A NOTE ON SOURCES AND AUTHORITIES

1. The point is made in two valuable historiographical studies, James B. Allen and Leonard J. Arrington, "Mormon Origins in New York: An Introductory Analysis," *B.Y.U. Studies,* 9 (Spring, 1969):242-43, and Thomas G. Alexander, "The Place of Joseph Smith in the Development of American Religion: A Historiographical Inquiry," *Journal of Mormon History,* 5 (1978):3. A useful summary of the bibliography relevant to early Mormon history is found in James B. Allen and Glen M. Leonard, *The Story of the Latter-day Saints* (Salt Lake City: Deseret Book Co., 1976), pp. 659-62, and more comprehensively in David J. Whittaker, "Early Mormon History: A Selected Bibliography, 1771-1847" (1973), unpublished compilation deposited in the Church Archives.

2. Solomon Mack's and Asael Smith's biographical writings and the larger part of John Smith's account are conveniently found in Anderson, *Joseph Smith's New England Heritage,* pp. 33-61, 124-29, 147-54. The most extensive statement of William Smith is *William Smith on Mormonism* (1883). George A. Smith's manuscript "Memoirs" are in the Church Archives.

Besides the printed *History of the Church,* additional information from Joseph Smith is found in the manuscript version, volume A-1, on microfilm at the Church Archives. The letters and diaries from the early period are described in Jeffery O. Johnson, *Register of the Joseph Smith Collection in the Church Archives, the Church of Jesus Christ of Latter-day Saints* (Salt Lake City: Historical Department, 1973). Richard L. Anderson appraised the Smiths as historians in "The Reliability of the Early History of Lucy and Joseph Smith," *Dialogue,* 4 (Summer, 1969):13-28.

3. Jessee, "Joseph Knight's Recollection" (1971); Joseph Knight, Jr., "Joseph Knight's Incidents," manuscript, Church Archives. Parley Pratt's *Autobiography,* 5th ed. (Salt Lake City: Deseret Book Co., 1961), describes the life of an early Mormon convert before he encountered the Book of Mormon.

4. Pomeroy Tucker, *Origin, Rise, and Progress of Mormonism* (New York: D. Appleton and Co., 1867), and Orasmus Turner, *History of the Pioneer Settlement of Phelps and Gorham's Purchase* (Rochester, N.Y.: William Alling, 1851), pp. 212-17.

5. The most detailed assessment of *Mormonism Unvailed* is Richard L. Anderson, "Joseph Smith's New York Reputation Reappraised," *B.Y.U. Studies,* 10 (Spring, 1970):288-314. Treating all the early critics, Hugh Nibley mixes satire with acute insight in *The Myth Makers* (Salt Lake City: Bookcraft, 1961).

6. For a history and analysis of the Muhammad comparison, see Arnold H. Green and Lawrence P. Goldrup, "Joseph Smith, an American Muhammad? An Essay on the Perils of Historical Analogy," *Dialogue,* 6 (Spring, 1971):46-58.

7. Riley's views of psychology were not doctrinaire. When he wrote *The Faith, the Falsity and the Failure of Christian Science* (New York: Fleming H. Revell Co., 1925), Riley applied Freudian psychoanalysis to account for Mary Baker Eddy.

8. Fawn M. Brodie, *No Man Knows My History: The Life of Joseph Smith,* 2d ed. (New York City: Alfred A. Knopf, 1971). For a vitriolic review of *No Man Knows My History,* see Hugh Nibley, *No Ma'am That's Not History* (Salt Lake City: Bookcraft, 1946), and for a judicious and scholarly critique, Marvin S. Hill, "Brodie Revisited: A Reappraisal," *Dialogue,* 7 (Winter, 1972):72-87, and "Secular or Sectarian History? A Critique of 'No Man Knows My History,' " *Church History,* 43 (Mar., 1974):78-96. Also critical is F. L. Stewart, *Exploding the Myth about Joseph Smith, the Mormon Prophet* (New York: F. L. Stewart, 1967).

Jan Shipps, "The Prophet Puzzle: Suggestions Leading toward a More Comprehensive Interpretation of Joseph Smith," *Journal of Mormon History,* 1 (1974):3-20, offers a mediating view. Shipps acknowledges the authenticity of Joseph's religious experiences but makes them and the Book of Mormon the product of cultural environment, genius, and a distinctive personality. Klaus Hansen suggests a variety of psychological explanations of Joseph Smith's visions in *Mormonism and the American Experience* (Chicago: University of Chicago Press, 1981), chap. 1.

9. Edward Tullidge, *Life of Joseph the Prophet* (New York: N.p., 1978);

George Q. Cannon, *Life of Joseph Smith, the Prophet* (Salt Lake City: Juvenile Instructor Office, 1888); John Henry Evans, *Joseph Smith: An American Prophet* (New York: Macmillan, 1933); John A. Widtsoe, *Joseph Smith: Seeker after Truth, Prophet of God* (Salt Lake City: Deseret News Press, 1951); Hyrum L. Andrus, *Joseph Smith, The Man and the Seer* (Salt Lake City: Deseret Book Co., 1962); Ivan J. Barrett, *Joseph Smith and the Restoration: A History of the Church to 1846* (Provo: Young House, 1973); Francis M. Gibbons, *Joseph Smith: Martyr, Prophet of God* (Salt Lake City: Deseret Book Co., 1977).

10. Mario S. DePillis, "The Quest for Religious Authority and the Rise of Mormonism," *Dialogue,* 1 (Spring, 1966):68-88; Marvin S. Hill, "The Role of Christian Primitivism in the Origin and Development of the Mormon Kingdom, 1830-1844" (Ph.D. diss., University of Chicago, 1968); "The Shaping of the Mormon Mind in New England and New York," *B.Y.U. Studies,* 9 (Spring, 1969):351-72; and "Quest for Refuge: An Hypothesis as to the Social Origins and Nature of the Mormon Political Kingdom," *Journal of Mormon History,* 2 (1975):3-20. William A. Clebsch reacted to DePillis in "Each Sect, the Sect to End All Sects," *Dialogue,* 1 (Summer, 1966):84-89. Klaus Hansen raised a number of issues in "Mormonism and American Culture: Some Tentative Hypotheses," in F. Mark McKiernan, Alma R. Blair, and Paul M. Edwards, eds., *The Restoration Movement: Essays in Mormon History* (Lawrence, Kans.: Coronado Press, 1973), pp. 1-25. For Christian primitivism, see Nathan O. Hatch, "The Christian Movement and the Demand for a Theology of the People," *Journal of American History,* 67 (Dec., 1980):545-67. Gordon Wood puts Mormonism into the context of a religious ferment that approached chaos in the first decades of the century, in "Evangelical America and Early Mormonism," *New York History,* 61 (Oct., 1980):359-86.

INDEX

Aaron (ancient prophet), 126
Aaronic Priesthood: conferred on Joseph Smith, Jr., and Oliver Cowdery, 101. *See also* Deacons; Priests; Teachers
Abraham (ancient prophet), 142, 185
Adair, James, 134; his *History of the American Indians,* 134
Adam (ancient prophet), 117-18, 186
Adams, John Quincy, 129
Albany, N.Y., 44, 45, 46, 87
Allen, Ethan: his *Only Oracle of Man,* 28
Alma (Book of Mormon prophet), 132
American Bible Society, 134-35, 137
American Home Missionary Society, 160
American Society for Meliorating the Condition of the Jews, 137
Amsterdam, N.Y., 58
Anthon, Charles, 80; edits *A Classical Dictionary,* 87; visited by Martin Harris, 87-88; on Book of Mormon characters, 219n
Anthon transcript, 86-89; and fulfillment of Isaiah 29, 219n; Lucy Harris counterfeits, 90; characters on, 219n
Anti-Masonry: and Book of Mormon, 128-31; and Mormonism, 232n
Apostles, 148, 163
Arbaugh, George B., 191
Arminianism, 27
Arminius, Jacobus, 27
Assyria, 135

Austin, David, 137
Austin, Seth, 19
Authority. *See* Priesthood

Bainbridge, Ohio, 173
Baltimore, Md., 44
Baptism: Joseph Smith, Jr., and Oliver Cowdery inquire about, 100-101; of Joseph Smith, Jr., and Oliver Cowdery, 101, 224-25n; required of converts, 153; of infants, 157; in Campbellite teachings, 181-82
Baptists: growth of, 5; in Palmyra area, 51-52, 53; Sidney Rigdon and, 150, 173; and Campbellites, 180-84 passim
Beaver (privateer), 15
Beckwith, George, 109, 112
Beeman (money-digger), 83-84
Belcher, Jack, 71
Ben Israel, Manasseh, 136-38; his *Hope of Israel,* 137
Bennett, James Gordon, 111, 219n
Benton, A. W., 160-61
Bering Straits, 135
Bible: influence on Smith family, 5; Lucy Mack Smith studies, 17, 38, 205n; Joseph Smith, Jr., and, 65, 94, 206n; prophecy in, confirmed by Anthon incident, 88-89; miracles in, 123; Book of Mormon purportedly copied from, 124-25, 127; Book of Mormon and, 126, 141-42, 230n; and lost tribes, 135; on future of Jews, 136; and church structure, 146; Mormon additions

249

Palestine, 126
Paley, William, 123
Palmyra Freeman, 111
Palmyra, N.Y., 63, 102, 106-8;
Smiths move to, 4, 42; churches
in, 5, 51; growth of, 43-46; Joseph
Smith, Sr., buys a farm near, 47-
48; asheries in, 48; revivals in, 52-
53, 65; affidavits against Smiths
collected in, 70; home of Martin
Harris in, 84; Book of Mormon
printed in, 107-11 passim; citizens
of, critical of Book of Mormon,
108-10, 119-20, 184; Lucy Mack
Smith joins Presbyterians in, 144;
Thomas Marsh moves to, 149;
and Sidney Rigdon, 175; members
in, leave New York, 176
Palmyra *Reflector,* 74, 111, 120
Palmyra Register, 54
Paris, 137
Parker, Dr., 32
Partridge, Edward, 173-74
Peck, Hezekiah, 171
Perkins, Cyrus, 33
Peter (the apostle), 146
Peter, James, and John, 188; send
John the Baptist, 101; visit Joseph
Smith, Jr., and Oliver Cowdery,
162-63; date of visit of, uncertain,
240-41n
Peterson, Ziba, 168-71
Phelps, Oliver, 43, 44
Phelps, W. W., 89, 124, 152
Pierce, Martha, 151
Pittsburgh, Pa., 173
Pontiac, Mich., 19
Postmillennialism, 170
Potsdam, N.Y., 25
Pratt, Orson, 171, 176, 194n
Pratt, Parley: and lost tribes of Israel,
135; and Book of Mormon, 140-41;
conversion, 150, 180; on mission
to Indians, 168-71; teaches Sidney
Rigdon, 173-74
Premillennialism, 139, 170
Presbyterianism, 181; growth of, 5;
Lucy Mack Smith and, 5-6, 38-39,
140, 144, 205n; and conversion,
37; in Palmyra, 51-52, 53; and

magic, 72; minister of, opposes
Mormons, 160
Priest, Josiah, 133-34; his *American
Antiquities and Discoveries in the
West,* 131
Priesthood: members ordained to,
143, 226n; Parley Pratt looks for,
150; licenses issued to holders of,
158; restoration of apostleship in,
163; and basis of Mormon belief,
187-88; Oliver Cowdery on resto-
ration of Melchizedek, 241n. *See
also* Aaronic Priesthood; Deacons;
Elders; Melchizedek Priesthood;
Priests; Teachers
Priests, 147-48
Primitive gospel movement, 183
Prince, Walter F., 232n
Puritanism, 3, 136-37, 166
Purple, W. D., 71, 75
Putnam, Israel, 12

Randolph, Vt., 43, 144; Smith fam-
ily opens a store in, 29
Red Sea, 105
Reflector, The. See Palmyra *Reflector*
Reid, John, 162; describes character
of Joseph Smith, Jr., 76
Religious infidelity, 52
Republicanism: and Book of Mor-
mon, 131-33; and church authority, 146
Restoration, 182-85 passim
Restorationist Movement, 154; and
Walter Scott, 150
Revelations. *See* Doctrine and Covenants; First Vision; Moroni
Revivals: time of, in Palmyra dis-
puted, 204-5n
Richards, Franklin D., 187
Richards, Willard, 9
Rigdon, Sidney: and Thomas Camp-
bell, 121, 183; believed to have
written Book of Mormon, 126-27,
191, 230-31n; and Parley Pratt,
150; and conversion, 152-53; challenged by Thomas Campbell, 155,
179; called to preach, 171; converted and preaches Mormonism,
173-75; leaves New York, 176; and
Walter Scott, 181

Riley, I. Woodbridge, 128, 191
Robinson, Gain, 67
Rochester, Mich., 19
Rochester, N.Y., 46-47, 81
Rochester (N.Y.) Daily Advertiser,
    111-12
Rochester (N.Y.) Gem, 71, 87, 89,
    111
Rochester (N.Y.) Republican, 111
Rochester (N.Y.) Telegraph, 107
Rockwell family, 151
Rockwell, Orrin, 144
Rockwell, Sarah, 144
Rod of Aaron, 98
Rogers (imposter), 121
Roget's Thesaurus, 191
Romantic nationalism, 139-40
Romanticism, 3
Royalton, Vt., 31, 39, 41, 151

Sacrament, 165
Salem, Mass., 33
Salem, N.H., 20
Samuel (Book of Mormon prophet),
    116
Samuel (son of Lehi), 116
Sandford, N.Y., 160
Sariah (Lehi's wife), 116
Satan, 117, 186
Schroeder, Theodore, 232n
Scott, Walter: and Sidney Rigdon,
    150, 173; and restored gospel, 181-
    82; and Enlightenment, 184
Second Coming of Christ: foretold
    by Moroni, 62, 170-71. See also
    Millennium
Second Great Awakening, 37
Seerstone: used by Joseph Smith, Jr.,
    69-70, 212n, 216n; Martin Harris
    substitutes a counterfeit for, 90;
    part in translation of Book of Mor-
    mon, 97, 221n; and David Whit-
    mer's journey to Harmony, 103;
    makes Joseph Smith, Jr., a seer,
    148; Hiram Page receives revela-
    tions through, 167; Joseph Smith,
    Jr., said to relinquish, 167, 238n;
    Joseph Smith, Jr., prizes, 184;
    brought from England, 215n
Seneca County, N.Y., 104
Seneca Falls, N.Y., 173

Seneca Lake, 43-47 passim, 102; site
    of baptisms, 149, 150
Seneca River, 46
Seneca township, N.Y., 44
Sewall, Samuel, 134
Seymour (attorney), 161-62
Shakers, 180
Sharon, Vt., 31
Shearer, Rev. Mr. (Presbyterian min-
    ister), 160
Shipps, Jan, 192
Skepticism. See Enlightenment
Slade, Mary Knight, 151
Smith family: influence on Joseph
    Smith, Jr., 4; witnesses of Book of
    Mormon, 4; influences on, 5-6; as
    martyrs, 10-11; source of converts,
    151-52
Smith, Alvin, 41, 42; attends school,
    32; earns money for family, 47,
    49; refuses to join Presbyterians,
    53-54, 144; plans house for family,
    60; chides Joseph Smith, Jr., 62-63;
    illness and death of, 64-65; effect
    of death on family economy, 66,
    68; Joseph and Emma Smith's first
    child named for, 91
Smith, Asael, 43; moves, 4, 22, 25;
    religion of, 5, 26-29, 198n; friend
    of Stephen Mack, 19; early career
    of, 20-21; takes over father's farm,
    21-22; gives farms to sons, 23, 29;
    his "A few words of advice," 24-
    25; character of, 24-25; death of,
    26; family of, reacts to Mormon-
    ism, 26, 198n; opposes Joseph
    Smith Sr.'s interest in Methodism,
    38; converted, 152
Smith, Asael, Jr., 26, 152
Smith, Catherine, 32, 172, 176
Smith, Don Carlos: born, 40, 83,
    172; accompanies father on mis-
    sion, 151-52
Smith, Emma, 162; and seerstone,
    69, 221n; marries Joseph Smith,
    Jr., 76-77, 210n, 215n; as a histori-
    cal source, 80; helps get gold
    plates, 81-83; and Martin Harris,
    84; moves, 85-86, 103, 173, 176,
    179; helps copy characters from
    plates, 86; gives birth to first

sought by Goodwin Wharton,
213n; described, 217n; called interpreters, 222n
Utica, N.Y., 42

Vermont, 22
Vienna (Phelps), N.Y., 53-54

Walters, the Magician, 120-27 pas-
sim
Waterloo, N.Y., 173, 176
Water-witching. *See* Rod of Aaron
Wayne County, N.Y., 46
Wayne Sentinel, 65, 110, 111
Weed, Thurlow, 107
Wells, Vt., 96
Wesley, John, 145, 146
West Bloomfield, N.Y., 51
Western Presbyterian Church, 53,
109
Wethersfield, Conn., 58
Wharton, Goodwin, 71
Whitefield, George, 145
Whitmer family, 151, 153, 166-68
Whitmer, Catherine, 103
Whitmer, Christian, 103-7 passim,
149, 167
Whitmer, David, 145; and money-
diggers' claims, 83; meets Oliver
Cowdery, 96-97; helps Joseph
Smith, Jr., move, 102; sees vision
of plates and angel, 105-6; witness
of plates, 106-7; and Canada expe-
dition, 110; at church organization, 143; revelation for, 145-46;
and appointment of apostles, 148;
and first ordinations of elders,
148; baptizes converts, 149, 154;
in Colesville, 159; in Harmony
and Colesville, 165; and seerstone,
167; and Sidney Rigdon, 174; later

testimony of, 190; and Joseph
Smith Jr.'s authority, 238n
Whitmer, Elizabeth Ann, 103
Whitmer, Jacob, 106-7
Whitmer, John, 103, 145; helps with
translation, 104; witness of plates,
106-7; in Colesville, 159, 165; par-
ticipates in Harmony church service, 165; compiles revelations,
166; on reaction of Colesville to
Sidney Rigdon, 175; sent to Ohio,
175; works on revision of Bible,
187
Whitmer, Mary, 103
Whitmer, Peter, Jr., 103, 106-7; mis-
sion to west, 120-21; on mission
to Indians, 120-21, 168-71; at
church organization, 143
Whitmer, Peter, 145; family of,
helps Joseph Smith, Jr., 102-3;
church organized at house of, 143;
offers hospitality to Joseph Smith,
Jr., 166; hosts conference, 175;
farm of, 177; vision in house of,
184
Whitney, Newell K., 179
Wild, Asa, 58
Wilkinson, Jemima, 121, 180
Willard, Samuel, 134
Winchell (treasure-hunter), 71
Windham, N.H., 20
Wirt, William, 129
Witnesses, 104-7, 124
Woodruff, Wilford, 69
Woods, Nathaniel, 71

Young, Brigham, 61, 69, 82, 141,
151, 177, 194n
Young, Joseph, 151
Young, Phineas, 141, 151

Zarahemla, 126
Zoramites, 145